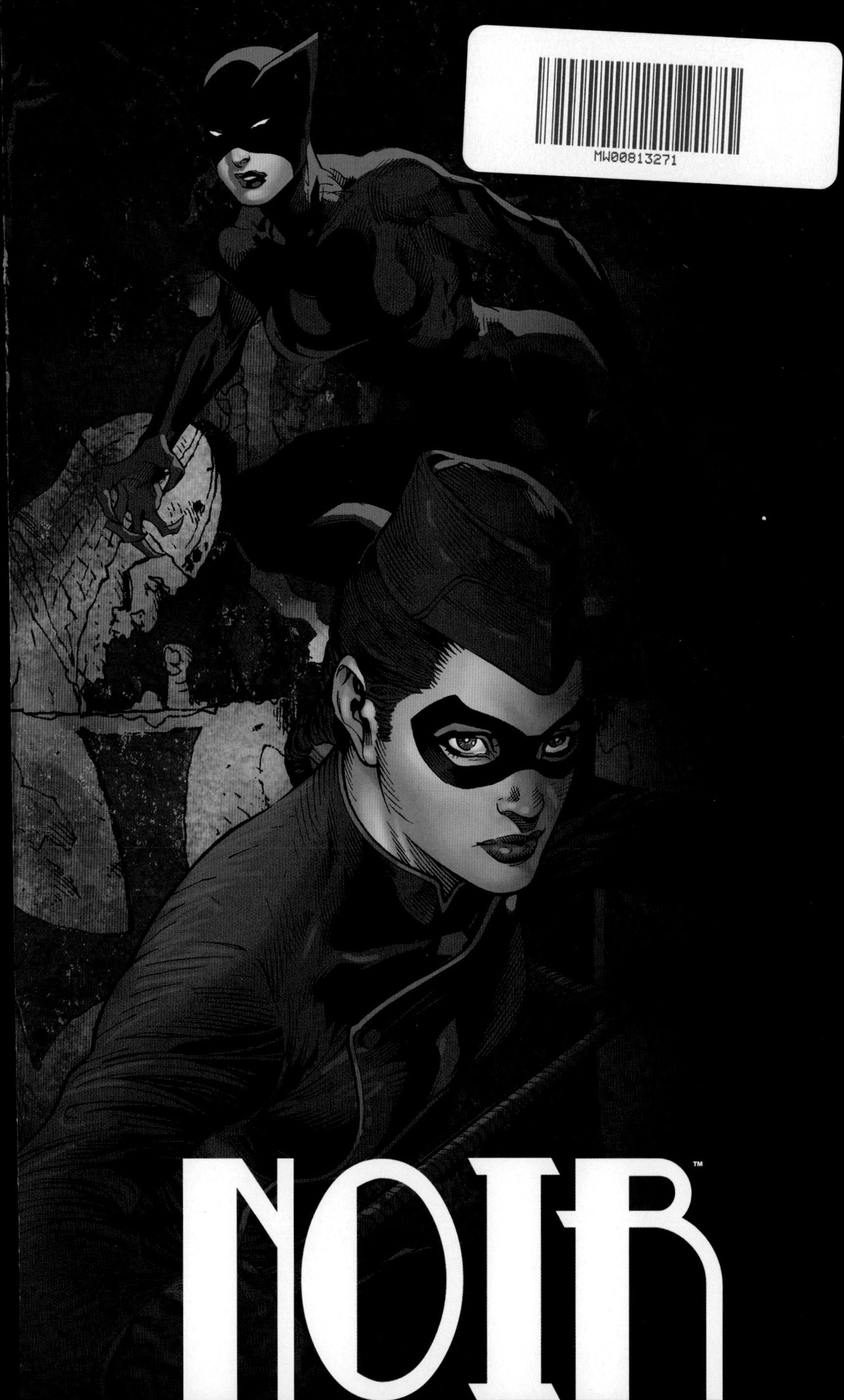

NOIR™

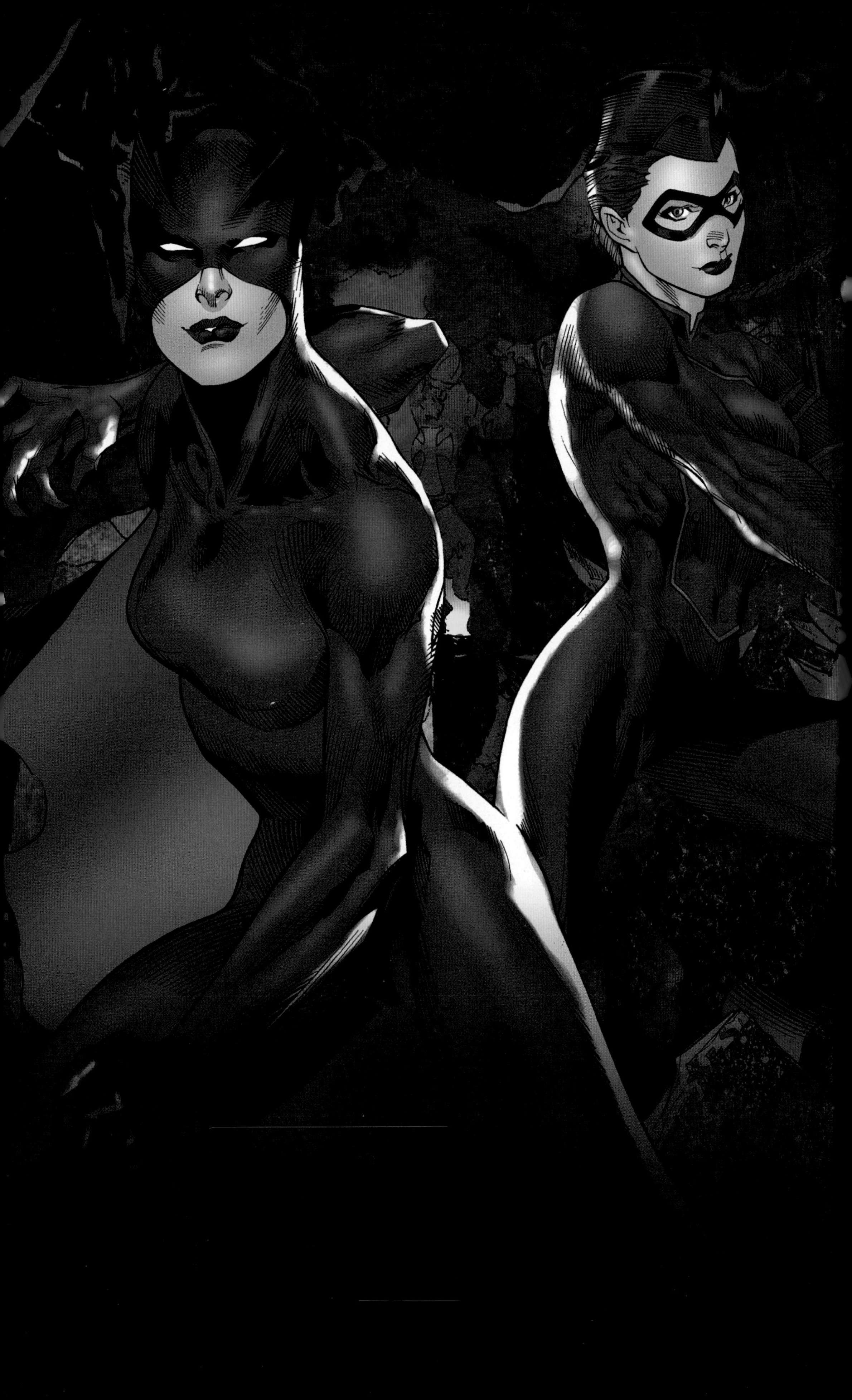

NOIR

THE MOHAWK TEMPLAR

Written by **VICTOR GISCHLER**

Illustrated by **ANDREA MUTTI**

Colored by **VLADIMIR POPOV**

Lettered by **ROB STEEN**

Collection Cover by **ARDIAN SYAF**

Collection Design by **KATIE HIDALGO**

SPECIAL THANKS TO
JERRY BIRENZ, ANTHONY TOLLIN
AND MICHAEL USLAN

THE SHADOW CREATED BY
WALTER B. GIBSON

This volume collects issues 1-5 of
Noir by Dynamite Entertainment.

DYNAMITE

Nick Barrucci, CEO / Publisher
Juan Collado, President / COO
Rich Young, Director Business Development
Keith Davidsen, Marketing Manager

Joe Rybandt, Senior Editor
Hannah Gorfinkel, Associate Editor
Josh Green, Traffic Coordinator
Molly Mahan, Assistant Editor

Josh Johnson, Art Director
Jason Ullmeyer, Senior Graphic Designer
Katie Hidalgo, Graphic Designer
Chris Caniano, Production Assistant

Visit us online at **www.DYNAMITE.com**
Follow us on Twitter **@dynamitecomics**
Like us on Facebook **/Dynamitecomics**
Watch us on YouTube **/Dynamitecomics**

ISBN-10: 1-60690-487-6   ISBN-13: 978-1-60690-487-9   First Printing   10 9 8 7 6 5 4 3 2 1

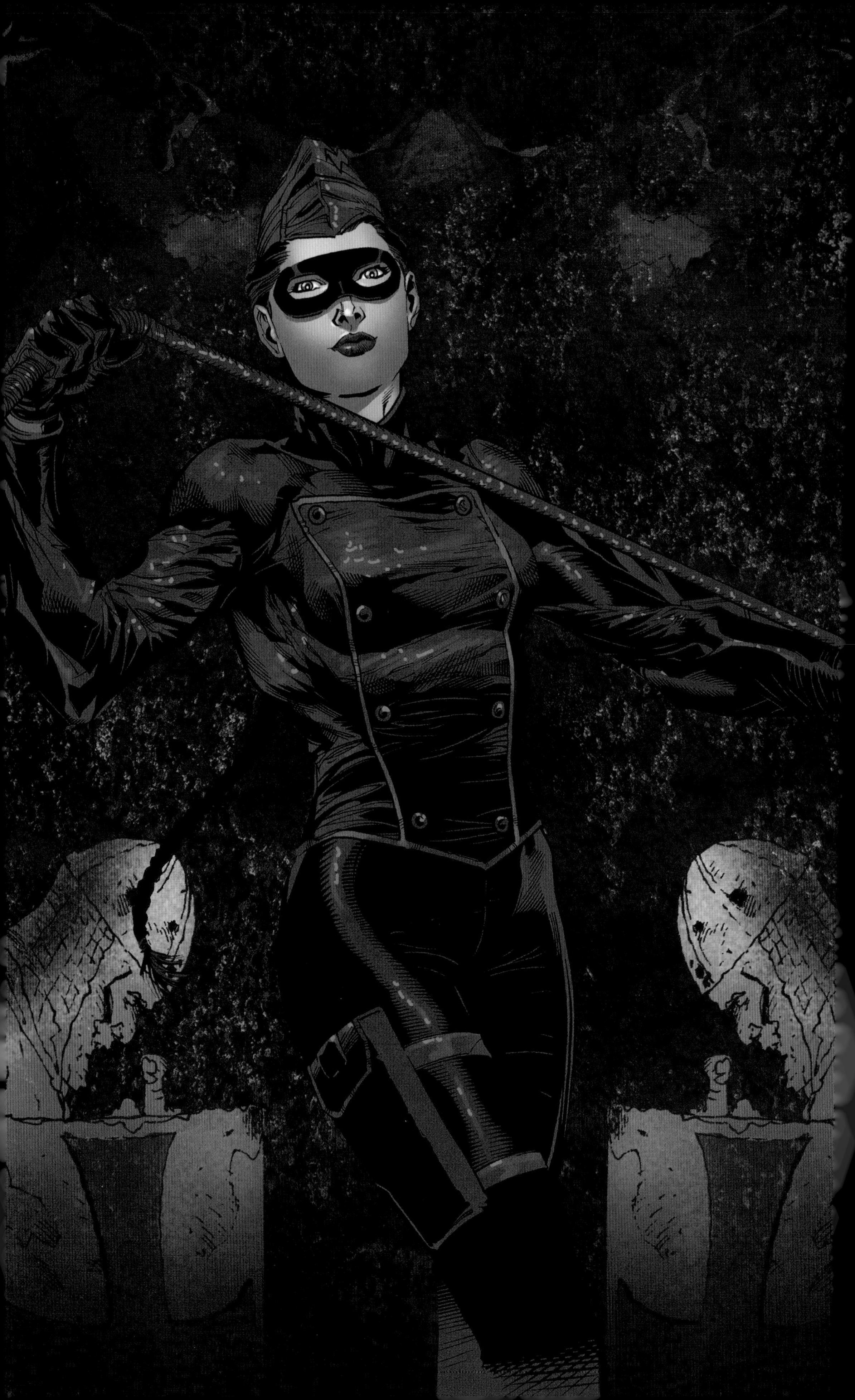

Bad Girls Make for Good Comics

When Nick Barrucci offered to let me write an arc of *The Shadow*, I jumped at the opportunity. I mean this was a cool, iconic pulp hero. I could not wait to put Lamont Cranston and his hat-wearing alter ego through their paces. I knew instinctively I would need a good villain. I wanted somebody who would be a match not only for The Shadow but for Cranston. I wanted to throw some sexual tension (and ... well some actual sex) in there too. So I came up with the beautiful and dangerous Black Sparrow!

That sounded good and pulpy, right? I described the cool costume I wanted, and the very first drawing of her was the #10 cover by Alex Ross. Alex Ross! She looked great! And that cover ended up being the cover for the trade as well. So we had an awesome character that looked fabulous and was totally kicking ass in the pages of *The Shadow*.

About that time the *Miss Fury* comic hit, helmed by the talented Rob Williams. The protagonist was ... *drum roll* ... a sexy, dangerous woman! While Miss Fury and Black Sparrow are different in some ways, they could certainly have belonged to the same sorority. Cut from the same cloth, a more manic and less suicidal Thelma & Louise. I said to Joe Rybandt, "Hey, we should get these two ladies together."

Possibly I am paraphrasing a tad, but my memory is that the pitch was that straight forward. Joe immediately saw the potential, and pretty soon I put on my thinking cap (i.e. drinking a beer) to come up with an adventure that suited these two daring babes. (Knowing too well that if I called them "babes" they would punch me in the groin.)

What followed developed into "The Mohawk Templar," an *Indiana Jones*-style adventure with a noir vibe. I wanted swashbuckling, but I also wanted deceit and betrayal and the very strong understanding that these ladies were just as capable of stabbing you in the back as they were likely to save the day. This isn't Superman or Captain America's world. This is *NOIR*, baby.

So, five issues later, here we are. Miss Fury lives on in Rob's excellent series, and my sincere hope is that Black Sparrow shows herself again soon. Fingers crossed.

Read on. Enjoy.

Victor Gischler
February 13, 2014

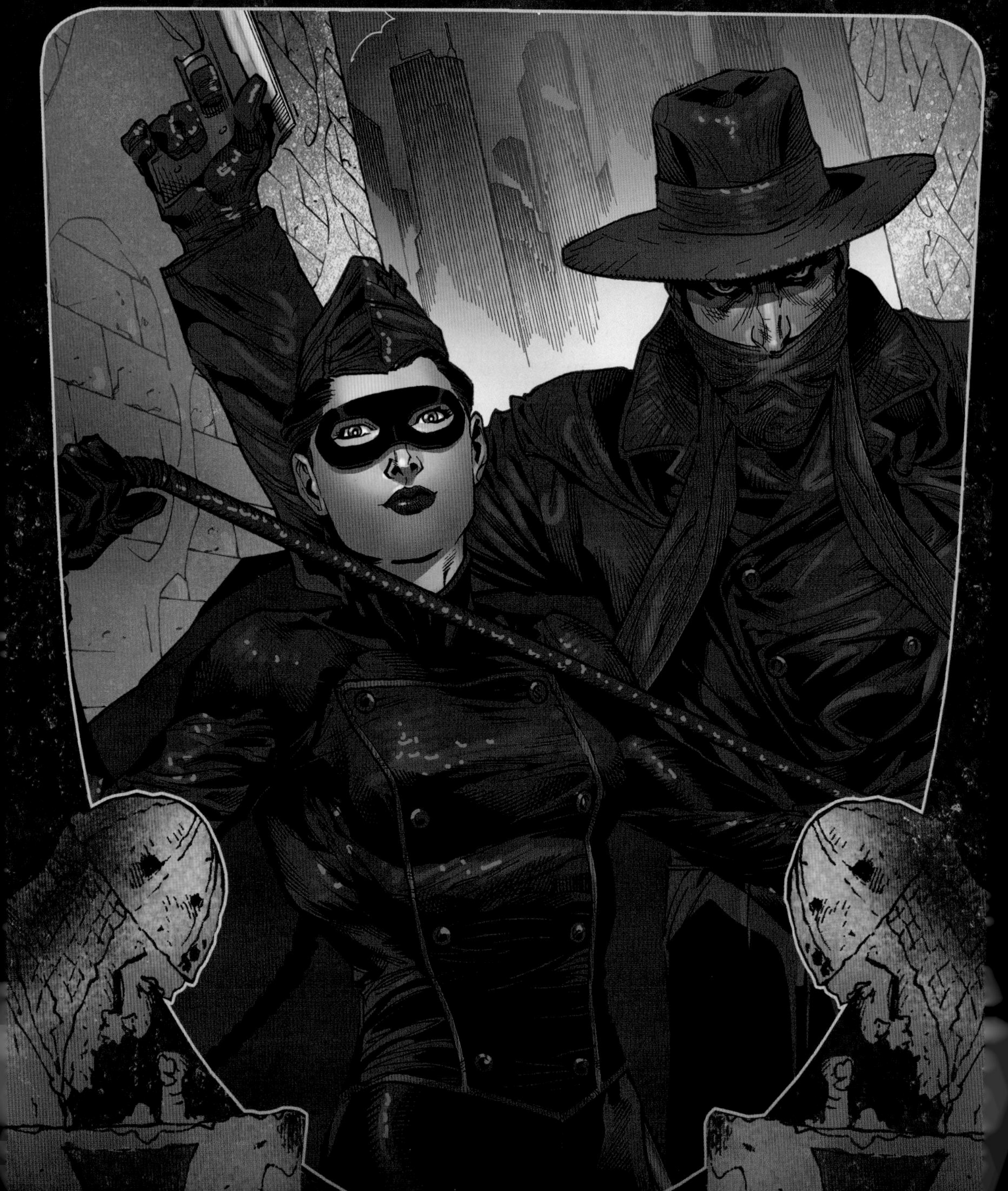

ISSUE 1

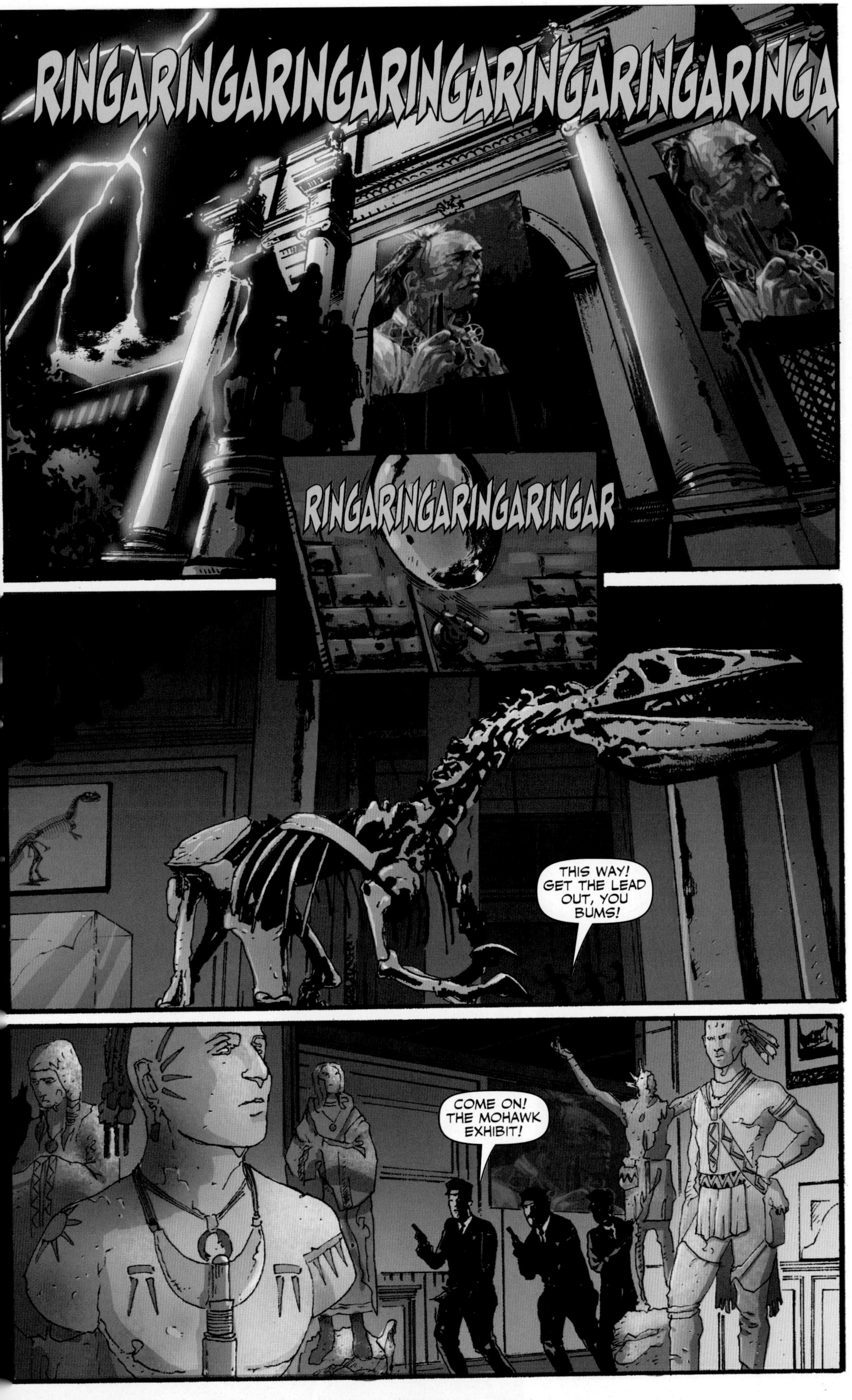
RINGARINGARINGARINGARINGARINGARINGA
RINGARINGARINGARINGAR
THIS WAY! GET THE LEAD OUT, YOU BUMS!
COME ON! THE MOHAWK EXHIBIT!

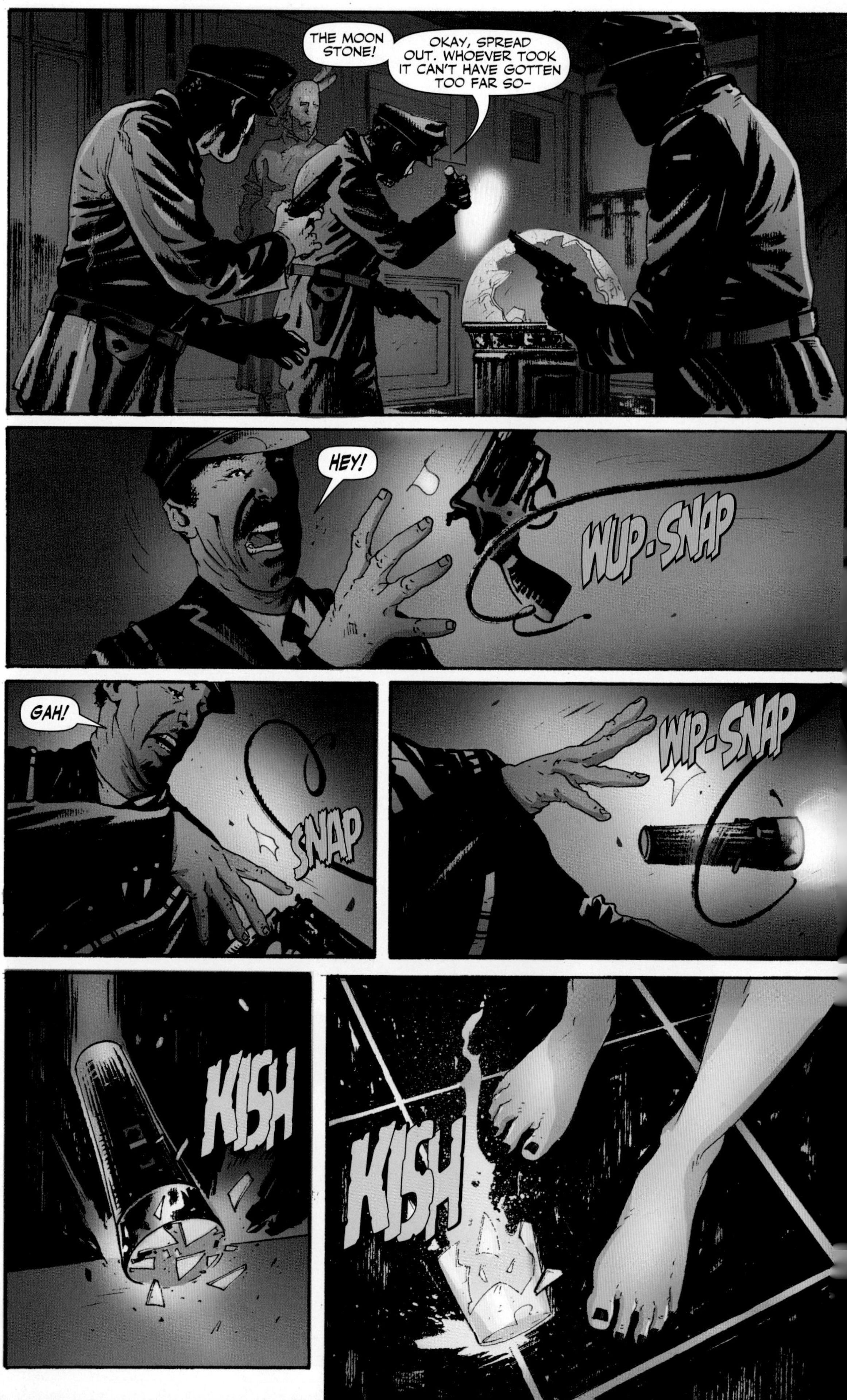
THE MOON STONE!
OKAY, SPREAD OUT. WHOEVER TOOK IT CAN'T HAVE GOTTEN TOO FAR SO-
HEY!
WUP-SNAP
GAH!
SNAP
WIP-SNAP
KISH
KISH

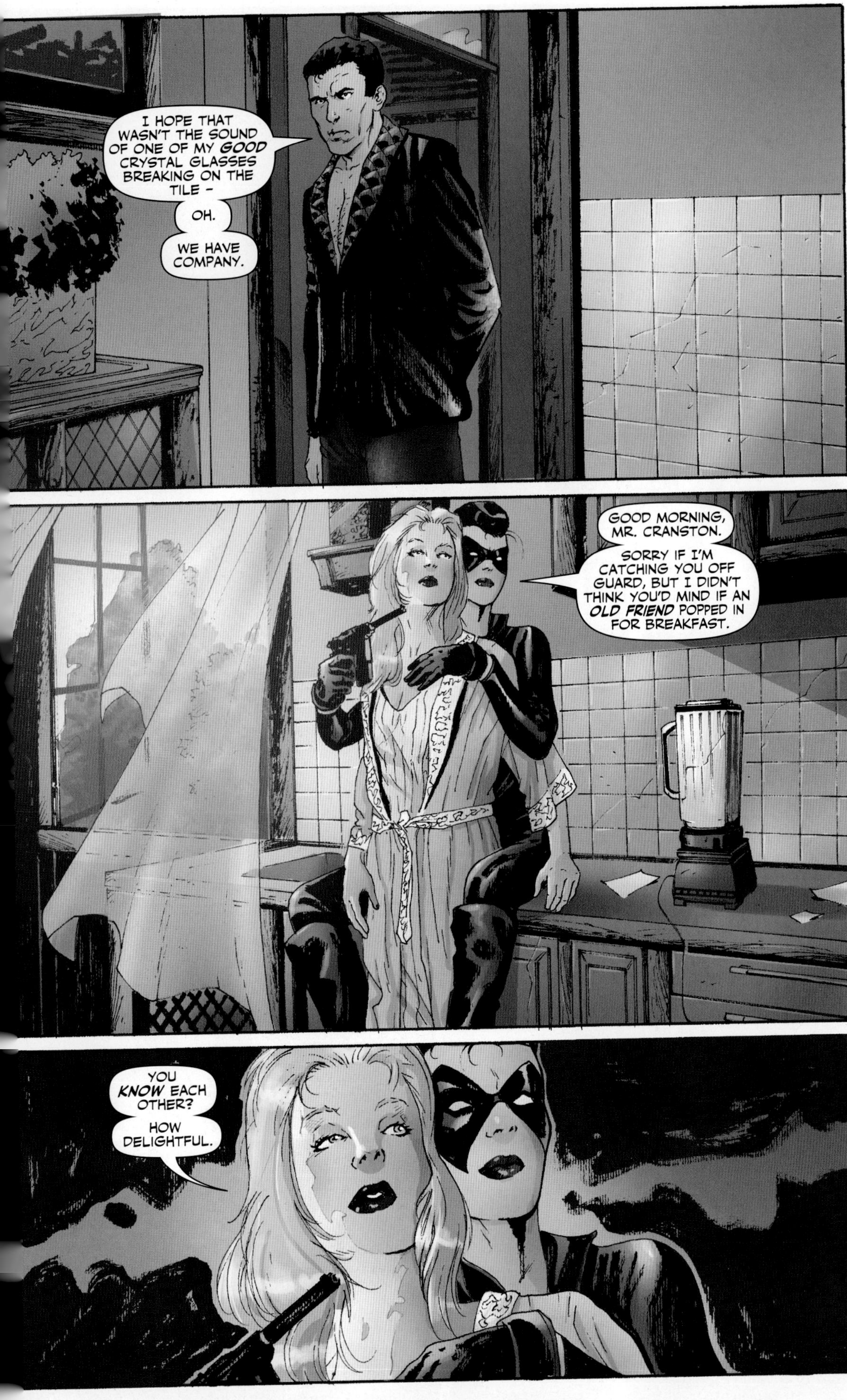

I HOPE THAT WASN'T THE SOUND OF ONE OF MY *GOOD* CRYSTAL GLASSES BREAKING ON THE TILE –
OH.
WE HAVE COMPANY.
GOOD MORNING, MR. CRANSTON.
SORRY IF I'M CATCHING YOU OFF GUARD, BUT I DIDN'T THINK YOU'D MIND IF AN *OLD FRIEND* POPPED IN FOR BREAKFAST.
YOU *KNOW* EACH OTHER?
HOW DELIGHTFUL.

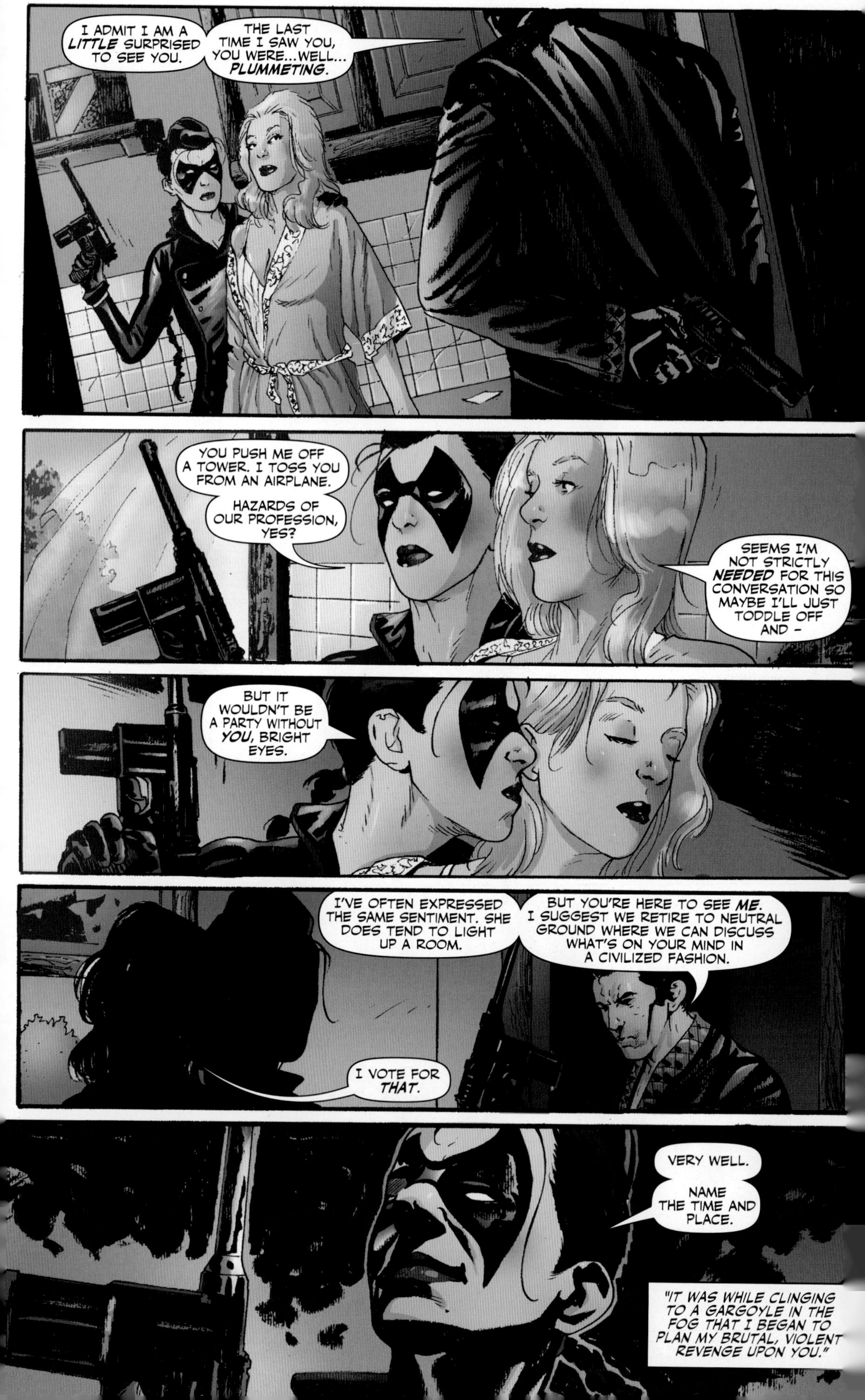
I ADMIT I AM A LITTLE SURPRISED TO SEE YOU.
THE LAST TIME I SAW YOU, YOU WERE...WELL... PLUMMETING.
YOU PUSH ME OFF A TOWER. I TOSS YOU FROM AN AIRPLANE.
HAZARDS OF OUR PROFESSION, YES?
SEEMS I'M NOT STRICTLY NEEDED FOR THIS CONVERSATION SO MAYBE I'LL JUST TODDLE OFF AND –
BUT IT WOULDN'T BE A PARTY WITHOUT YOU, BRIGHT EYES.
I'VE OFTEN EXPRESSED THE SAME SENTIMENT. SHE DOES TEND TO LIGHT UP A ROOM.
BUT YOU'RE HERE TO SEE ME. I SUGGEST WE RETIRE TO NEUTRAL GROUND WHERE WE CAN DISCUSS WHAT'S ON YOUR MIND IN A CIVILIZED FASHION.
I VOTE FOR THAT.
VERY WELL.
NAME THE TIME AND PLACE.
"IT WAS WHILE CLINGING TO A GARGOYLE IN THE FOG THAT I BEGAN TO PLAN MY BRUTAL, VIOLENT REVENGE UPON YOU."

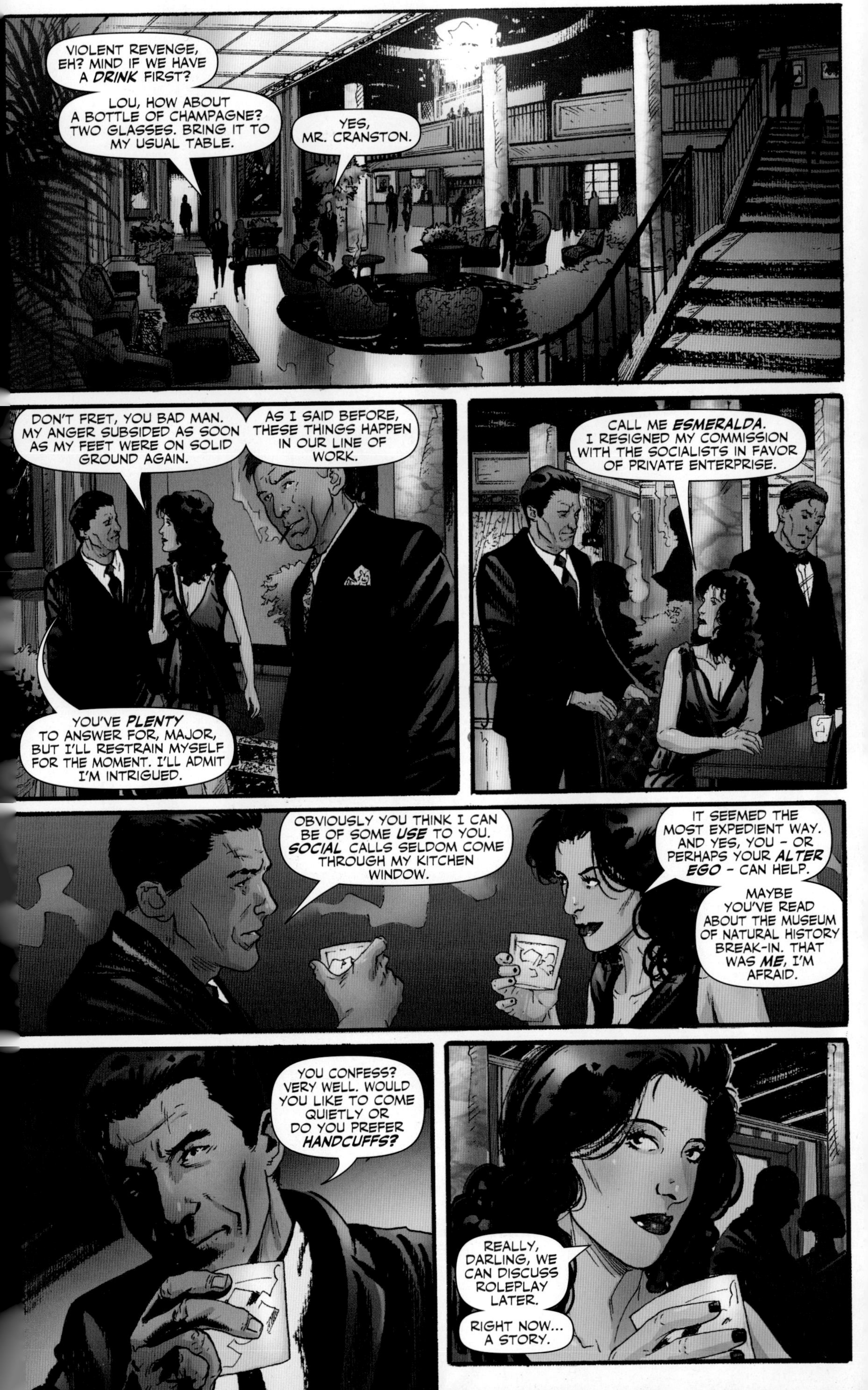
VIOLENT REVENGE, EH? MIND IF WE HAVE A DRINK FIRST?
LOU, HOW ABOUT A BOTTLE OF CHAMPAGNE? TWO GLASSES. BRING IT TO MY USUAL TABLE.
YES, MR. CRANSTON.
DON'T FRET, YOU BAD MAN. MY ANGER SUBSIDED AS SOON AS MY FEET WERE ON SOLID GROUND AGAIN.
AS I SAID BEFORE, THESE THINGS HAPPEN IN OUR LINE OF WORK.
YOU'VE PLENTY TO ANSWER FOR, MAJOR, BUT I'LL RESTRAIN MYSELF FOR THE MOMENT. I'LL ADMIT I'M INTRIGUED.
CALL ME ESMERALDA. I RESIGNED MY COMMISSION WITH THE SOCIALISTS IN FAVOR OF PRIVATE ENTERPRISE.
OBVIOUSLY YOU THINK I CAN BE OF SOME USE TO YOU. SOCIAL CALLS SELDOM COME THROUGH MY KITCHEN WINDOW.
IT SEEMED THE MOST EXPEDIENT WAY. AND YES, YOU - OR PERHAPS YOUR ALTER EGO - CAN HELP.
MAYBE YOU'VE READ ABOUT THE MUSEUM OF NATURAL HISTORY BREAK-IN. THAT WAS ME, I'M AFRAID.
YOU CONFESS? VERY WELL. WOULD YOU LIKE TO COME QUIETLY OR DO YOU PREFER HANDCUFFS?
REALLY, DARLING, WE CAN DISCUSS ROLEPLAY LATER.
RIGHT NOW... A STORY.

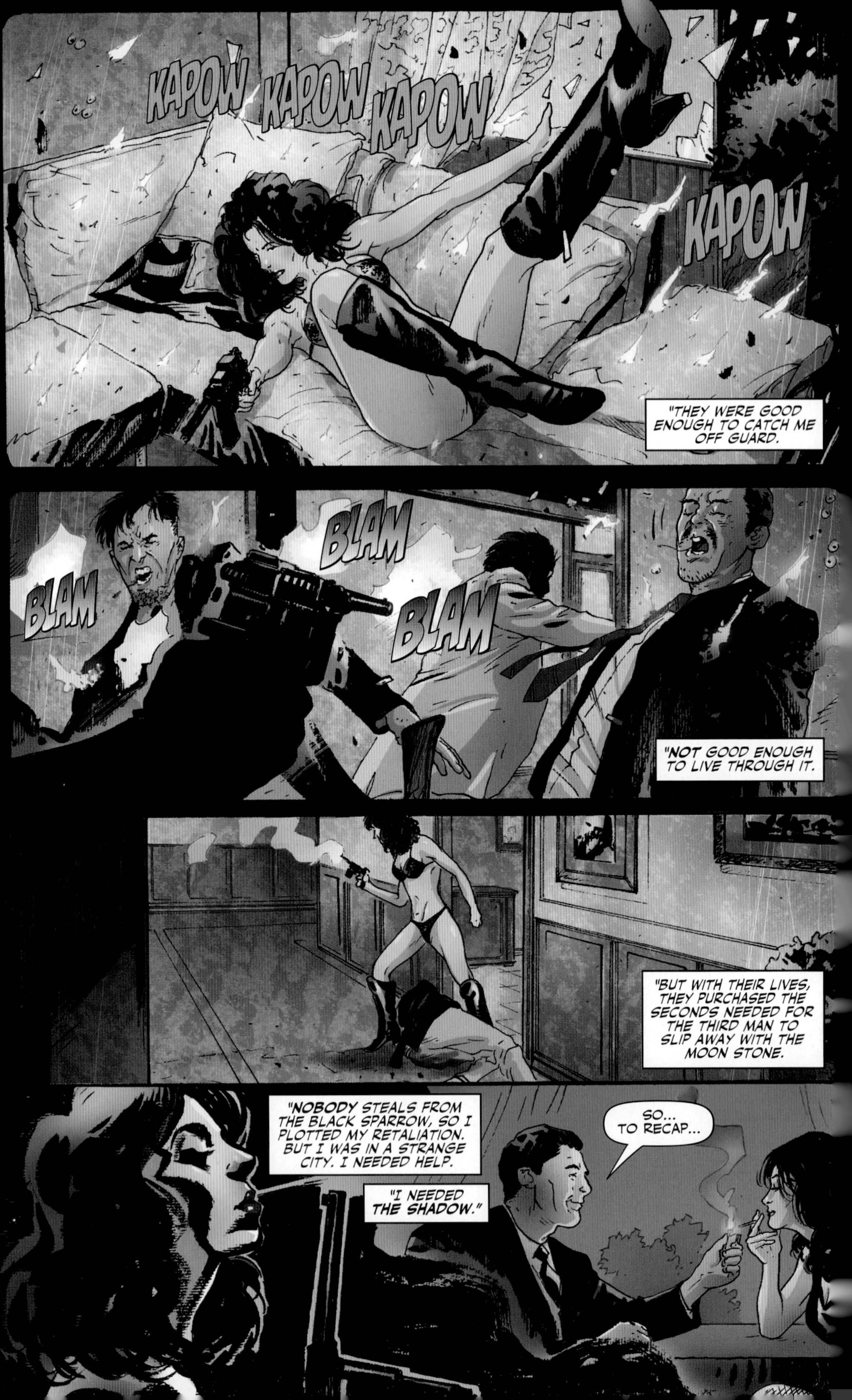
KAPOW KAPOW KAPOW
KAPOW
"THEY WERE GOOD ENOUGH TO CATCH ME OFF GUARD.
BLAM
BLAM
BLAM
"NOT GOOD ENOUGH TO LIVE THROUGH IT.
"BUT WITH THEIR LIVES, THEY PURCHASED THE SECONDS NEEDED FOR THE THIRD MAN TO SLIP AWAY WITH THE MOON STONE.
"NOBODY STEALS FROM THE BLACK SPARROW, SO I PLOTTED MY RETALIATION. BUT I WAS IN A STRANGE CITY. I NEEDED HELP.
"I NEEDED THE SHADOW."
SO... TO RECAP...

A SHADY CHARACTER HIRES YOU TO **STEAL** THE MOON STONE. YOU THEN **DOUBLE-CROSS** HIM. THEN THEY GET THE DROP ON YOU AND STEAL IT BACK.

AND **NOW** YOU'RE ASKING FOR HELP.

FROM SOMEBODY WHO'S ALREADY TRIED TO **KILL** YOU ONCE.

DID I LEAVE ANYTHING OUT?

JUST THIS.

ALL I WANT IS WHAT I STOLE FAIR AND SQUARE.

BUT **ARGUS** HAS A NETWORK OF THIEVES AND SMUGGLERS ALL UP AND DOWN THE EAST COAST. YOU TURN A BLIND EYE TO **MY** MINOR INDISCRETIONS, AND I SERVE **HIM** AND HIS OPERATION UP ON A SILVER PLATTER.

FOR A LONG TIME NOW I'VE BEEN **TWO** MEN.

WELL, ONE MAN AND ONE **SHADOW** OF A MAN.

TOO OFTEN PEOPLE THINK THEY NEED THE ONE WHEN THEY REALLY NEED THE OTHER.

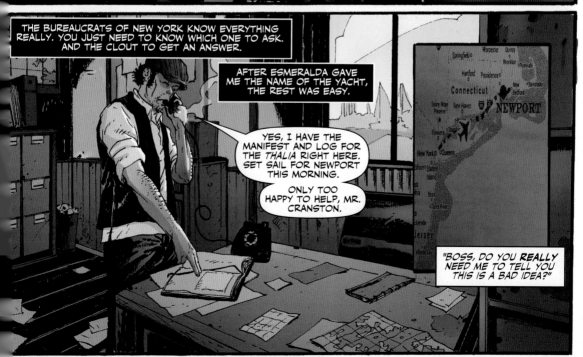

THE BUREAUCRATS OF NEW YORK KNOW EVERYTHING REALLY. YOU JUST NEED TO KNOW WHICH ONE TO ASK. AND THE CLOUT TO GET AN ANSWER.

AFTER ESMERALDA GAVE ME THE NAME OF THE YACHT, THE REST WAS EASY.

YES, I HAVE THE MANIFEST AND LOG FOR THE *THALIA* RIGHT HERE. SET SAIL FOR NEWPORT THIS MORNING.

ONLY TOO HAPPY TO HELP, MR. CRANSTON.

"BOSS, DO YOU **REALLY** NEED ME TO TELL YOU THIS IS A BAD IDEA?"

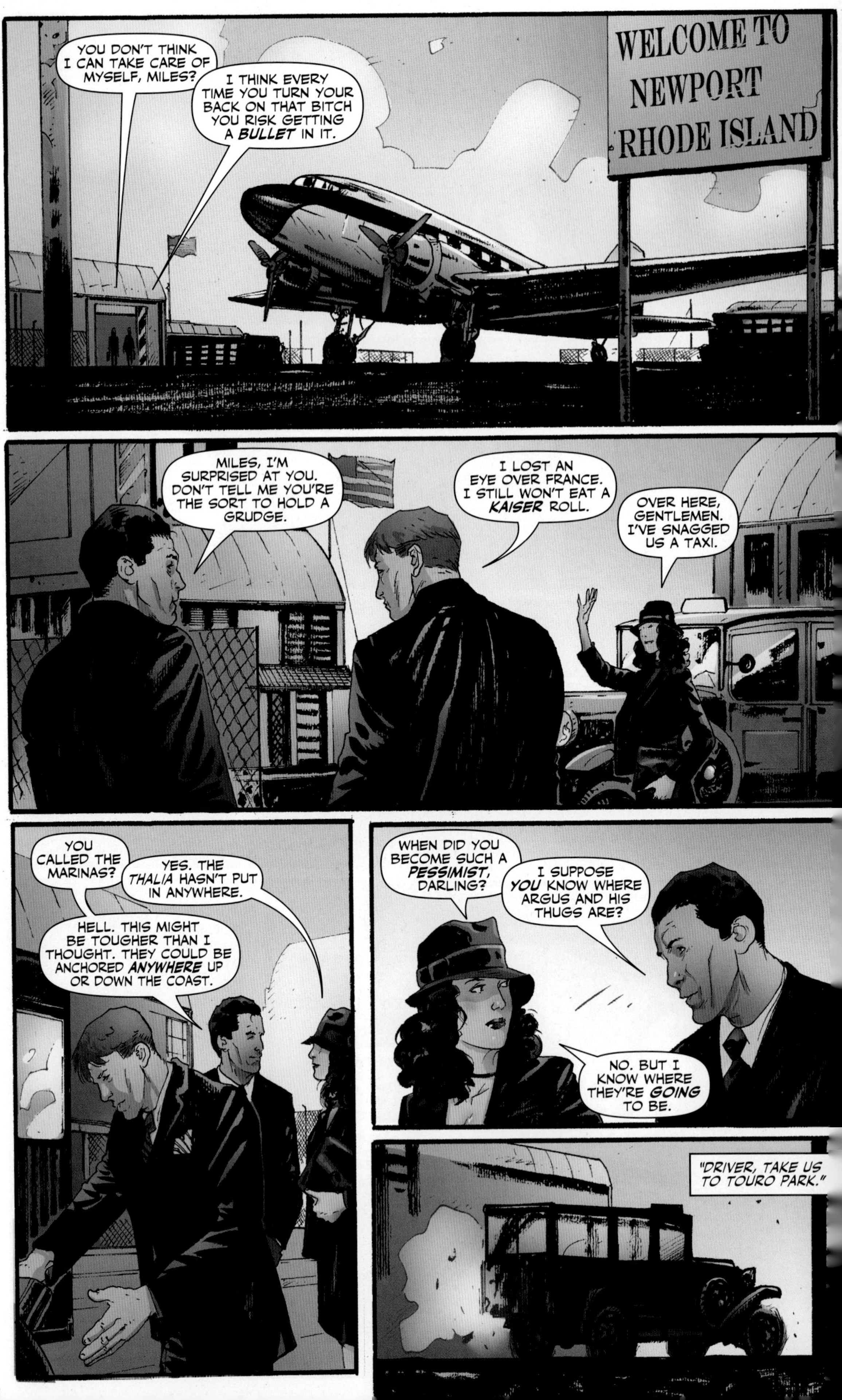
WELCOME TO NEWPORT RHODE ISLAND
YOU DON'T THINK I CAN TAKE CARE OF MYSELF, MILES?
I THINK EVERY TIME YOU TURN YOUR BACK ON THAT BITCH YOU RISK GETTING A *BULLET* IN IT.
MILES, I'M SURPRISED AT YOU. DON'T TELL ME YOU'RE THE SORT TO HOLD A GRUDGE.
I LOST AN EYE OVER FRANCE. I STILL WON'T EAT A *KAISER* ROLL.
OVER HERE, GENTLEMEN. I'VE SNAGGED US A TAXI.
YOU CALLED THE MARINAS?
YES. THE *THALIA* HASN'T PUT IN ANYWHERE.
HELL. THIS MIGHT BE TOUGHER THAN I THOUGHT. THEY COULD BE ANCHORED *ANYWHERE* UP OR DOWN THE COAST.
WHEN DID YOU BECOME SUCH A *PESSIMIST*, DARLING?
I SUPPOSE *YOU* KNOW WHERE ARGUS AND HIS THUGS ARE?
NO. BUT I KNOW WHERE THEY'RE *GOING* TO BE.
"DRIVER, TAKE US TO TOURO PARK."

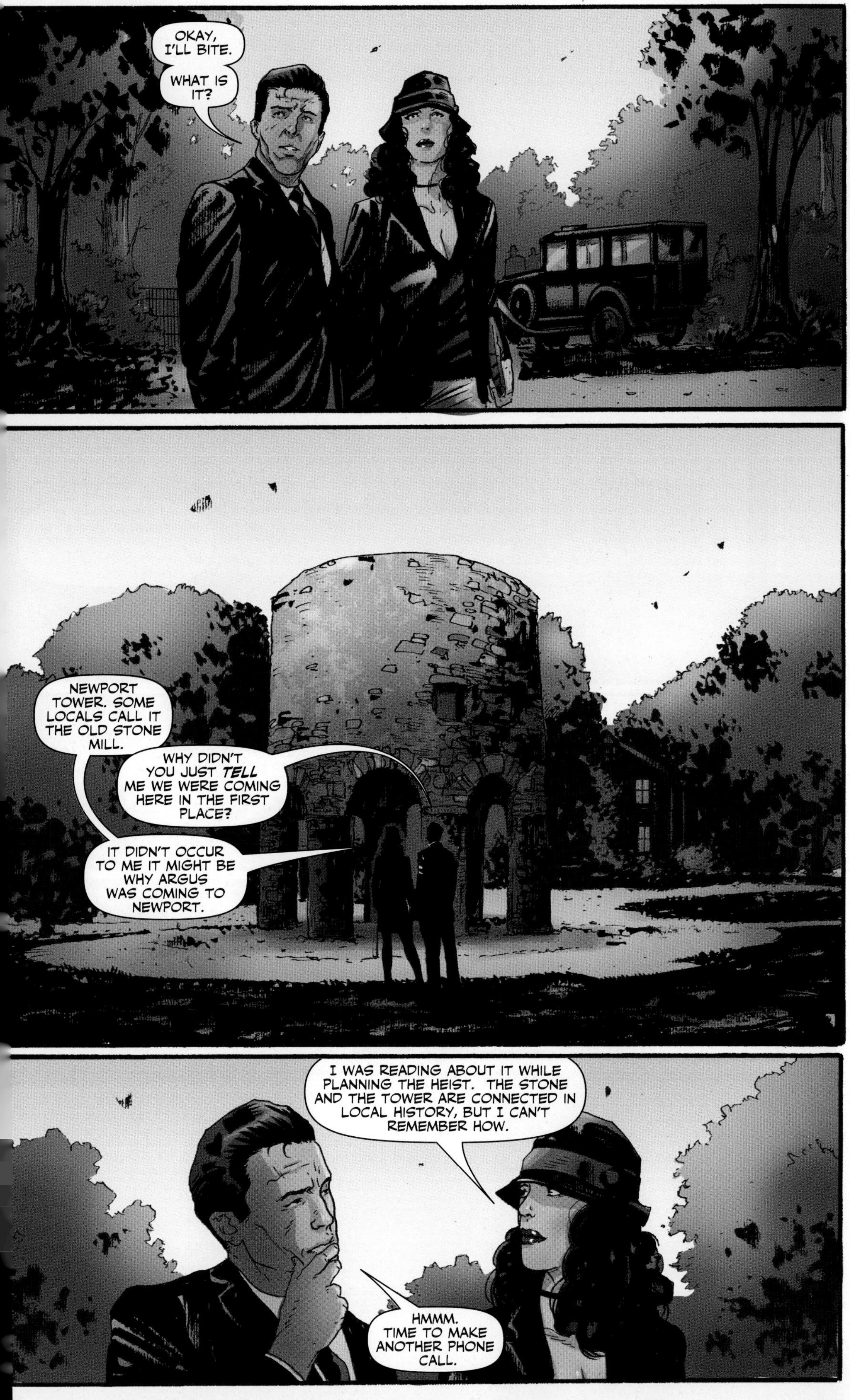
OKAY, I'LL BITE.
WHAT IS IT?
NEWPORT TOWER. SOME LOCALS CALL IT THE OLD STONE MILL.
WHY DIDN'T YOU JUST *TELL* ME WE WERE COMING HERE IN THE FIRST PLACE?
IT DIDN'T OCCUR TO ME IT MIGHT BE WHY ARGUS WAS COMING TO NEWPORT.
I WAS READING ABOUT IT WHILE PLANNING THE HEIST. THE STONE AND THE TOWER ARE CONNECTED IN LOCAL HISTORY, BUT I CAN'T REMEMBER HOW.
HMMM. TIME TO MAKE ANOTHER PHONE CALL.

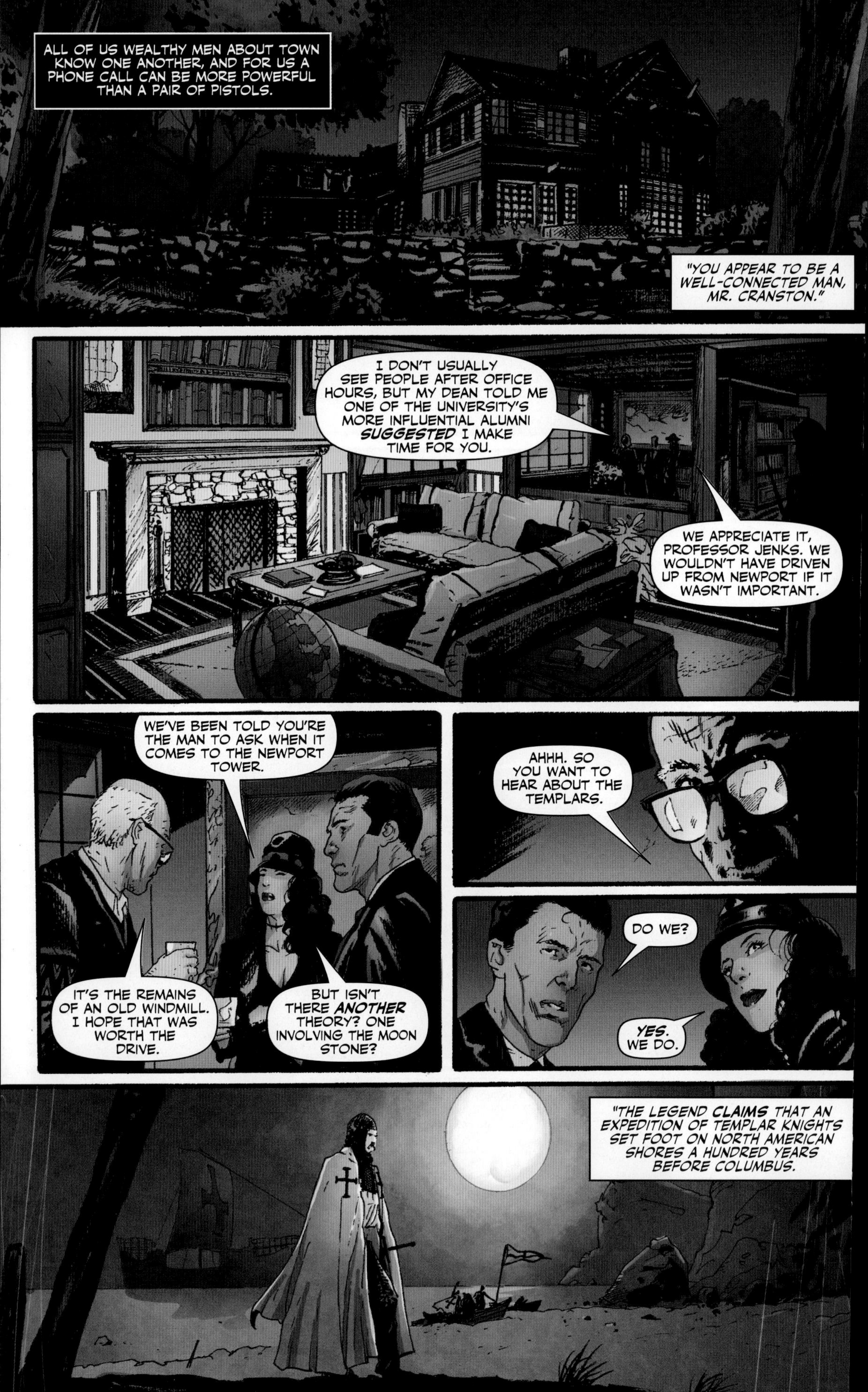
ALL OF US WEALTHY MEN ABOUT TOWN KNOW ONE ANOTHER, AND FOR US A PHONE CALL CAN BE MORE POWERFUL THAN A PAIR OF PISTOLS.
"YOU APPEAR TO BE A WELL-CONNECTED MAN, MR. CRANSTON."
I DON'T USUALLY SEE PEOPLE AFTER OFFICE HOURS, BUT MY DEAN TOLD ME ONE OF THE UNIVERSITY'S MORE INFLUENTIAL ALUMNI SUGGESTED I MAKE TIME FOR YOU.
WE APPRECIATE IT, PROFESSOR JENKS. WE WOULDN'T HAVE DRIVEN UP FROM NEWPORT IF IT WASN'T IMPORTANT.
WE'VE BEEN TOLD YOU'RE THE MAN TO ASK WHEN IT COMES TO THE NEWPORT TOWER.
IT'S THE REMAINS OF AN OLD WINDMILL. I HOPE THAT WAS WORTH THE DRIVE.
BUT ISN'T THERE ANOTHER THEORY? ONE INVOLVING THE MOON STONE?
AHHH. SO YOU WANT TO HEAR ABOUT THE TEMPLARS.
DO WE?
YES. WE DO.
"THE LEGEND CLAIMS THAT AN EXPEDITION OF TEMPLAR KNIGHTS SET FOOT ON NORTH AMERICAN SHORES A HUNDRED YEARS BEFORE COLUMBUS.

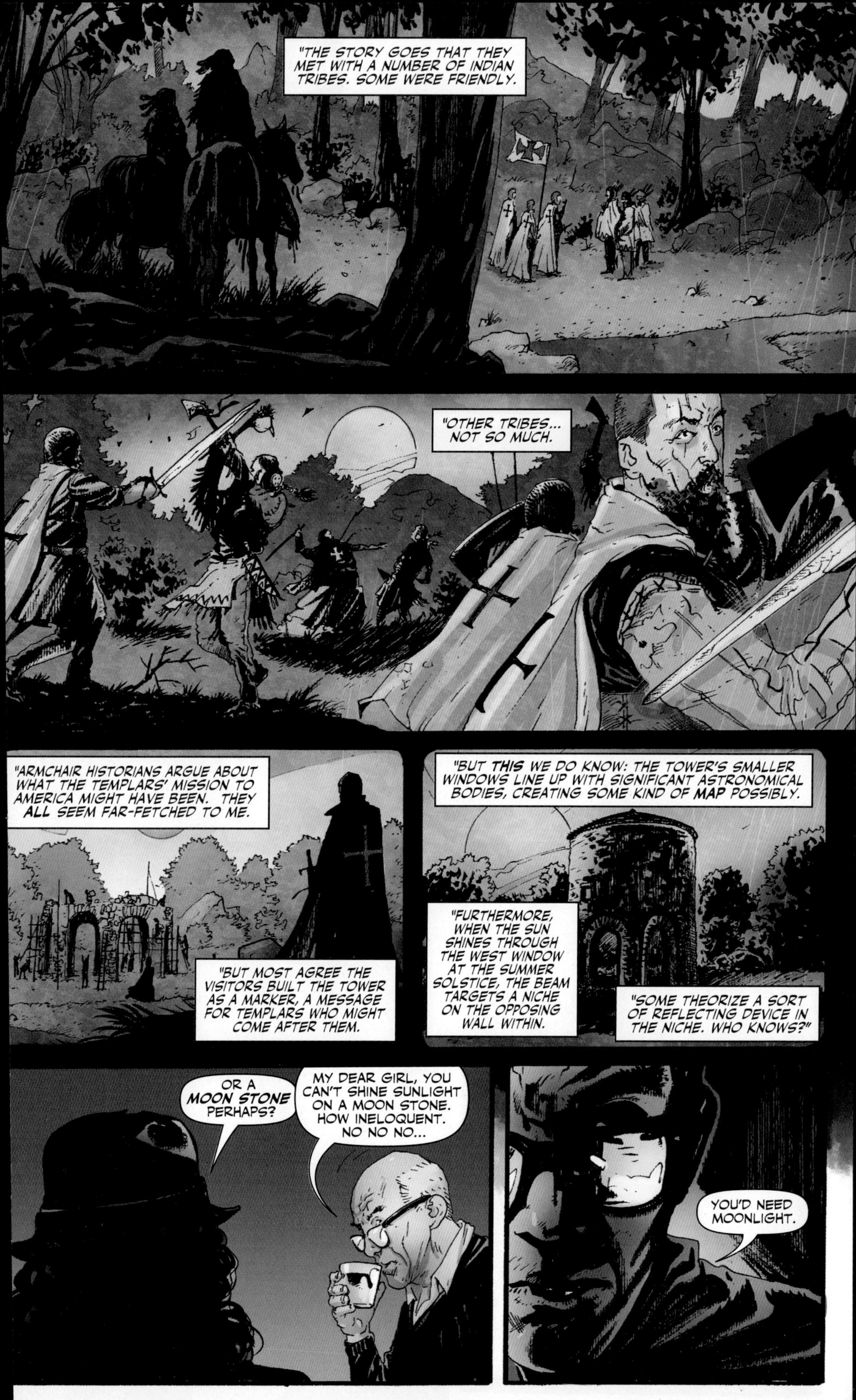
"THE STORY GOES THAT THEY MET WITH A NUMBER OF INDIAN TRIBES. SOME WERE FRIENDLY.
"OTHER TRIBES... NOT SO MUCH.
"ARMCHAIR HISTORIANS ARGUE ABOUT WHAT THE TEMPLARS' MISSION TO AMERICA MIGHT HAVE BEEN. THEY ALL SEEM FAR-FETCHED TO ME.
"BUT MOST AGREE THE VISITORS BUILT THE TOWER AS A MARKER, A MESSAGE FOR TEMPLARS WHO MIGHT COME AFTER THEM.
"BUT THIS WE DO KNOW: THE TOWER'S SMALLER WINDOWS LINE UP WITH SIGNIFICANT ASTRONOMICAL BODIES, CREATING SOME KIND OF MAP POSSIBLY.
"FURTHERMORE, WHEN THE SUN SHINES THROUGH THE WEST WINDOW AT THE SUMMER SOLSTICE, THE BEAM TARGETS A NICHE ON THE OPPOSING WALL WITHIN.
"SOME THEORIZE A SORT OF REFLECTING DEVICE IN THE NICHE. WHO KNOWS?"
OR A MOON STONE PERHAPS?
MY DEAR GIRL, YOU CAN'T SHINE SUNLIGHT ON A MOON STONE. HOW INELOQUENT. NO NO NO...
YOU'D NEED MOONLIGHT.

AND *WHY* IS THIS IMPORTANT?

IT'S *NOT* IMPORTANT. IT'S ALL *BUNK*.

THE STONE IS SUPPOSED TO AMPLIFY AND REFLECT MOONLIGHT, REVEALING... *SOMETHING*. A MESSAGE. A TREASURE MAP. ALL PURE FANTASY.

I SUPPOSE *ONE* MORE GLASS WOULDN'T HURT...

FORGIVE ME, PROFESSOR, BUT YOU SEEM TO KNOW A *LOT* ABOUT THESE LEGENDS FOR SOMEONE WHO DOESN'T BELIEVE THEM.

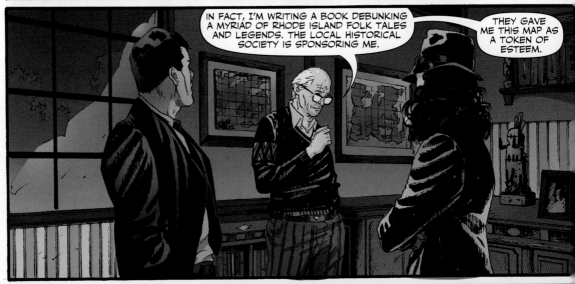

IN FACT, I'M WRITING A BOOK DEBUNKING A MYRIAD OF RHODE ISLAND FOLK TALES AND LEGENDS. THE LOCAL HISTORICAL SOCIETY IS SPONSORING ME.

THEY GAVE ME THIS MAP AS A TOKEN OF ESTEEM.

IT DATES BACK TO 1770 AND WAS RECENTLY DISCOVERED AT AN ESTATE SALE. AS YOU CAN SEE, THERE ARE NO TOWNS OR LANDMARKS, SO IT'S REALLY QUITE USELESS.

BUT IT HAS THE MARK OF THE *TEMPLAR* ON IT, AND THE SOCIETY THOUGHT I MIGHT BE AMUSED.

A NUMBER OF PEOPLE HAVE OFFERED TO BUY IT, BUT AS I TOLD THE YOUNG GENTLEMAN THIS AFTERNOON, I HAVE *NO* INTENTION OF SELLING. GROWN RATHER FOND OF IT ACTUALLY.

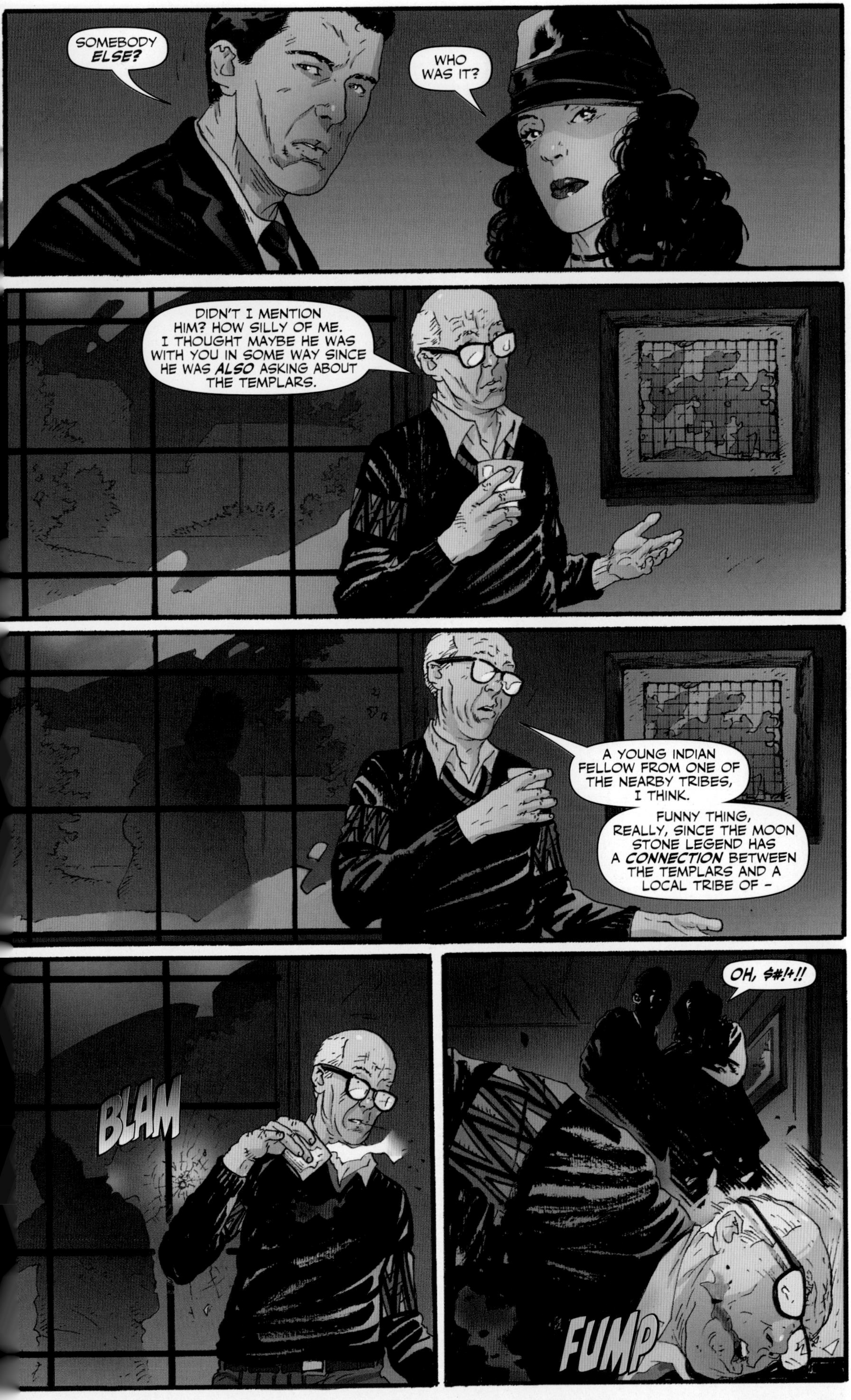
SOMEBODY ELSE?
WHO WAS IT?
DIDN'T I MENTION HIM? HOW SILLY OF ME. I THOUGHT MAYBE HE WAS WITH YOU IN SOME WAY SINCE HE WAS ALSO ASKING ABOUT THE TEMPLARS.
A YOUNG INDIAN FELLOW FROM ONE OF THE NEARBY TRIBES, I THINK.
FUNNY THING, REALLY, SINCE THE MOON STONE LEGEND HAS A CONNECTION BETWEEN THE TEMPLARS AND A LOCAL TRIBE OF –
BLAM
OH, $#!+!!
FUMP

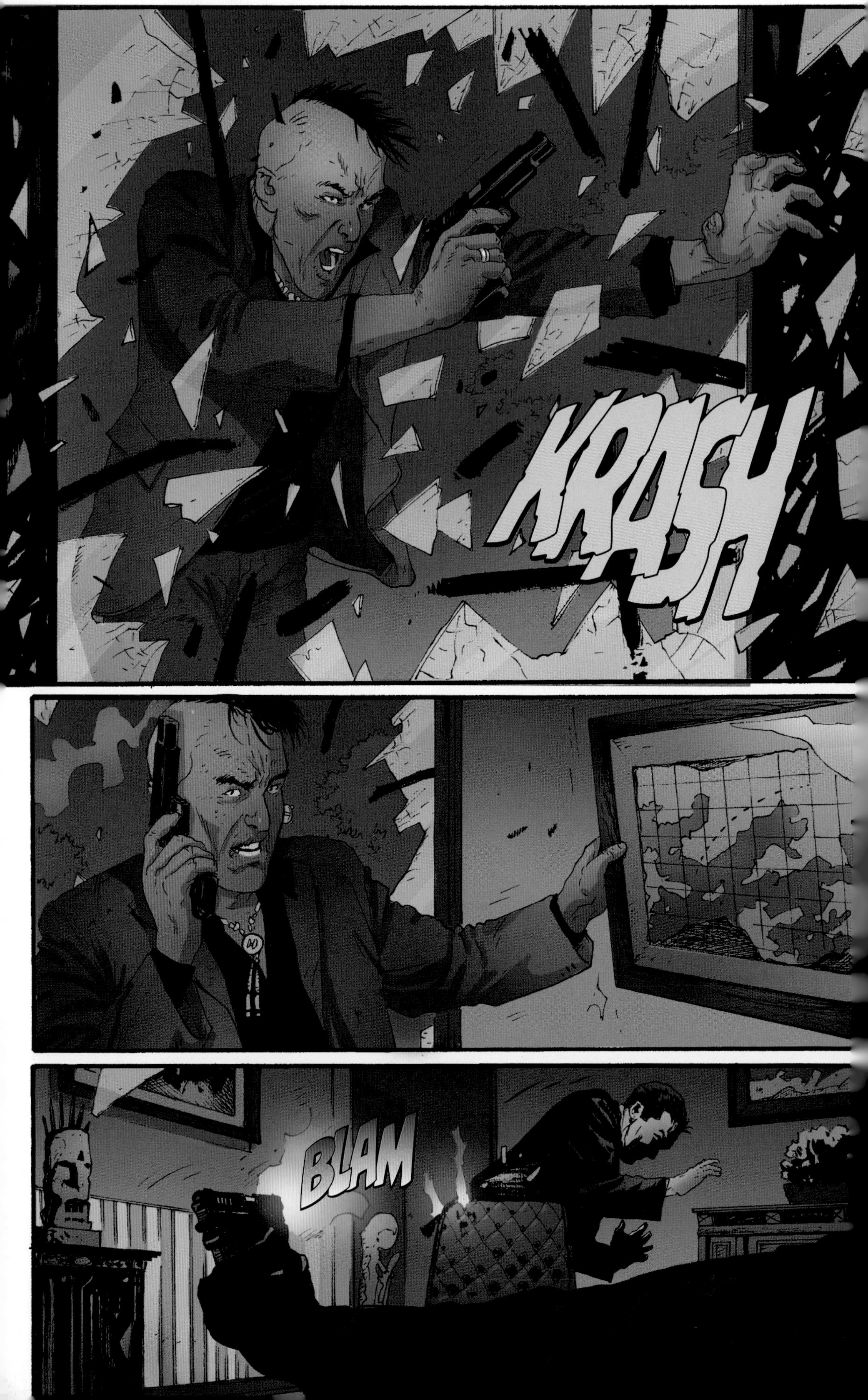
KRASH
BLAM

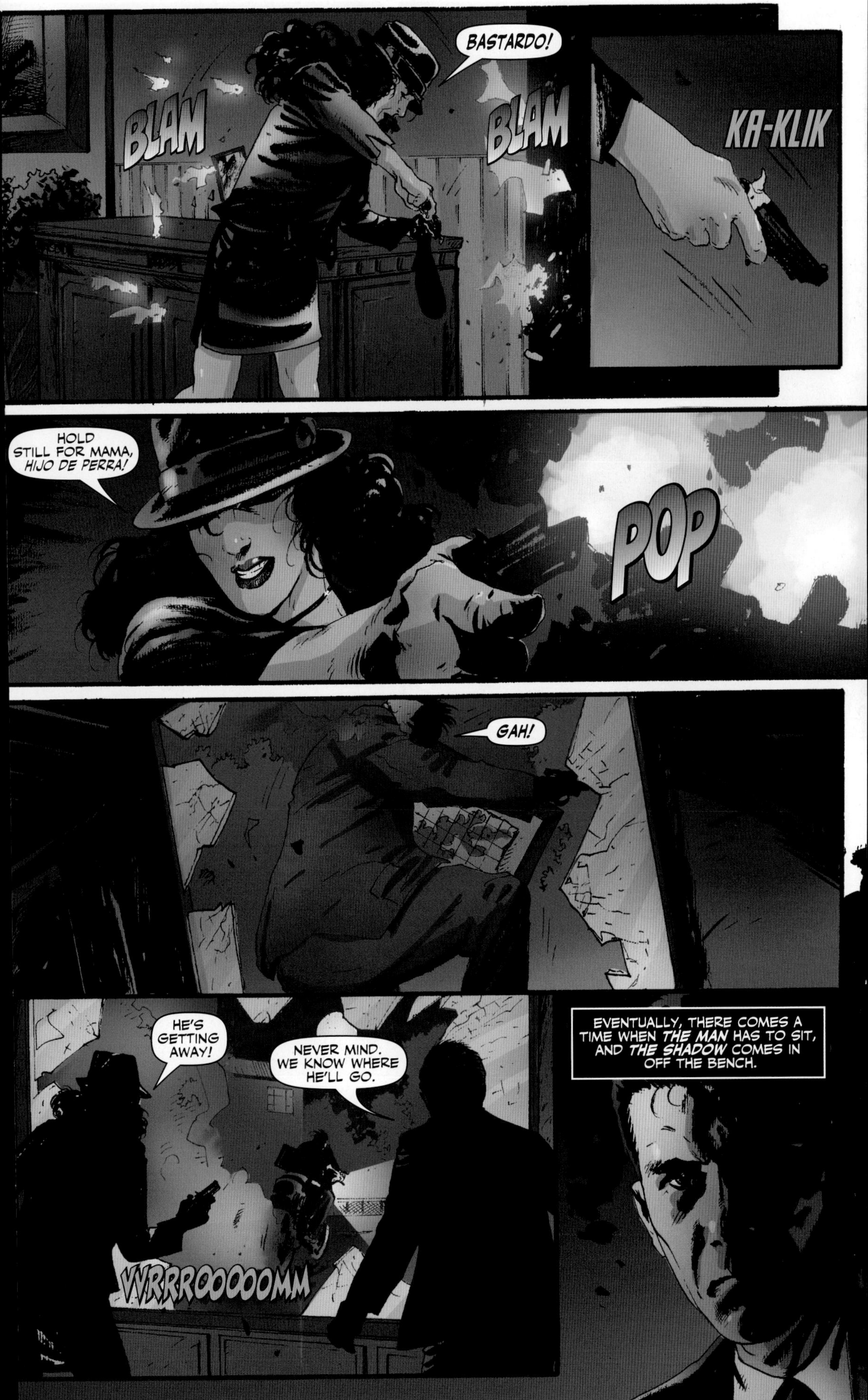
BASTARDO!
BLAM
BLAM
KA-KLIK
HOLD STILL FOR MAMA, HIJO DE PERRA!
POP
GAH!
HE'S GETTING AWAY!
NEVER MIND. WE KNOW WHERE HE'LL GO.
VVRRROOOOOMM
EVENTUALLY, THERE COMES A TIME WHEN THE MAN HAS TO SIT, AND THE SHADOW COMES IN OFF THE BENCH.

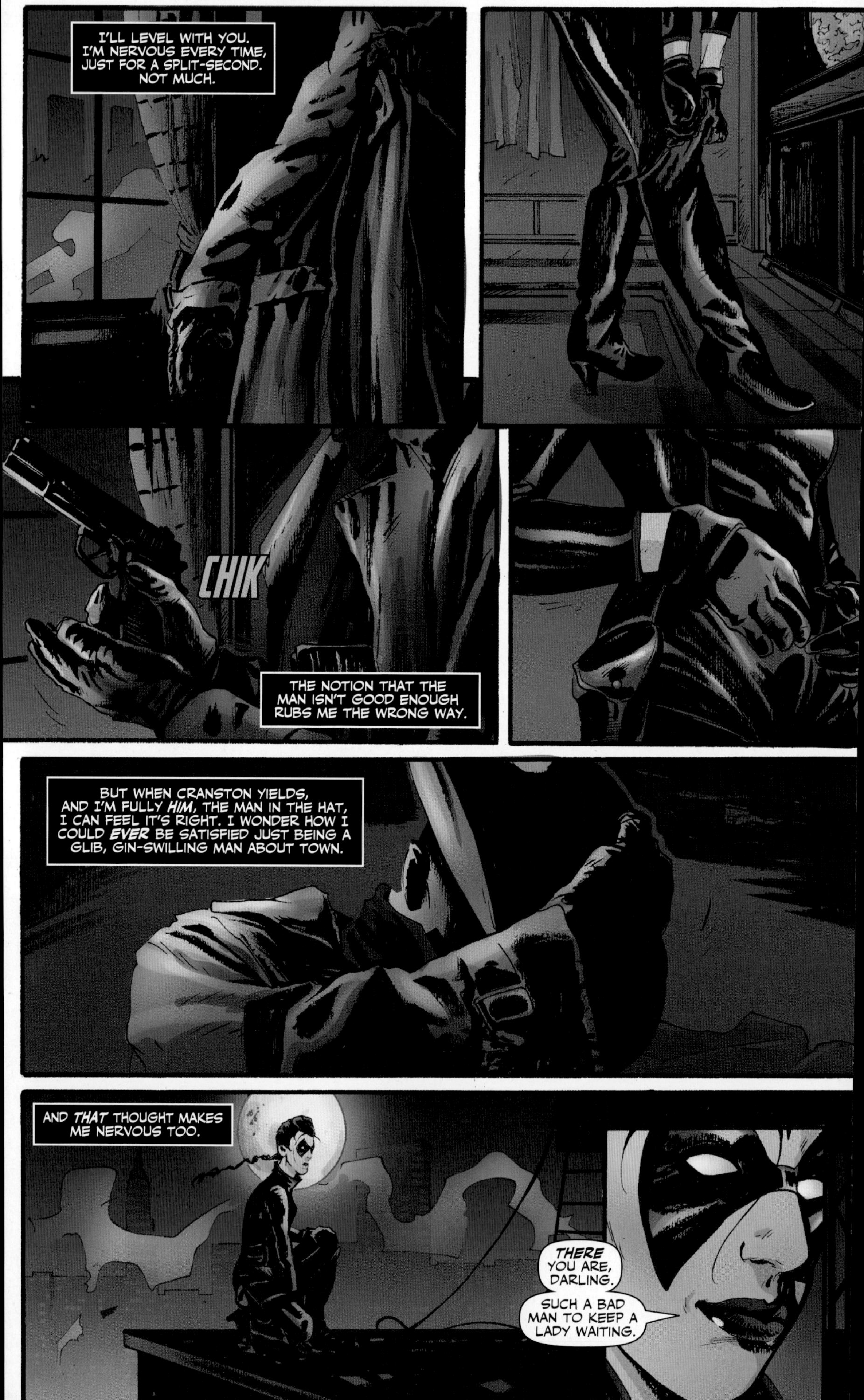
I'LL LEVEL WITH YOU. I'M NERVOUS EVERY TIME, JUST FOR A SPLIT-SECOND. NOT MUCH.
CHIK
THE NOTION THAT THE MAN ISN'T GOOD ENOUGH RUBS ME THE WRONG WAY.
BUT WHEN CRANSTON YIELDS, AND I'M FULLY *HIM*, THE MAN IN THE HAT, I CAN FEEL IT'S RIGHT. I WONDER HOW I COULD *EVER* BE SATISFIED JUST BEING A GLIB, GIN-SWILLING MAN ABOUT TOWN.
AND *THAT* THOUGHT MAKES ME NERVOUS TOO.
THERE YOU ARE, DARLING.
SUCH A BAD MAN TO KEEP A LADY WAITING.

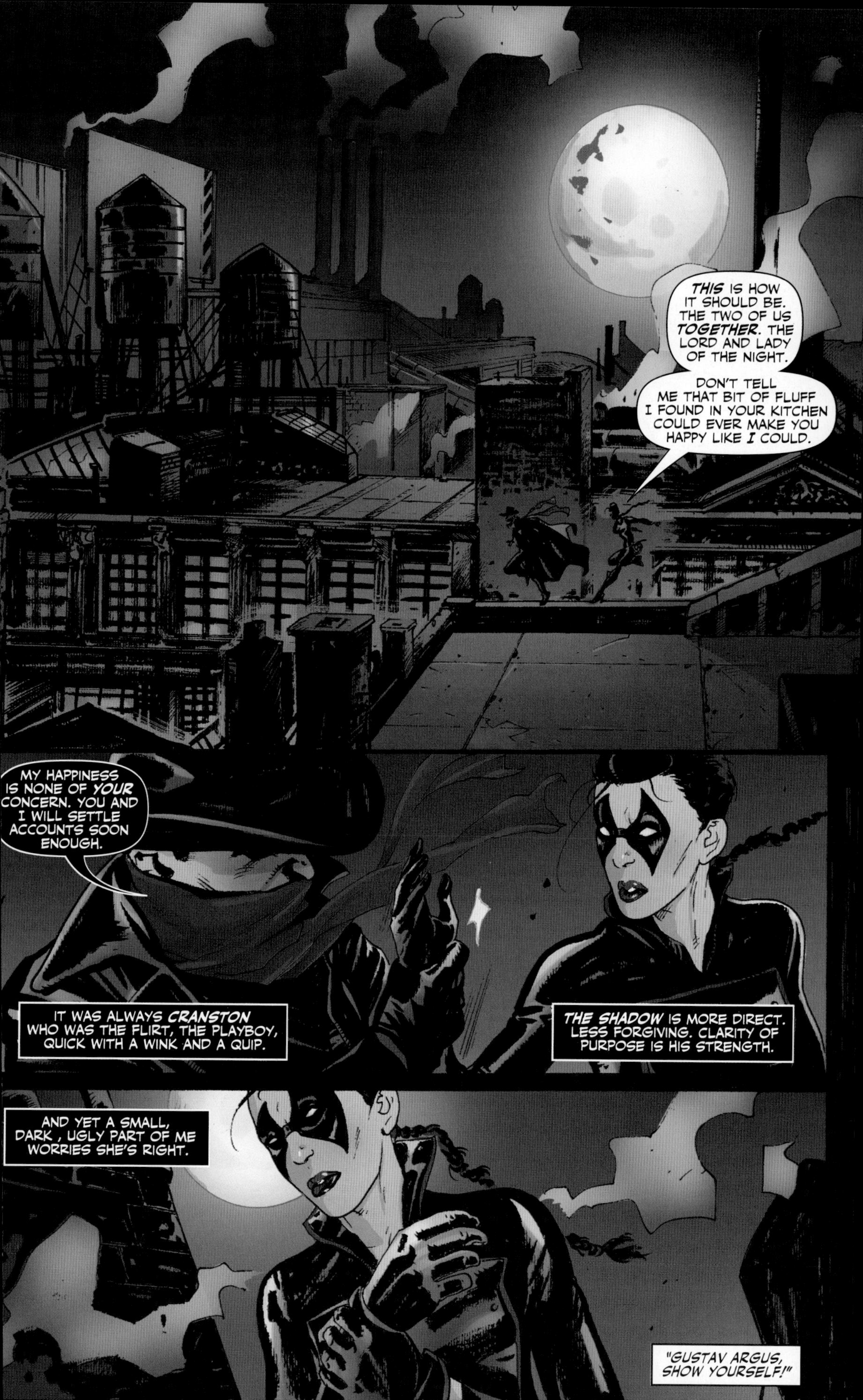
THIS IS HOW IT SHOULD BE. THE TWO OF US TOGETHER. THE LORD AND LADY OF THE NIGHT.
DON'T TELL ME THAT BIT OF FLUFF I FOUND IN YOUR KITCHEN COULD EVER MAKE YOU HAPPY LIKE I COULD.
MY HAPPINESS IS NONE OF YOUR CONCERN. YOU AND I WILL SETTLE ACCOUNTS SOON ENOUGH.
IT WAS ALWAYS CRANSTON WHO WAS THE FLIRT, THE PLAYBOY, QUICK WITH A WINK AND A QUIP.
THE SHADOW IS MORE DIRECT. LESS FORGIVING. CLARITY OF PURPOSE IS HIS STRENGTH.
AND YET A SMALL, DARK, UGLY PART OF ME WORRIES SHE'S RIGHT.
"GUSTAV ARGUS, SHOW YOURSELF!"

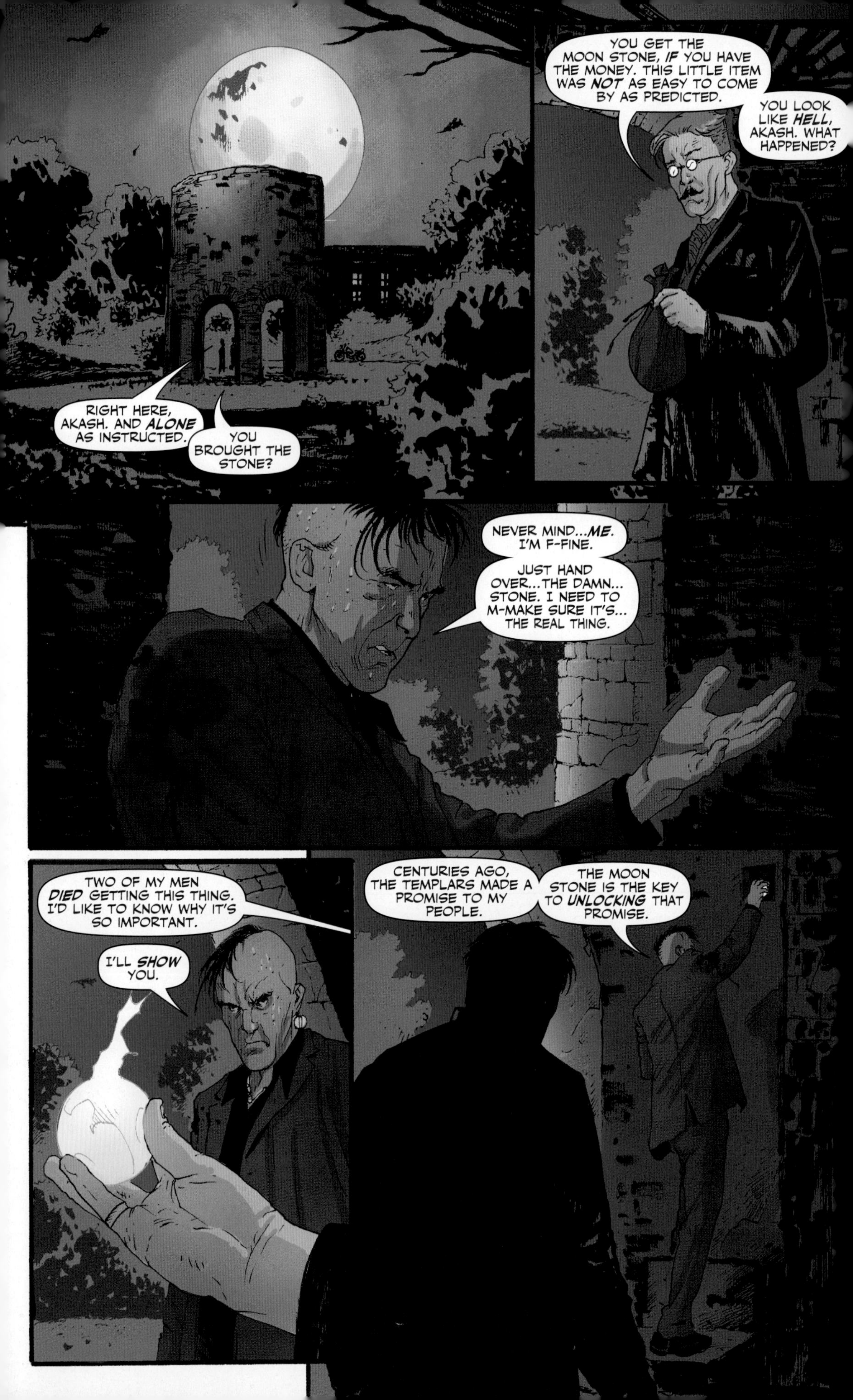

RIGHT HERE, AKASH. AND ALONE AS INSTRUCTED.
YOU BROUGHT THE STONE?
YOU GET THE MOON STONE, IF YOU HAVE THE MONEY. THIS LITTLE ITEM WAS NOT AS EASY TO COME BY AS PREDICTED.
YOU LOOK LIKE HELL, AKASH. WHAT HAPPENED?
NEVER MIND...ME. I'M F-FINE.
JUST HAND OVER...THE DAMN... STONE. I NEED TO M-MAKE SURE IT'S... THE REAL THING.
TWO OF MY MEN DIED GETTING THIS THING. I'D LIKE TO KNOW WHY IT'S SO IMPORTANT.
I'LL SHOW YOU.
CENTURIES AGO, THE TEMPLARS MADE A PROMISE TO MY PEOPLE.
THE MOON STONE IS THE KEY TO UNLOCKING THAT PROMISE.

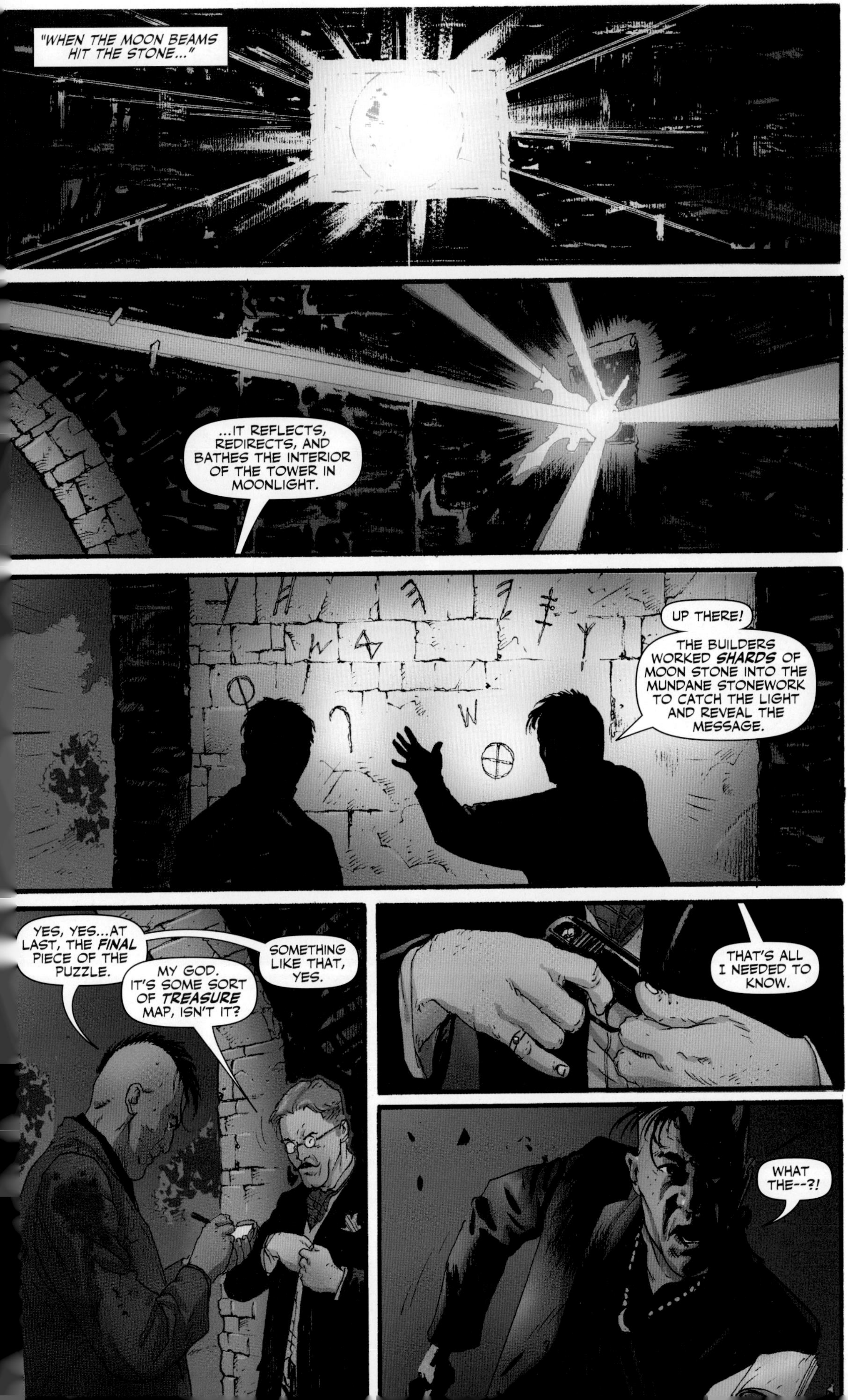
"WHEN THE MOON BEAMS HIT THE STONE..."
...IT REFLECTS, REDIRECTS, AND BATHES THE INTERIOR OF THE TOWER IN MOONLIGHT.
UP THERE!
THE BUILDERS WORKED SHARDS OF MOON STONE INTO THE MUNDANE STONEWORK TO CATCH THE LIGHT AND REVEAL THE MESSAGE.
YES, YES...AT LAST, THE FINAL PIECE OF THE PUZZLE.
MY GOD. IT'S SOME SORT OF TREASURE MAP, ISN'T IT?
SOMETHING LIKE THAT, YES.
THAT'S ALL I NEEDED TO KNOW.
WHAT THE--?!

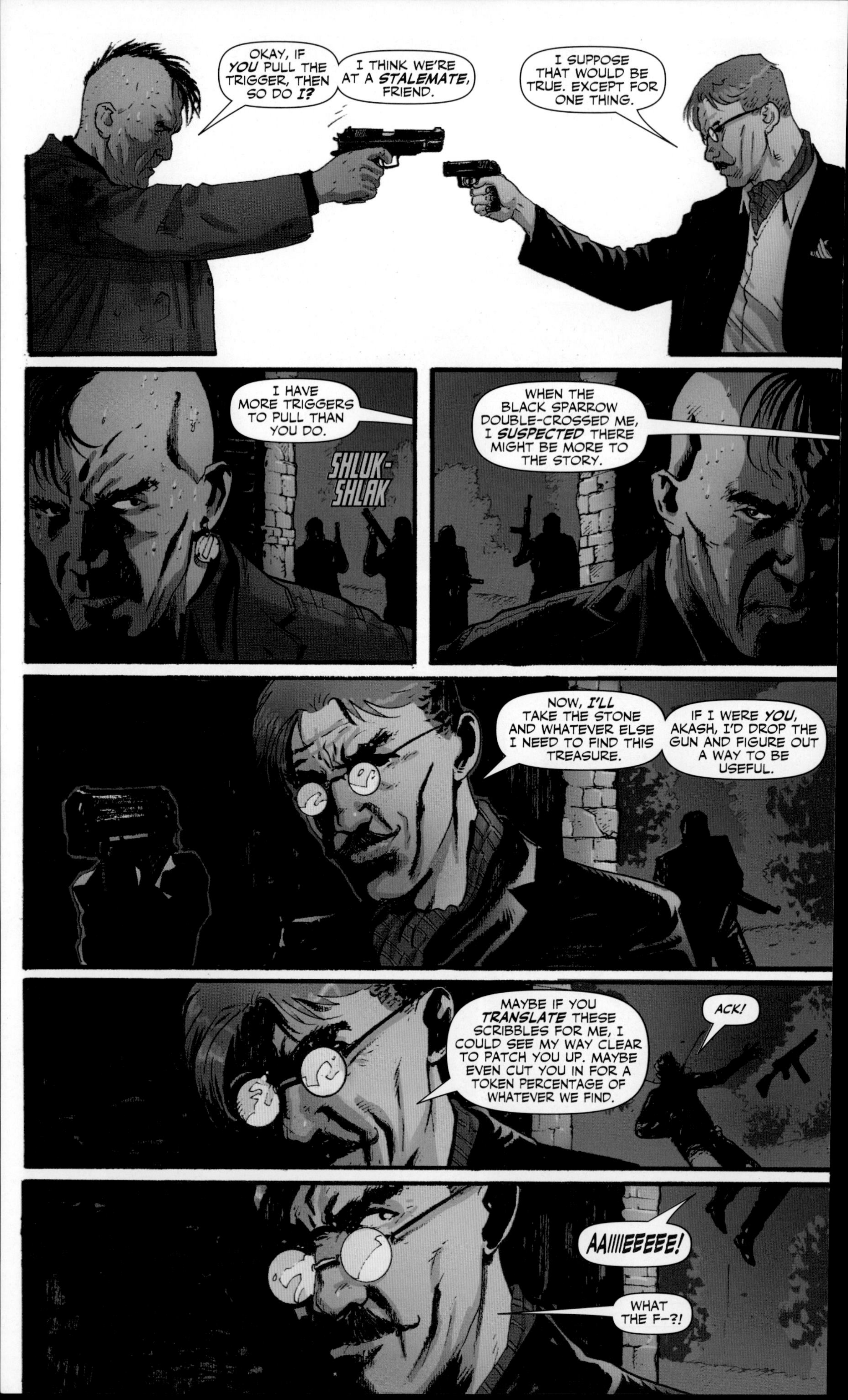
OKAY, IF *YOU* PULL THE TRIGGER, THEN SO DO *I?*
I THINK WE'RE AT A *STALEMATE*, FRIEND.
I SUPPOSE THAT WOULD BE TRUE. EXCEPT FOR ONE THING.
I HAVE MORE TRIGGERS TO PULL THAN YOU DO.
SHLUK-SHLAK
WHEN THE BLACK SPARROW DOUBLE-CROSSED ME, I *SUSPECTED* THERE MIGHT BE MORE TO THE STORY.
NOW, *I'LL* TAKE THE STONE AND WHATEVER ELSE I NEED TO FIND THIS TREASURE.
IF I WERE *YOU*, AKASH, I'D DROP THE GUN AND FIGURE OUT A WAY TO BE USEFUL.
MAYBE IF YOU *TRANSLATE* THESE SCRIBBLES FOR ME, I COULD SEE MY WAY CLEAR TO PATCH YOU UP. MAYBE EVEN CUT YOU IN FOR A TOKEN PERCENTAGE OF WHATEVER WE FIND.
ACK!
AAIIIIEEEEE!
WHAT THE F–?!

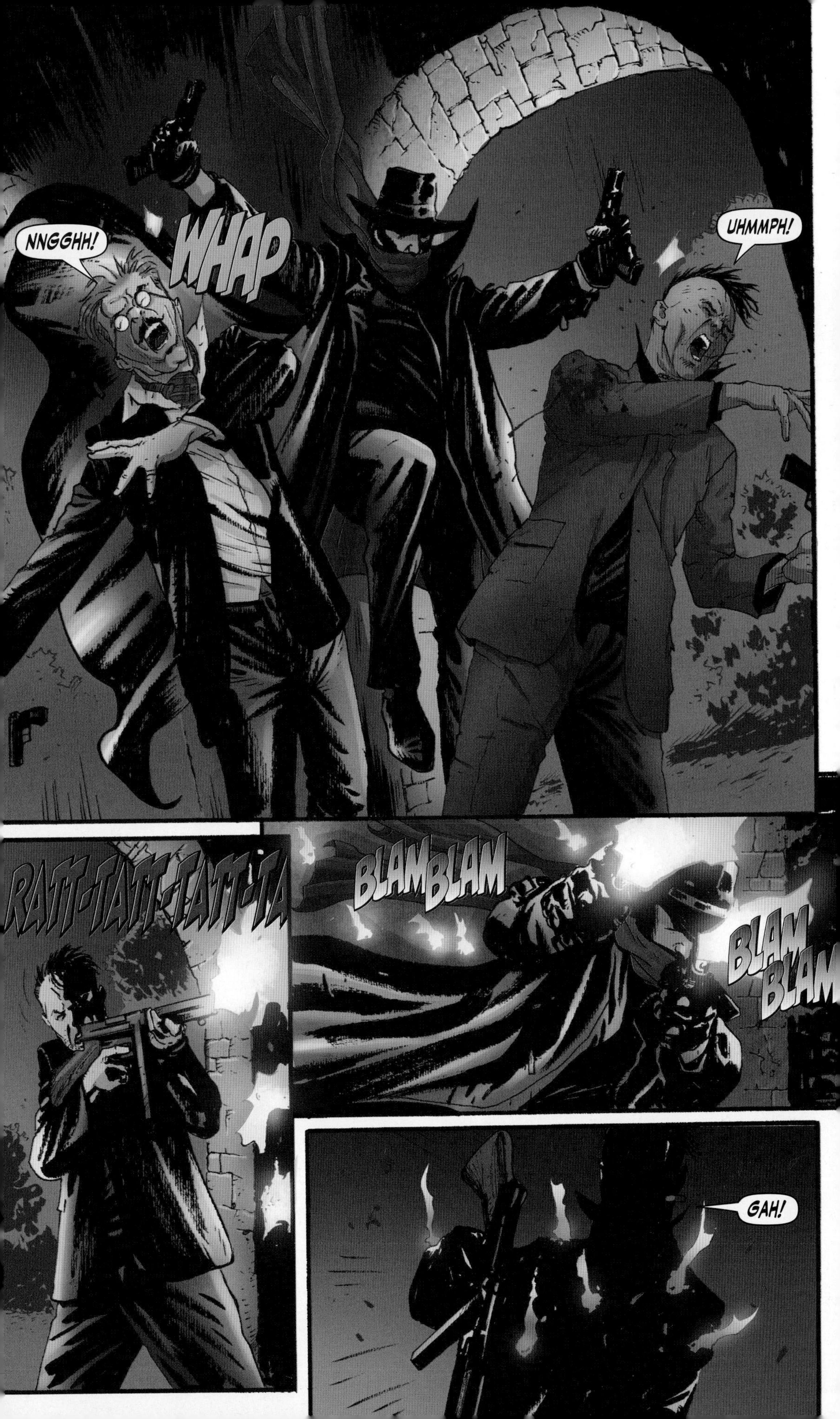
NNGGHH!
WHAP
UHMMPH!
RATT-TATT-TATT-TA
BLAMBLAM
BLAM
BLAM
GAH!

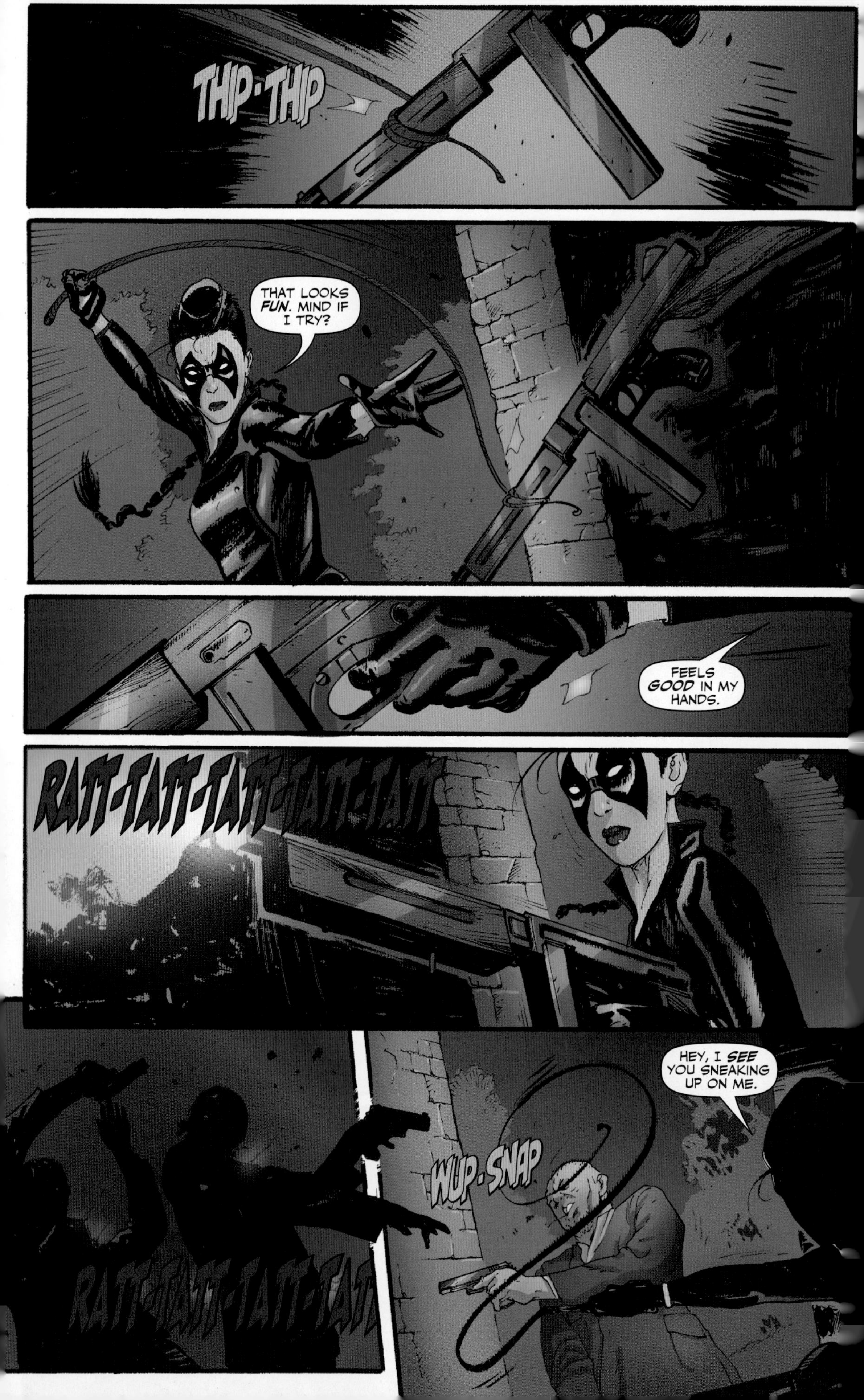
THIP-THIP
THAT LOOKS FUN. MIND IF I TRY?
FEELS GOOD IN MY HANDS.
RATT-TATT-TATT-TATT-TATT
RATT-TATT-TATT-TATT
WUP-SNAP
HEY, I SEE YOU SNEAKING UP ON ME.

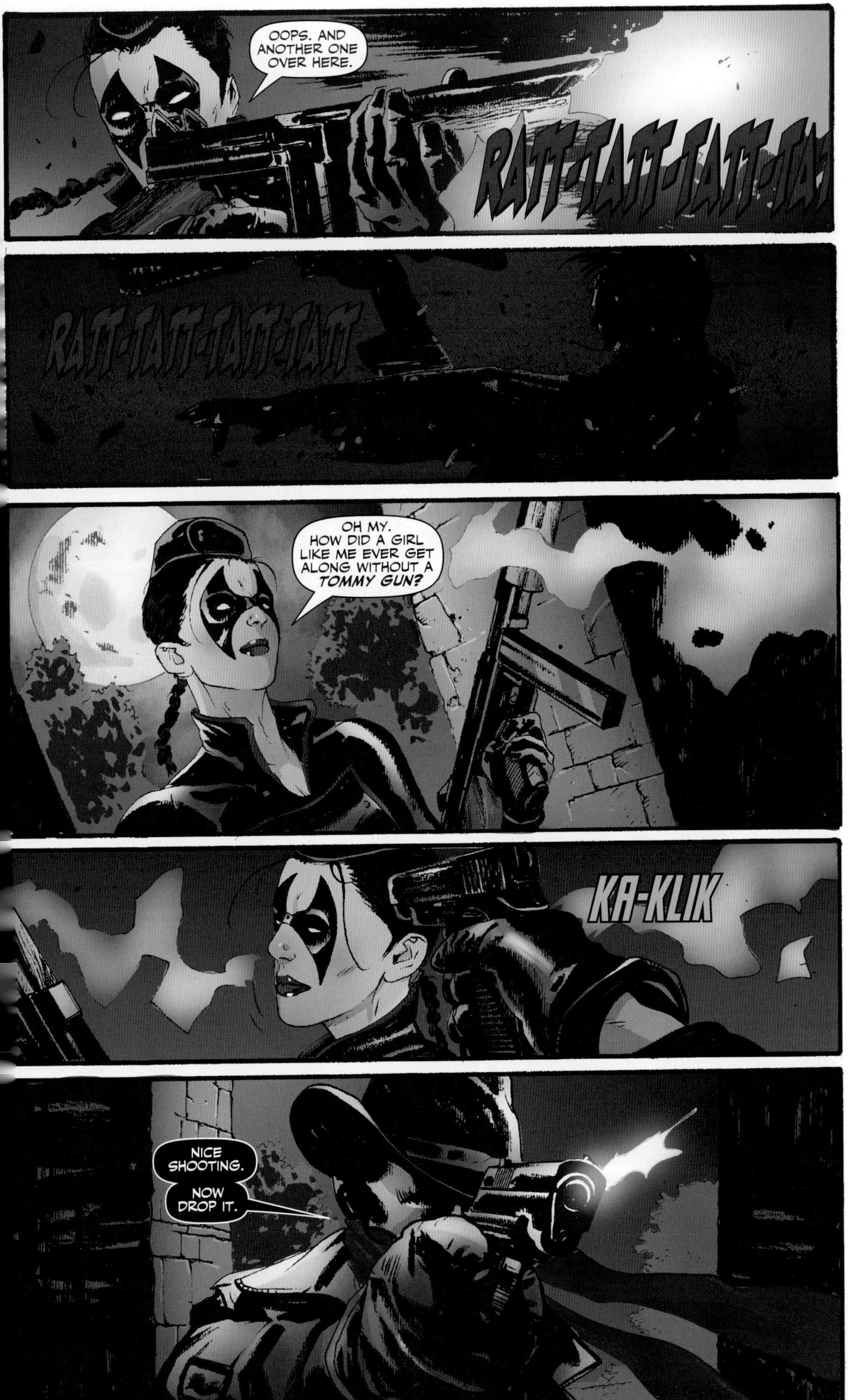

OOPS. AND ANOTHER ONE OVER HERE.
RATT-TATT-TATT-TAT
RATT-TATT-TATT-TATT
OH MY. HOW DID A GIRL LIKE ME EVER GET ALONG WITHOUT A *TOMMY GUN?*
KA-KLIK
NICE SHOOTING.
NOW DROP IT.

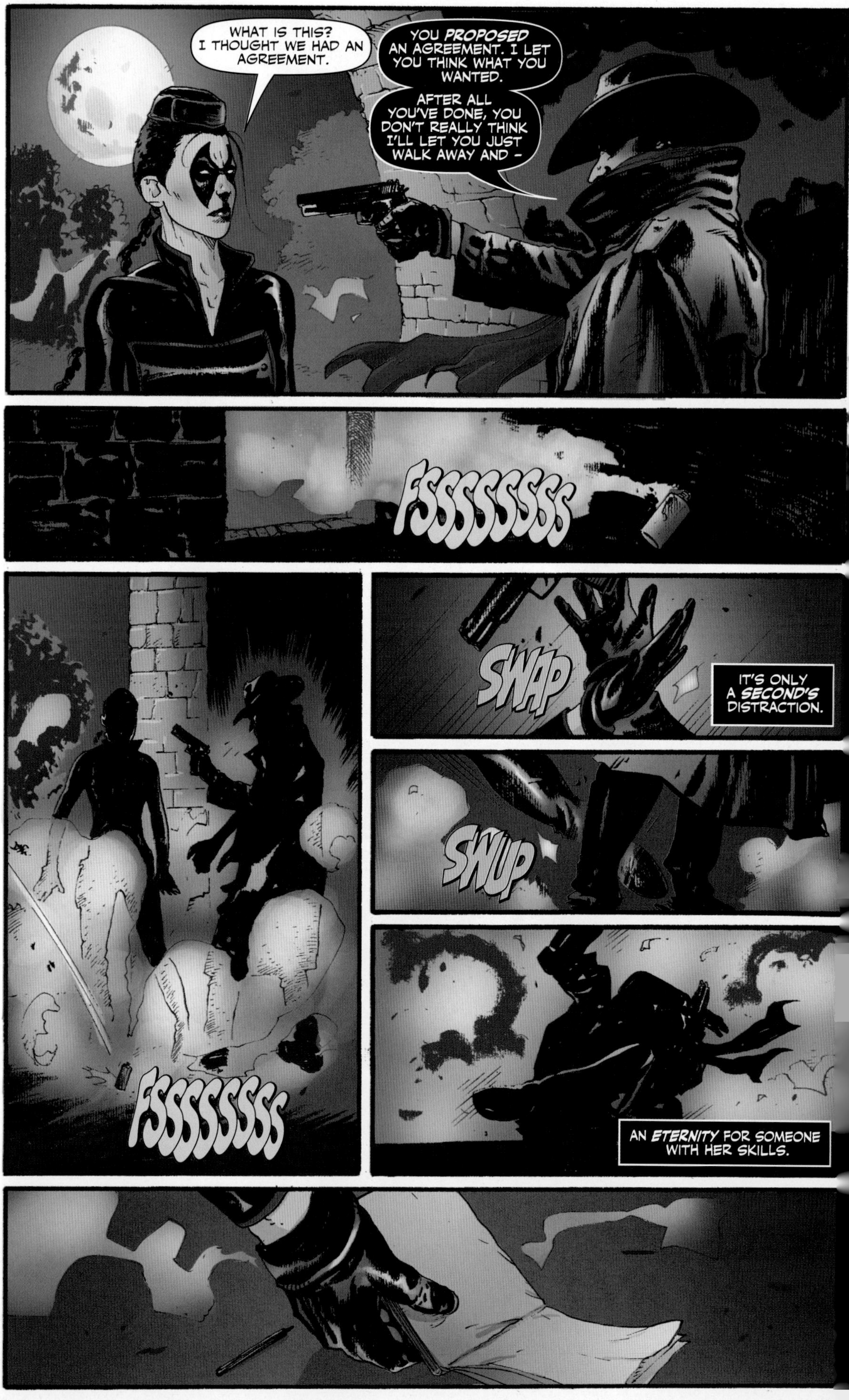
WHAT IS THIS? I THOUGHT WE HAD AN AGREEMENT.
YOU PROPOSED AN AGREEMENT. I LET YOU THINK WHAT YOU WANTED.
AFTER ALL YOU'VE DONE, YOU DON'T REALLY THINK I'LL LET YOU JUST WALK AWAY AND –
FSSSSSSSS
FSSSSSSSS
SWAP
IT'S ONLY A SECOND'S DISTRACTION.
SWUP
AN ETERNITY FOR SOMEONE WITH HER SKILLS.

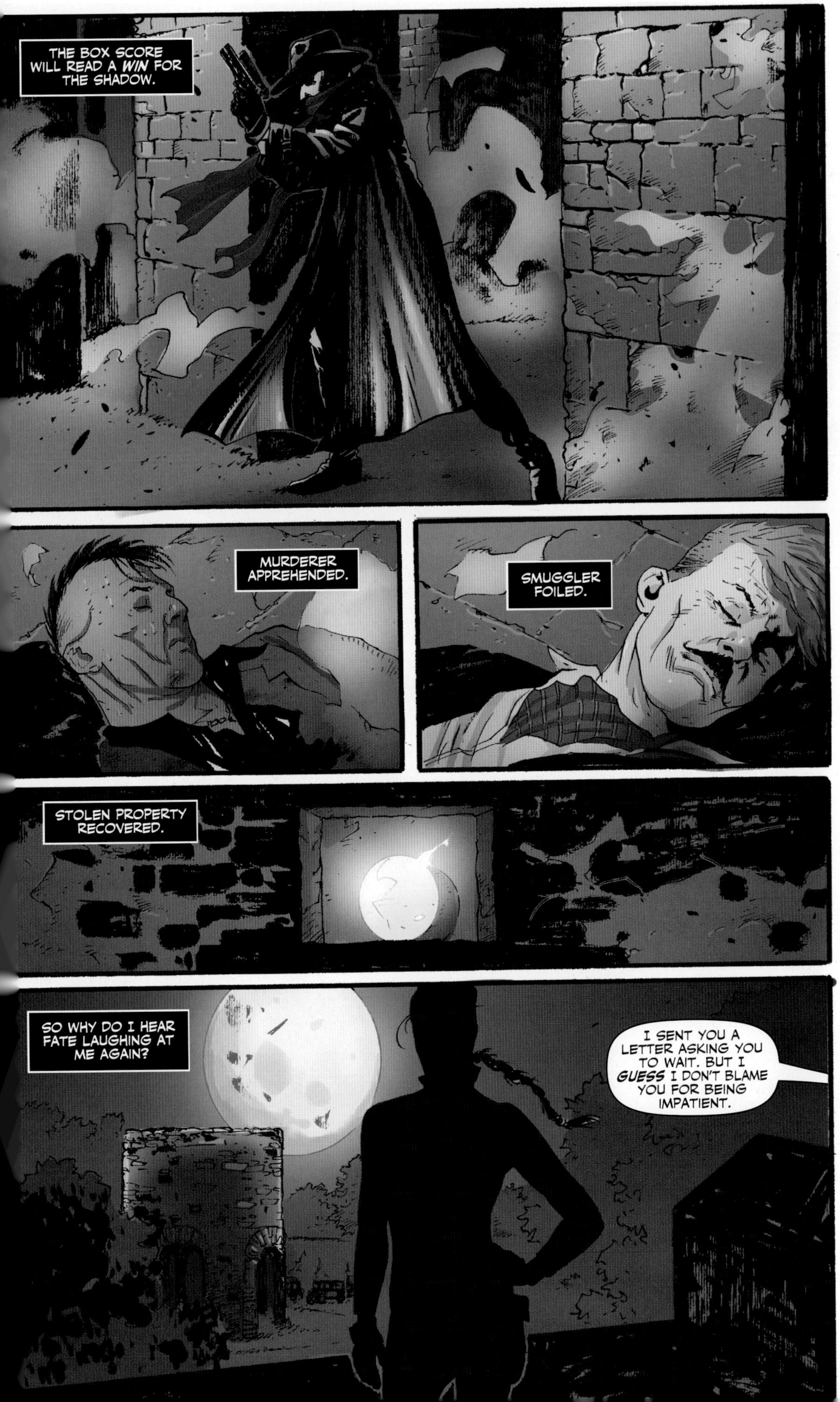
THE BOX SCORE WILL READ A *WIN* FOR THE SHADOW.
MURDERER APPREHENDED.
SMUGGLER FOILED.
STOLEN PROPERTY RECOVERED.
SO WHY DO I HEAR FATE LAUGHING AT ME AGAIN?
I SENT YOU A LETTER ASKING YOU TO WAIT. BUT I *GUESS* I DON'T BLAME YOU FOR BEING IMPATIENT.

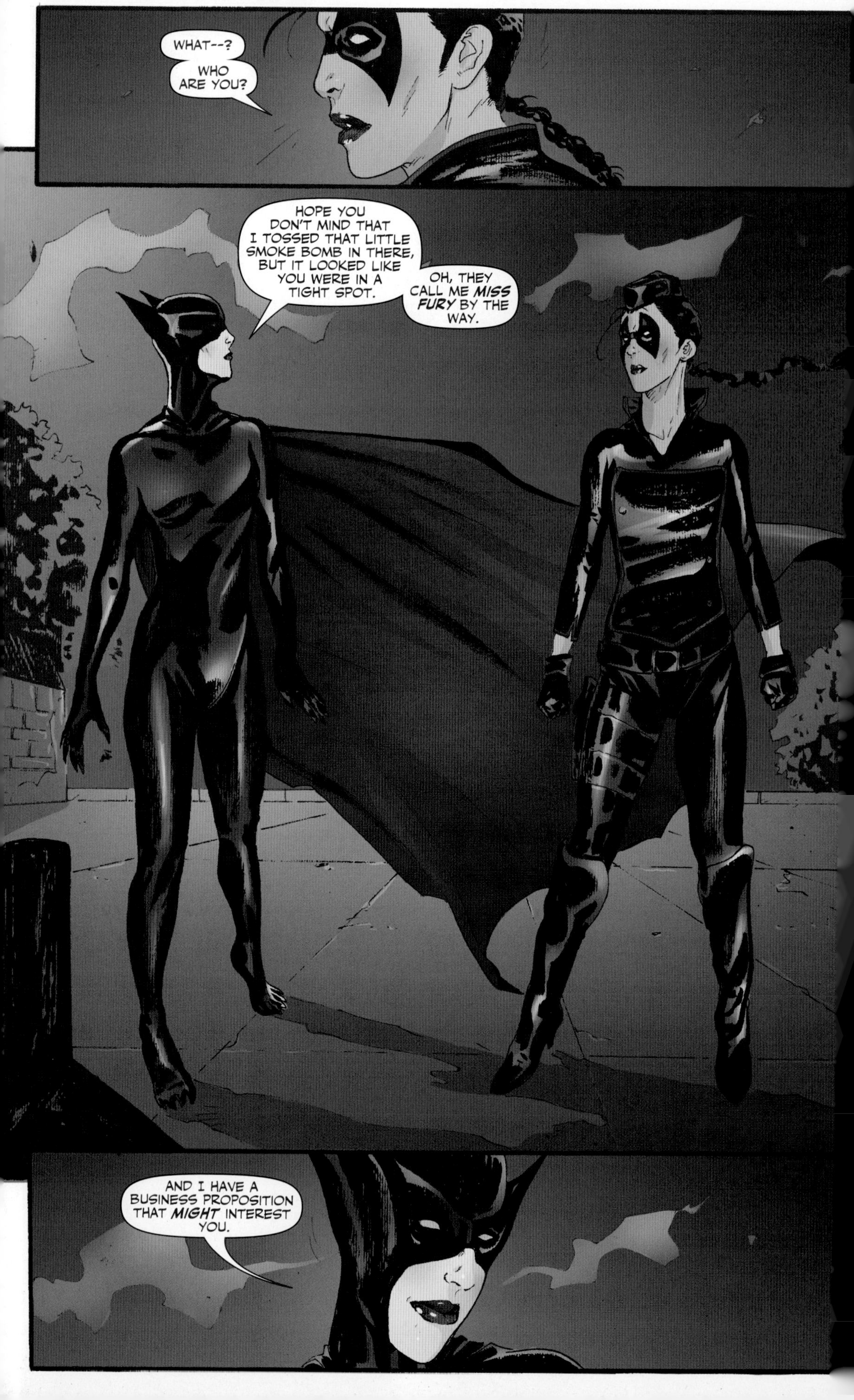
WHAT--?
WHO ARE YOU?
HOPE YOU DON'T MIND THAT I TOSSED THAT LITTLE SMOKE BOMB IN THERE, BUT IT LOOKED LIKE YOU WERE IN A TIGHT SPOT.
OH, THEY CALL ME *MISS FURY* BY THE WAY.
AND I HAVE A BUSINESS PROPOSITION THAT *MIGHT* INTEREST YOU.

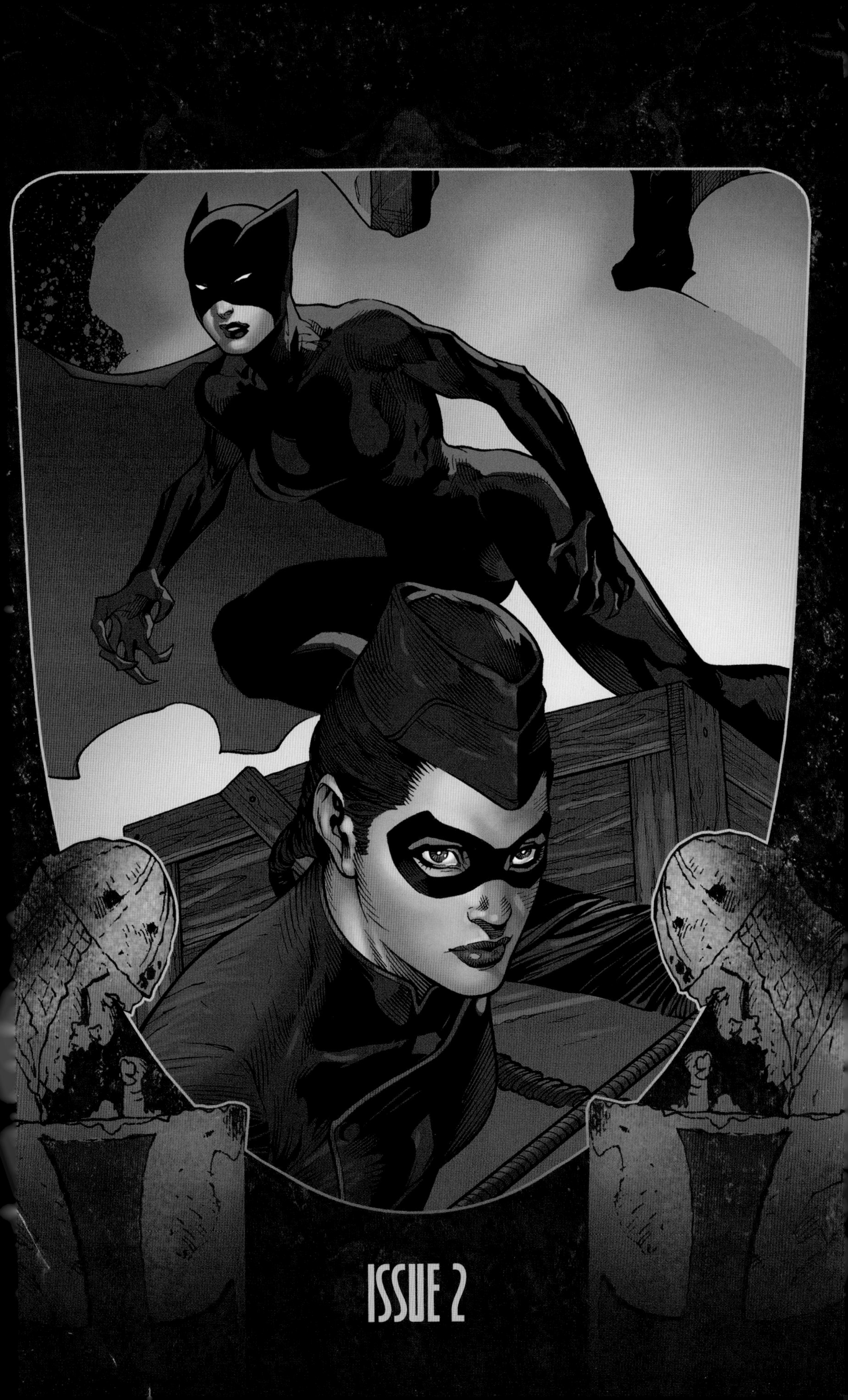

ISSUE 2

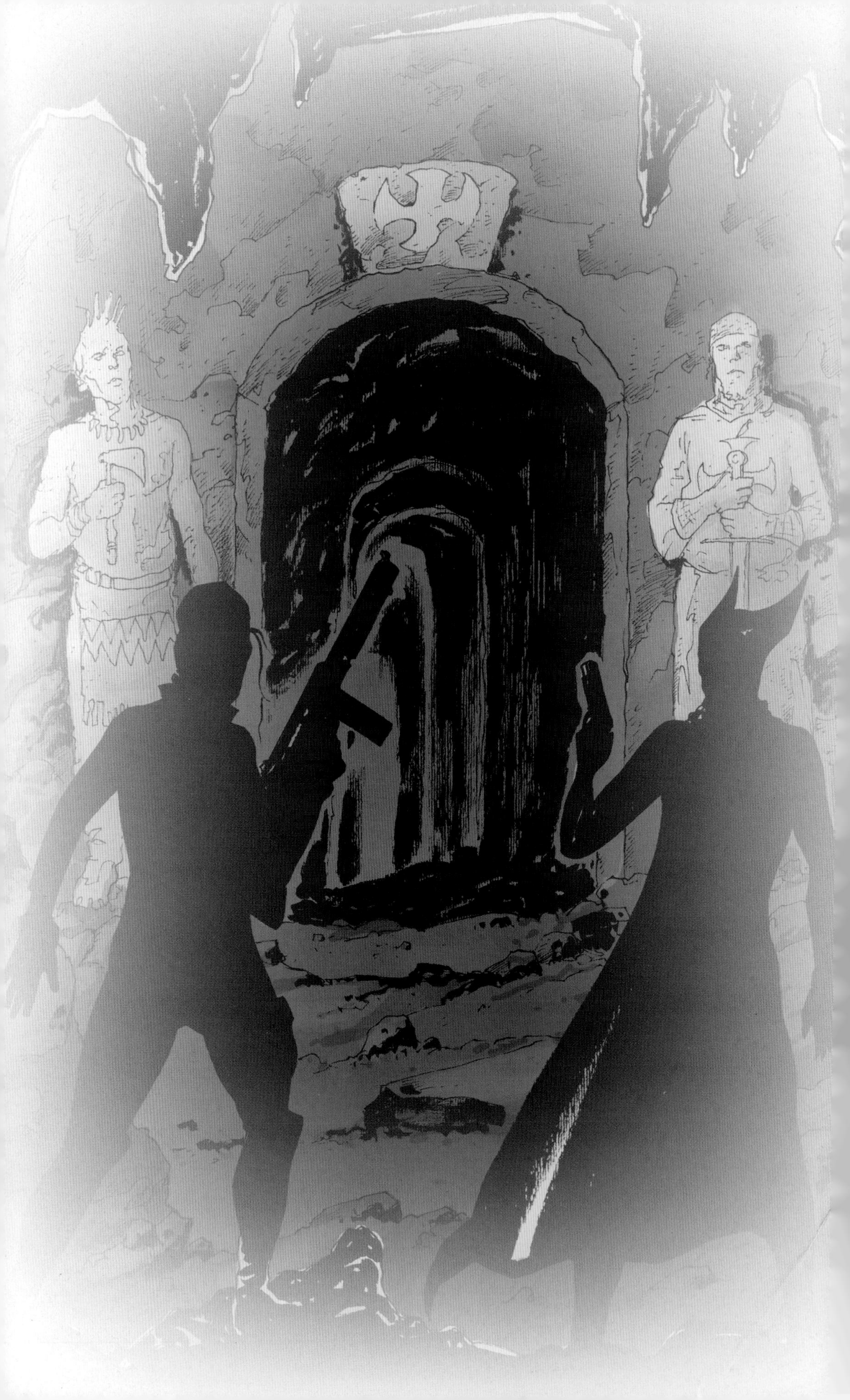

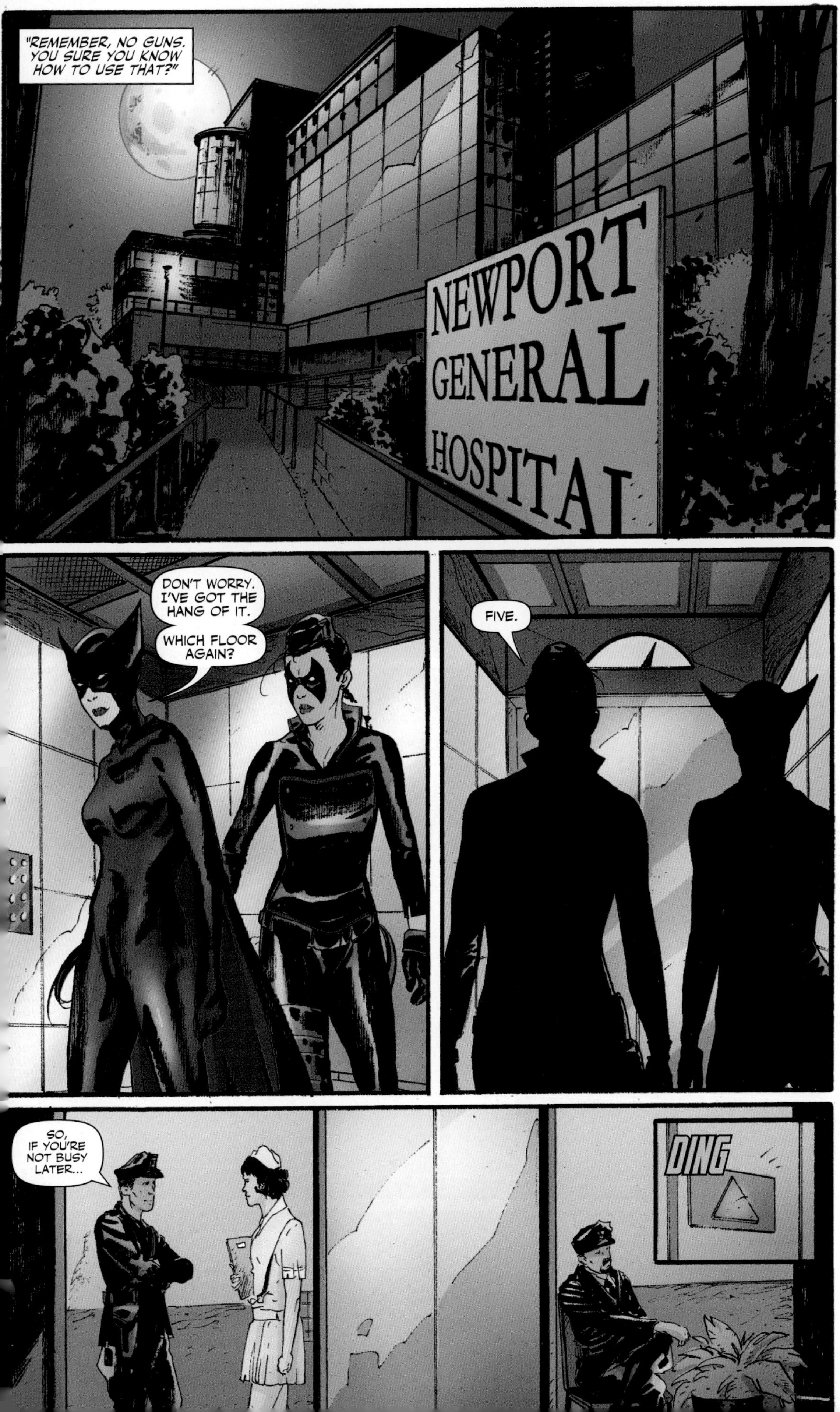
"REMEMBER, NO GUNS. YOU SURE YOU KNOW HOW TO USE THAT?"
NEWPORT GENERAL HOSPITAL
DON'T WORRY. I'VE GOT THE HANG OF IT.
WHICH FLOOR AGAIN?
FIVE.
SO, IF YOU'RE NOT BUSY LATER...
DING

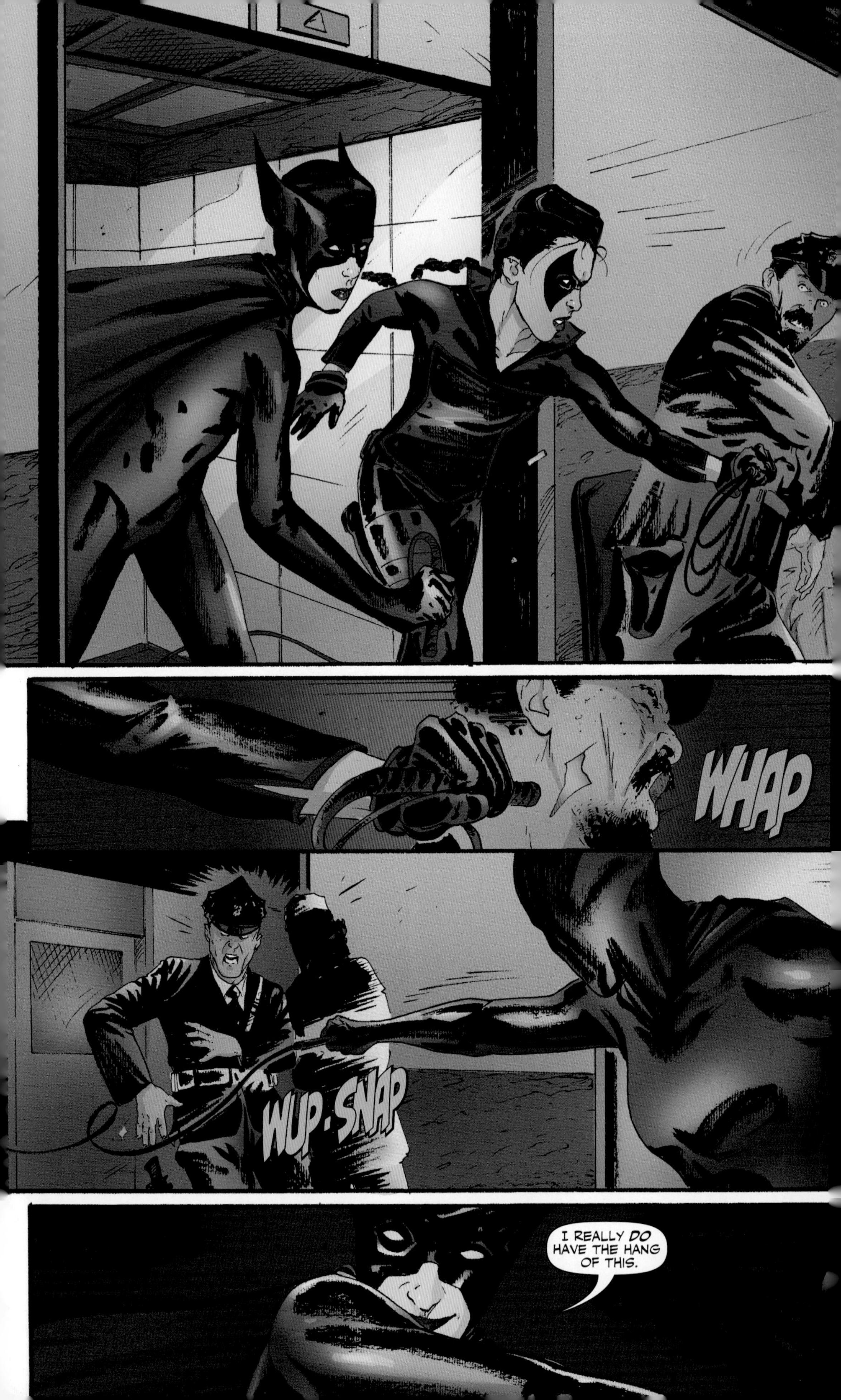
WHAP
WUP-SNAP
I REALLY DO HAVE THE HANG OF THIS.

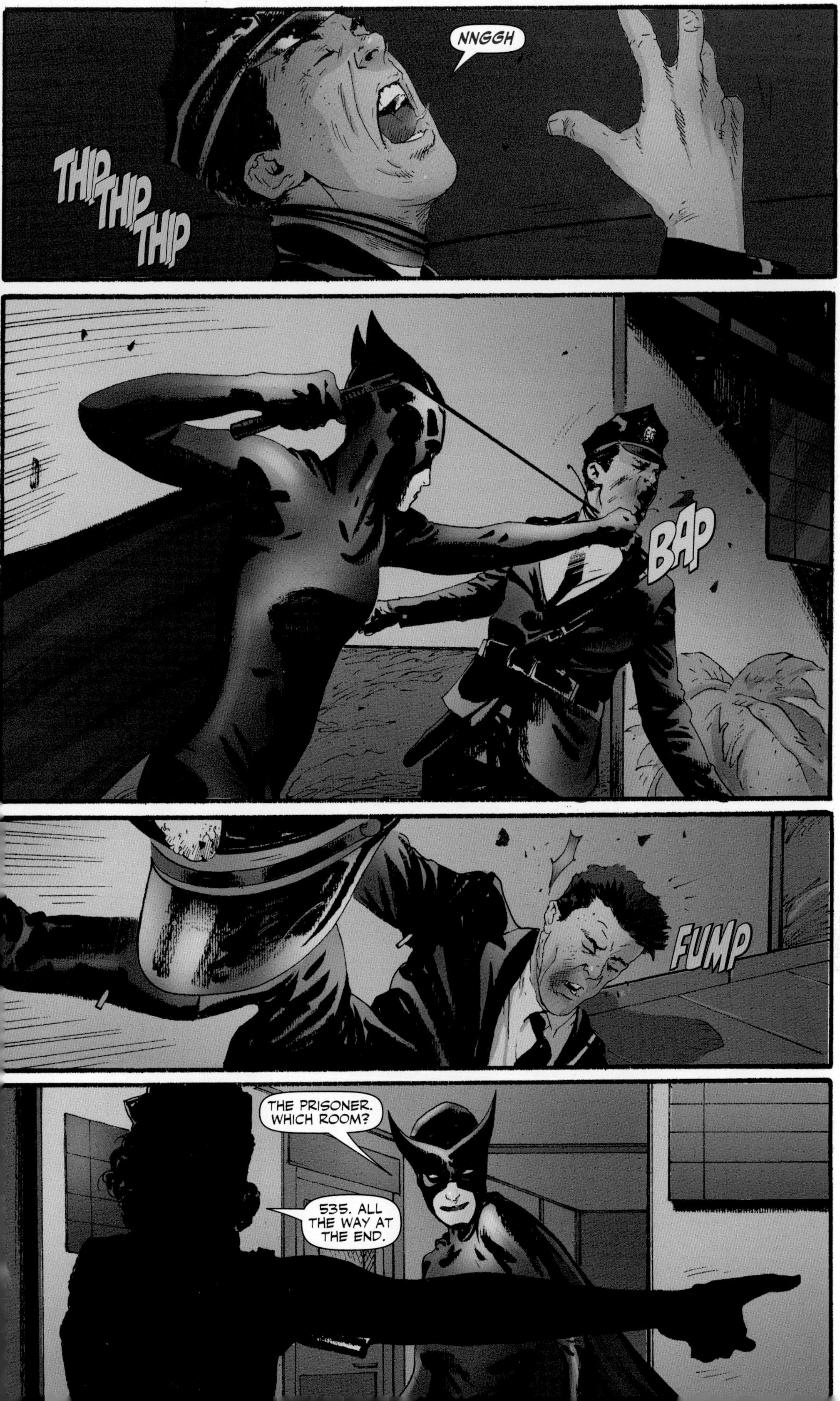
NNGGH
THIP THIP THIP
BAP
FUMP
THE PRISONER. WHICH ROOM?
535. ALL THE WAY AT THE END.

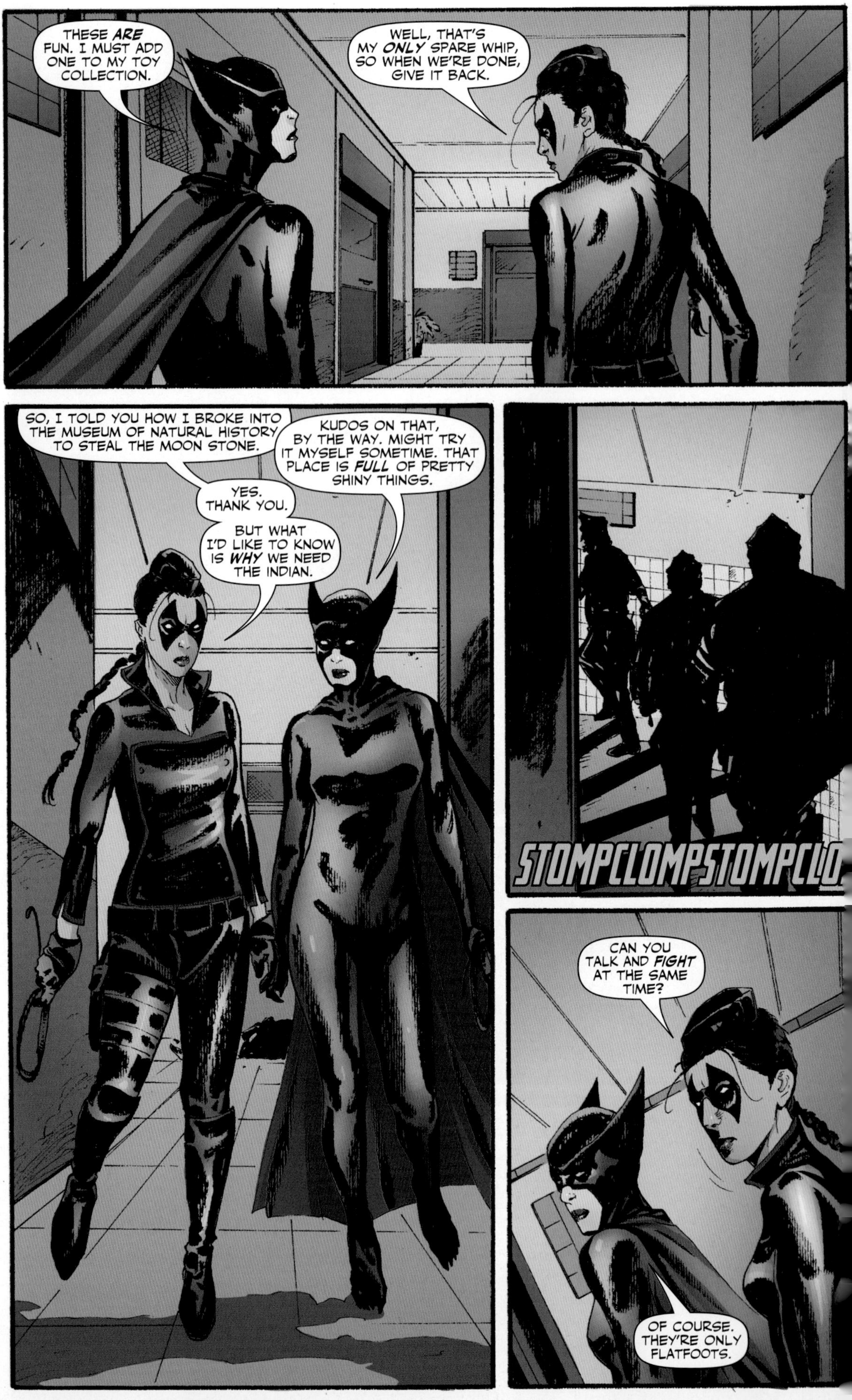
THESE ARE FUN. I MUST ADD ONE TO MY TOY COLLECTION.
WELL, THAT'S MY ONLY SPARE WHIP, SO WHEN WE'RE DONE, GIVE IT BACK.
SO, I TOLD YOU HOW I BROKE INTO THE MUSEUM OF NATURAL HISTORY TO STEAL THE MOON STONE.
KUDOS ON THAT, BY THE WAY. MIGHT TRY IT MYSELF SOMETIME. THAT PLACE IS FULL OF PRETTY SHINY THINGS.
YES. THANK YOU.
BUT WHAT I'D LIKE TO KNOW IS WHY WE NEED THE INDIAN.
STOMPCLOMPSTOMPCLO
CAN YOU TALK AND FIGHT AT THE SAME TIME?
OF COURSE. THEY'RE ONLY FLATFOOTS.

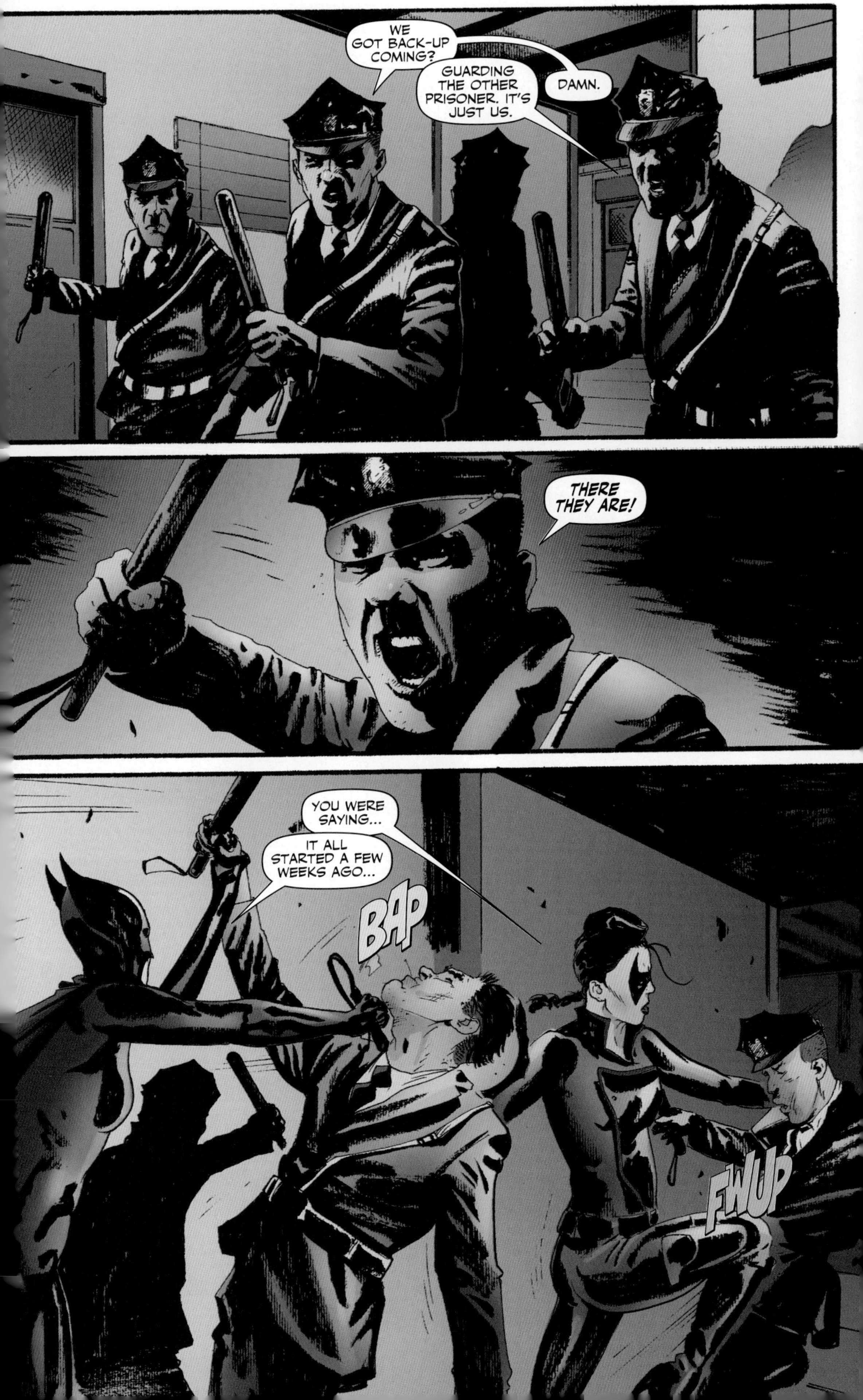
WE GOT BACK-UP COMING?
GUARDING THE OTHER PRISONER. IT'S JUST US.
DAMN.
THERE THEY ARE!
YOU WERE SAYING...
IT ALL STARTED A FEW WEEKS AGO...
BAP
FWUP

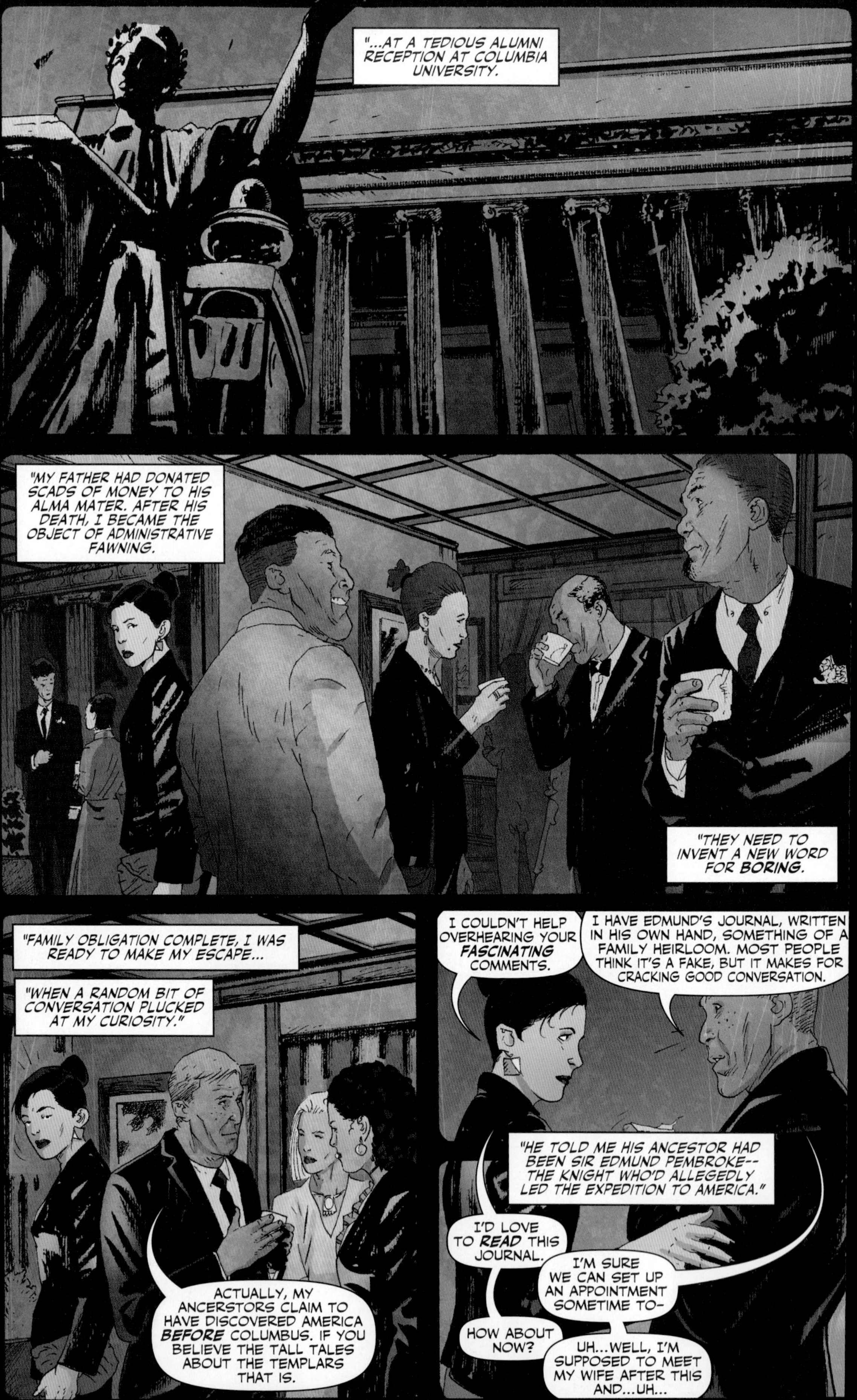
"...AT A TEDIOUS ALUMNI RECEPTION AT COLUMBIA UNIVERSITY.
"MY FATHER HAD DONATED SCADS OF MONEY TO HIS ALMA MATER. AFTER HIS DEATH, I BECAME THE OBJECT OF ADMINISTRATIVE FAWNING.
"THEY NEED TO INVENT A NEW WORD FOR BORING.
"FAMILY OBLIGATION COMPLETE, I WAS READY TO MAKE MY ESCAPE...
"WHEN A RANDOM BIT OF CONVERSATION PLUCKED AT MY CURIOSITY."
ACTUALLY, MY ANCERSTORS CLAIM TO HAVE DISCOVERED AMERICA BEFORE COLUMBUS. IF YOU BELIEVE THE TALL TALES ABOUT THE TEMPLARS THAT IS.
I COULDN'T HELP OVERHEARING YOUR FASCINATING COMMENTS.
I HAVE EDMUND'S JOURNAL, WRITTEN IN HIS OWN HAND, SOMETHING OF A FAMILY HEIRLOOM. MOST PEOPLE THINK IT'S A FAKE, BUT IT MAKES FOR CRACKING GOOD CONVERSATION.
"HE TOLD ME HIS ANCESTOR HAD BEEN SIR EDMUND PEMBROKE-- THE KNIGHT WHO'D ALLEGEDLY LED THE EXPEDITION TO AMERICA."
I'D LOVE TO READ THIS JOURNAL.
I'M SURE WE CAN SET UP AN APPOINTMENT SOMETIME TO-
HOW ABOUT NOW?
UH...WELL, I'M SUPPOSED TO MEET MY WIFE AFTER THIS AND...UH...

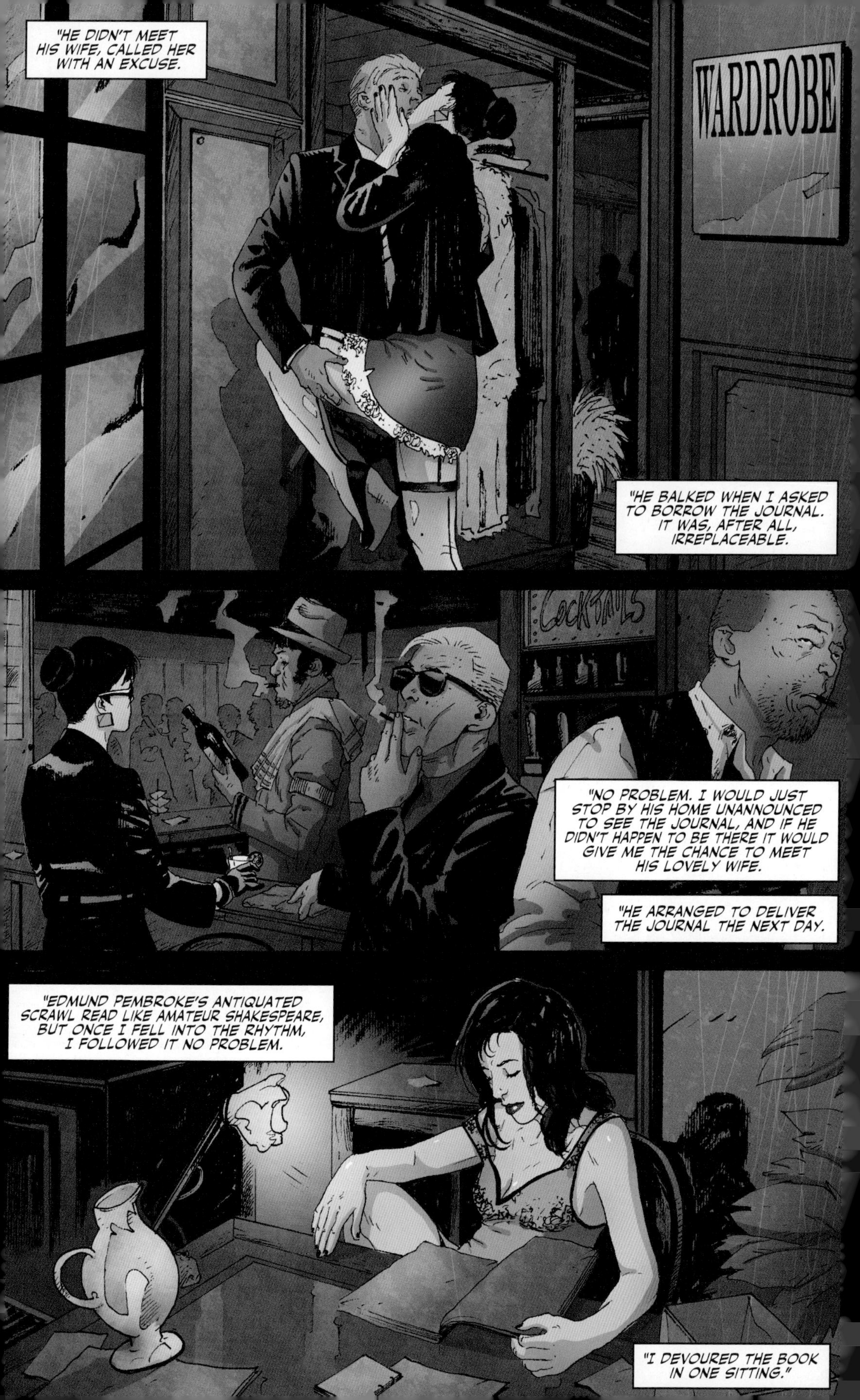
"HE DIDN'T MEET HIS WIFE, CALLED HER WITH AN EXCUSE.
WARDROBE
"HE BALKED WHEN I ASKED TO BORROW THE JOURNAL. IT WAS, AFTER ALL, IRREPLACEABLE.
"NO PROBLEM. I WOULD JUST STOP BY HIS HOME UNANNOUNCED TO SEE THE JOURNAL, AND IF HE DIDN'T HAPPEN TO BE THERE IT WOULD GIVE ME THE CHANCE TO MEET HIS LOVELY WIFE.
"HE ARRANGED TO DELIVER THE JOURNAL THE NEXT DAY.
"EDMUND PEMBROKE'S ANTIQUATED SCRAWL READ LIKE AMATEUR SHAKESPEARE, BUT ONCE I FELL INTO THE RHYTHM, I FOLLOWED IT NO PROBLEM.
"I DEVOURED THE BOOK IN ONE SITTING."

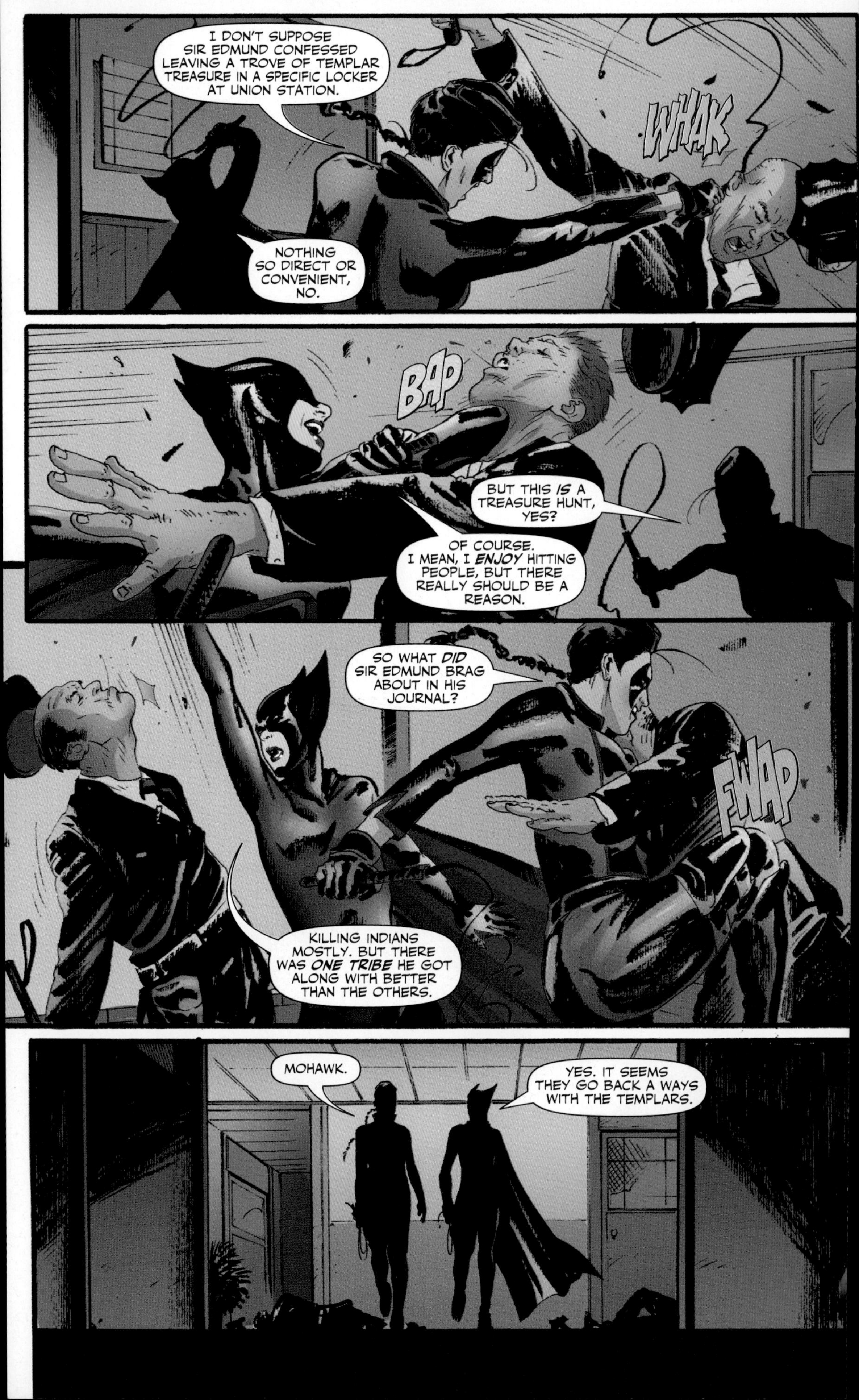

I DON'T SUPPOSE SIR EDMUND CONFESSED LEAVING A TROVE OF TEMPLAR TREASURE IN A SPECIFIC LOCKER AT UNION STATION.
WHAK
NOTHING SO DIRECT OR CONVENIENT, NO.
BAP
BUT THIS IS A TREASURE HUNT, YES?
OF COURSE. I MEAN, I ENJOY HITTING PEOPLE, BUT THERE REALLY SHOULD BE A REASON.
SO WHAT DID SIR EDMUND BRAG ABOUT IN HIS JOURNAL?
FWAP
KILLING INDIANS MOSTLY. BUT THERE WAS ONE TRIBE HE GOT ALONG WITH BETTER THAN THE OTHERS.
MOHAWK.
YES. IT SEEMS THEY GO BACK A WAYS WITH THE TEMPLARS.

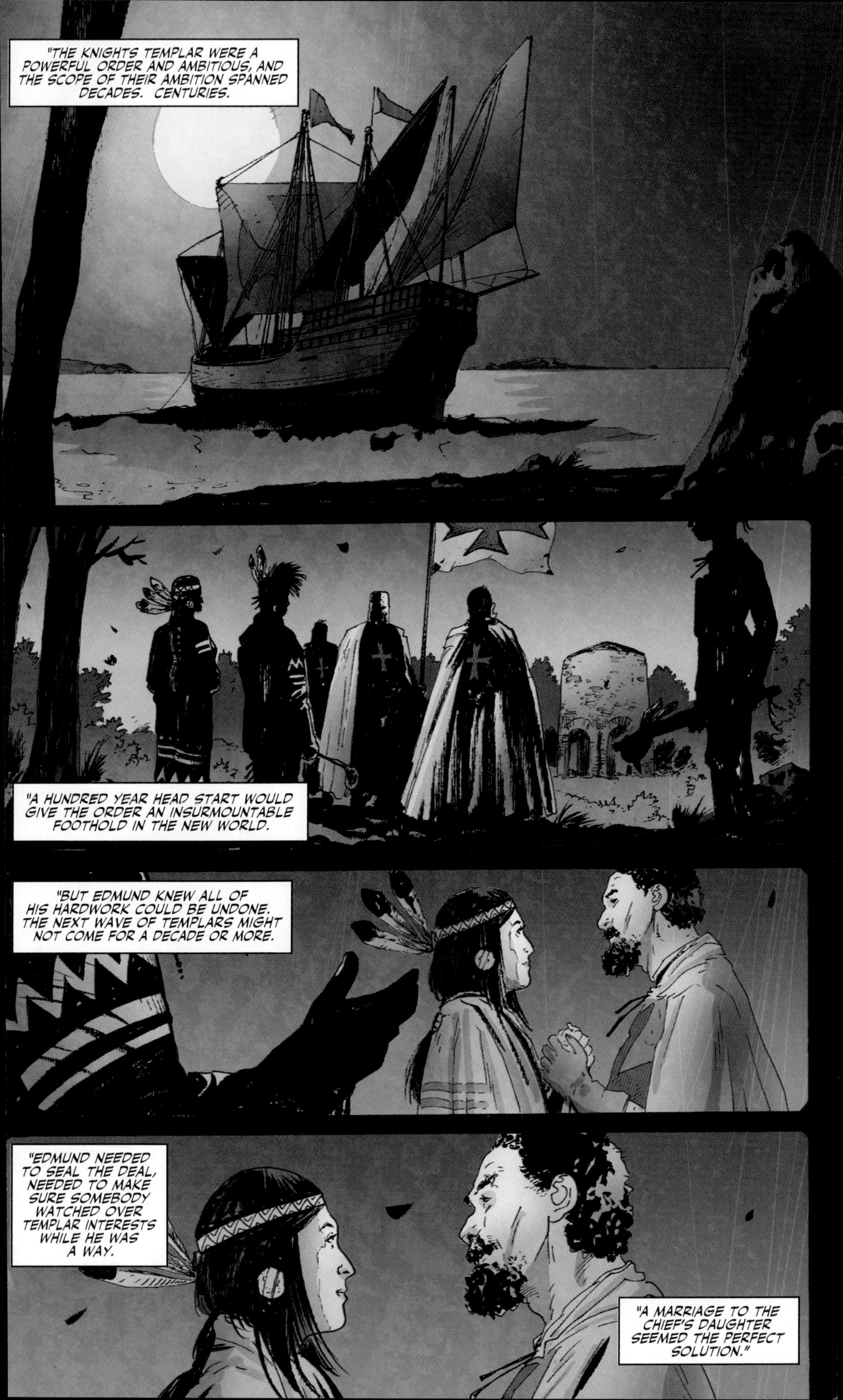
"THE KNIGHTS TEMPLAR WERE A POWERFUL ORDER AND AMBITIOUS, AND THE SCOPE OF THEIR AMBITION SPANNED DECADES. CENTURIES.
"A HUNDRED YEAR HEAD START WOULD GIVE THE ORDER AN INSURMOUNTABLE FOOTHOLD IN THE NEW WORLD.
"BUT EDMUND KNEW ALL OF HIS HARDWORK COULD BE UNDONE. THE NEXT WAVE OF TEMPLARS MIGHT NOT COME FOR A DECADE OR MORE.
"EDMUND NEEDED TO SEAL THE DEAL, NEEDED TO MAKE SURE SOMEBODY WATCHED OVER TEMPLAR INTERESTS WHILE HE WAS A WAY.
"A MARRIAGE TO THE CHIEF'S DAUGHTER SEEMED THE PERFECT SOLUTION."

THIS ALL SEEMS VERY THIN. TALL TALES AND STORIES. I'M IN THIS TO GET *PAID*.

PAID? SURELY. BUT AREN'T YOU EXCITED BY THE *ADVENTURE* OF IT?

LOOK, I'M ALWAYS DOWN FOR A BIT OF ADVENTURE, BUT THAT DOESN'T MEAN—

OH, HELL.

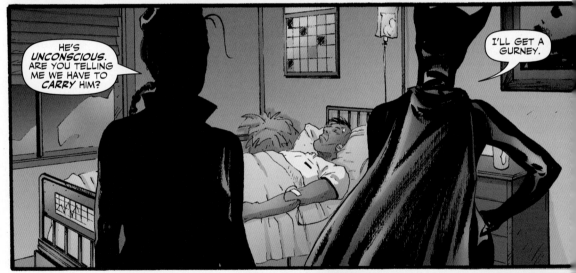

HE'S *UNCONSCIOUS*. ARE YOU TELLING ME WE HAVE TO *CARRY* HIM?

I'LL GET A GURNEY.

YOU DIDN'T ANSWER THE *QUESTION*, BY THE WAY. DON'T THINK I DIDN'T NOTICE.

WHAT QUESTION?

WHY DO WE NEED THE INDIAN?

WELL, LET ME TELL YOU ABOUT KNIGHTS TEMPLAR, DARLING. OR *ANY* MAN FOR THAT MATTER.

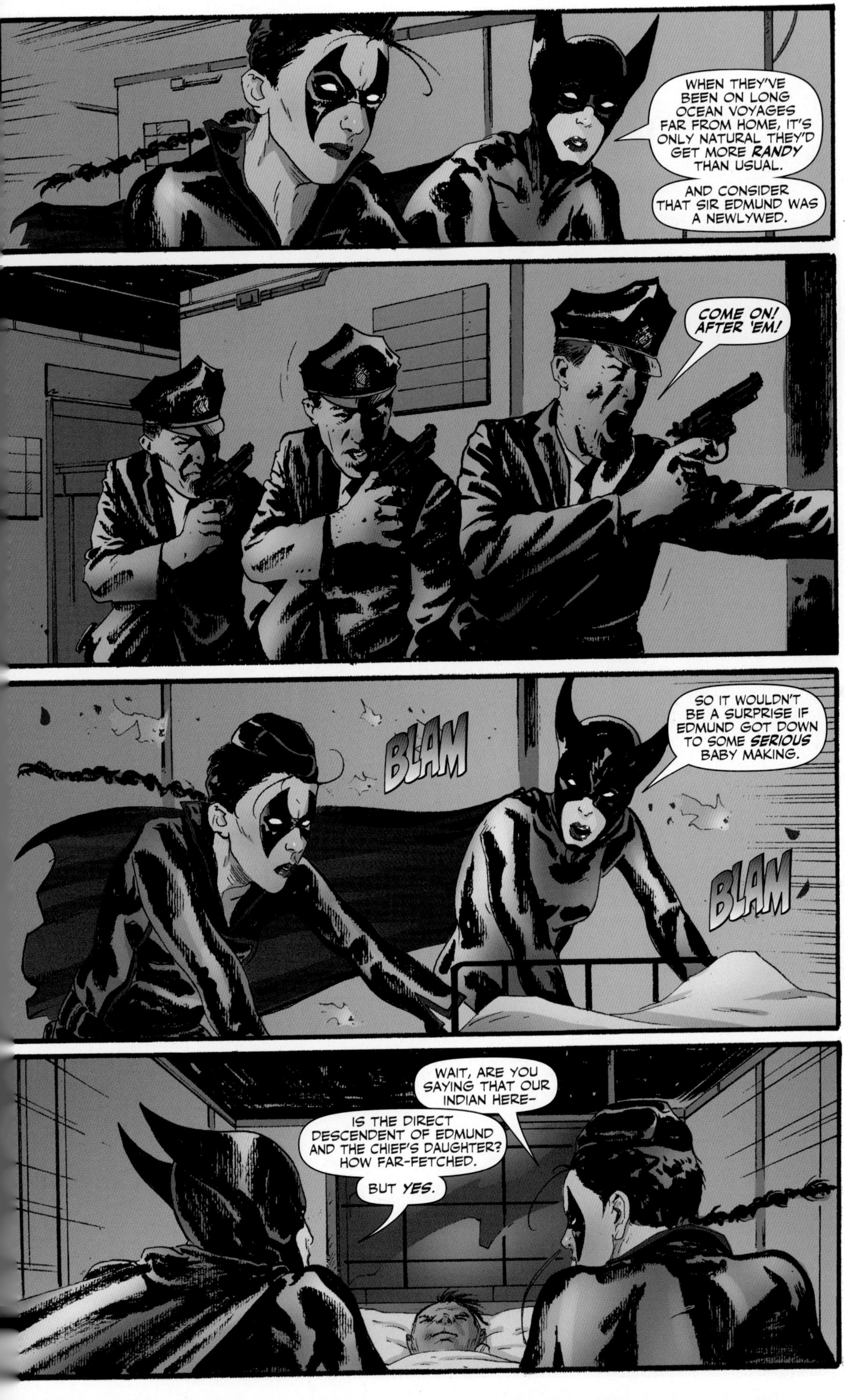
WHEN THEY'VE BEEN ON LONG OCEAN VOYAGES FAR FROM HOME, IT'S ONLY NATURAL THEY'D GET MORE RANDY THAN USUAL.
AND CONSIDER THAT SIR EDMUND WAS A NEWLYWED.
COME ON! AFTER 'EM!
BLAM
SO IT WOULDN'T BE A SURPRISE IF EDMUND GOT DOWN TO SOME SERIOUS BABY MAKING.
BLAM
WAIT, ARE YOU SAYING THAT OUR INDIAN HERE-
IS THE DIRECT DESCENDENT OF EDMUND AND THE CHIEF'S DAUGHTER? HOW FAR-FETCHED.
BUT YES.

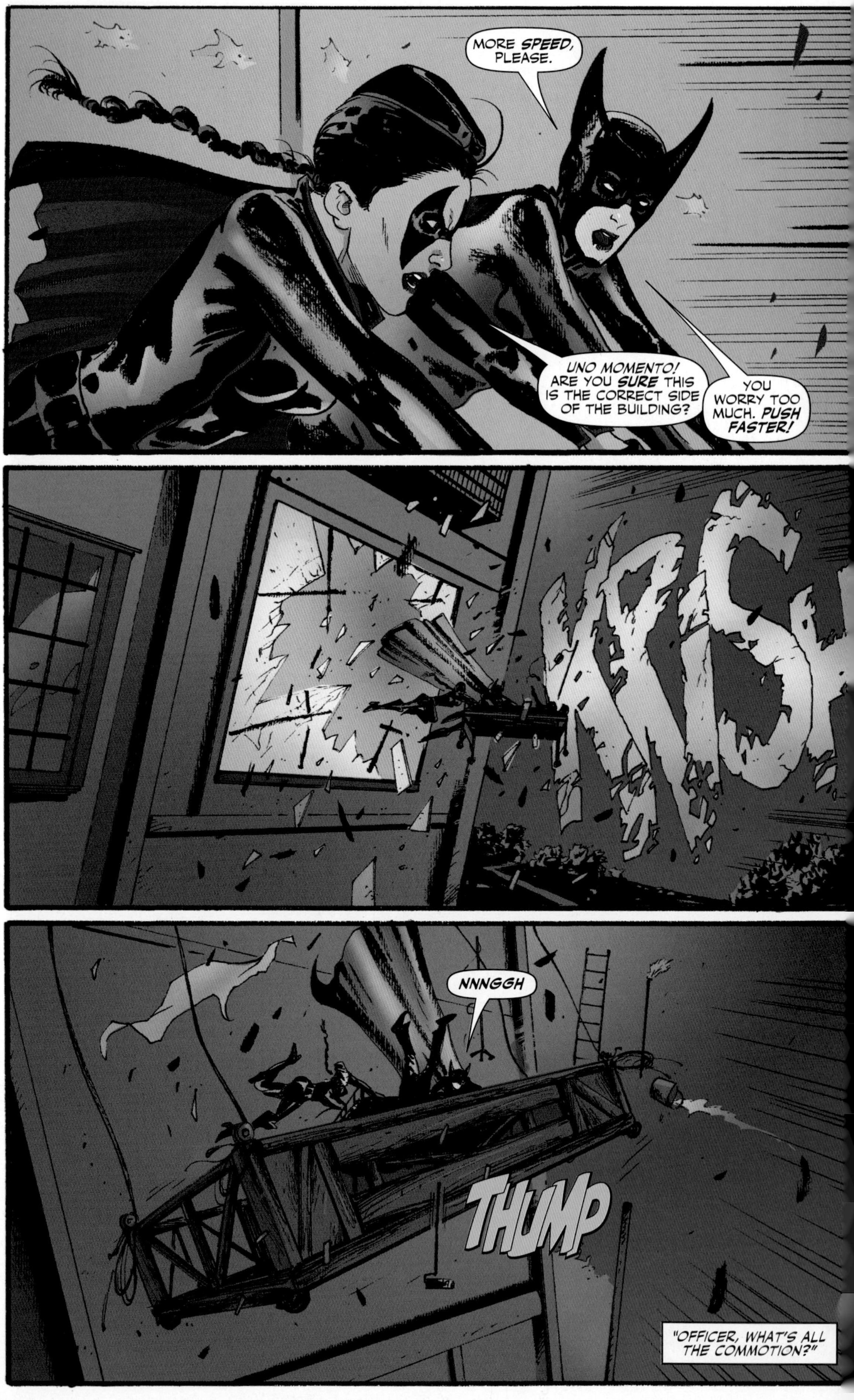
MORE SPEED, PLEASE.
UNO MOMENTO! ARE YOU SURE THIS IS THE CORRECT SIDE OF THE BUILDING?
YOU WORRY TOO MUCH. PUSH FASTER!
KRISH
NNNGGH
THUMP
"OFFICER, WHAT'S ALL THE COMMOTION?"

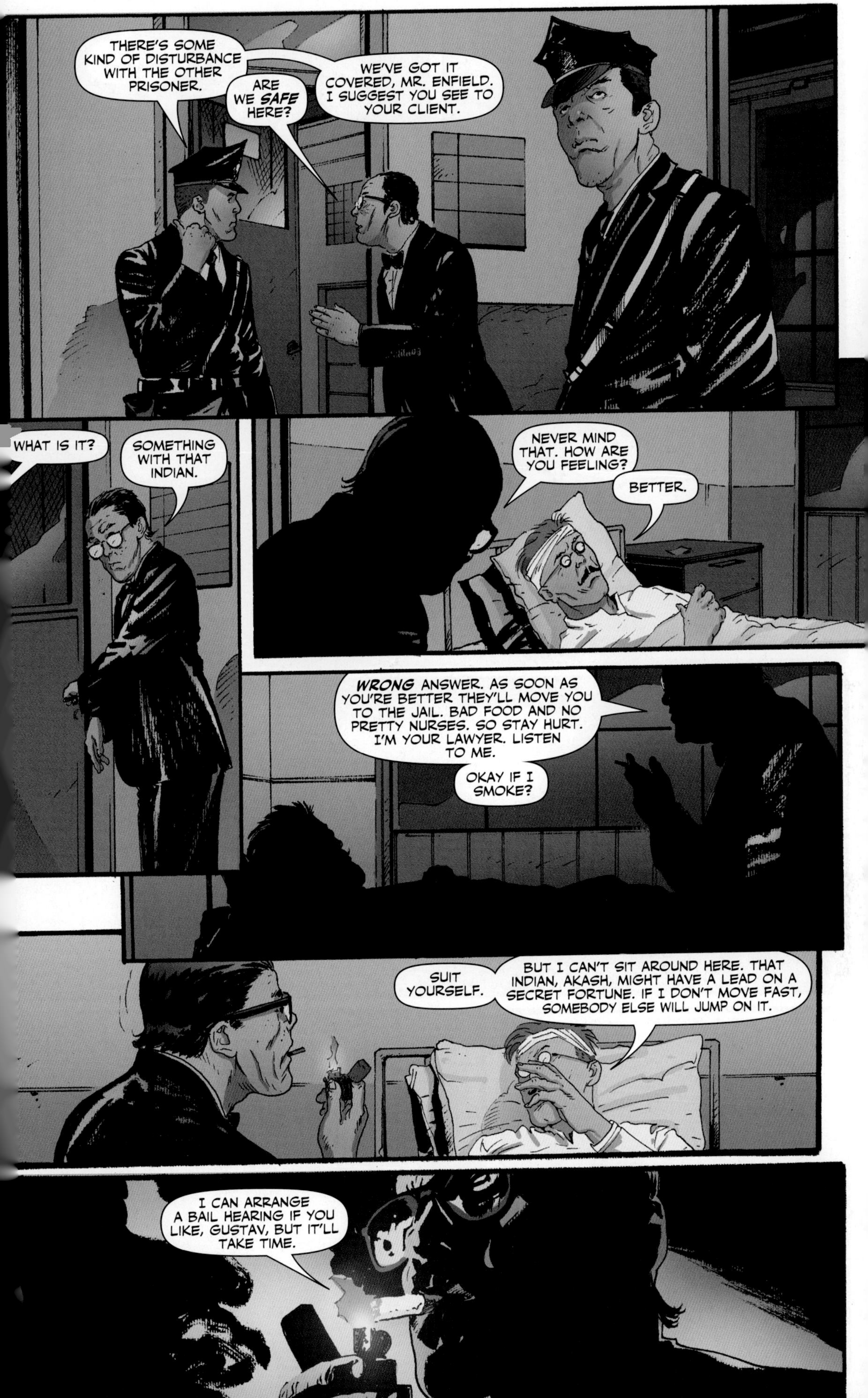
THERE'S SOME KIND OF DISTURBANCE WITH THE OTHER PRISONER.
ARE WE SAFE HERE?
WE'VE GOT IT COVERED, MR. ENFIELD. I SUGGEST YOU SEE TO YOUR CLIENT.
WHAT IS IT?
SOMETHING WITH THAT INDIAN.
NEVER MIND THAT. HOW ARE YOU FEELING?
BETTER.
WRONG ANSWER. AS SOON AS YOU'RE BETTER THEY'LL MOVE YOU TO THE JAIL. BAD FOOD AND NO PRETTY NURSES. SO STAY HURT. I'M YOUR LAWYER. LISTEN TO ME.
OKAY IF I SMOKE?
SUIT YOURSELF.
BUT I CAN'T SIT AROUND HERE. THAT INDIAN, AKASH, MIGHT HAVE A LEAD ON A SECRET FORTUNE. IF I DON'T MOVE FAST, SOMEBODY ELSE WILL JUMP ON IT.
I CAN ARRANGE A BAIL HEARING IF YOU LIKE, GUSTAV, BUT IT'LL TAKE TIME.

THERE *IS* NO TIME. THAT'S THE POINT.

UNLESS... ORLANDO.

YOUR BROTHER? THAT... *MIGHT* NOT BE A GOOD IDEA.

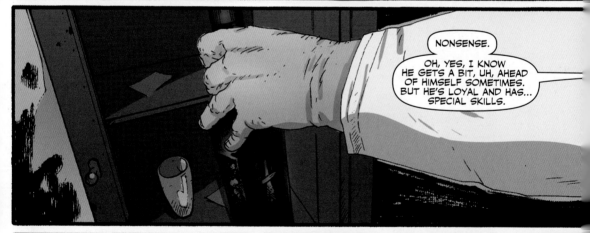

NONSENSE.

OH, YES, I KNOW HE GETS A BIT, UH, AHEAD OF HIMSELF SOMETIMES. BUT HE'S LOYAL AND HAS... SPECIAL SKILLS.

AND IF *ANYONE* GETS IN HIS WAY, ORLANDO WON'T HESITATE TO *ELIMINATE* THEM. CREATIVELY.

WRITE DOWN THESE SPECIFIC INSTRUCTIONS AND MAKE SURE HE GETS THEM AS SOON AS POSSIBLE. I WANT HIM TO –

NOW WHAT?

BLAM BLAM

"WORK THE ROPES, *DAMN IT!*"

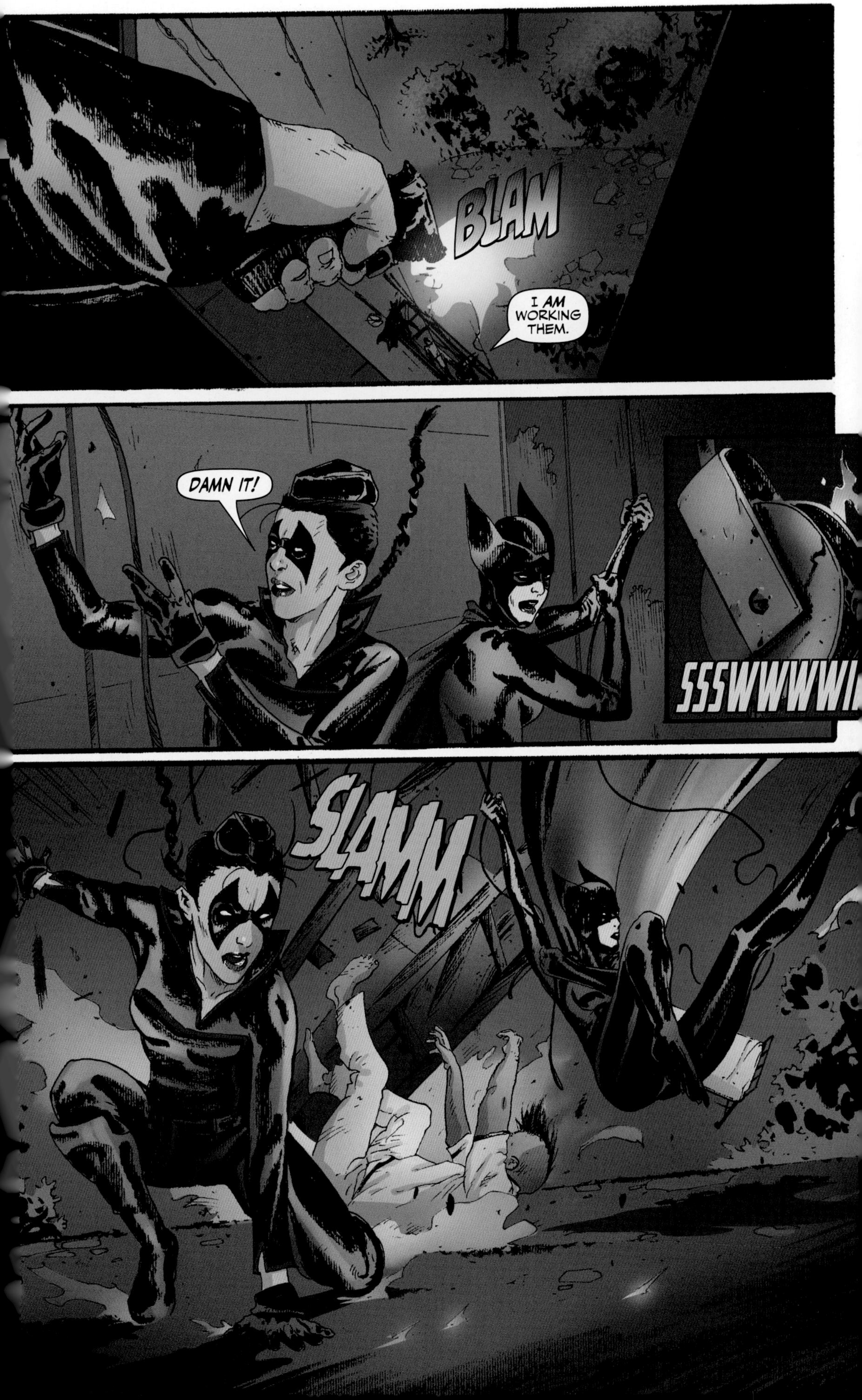

BLAM
I AM WORKING THEM.
DAMN IT!
SSSWWWWI
SLAMM

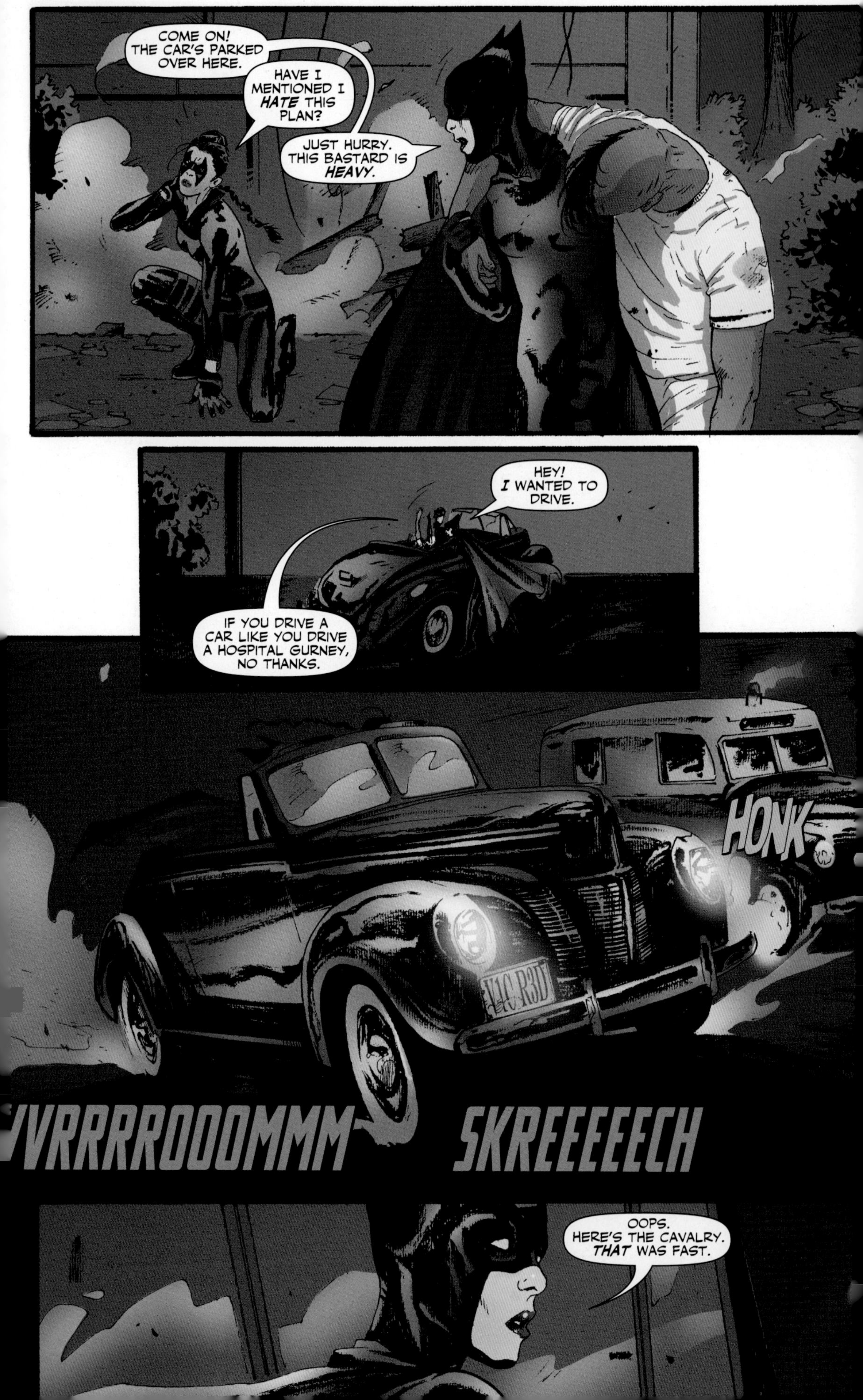
COME ON! THE CAR'S PARKED OVER HERE.
HAVE I MENTIONED I HATE THIS PLAN?
JUST HURRY. THIS BASTARD IS HEAVY.
HEY! I WANTED TO DRIVE.
IF YOU DRIVE A CAR LIKE YOU DRIVE A HOSPITAL GURNEY, NO THANKS.
HONK
V1C R3D
VRRRROOOMMM
SKREEEEECH
OOPS. HERE'S THE CAVALRY. THAT WAS FAST.

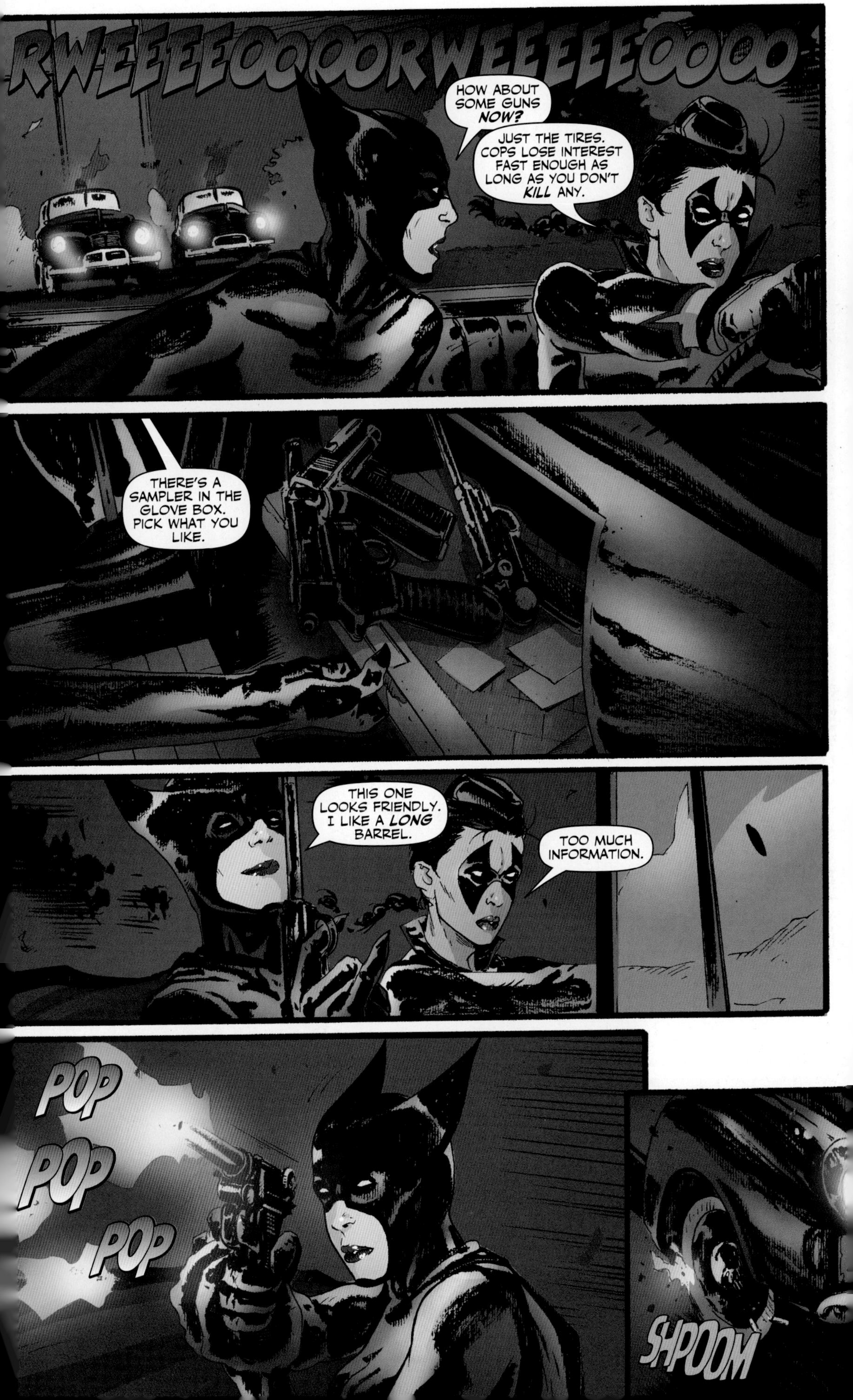
RWEEEEOOOORWEEEEEOOOO
HOW ABOUT SOME GUNS *NOW?*
JUST THE TIRES. COPS LOSE INTEREST FAST ENOUGH AS LONG AS YOU DON'T *KILL* ANY.
THERE'S A SAMPLER IN THE GLOVE BOX. PICK WHAT YOU LIKE.
THIS ONE LOOKS FRIENDLY. I LIKE A *LONG* BARREL.
TOO MUCH INFORMATION.
POP
POP
POP
SHPOOM

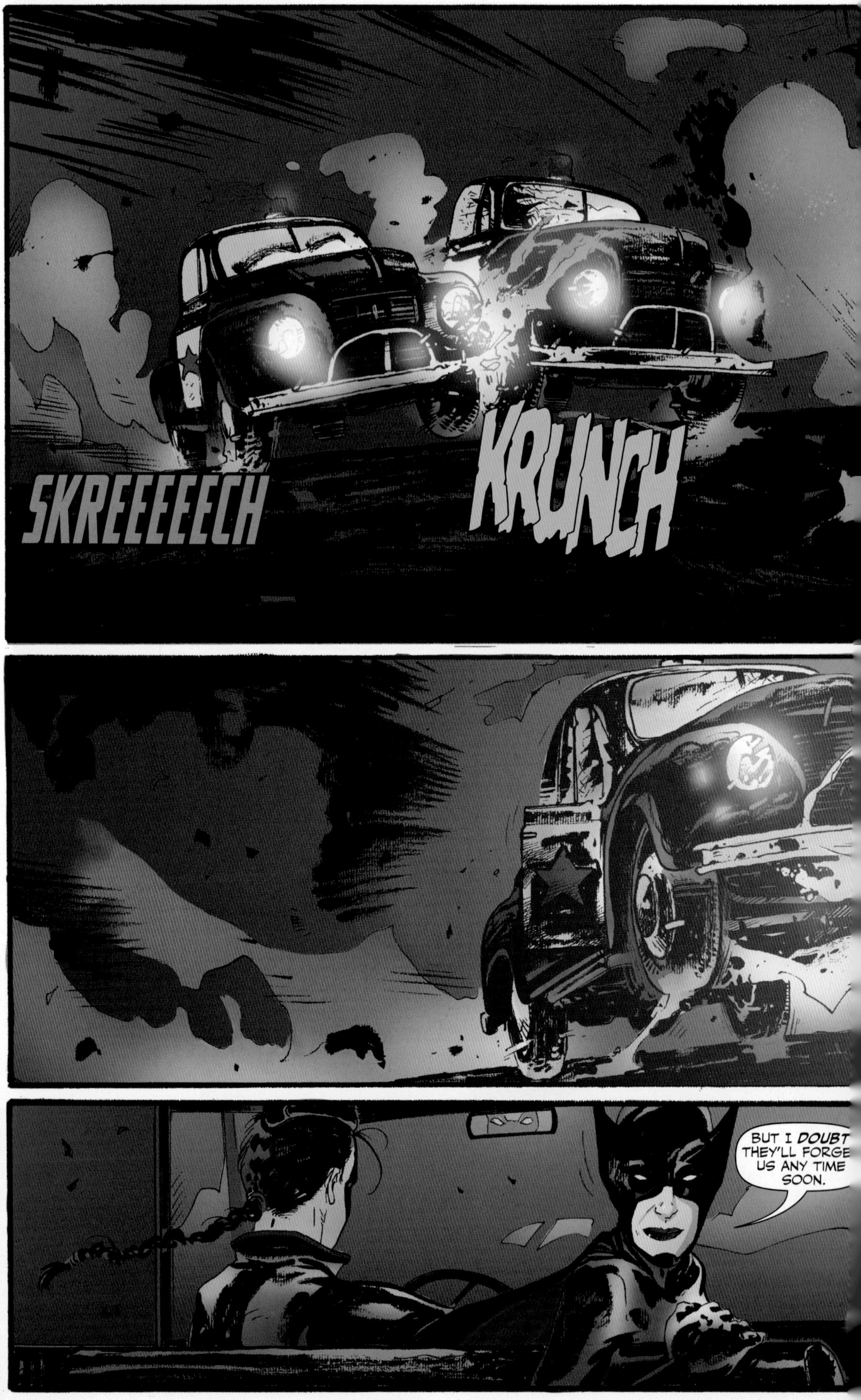
SKREEEEECH
KRUNCH
BUT I DOUBT THEY'LL FORGE US ANY TIME SOON.

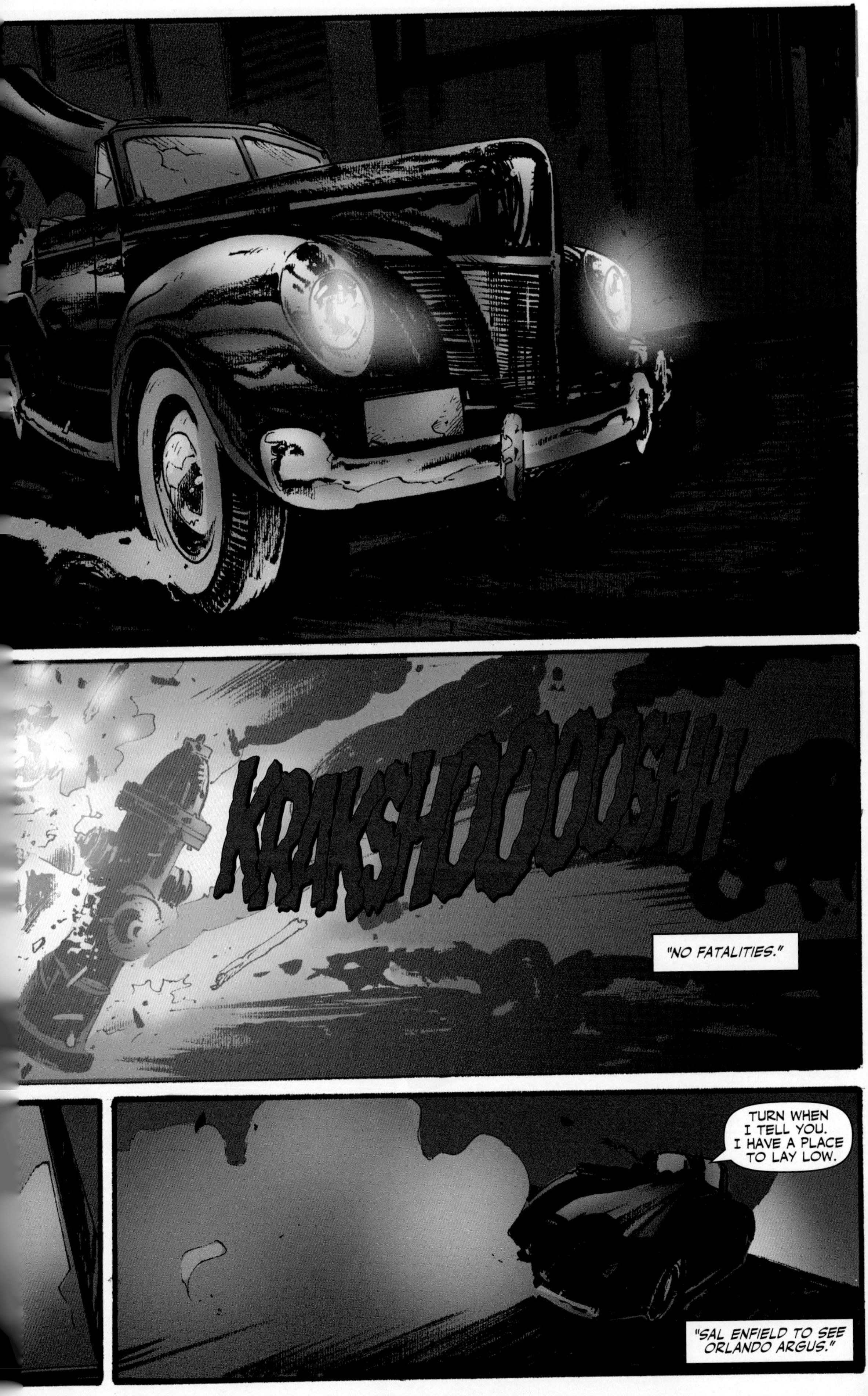
KRAKSHOOOOSHH
"NO FATALITIES."
TURN WHEN I TELL YOU. I HAVE A PLACE TO LAY LOW.
"SAL ENFIELD TO SEE ORLANDO ARGUS."

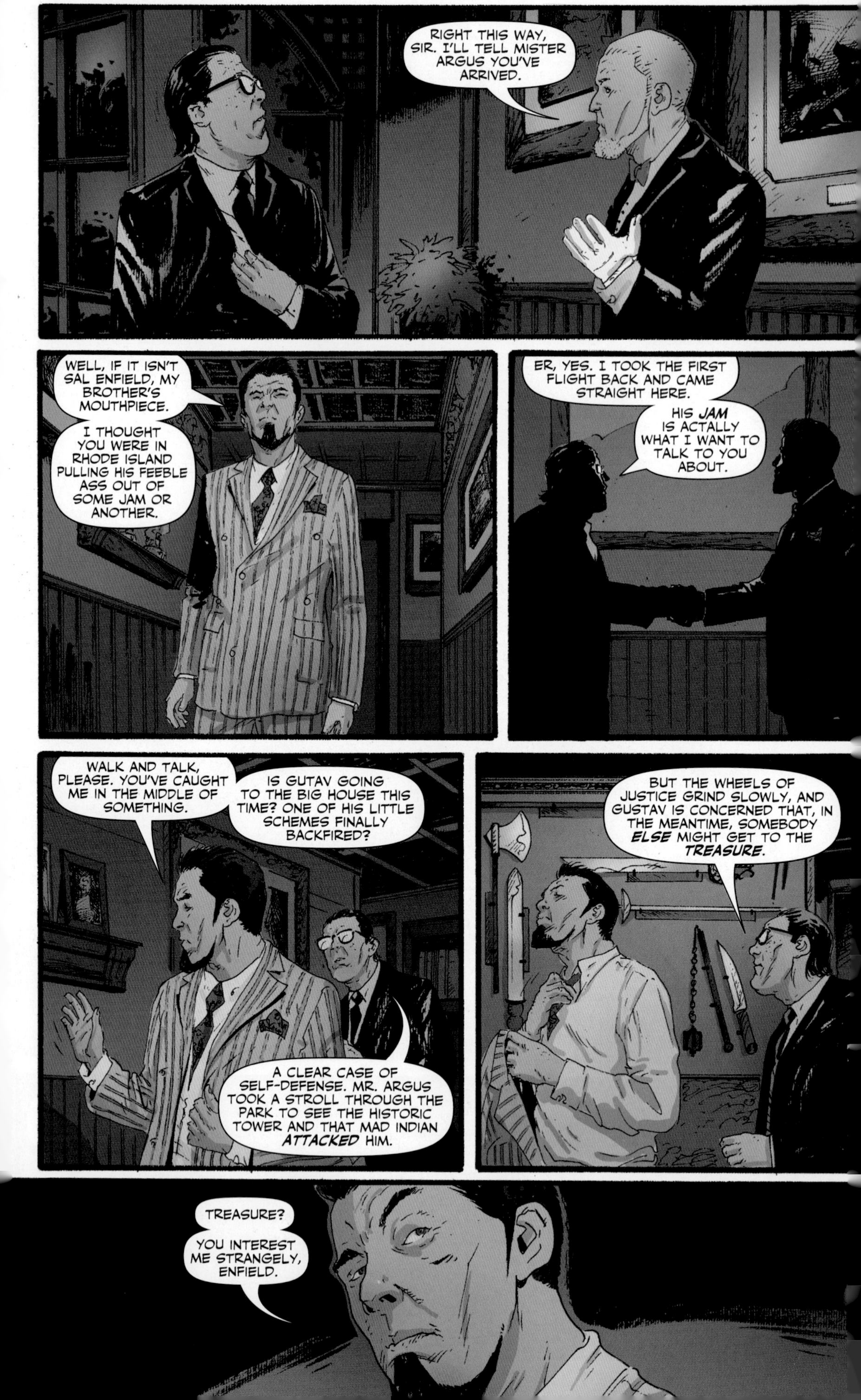
RIGHT THIS WAY, SIR. I'LL TELL MISTER ARGUS YOU'VE ARRIVED.
WELL, IF IT ISN'T SAL ENFIELD, MY BROTHER'S MOUTHPIECE.
I THOUGHT YOU WERE IN RHODE ISLAND PULLING HIS FEEBLE ASS OUT OF SOME JAM OR ANOTHER.
ER, YES. I TOOK THE FIRST FLIGHT BACK AND CAME STRAIGHT HERE.
HIS *JAM* IS ACTALLY WHAT I WANT TO TALK TO YOU ABOUT.
WALK AND TALK, PLEASE. YOU'VE CAUGHT ME IN THE MIDDLE OF SOMETHING.
IS GUTAV GOING TO THE BIG HOUSE THIS TIME? ONE OF HIS LITTLE SCHEMES FINALLY BACKFIRED?
A CLEAR CASE OF SELF-DEFENSE. MR. ARGUS TOOK A STROLL THROUGH THE PARK TO SEE THE HISTORIC TOWER AND THAT MAD INDIAN *ATTACKED* HIM.
BUT THE WHEELS OF JUSTICE GRIND SLOWLY, AND GUSTAV IS CONCERNED THAT, IN THE MEANTIME, SOMEBODY *ELSE* MIGHT GET TO THE *TREASURE*.
TREASURE?
YOU INTEREST ME STRANGELY, ENFIELD.

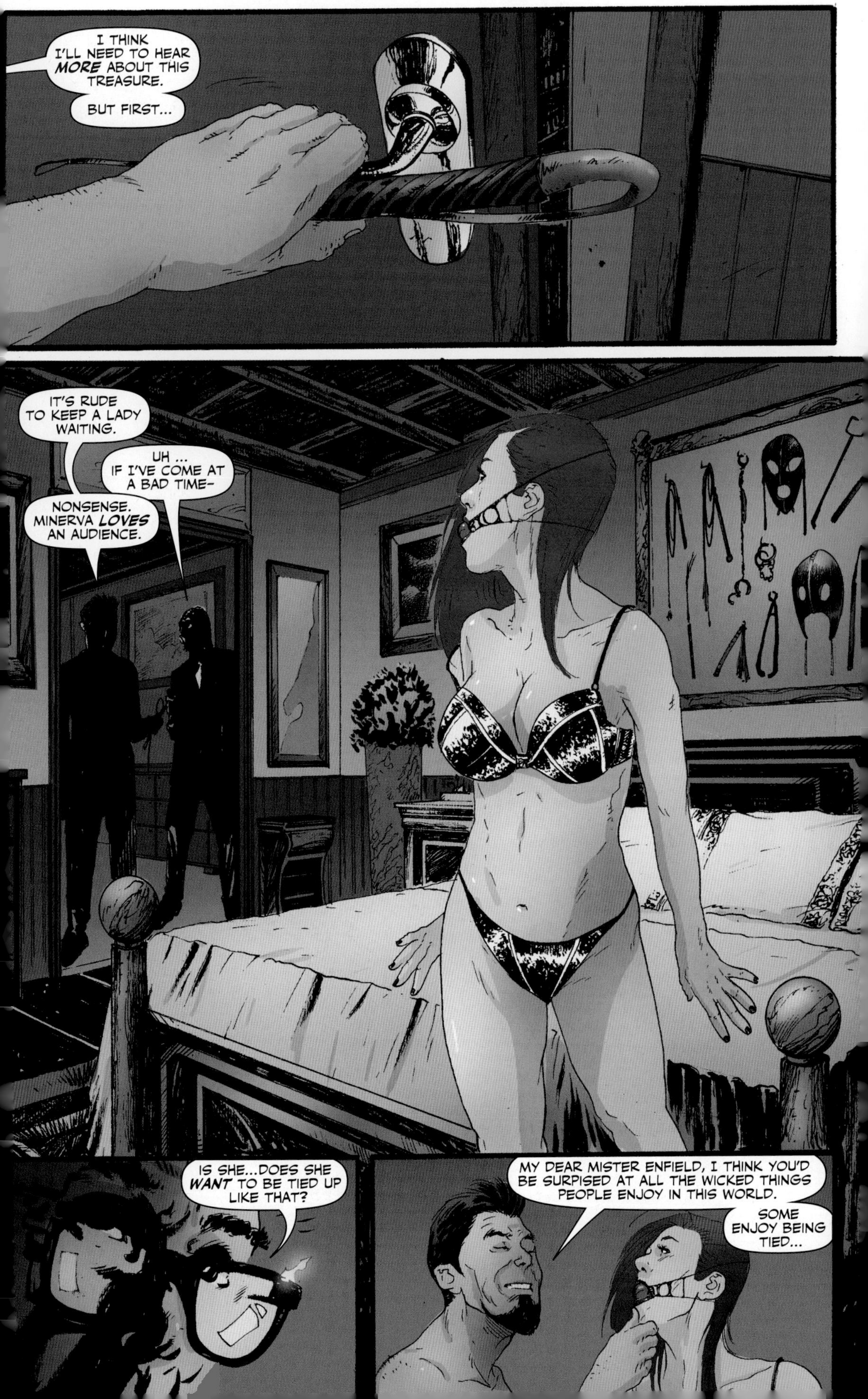
I THINK I'LL NEED TO HEAR MORE ABOUT THIS TREASURE.
BUT FIRST...
IT'S RUDE TO KEEP A LADY WAITING.
UH ... IF I'VE COME AT A BAD TIME-
NONSENSE. MINERVA LOVES AN AUDIENCE.
IS SHE...DOES SHE WANT TO BE TIED UP LIKE THAT?
MY DEAR MISTER ENFIELD, I THINK YOU'D BE SURPISED AT ALL THE WICKED THINGS PEOPLE ENJOY IN THIS WORLD.
SOME ENJOY BEING TIED...

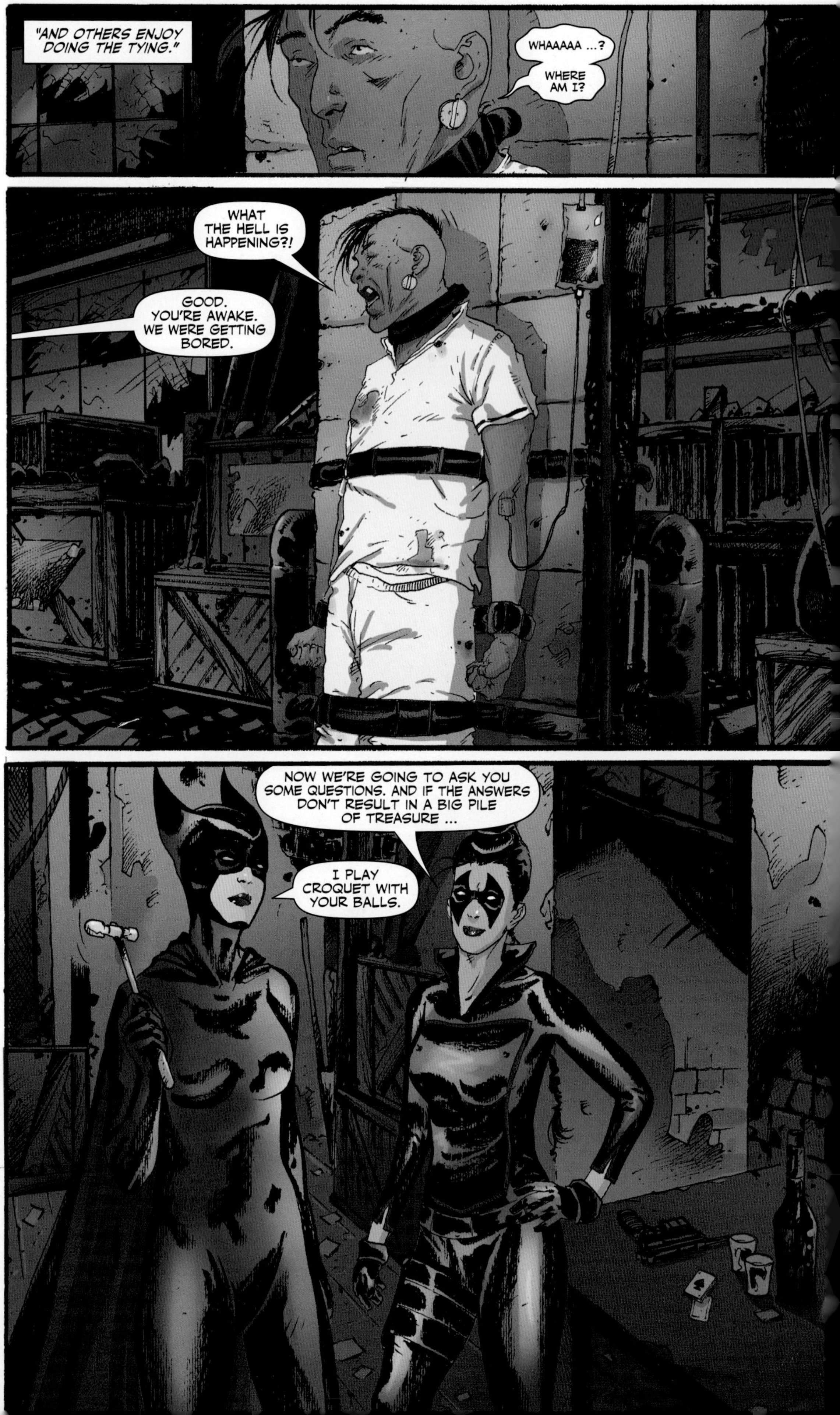
"AND OTHERS ENJOY DOING THE TYING."
WHAAAAA ...?
WHERE AM I?
WHAT THE HELL IS HAPPENING?!
GOOD. YOU'RE AWAKE. WE WERE GETTING BORED.
NOW WE'RE GOING TO ASK YOU SOME QUESTIONS. AND IF THE ANSWERS DON'T RESULT IN A BIG PILE OF TREASURE ...
I PLAY CROQUET WITH YOUR BALLS.

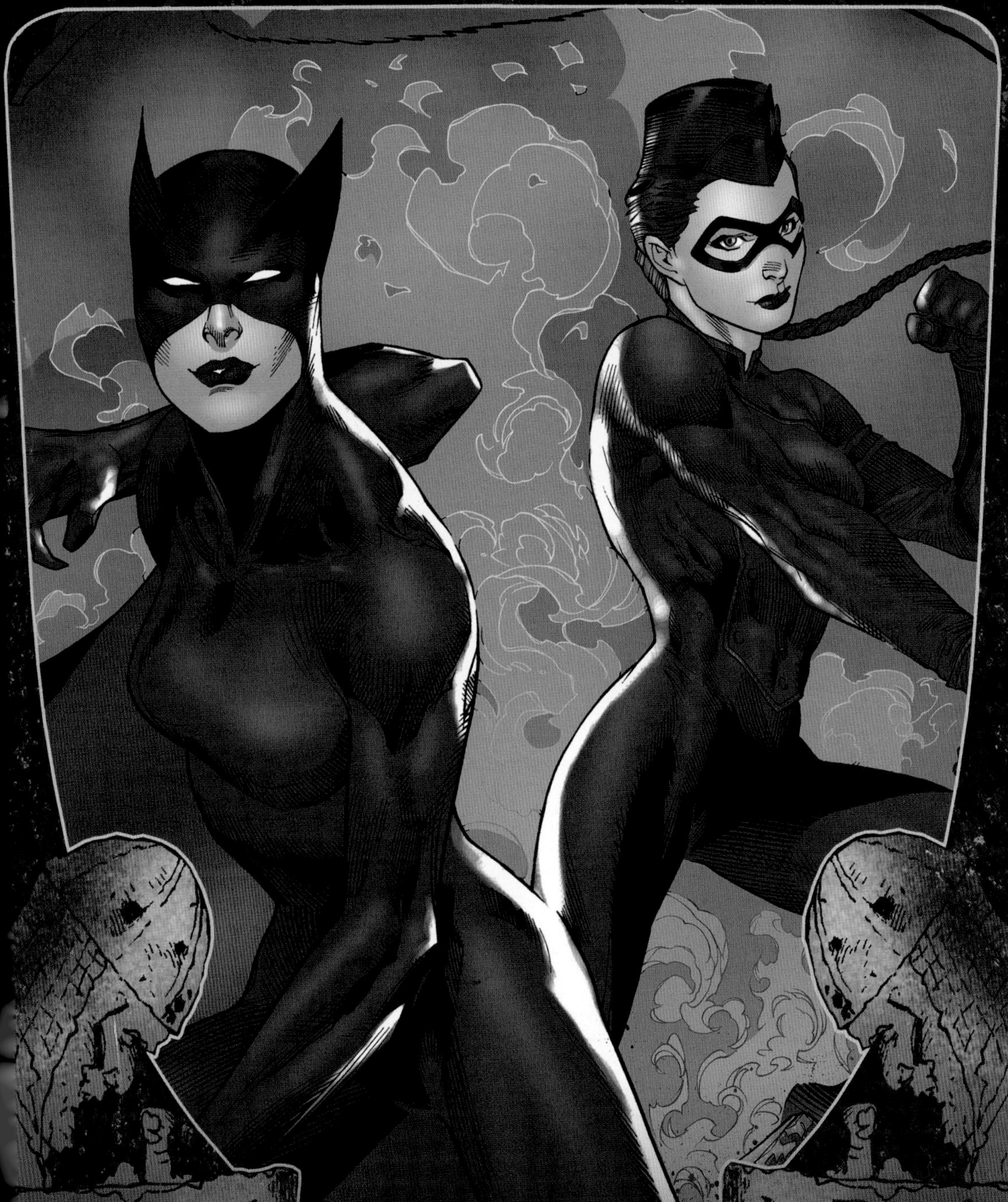

ISSUE 3

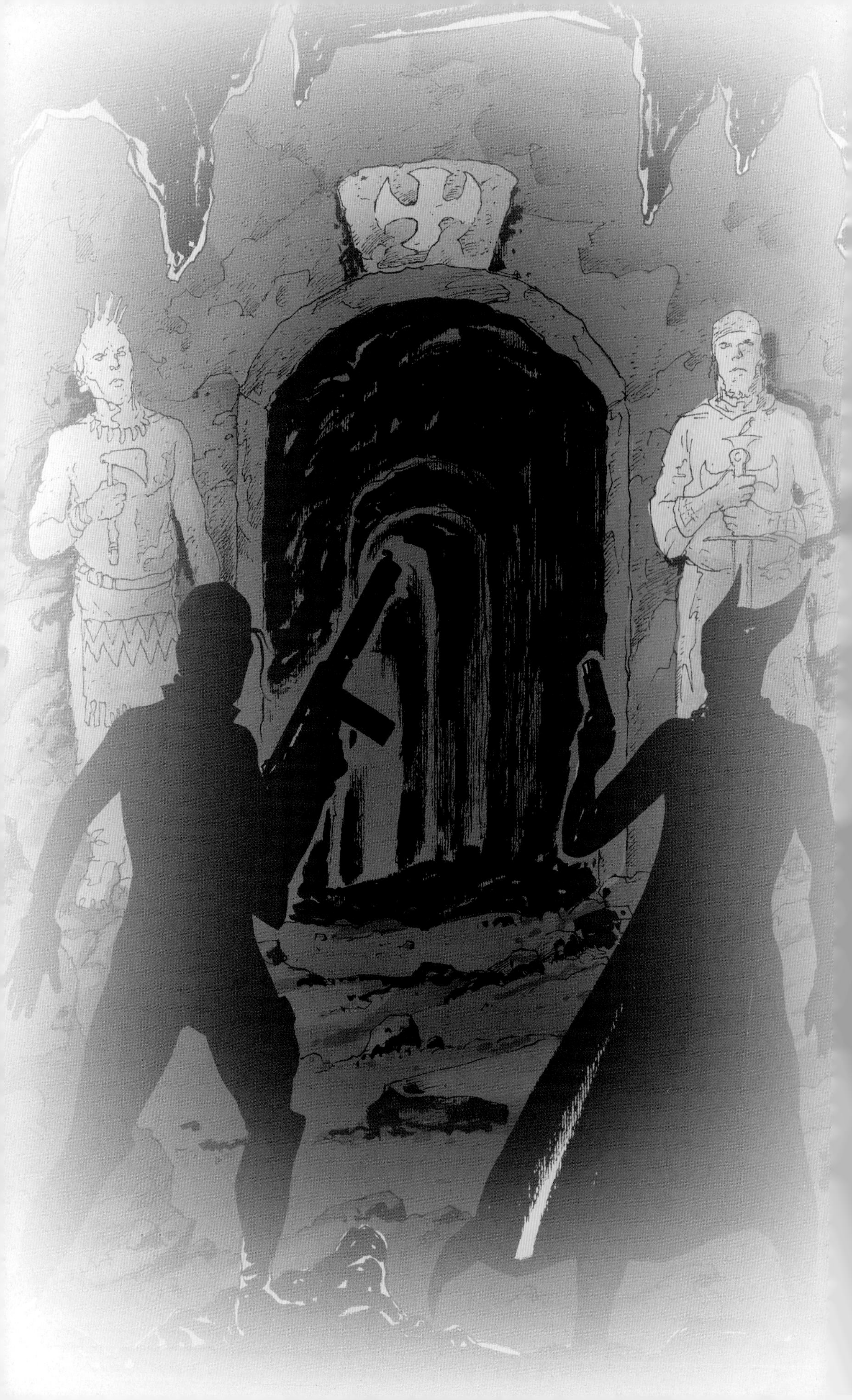

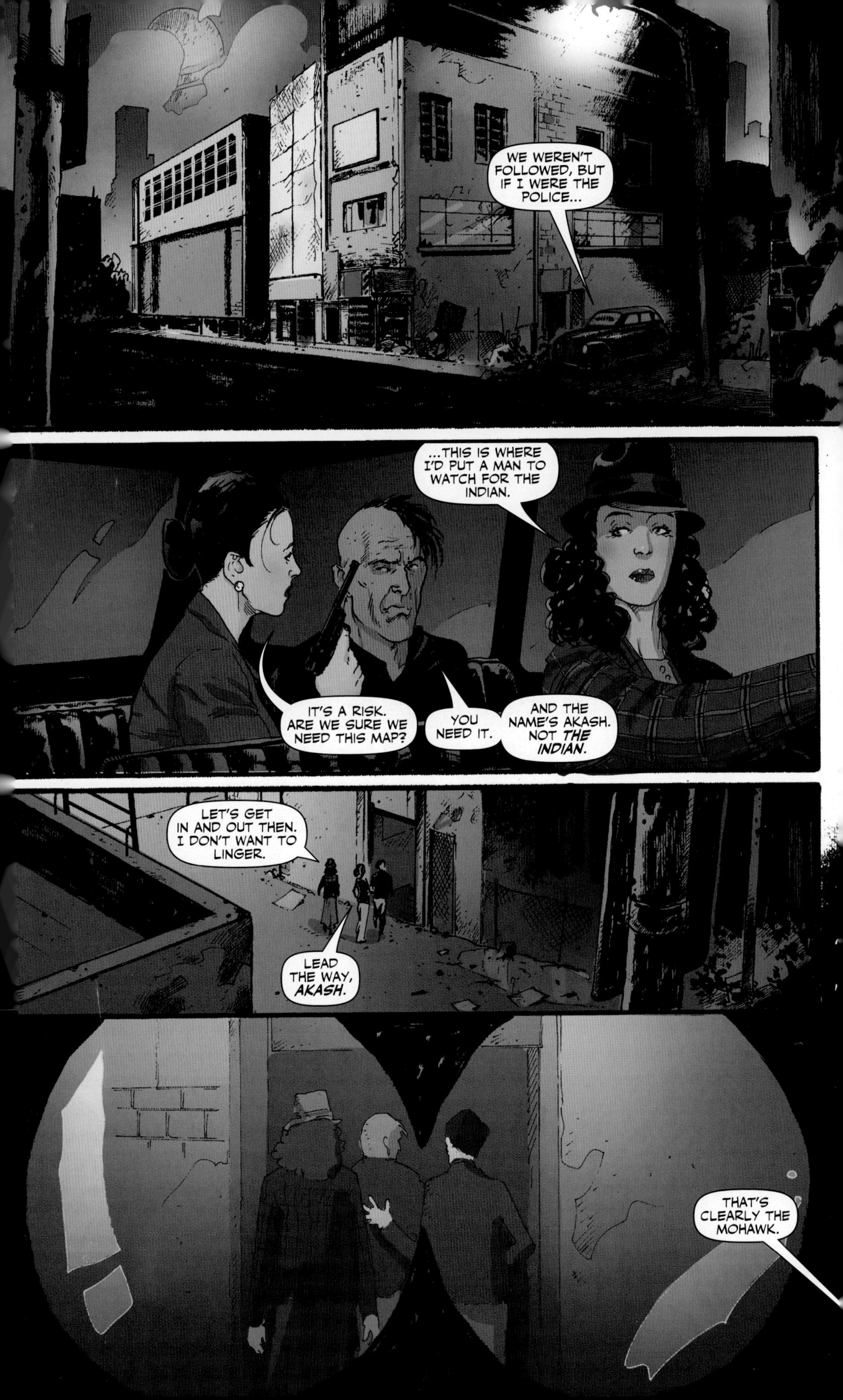
WE WEREN'T FOLLOWED, BUT IF I WERE THE POLICE...
...THIS IS WHERE I'D PUT A MAN TO WATCH FOR THE INDIAN.
IT'S A RISK. ARE WE SURE WE NEED THIS MAP?
YOU NEED IT.
AND THE NAME'S AKASH. NOT *THE INDIAN*.
LET'S GET IN AND OUT THEN. I DON'T WANT TO LINGER.
LEAD THE WAY, *AKASH*.
THAT'S CLEARLY THE MOHAWK.

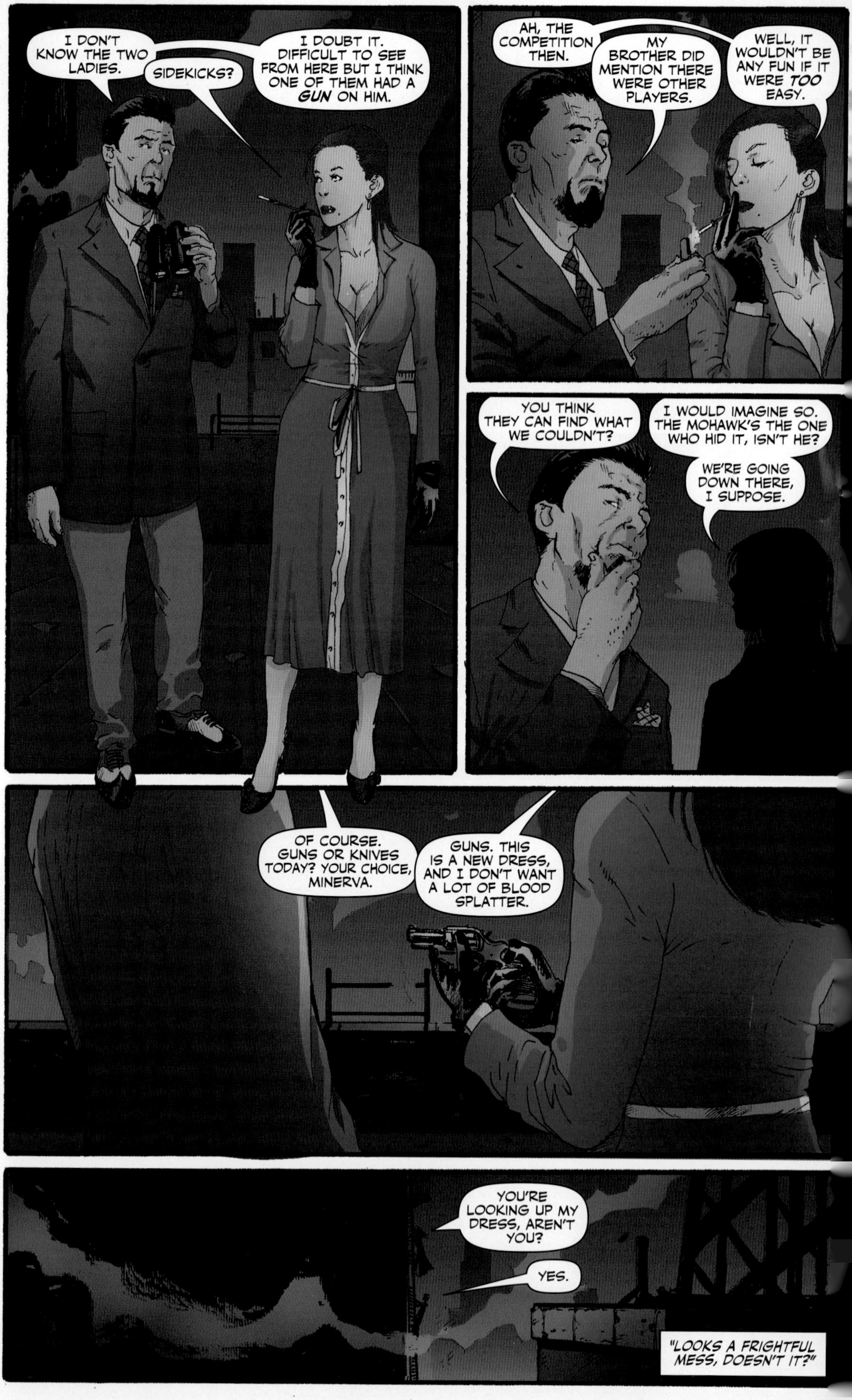
I DON'T KNOW THE TWO LADIES.
SIDEKICKS?
I DOUBT IT. DIFFICULT TO SEE FROM HERE BUT I THINK ONE OF THEM HAD A *GUN* ON HIM.
AH, THE COMPETITION THEN.
MY BROTHER DID MENTION THERE WERE OTHER PLAYERS.
WELL, IT WOULDN'T BE ANY FUN IF IT WERE *TOO* EASY.
YOU THINK THEY CAN FIND WHAT WE COULDN'T?
I WOULD IMAGINE SO. THE MOHAWK'S THE ONE WHO HID IT, ISN'T HE?
WE'RE GOING DOWN THERE, I SUPPOSE.
OF COURSE. GUNS OR KNIVES TODAY? YOUR CHOICE, MINERVA.
GUNS. THIS IS A NEW DRESS, AND I DON'T WANT A LOT OF BLOOD SPLATTER.
YOU'RE LOOKING UP MY DRESS, AREN'T YOU?
YES.
"LOOKS A FRIGHTFUL MESS, DOESN'T IT?"

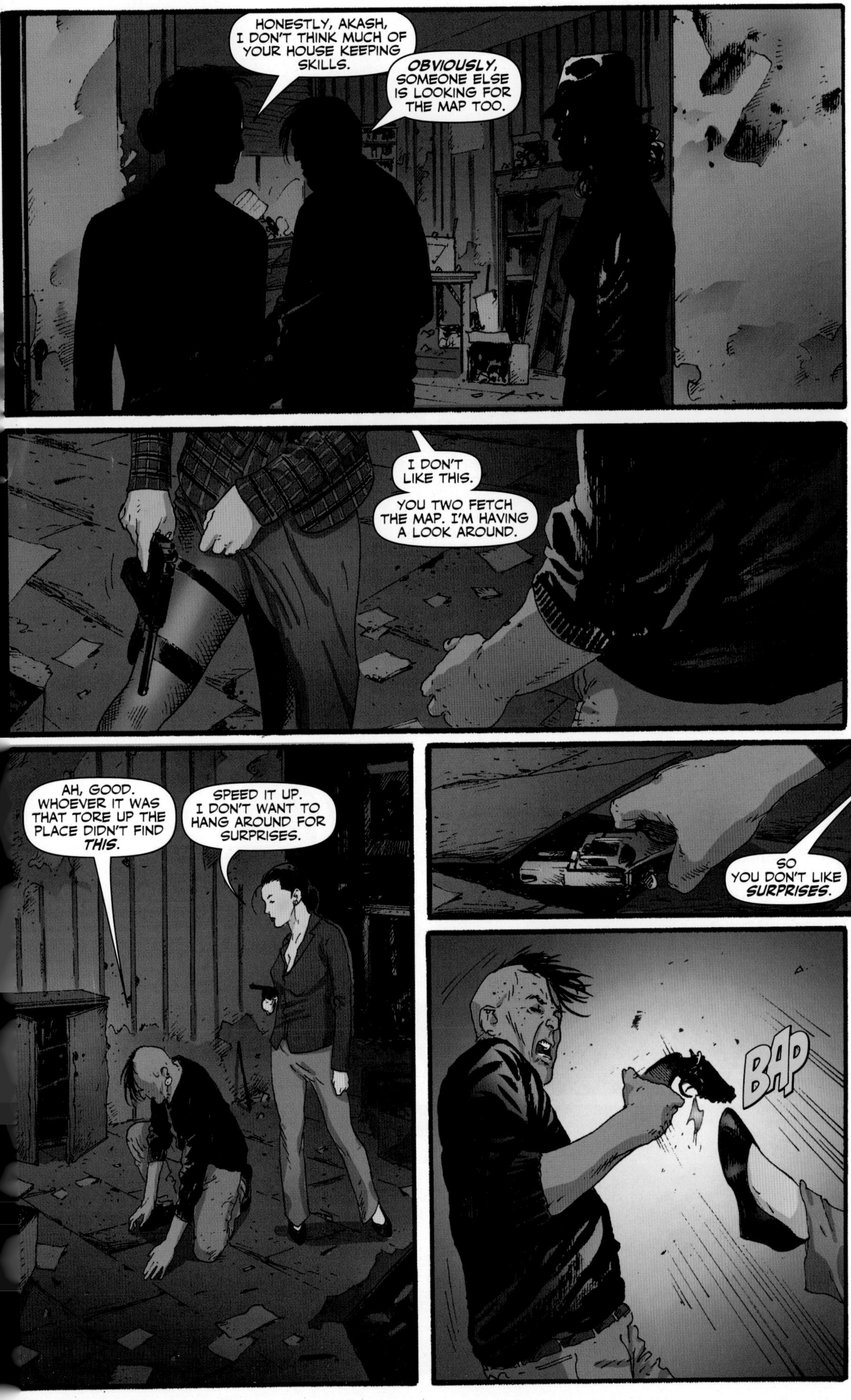
HONESTLY, AKASH, I DON'T THINK MUCH OF YOUR HOUSE KEEPING SKILLS.
OBVIOUSLY, SOMEONE ELSE IS LOOKING FOR THE MAP TOO.
I DON'T LIKE THIS.
YOU TWO FETCH THE MAP. I'M HAVING A LOOK AROUND.
AH, GOOD. WHOEVER IT WAS THAT TORE UP THE PLACE DIDN'T FIND *THIS*.
SPEED IT UP. I DON'T WANT TO HANG AROUND FOR SURPRISES.
SO YOU DON'T LIKE *SURPRISES*.
BAP

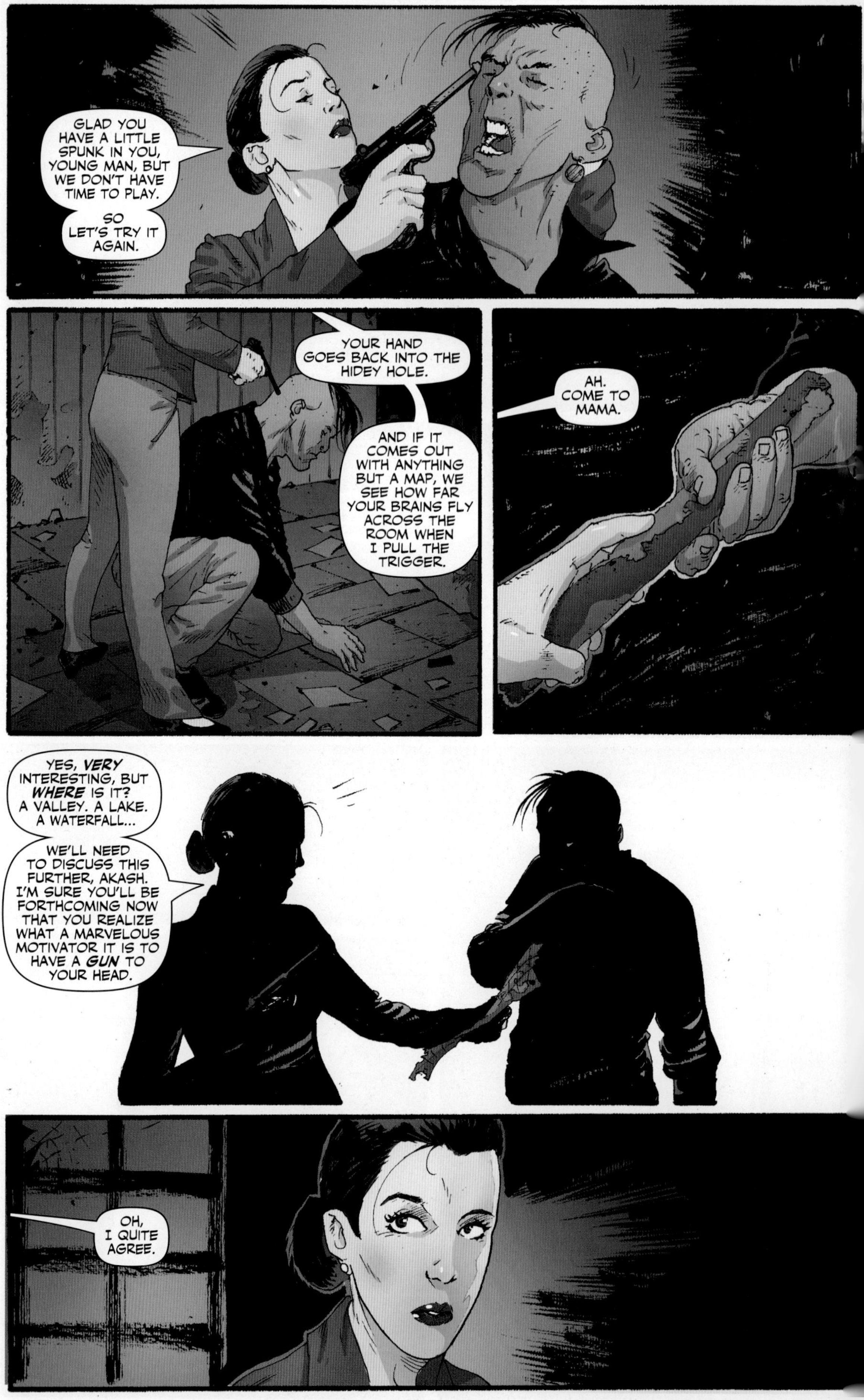
GLAD YOU HAVE A LITTLE SPUNK IN YOU, YOUNG MAN, BUT WE DON'T HAVE TIME TO PLAY.
SO LET'S TRY IT AGAIN.
YOUR HAND GOES BACK INTO THE HIDEY HOLE.
AND IF IT COMES OUT WITH ANYTHING BUT A MAP, WE SEE HOW FAR YOUR BRAINS FLY ACROSS THE ROOM WHEN I PULL THE TRIGGER.
AH. COME TO MAMA.
YES, *VERY* INTERESTING, BUT *WHERE* IS IT? A VALLEY. A LAKE. A WATERFALL...
WE'LL NEED TO DISCUSS THIS FURTHER, AKASH. I'M SURE YOU'LL BE FORTHCOMING NOW THAT YOU REALIZE WHAT A MARVELOUS MOTIVATOR IT IS TO HAVE A *GUN* TO YOUR HEAD.
OH, I QUITE AGREE.

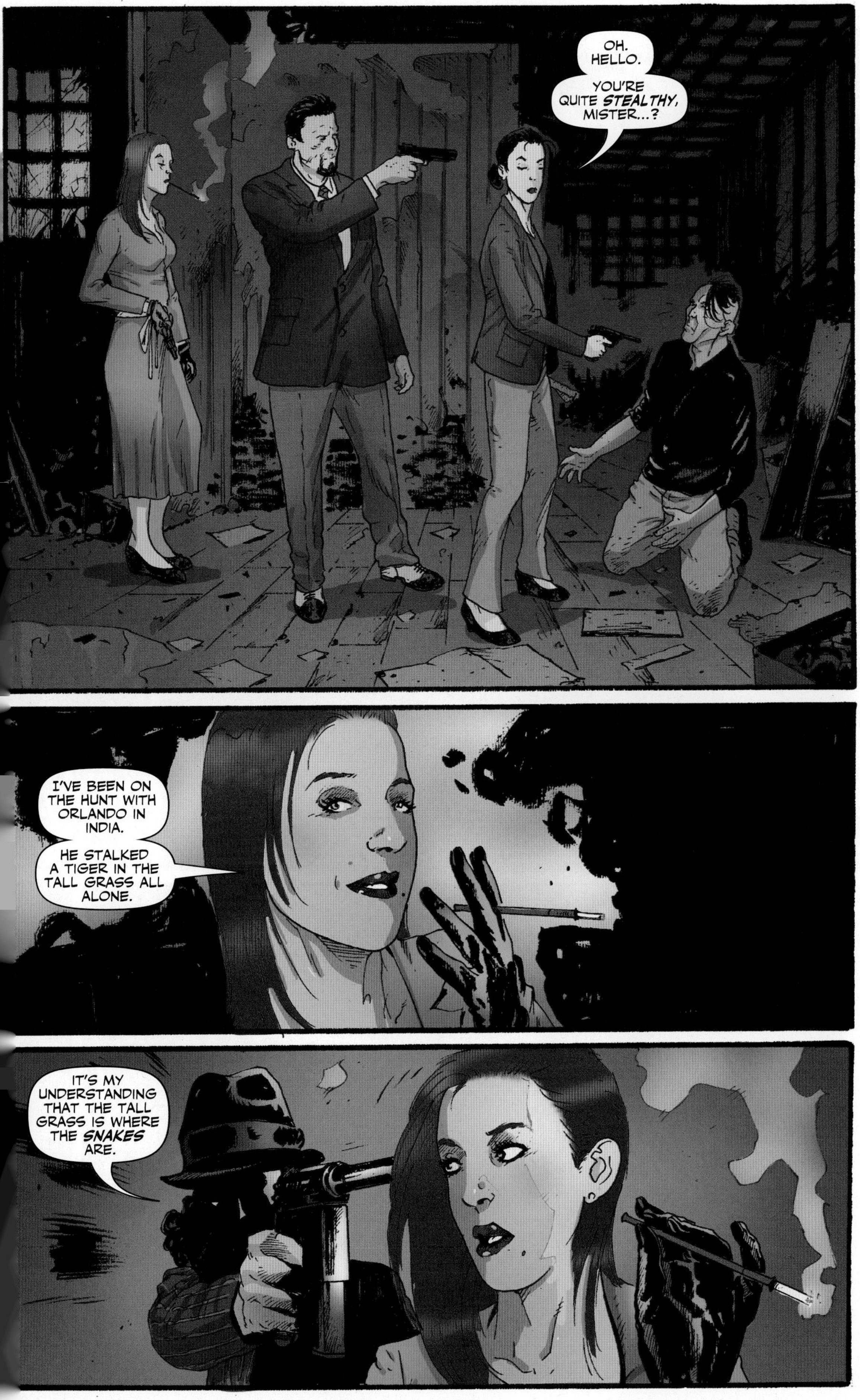
OH. HELLO.
YOU'RE QUITE STEALTHY, MISTER...?
I'VE BEEN ON THE HUNT WITH ORLANDO IN INDIA.
HE STALKED A TIGER IN THE TALL GRASS ALL ALONE.
IT'S MY UNDERSTANDING THAT THE TALL GRASS IS WHERE THE SNAKES ARE.

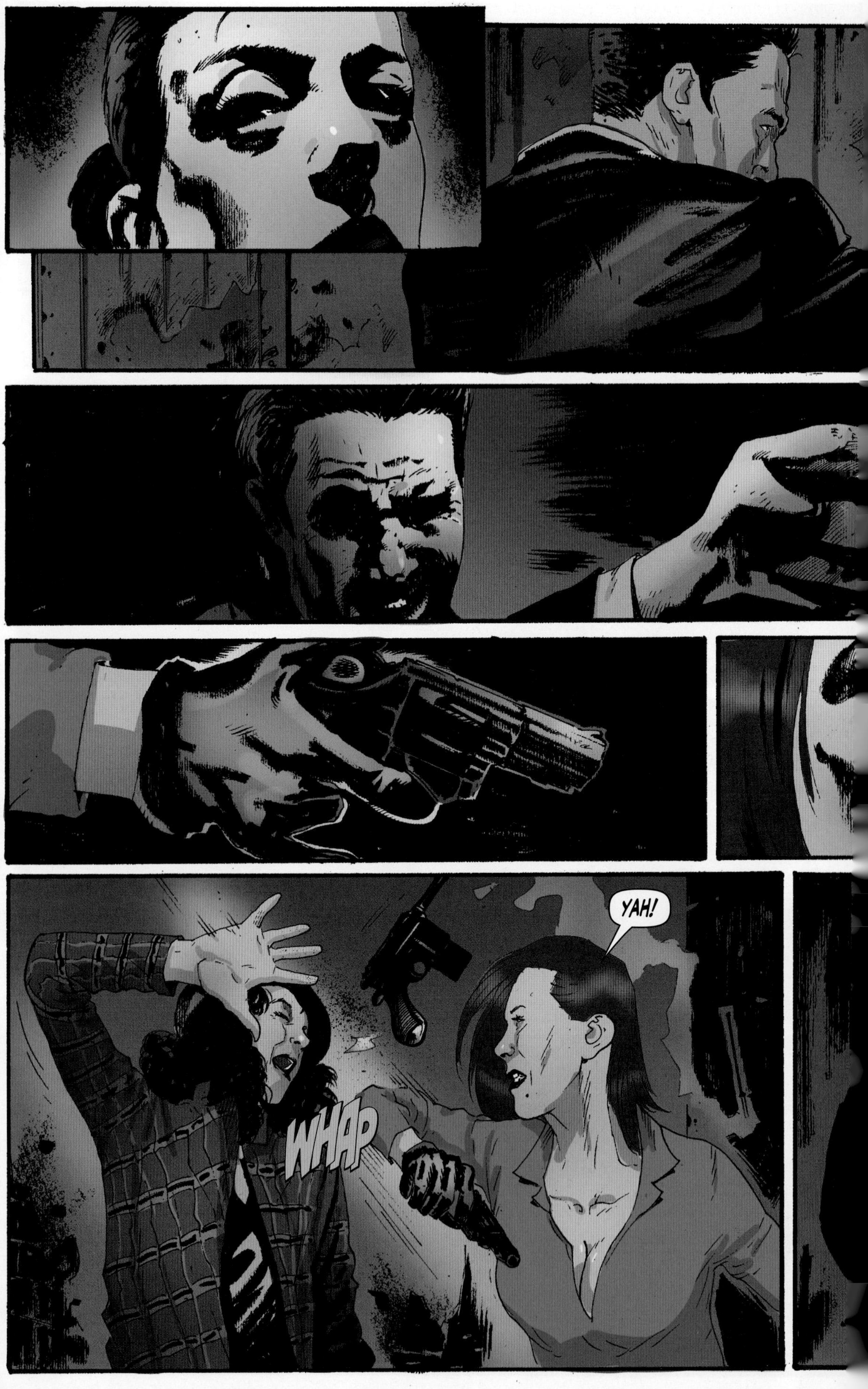
YAH!
WHAP

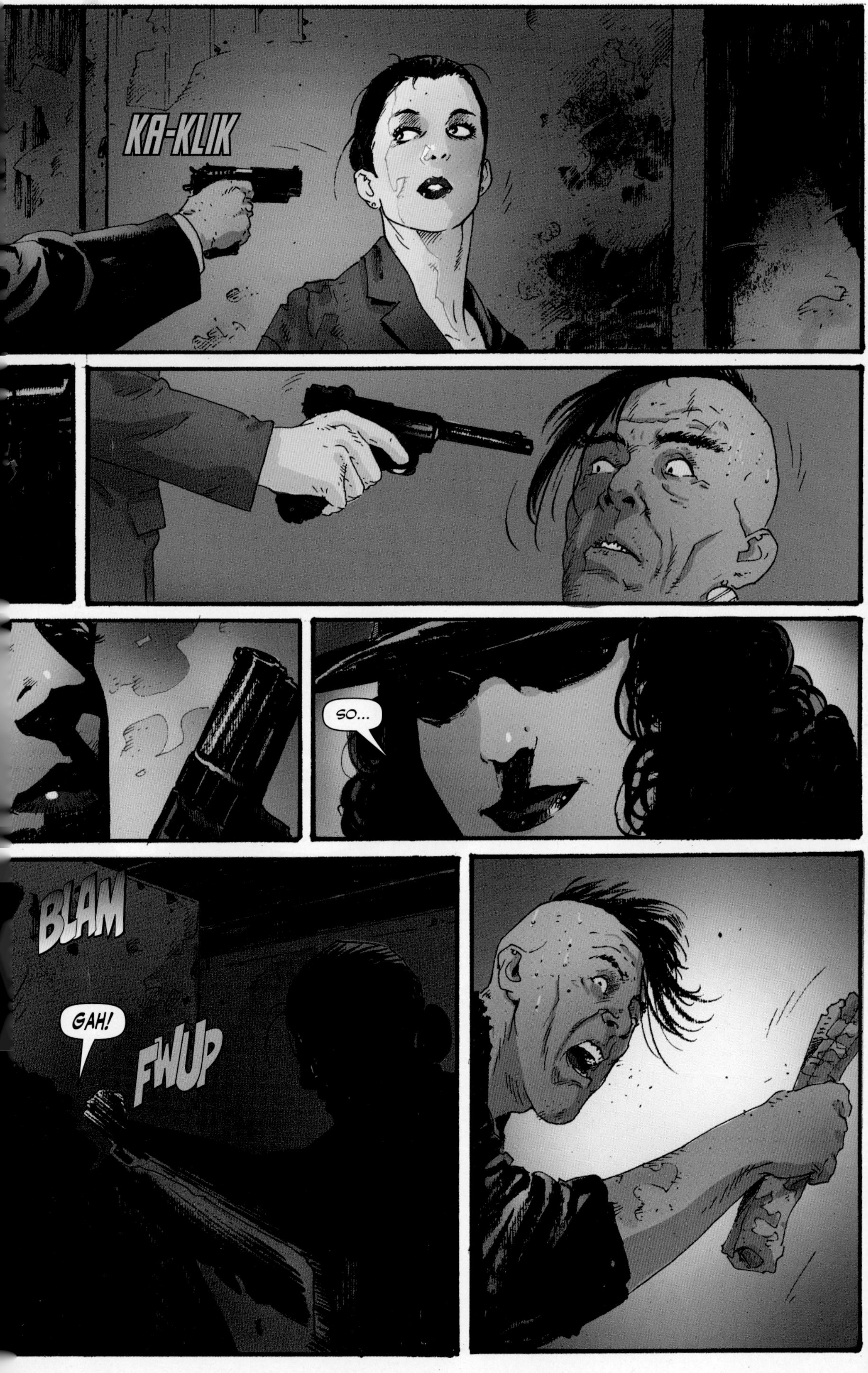
KA-KLIK
SO...
BLAM
GAH!
FWUP

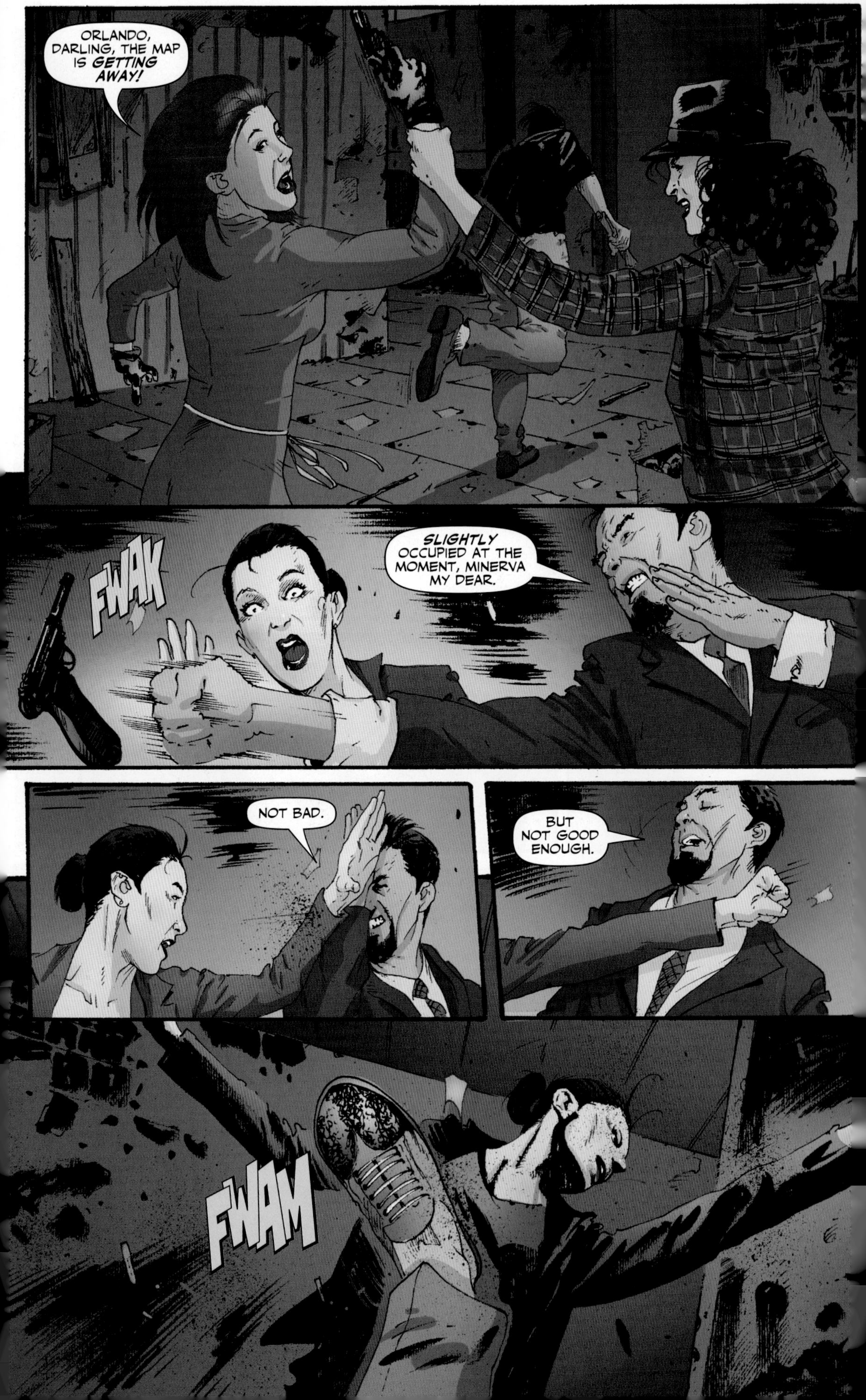
ORLANDO, DARLING, THE MAP IS *GETTING AWAY!*
FWAK
SLIGHTLY OCCUPIED AT THE MOMENT, MINERVA MY DEAR.
NOT BAD.
BUT NOT GOOD ENOUGH.
FWAM

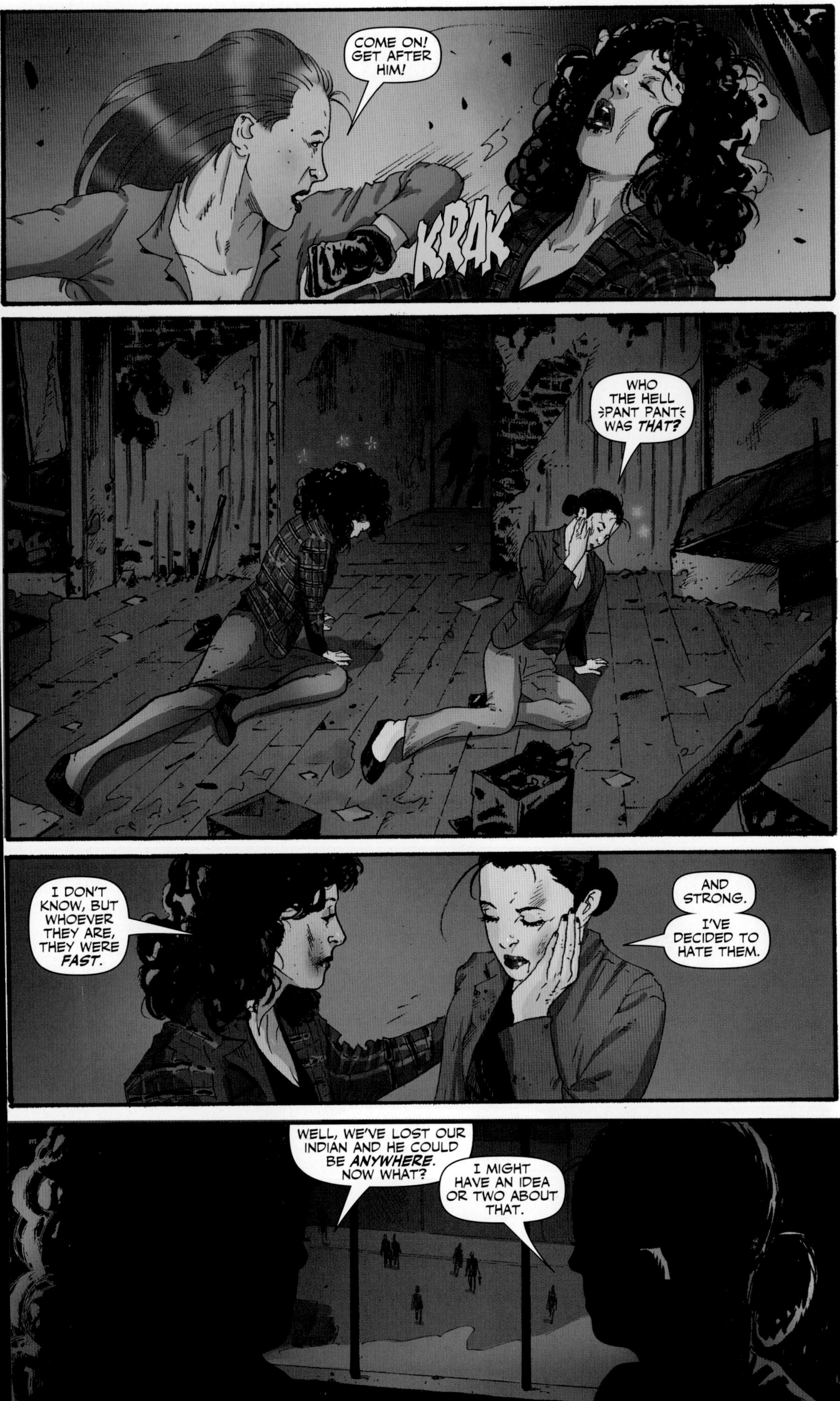
COME ON! GET AFTER HIM!
KRAK
WHO THE HELL PANT PANT WAS THAT?
I DON'T KNOW, BUT WHOEVER THEY ARE, THEY WERE FAST.
AND STRONG.
I'VE DECIDED TO HATE THEM.
WELL, WE'VE LOST OUR INDIAN AND HE COULD BE ANYWHERE. NOW WHAT?
I MIGHT HAVE AN IDEA OR TWO ABOUT THAT.

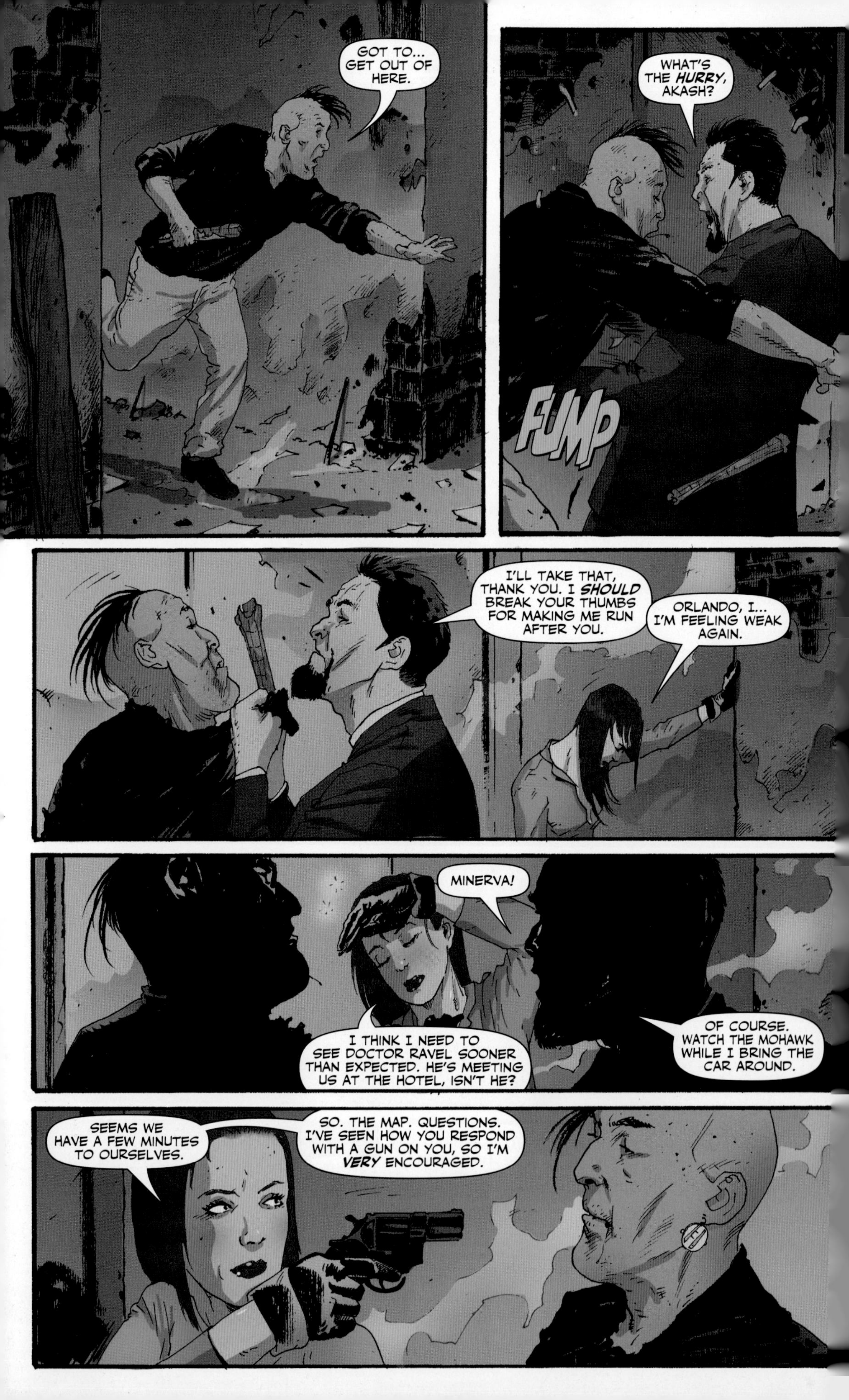

GOT TO... GET OUT OF HERE.
WHAT'S THE *HURRY*, AKASH?
FUMP
I'LL TAKE THAT, THANK YOU. I *SHOULD* BREAK YOUR THUMBS FOR MAKING ME RUN AFTER YOU.
ORLANDO, I... I'M FEELING WEAK AGAIN.
MINERVA!
I THINK I NEED TO SEE DOCTOR RAVEL SOONER THAN EXPECTED. HE'S MEETING US AT THE HOTEL, ISN'T HE?
OF COURSE. WATCH THE MOHAWK WHILE I BRING THE CAR AROUND.
SEEMS WE HAVE A FEW MINUTES TO OURSELVES.
SO. THE MAP. QUESTIONS. I'VE SEEN HOW YOU RESPOND WITH A GUN ON YOU, SO I'M *VERY* ENCOURAGED.

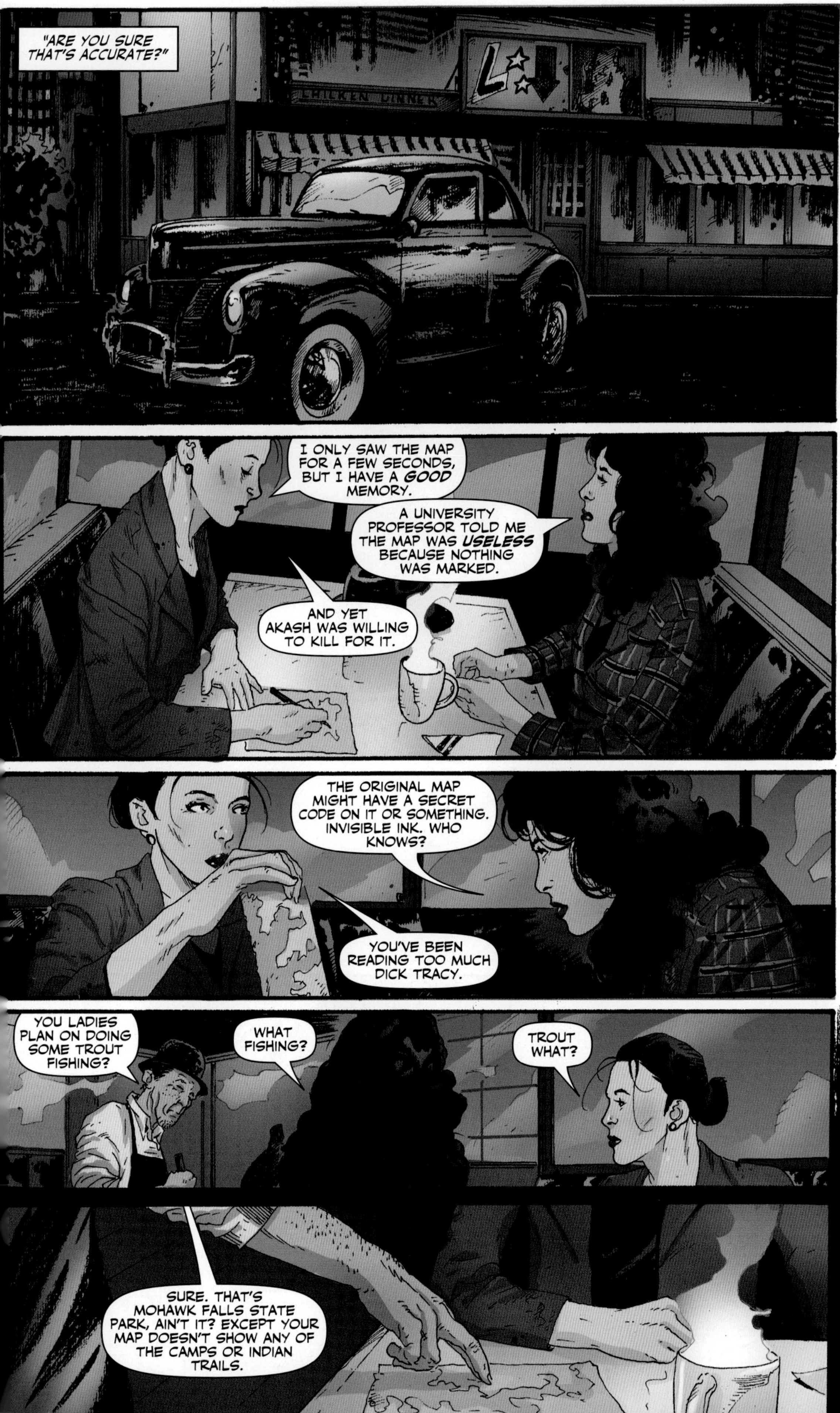
"ARE YOU SURE THAT'S ACCURATE?"
CHICKEN DINNER
I ONLY SAW THE MAP FOR A FEW SECONDS, BUT I HAVE A *GOOD* MEMORY.
A UNIVERSITY PROFESSOR TOLD ME THE MAP WAS *USELESS* BECAUSE NOTHING WAS MARKED.
AND YET AKASH WAS WILLING TO KILL FOR IT.
THE ORIGINAL MAP MIGHT HAVE A SECRET CODE ON IT OR SOMETHING. INVISIBLE INK. WHO KNOWS?
YOU'VE BEEN READING TOO MUCH DICK TRACY.
YOU LADIES PLAN ON DOING SOME TROUT FISHING?
WHAT FISHING?
TROUT WHAT?
SURE. THAT'S MOHAWK FALLS STATE PARK, AIN'T IT? EXCEPT YOUR MAP DOESN'T SHOW ANY OF THE CAMPS OR INDIAN TRAILS.

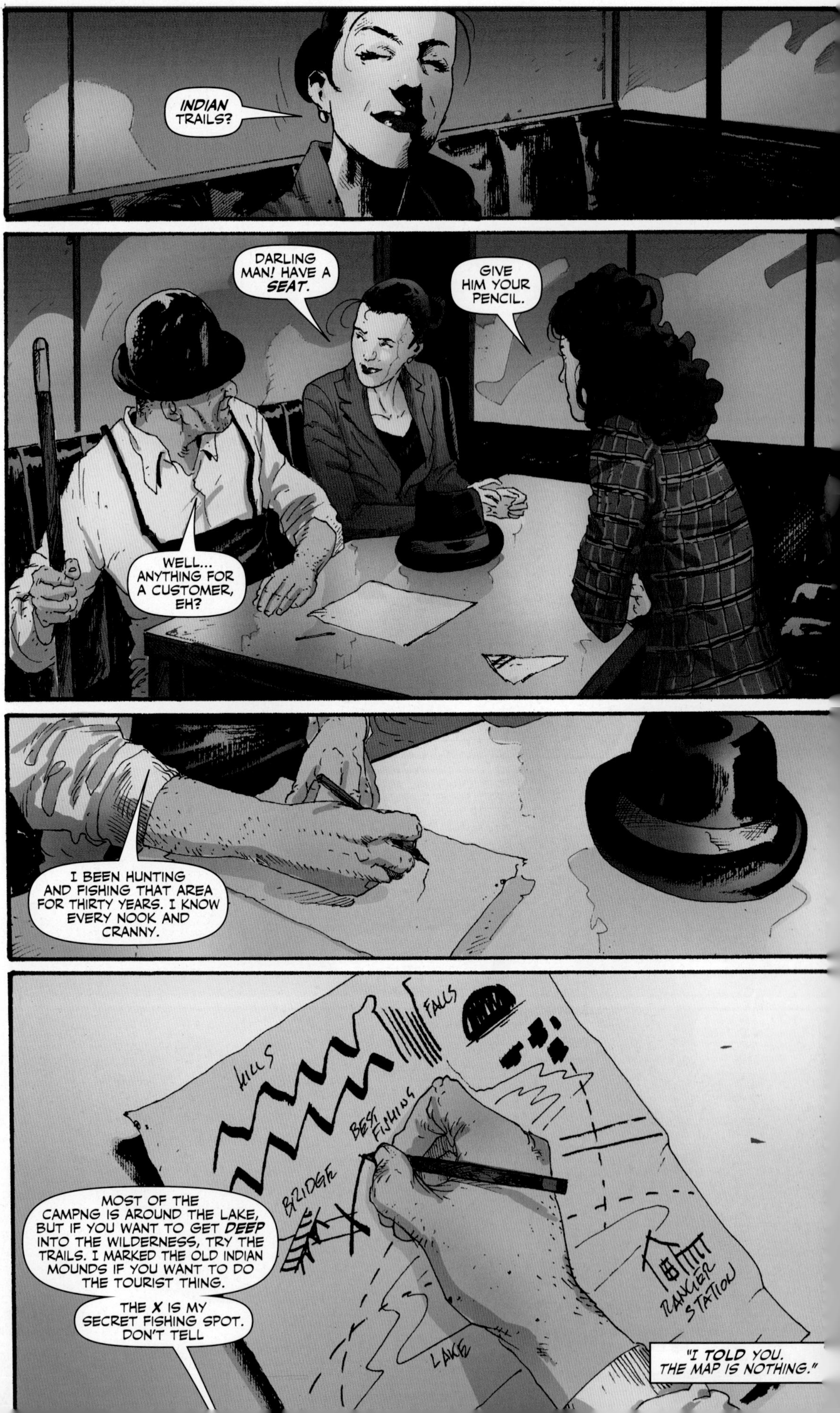
INDIAN TRAILS?
DARLING MAN! HAVE A SEAT.
GIVE HIM YOUR PENCIL.
WELL... ANYTHING FOR A CUSTOMER, EH?
I BEEN HUNTING AND FISHING THAT AREA FOR THIRTY YEARS. I KNOW EVERY NOOK AND CRANNY.
HILLS
FALLS
BEST FISHING
BRIDGE
RANGER STATION
LAKE
MOST OF THE CAMPNG IS AROUND THE LAKE, BUT IF YOU WANT TO GET DEEP INTO THE WILDERNESS, TRY THE TRAILS. I MARKED THE OLD INDIAN MOUNDS IF YOU WANT TO DO THE TOURIST THING.
THE X IS MY SECRET FISHING SPOT. DON'T TELL
"I TOLD YOU. THE MAP IS NOTHING."

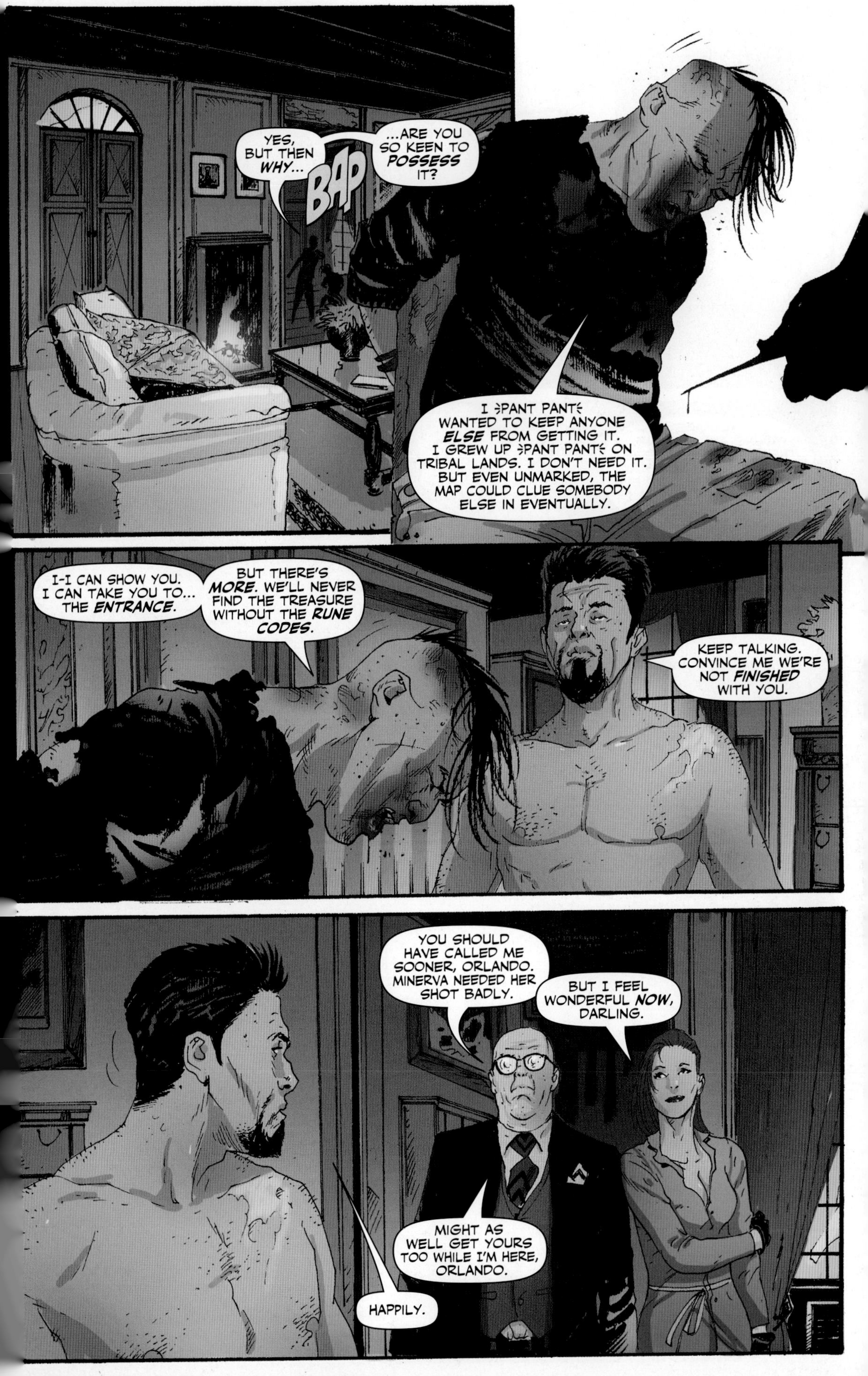
YES, BUT THEN WHY...
BAP
...ARE YOU SO KEEN TO POSSESS IT?
I ⋛PANT PANT⋚ WANTED TO KEEP ANYONE ELSE FROM GETTING IT. I GREW UP ⋛PANT PANT⋚ ON TRIBAL LANDS. I DON'T NEED IT. BUT EVEN UNMARKED, THE MAP COULD CLUE SOMEBODY ELSE IN EVENTUALLY.
I-I CAN SHOW YOU. I CAN TAKE YOU TO... THE ENTRANCE.
BUT THERE'S MORE. WE'LL NEVER FIND THE TREASURE WITHOUT THE RUNE CODES.
KEEP TALKING. CONVINCE ME WE'RE NOT FINISHED WITH YOU.
YOU SHOULD HAVE CALLED ME SOONER, ORLANDO. MINERVA NEEDED HER SHOT BADLY.
BUT I FEEL WONDERFUL NOW, DARLING.
MIGHT AS WELL GET YOURS TOO WHILE I'M HERE, ORLANDO.
HAPPILY.

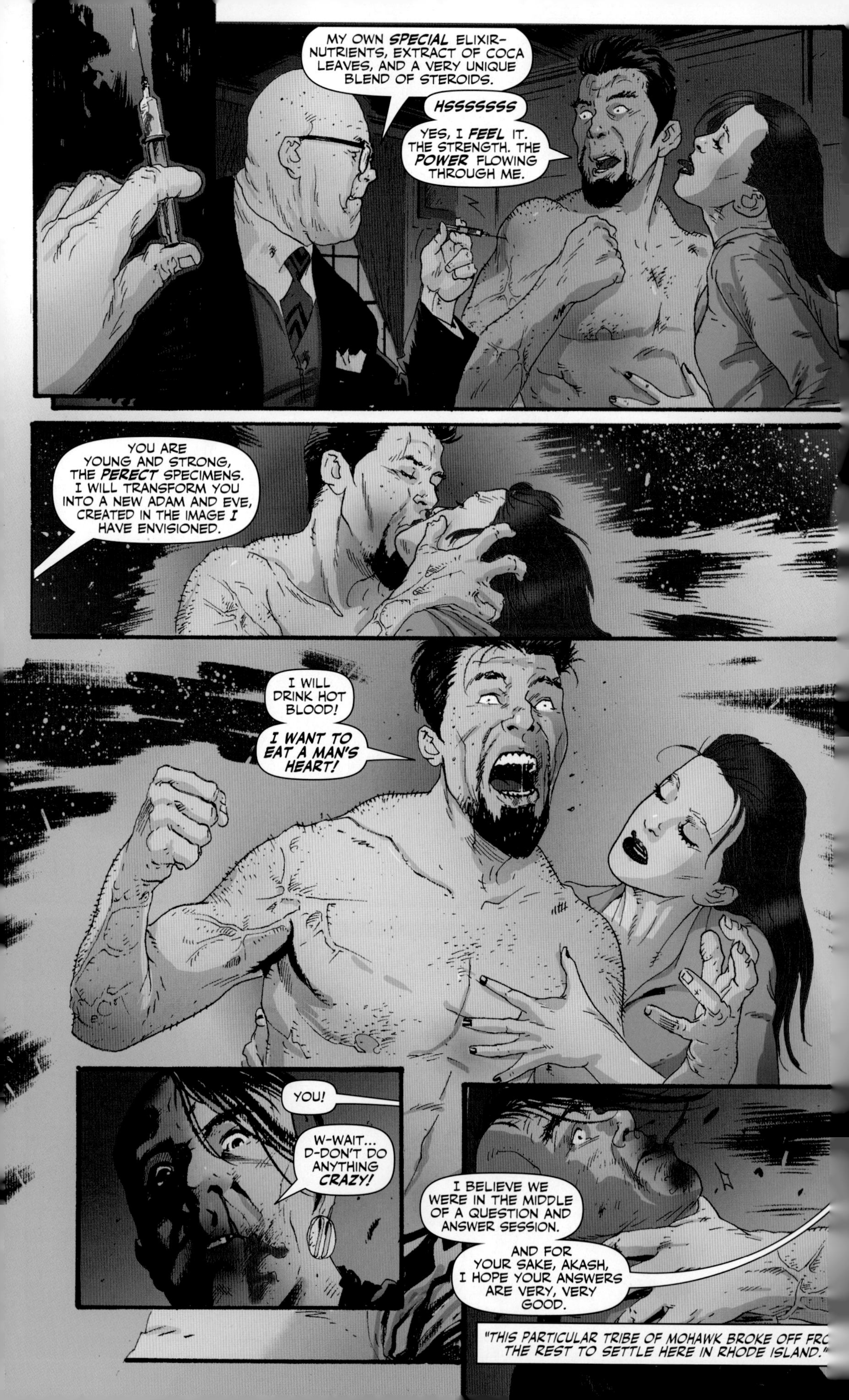

MY OWN SPECIAL ELIXIR- NUTRIENTS, EXTRACT OF COCA LEAVES, AND A VERY UNIQUE BLEND OF STEROIDS.
HSSSSSSS
YES, I FEEL IT. THE STRENGTH. THE POWER FLOWING THROUGH ME.
YOU ARE YOUNG AND STRONG, THE PERECT SPECIMENS. I WILL TRANSFORM YOU INTO A NEW ADAM AND EVE, CREATED IN THE IMAGE I HAVE ENVISIONED.
I WILL DRINK HOT BLOOD!
I WANT TO EAT A MAN'S HEART!
YOU!
W-WAIT... D-DON'T DO ANYTHING CRAZY!
I BELIEVE WE WERE IN THE MIDDLE OF A QUESTION AND ANSWER SESSION.
AND FOR YOUR SAKE, AKASH, I HOPE YOUR ANSWERS ARE VERY, VERY GOOD.
"THIS PARTICULAR TRIBE OF MOHAWK BROKE OFF FRO THE REST TO SETTLE HERE IN RHODE ISLAND."

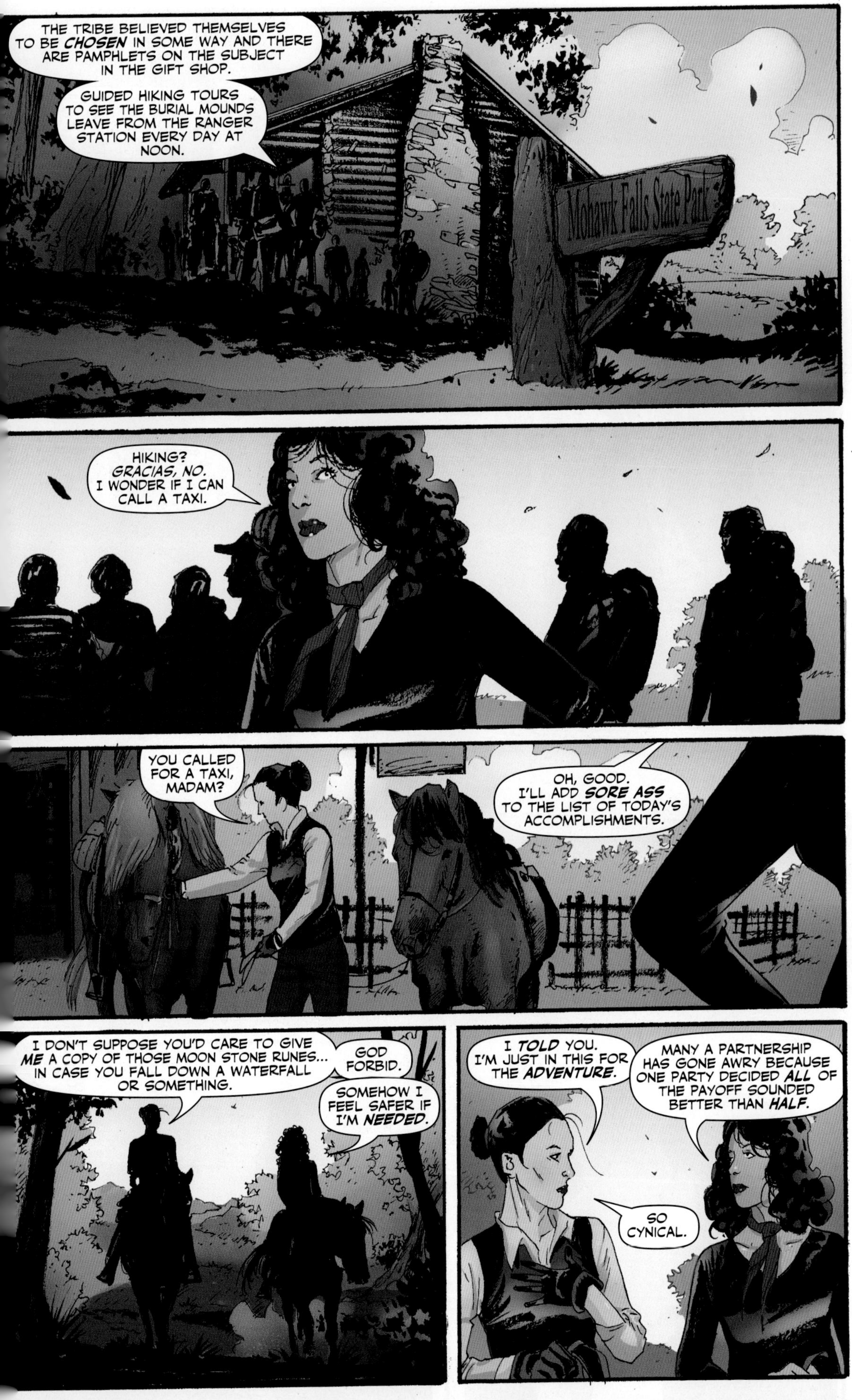
THE TRIBE BELIEVED THEMSELVES TO BE CHOSEN IN SOME WAY AND THERE ARE PAMPHLETS ON THE SUBJECT IN THE GIFT SHOP.
GUIDED HIKING TOURS TO SEE THE BURIAL MOUNDS LEAVE FROM THE RANGER STATION EVERY DAY AT NOON.
Mohawk Falls State Park
HIKING? GRACIAS, NO. I WONDER IF I CAN CALL A TAXI.
YOU CALLED FOR A TAXI, MADAM?
OH, GOOD. I'LL ADD SORE ASS TO THE LIST OF TODAY'S ACCOMPLISHMENTS.
I DON'T SUPPOSE YOU'D CARE TO GIVE ME A COPY OF THOSE MOON STONE RUNES... IN CASE YOU FALL DOWN A WATERFALL OR SOMETHING.
GOD FORBID.
SOMEHOW I FEEL SAFER IF I'M NEEDED.
I TOLD YOU. I'M JUST IN THIS FOR THE ADVENTURE.
MANY A PARTNERSHIP HAS GONE AWRY BECAUSE ONE PARTY DECIDED ALL OF THE PAYOFF SOUNDED BETTER THAN HALF.
SO CYNICAL.

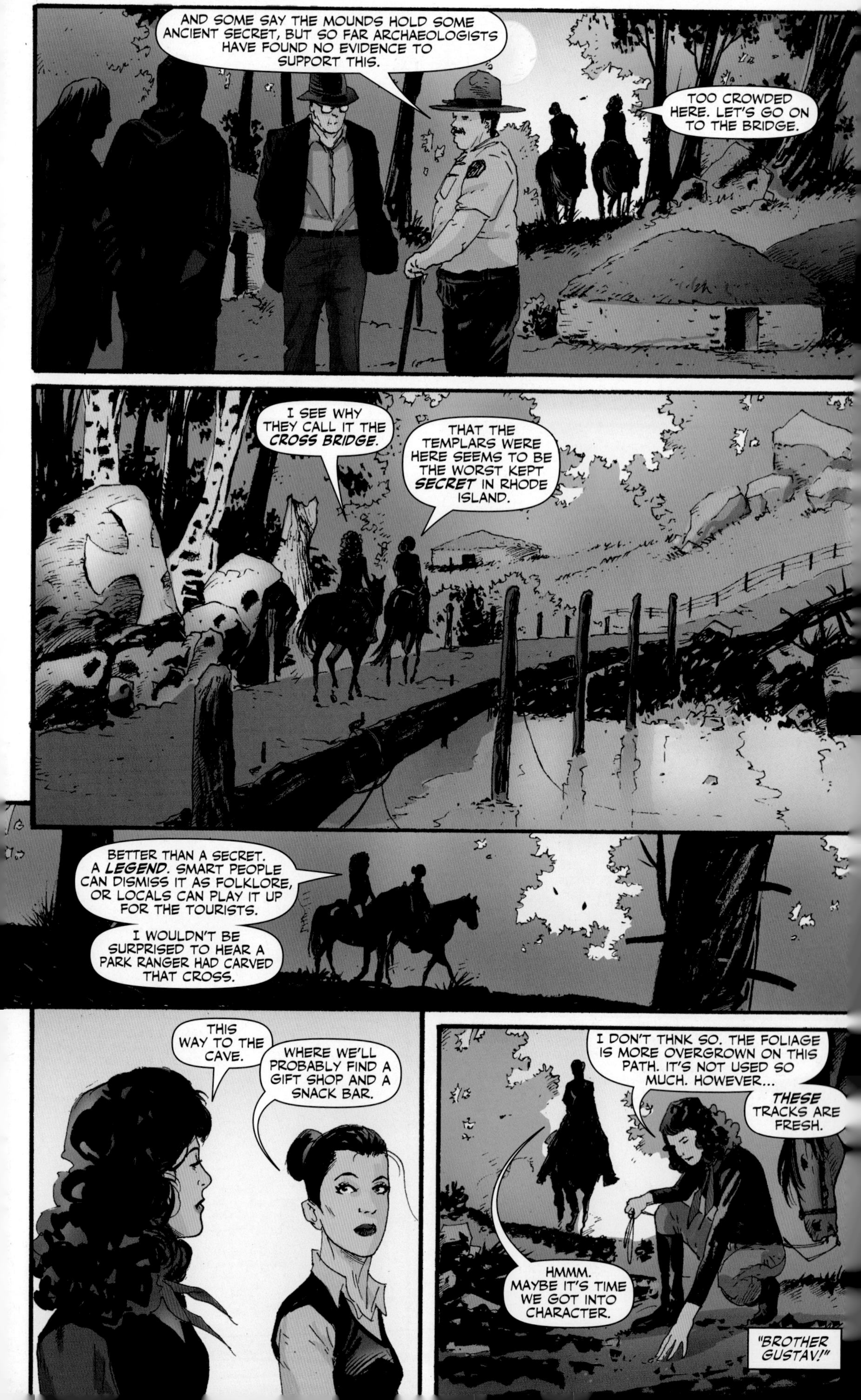
AND SOME SAY THE MOUNDS HOLD SOME ANCIENT SECRET, BUT SO FAR ARCHAEOLOGISTS HAVE FOUND NO EVIDENCE TO SUPPORT THIS.
TOO CROWDED HERE. LET'S GO ON TO THE BRIDGE.
I SEE WHY THEY CALL IT THE CROSS BRIDGE.
THAT THE TEMPLARS WERE HERE SEEMS TO BE THE WORST KEPT SECRET IN RHODE ISLAND.
BETTER THAN A SECRET. A LEGEND. SMART PEOPLE CAN DISMISS IT AS FOLKLORE, OR LOCALS CAN PLAY IT UP FOR THE TOURISTS.
I WOULDN'T BE SURPRISED TO HEAR A PARK RANGER HAD CARVED THAT CROSS.
THIS WAY TO THE CAVE.
WHERE WE'LL PROBABLY FIND A GIFT SHOP AND A SNACK BAR.
I DON'T THNK SO. THE FOLIAGE IS MORE OVERGROWN ON THIS PATH. IT'S NOT USED SO MUCH. HOWEVER...
THESE TRACKS ARE FRESH.
HMMM. MAYBE IT'S TIME WE GOT INTO CHARACTER.
"BROTHER GUSTAV!"

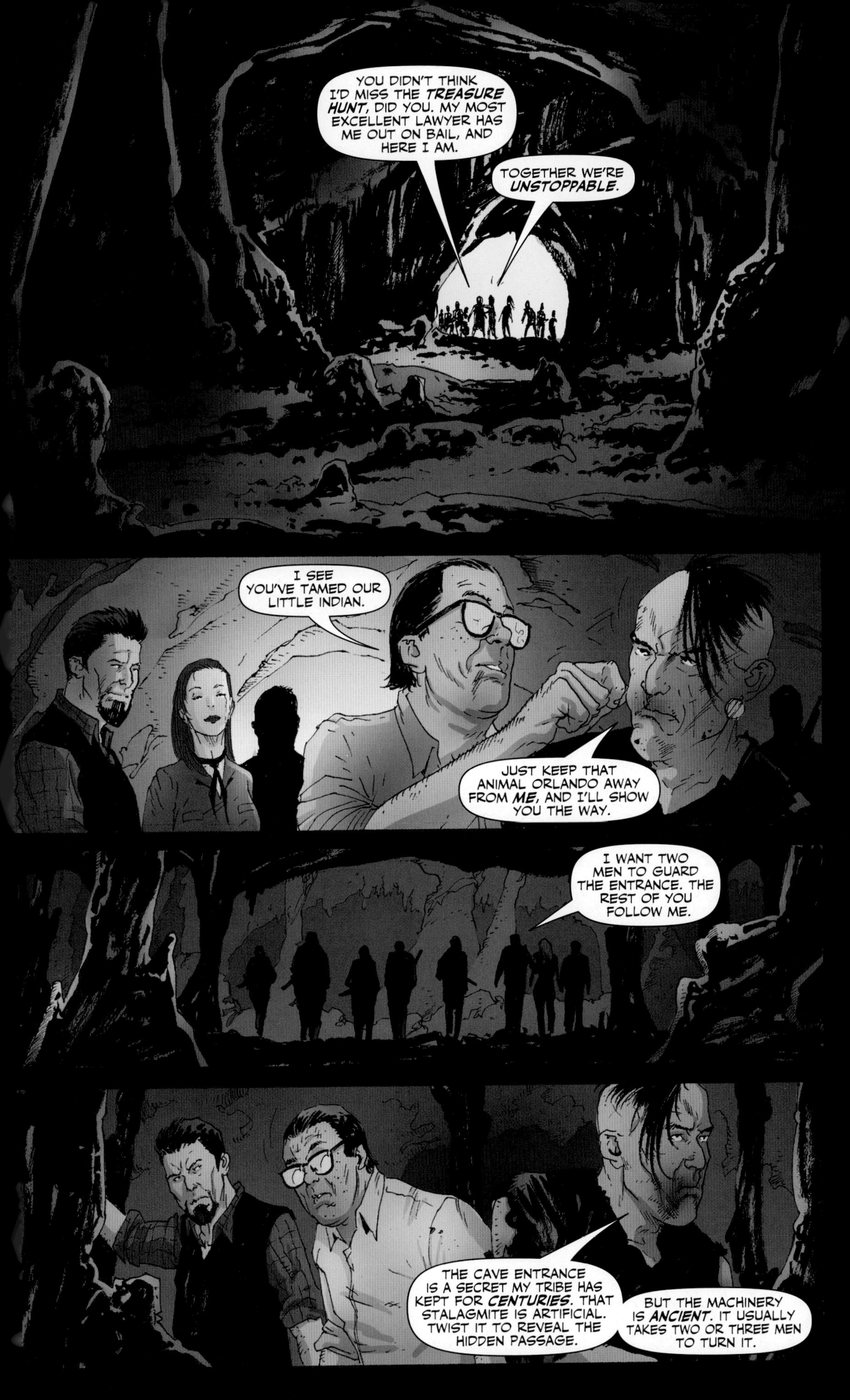
YOU DIDN'T THINK I'D MISS THE *TREASURE HUNT*, DID YOU. MY MOST EXCELLENT LAWYER HAS ME OUT ON BAIL, AND HERE I AM.
TOGETHER WE'RE *UNSTOPPABLE*.
I SEE YOU'VE TAMED OUR LITTLE INDIAN.
JUST KEEP THAT ANIMAL ORLANDO AWAY FROM *ME*, AND I'LL SHOW YOU THE WAY.
I WANT TWO MEN TO GUARD THE ENTRANCE. THE REST OF YOU FOLLOW ME.
THE CAVE ENTRANCE IS A SECRET MY TRIBE HAS KEPT FOR *CENTURIES*. THAT STALAGMITE IS ARTIFICIAL. TWIST IT TO REVEAL THE HIDDEN PASSAGE.
BUT THE MACHINERY IS *ANCIENT*. IT USUALLY TAKES TWO OR THREE MEN TO TURN IT.

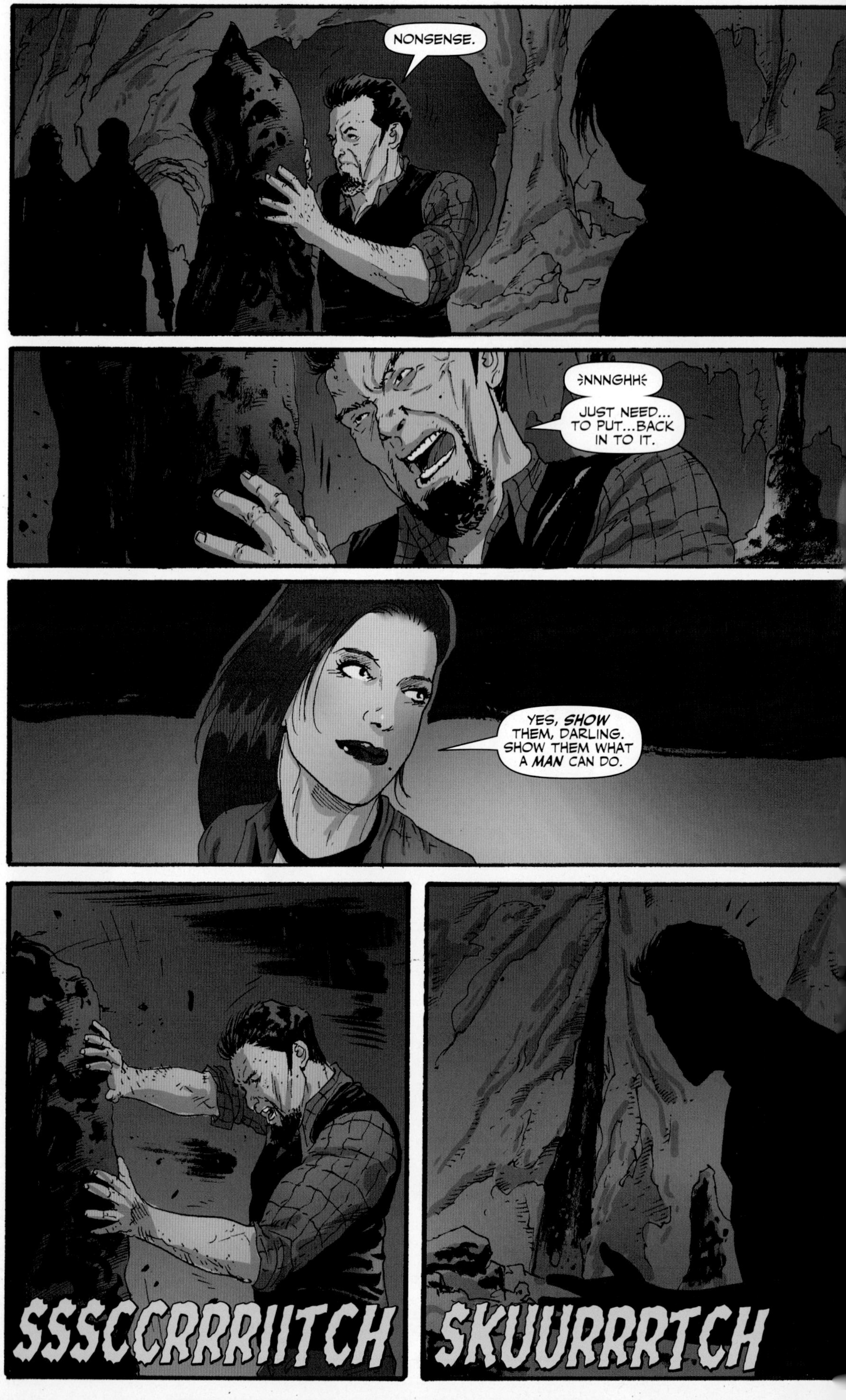
NONSENSE.
NNNGHH
JUST NEED... TO PUT...BACK IN TO IT.
YES, SHOW THEM, DARLING. SHOW THEM WHAT A MAN CAN DO.
SSSCCRRRRIITCH
SKUURRRRTCH

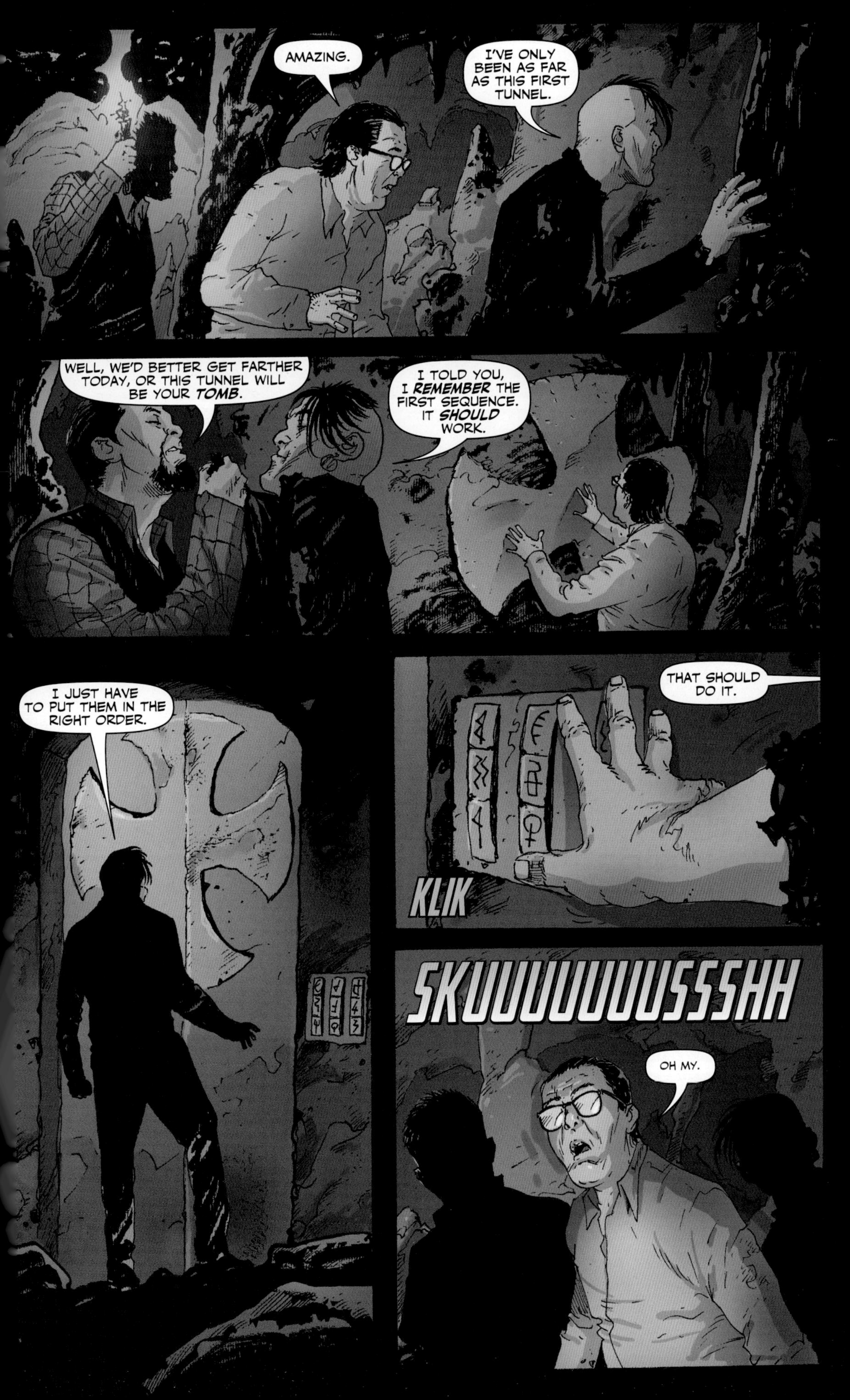
AMAZING.
I'VE ONLY BEEN AS FAR AS THIS FIRST TUNNEL.
WELL, WE'D BETTER GET FARTHER TODAY, OR THIS TUNNEL WILL BE YOUR TOMB.
I TOLD YOU, I REMEMBER THE FIRST SEQUENCE. IT SHOULD WORK.
I JUST HAVE TO PUT THEM IN THE RIGHT ORDER.
THAT SHOULD DO IT.
KLIK
SKUUUUUUUUSSSHH
OH MY.

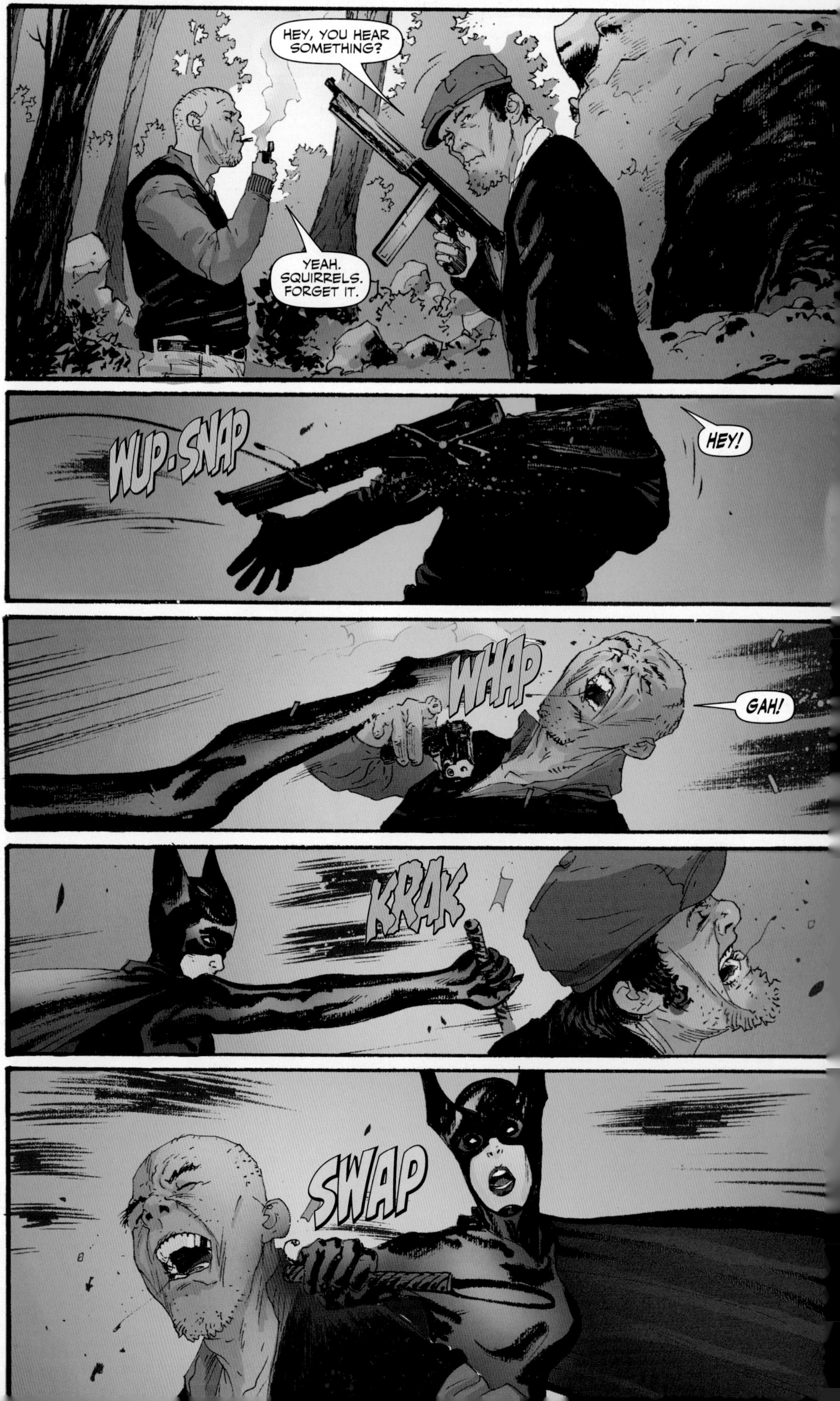
HEY, YOU HEAR SOMETHING?
YEAH. SQUIRRELS. FORGET IT.
WUP-SNAP
HEY!
WHAP
GAH!
KRAK
SWAP

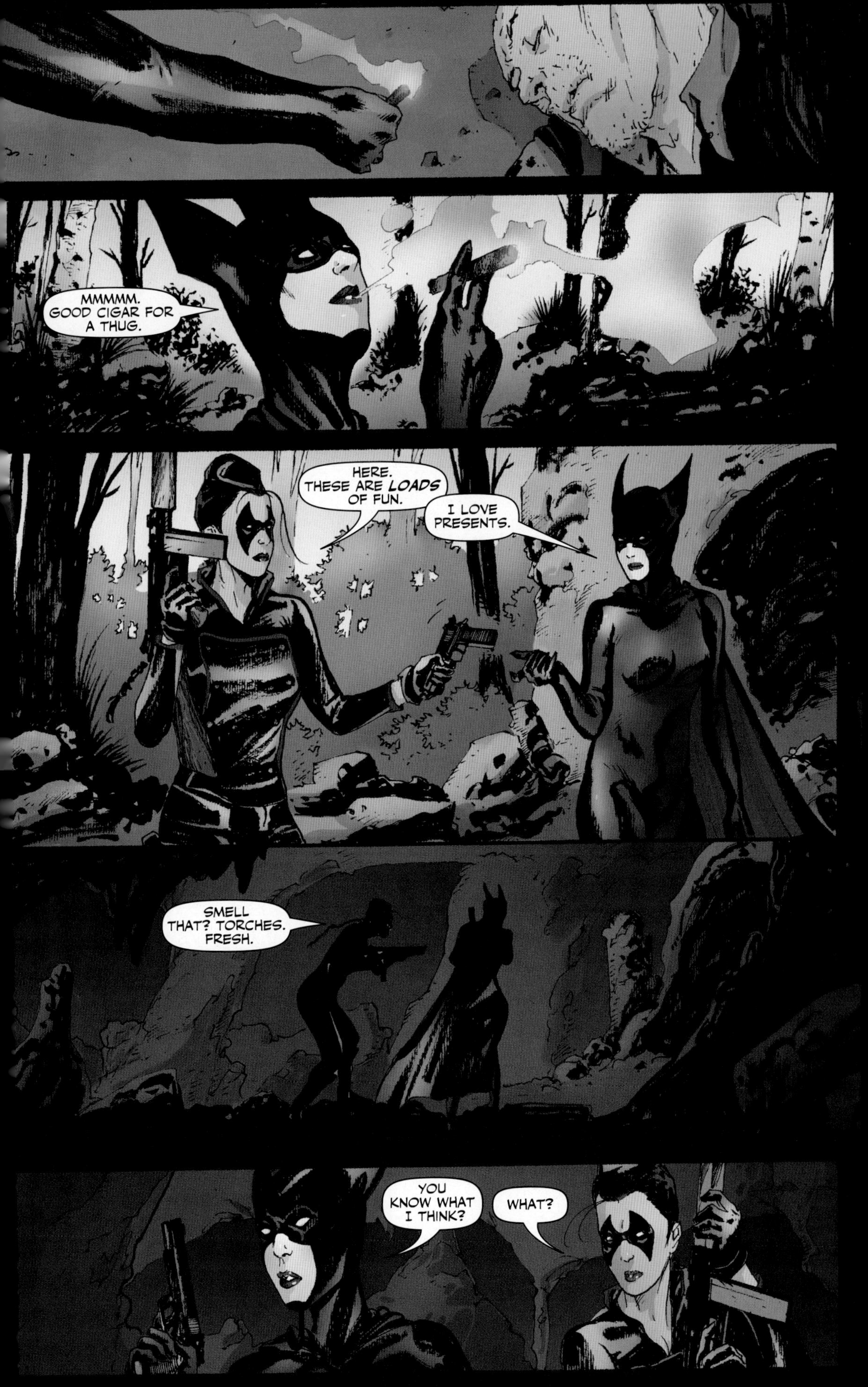

MMMMM. GOOD CIGAR FOR A THUG.
HERE. THESE ARE *LOADS* OF FUN.
I LOVE PRESENTS.
SMELL THAT? TORCHES. FRESH.
YOU KNOW WHAT I THINK?
WHAT?

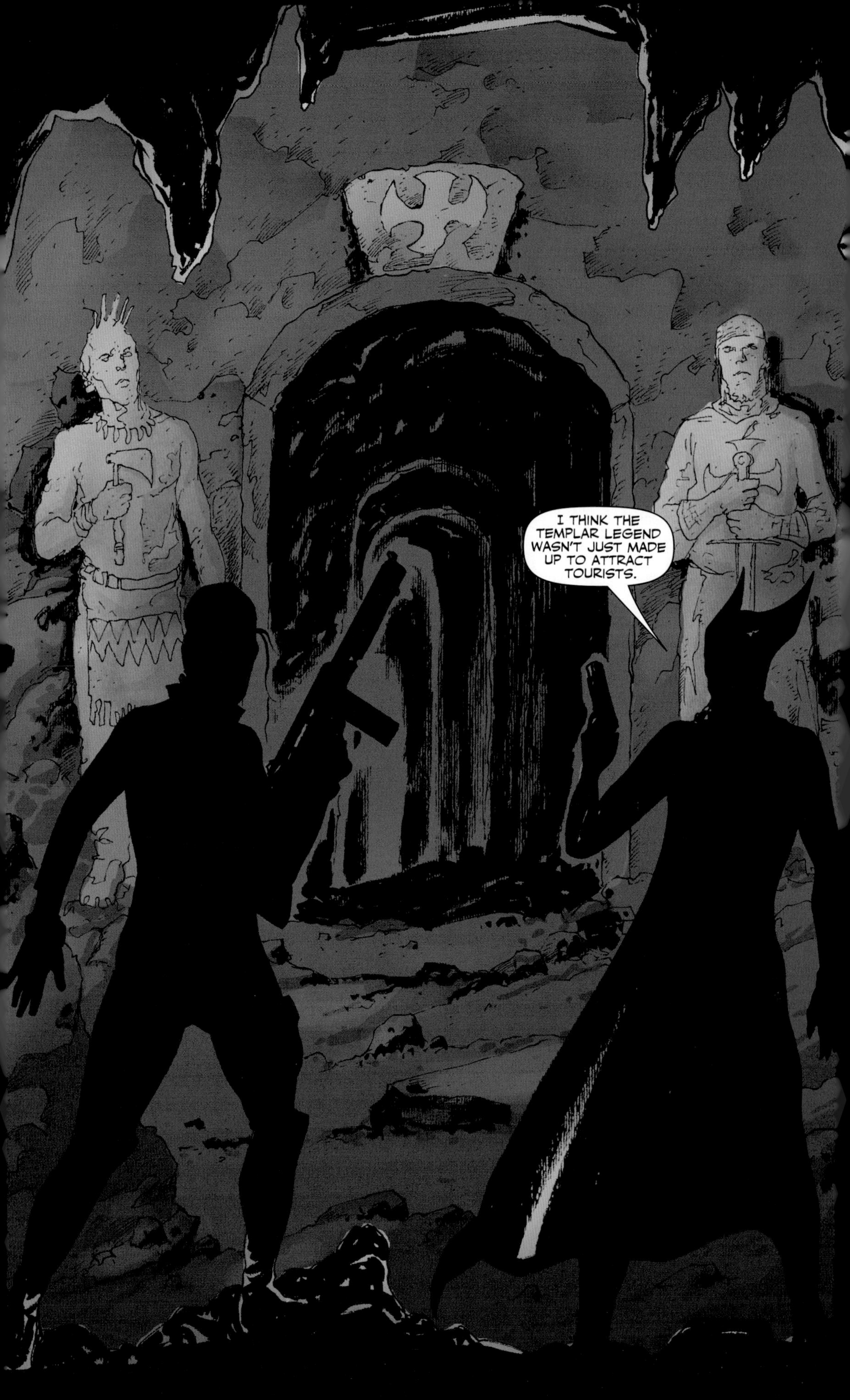
I THINK THE TEMPLAR LEGEND WASN'T JUST MADE UP TO ATTRACT TOURISTS.

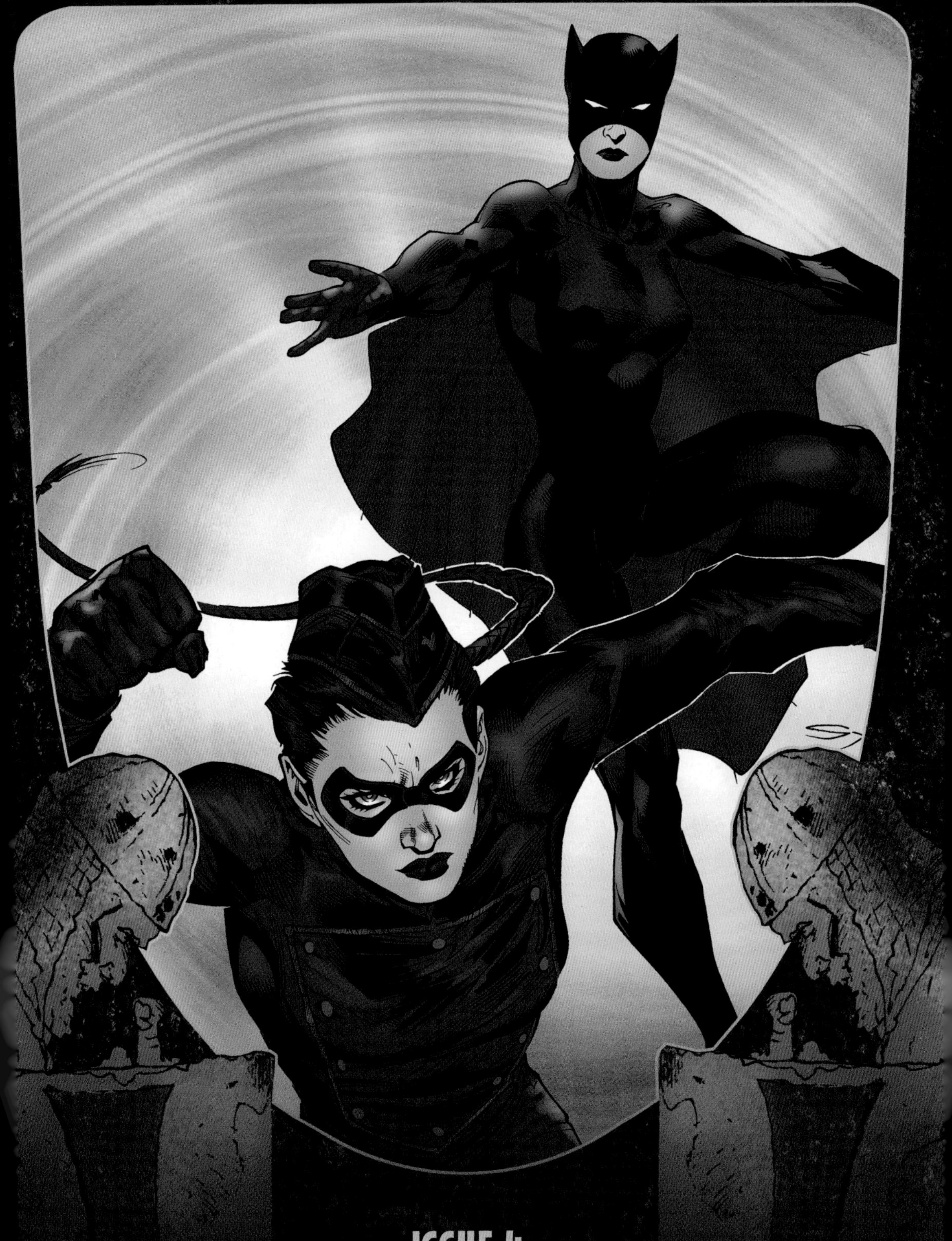

ISSUE 4

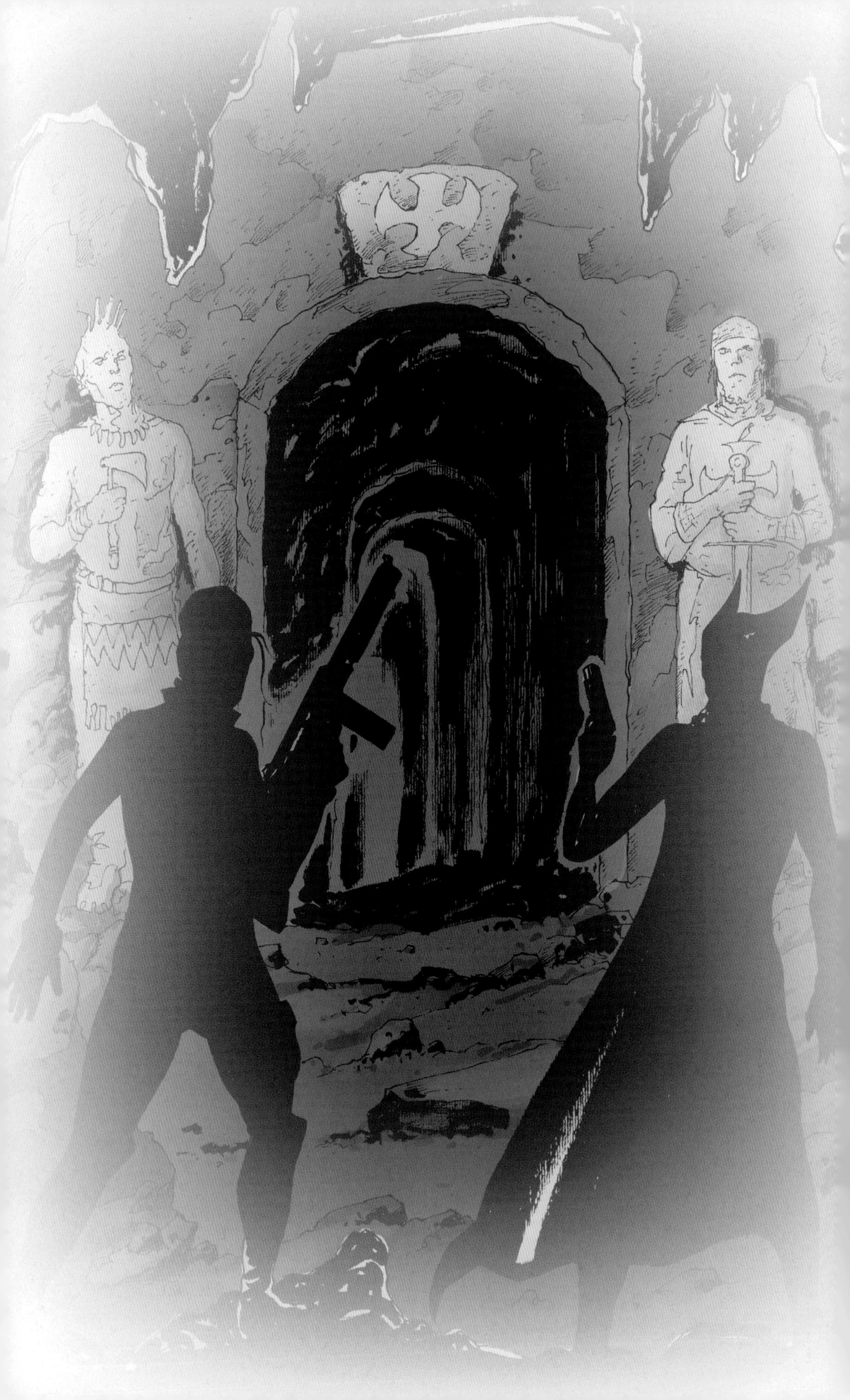

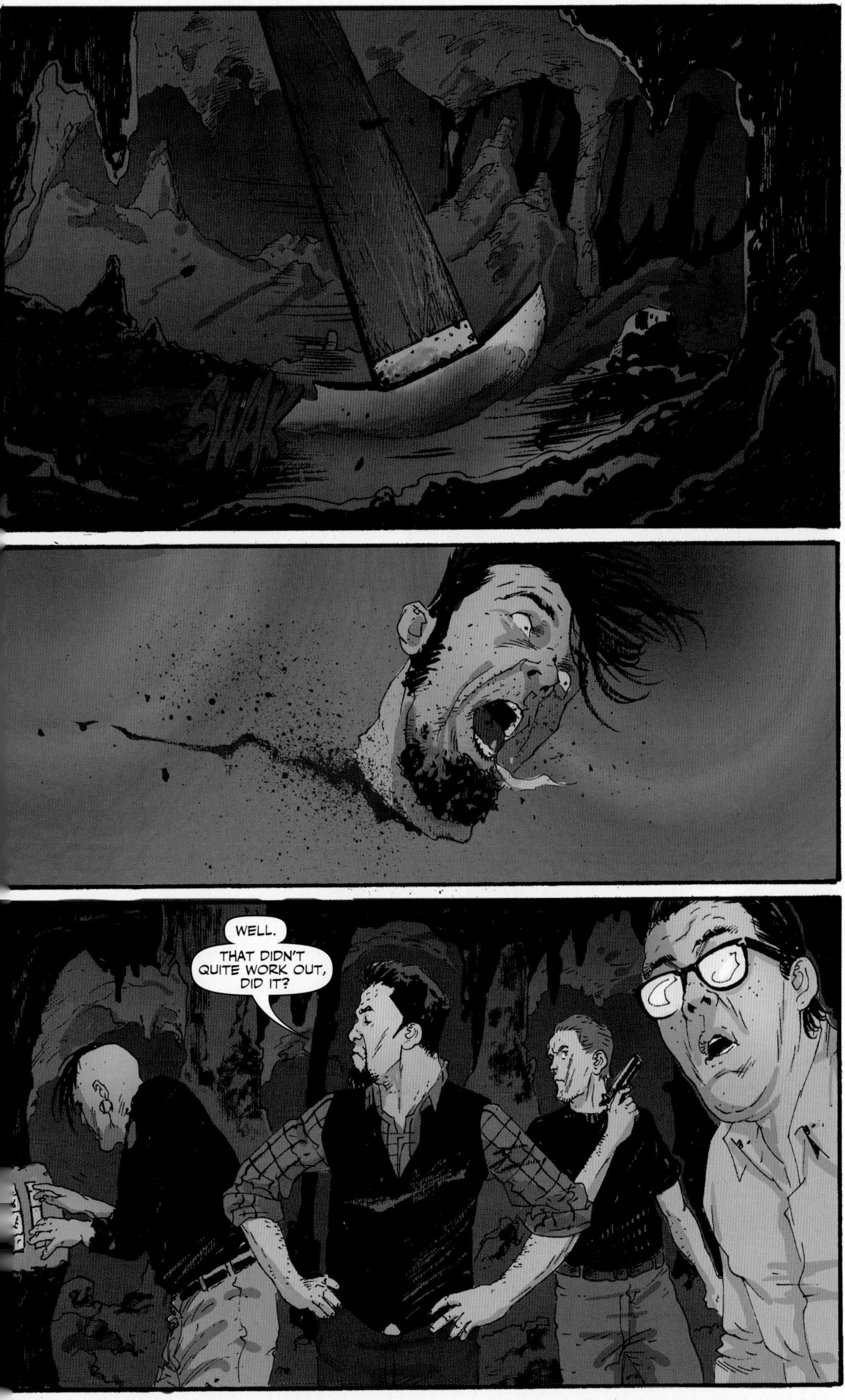
SNAK
WELL.
THAT DIDN'T QUITE WORK OUT, DID IT?

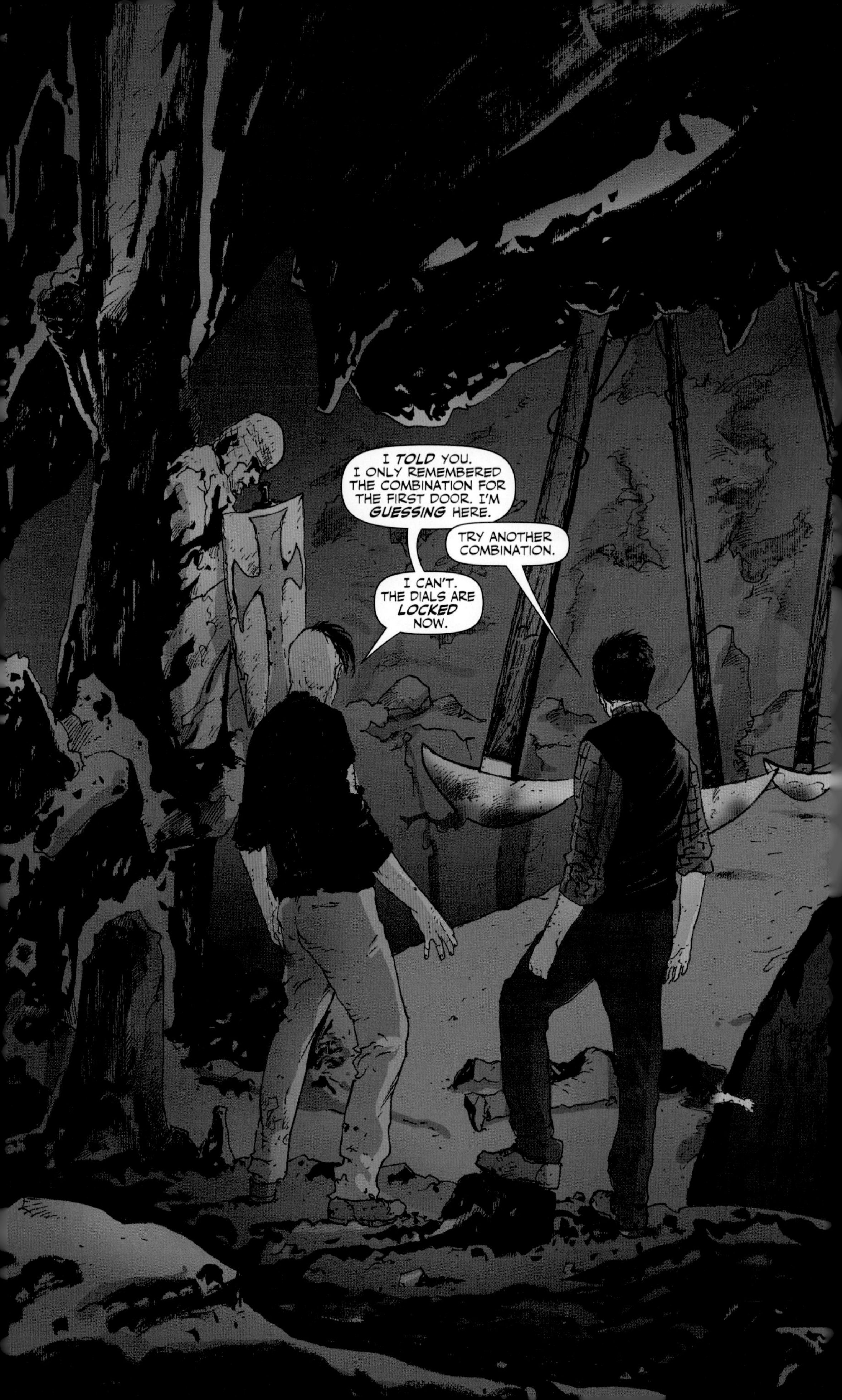
I *TOLD* YOU. I ONLY REMEMBERED THE COMBINATION FOR THE FIRST DOOR. I'M *GUESSING* HERE.
TRY ANOTHER COMBINATION.
I CAN'T. THE DIALS ARE *LOCKED* NOW.

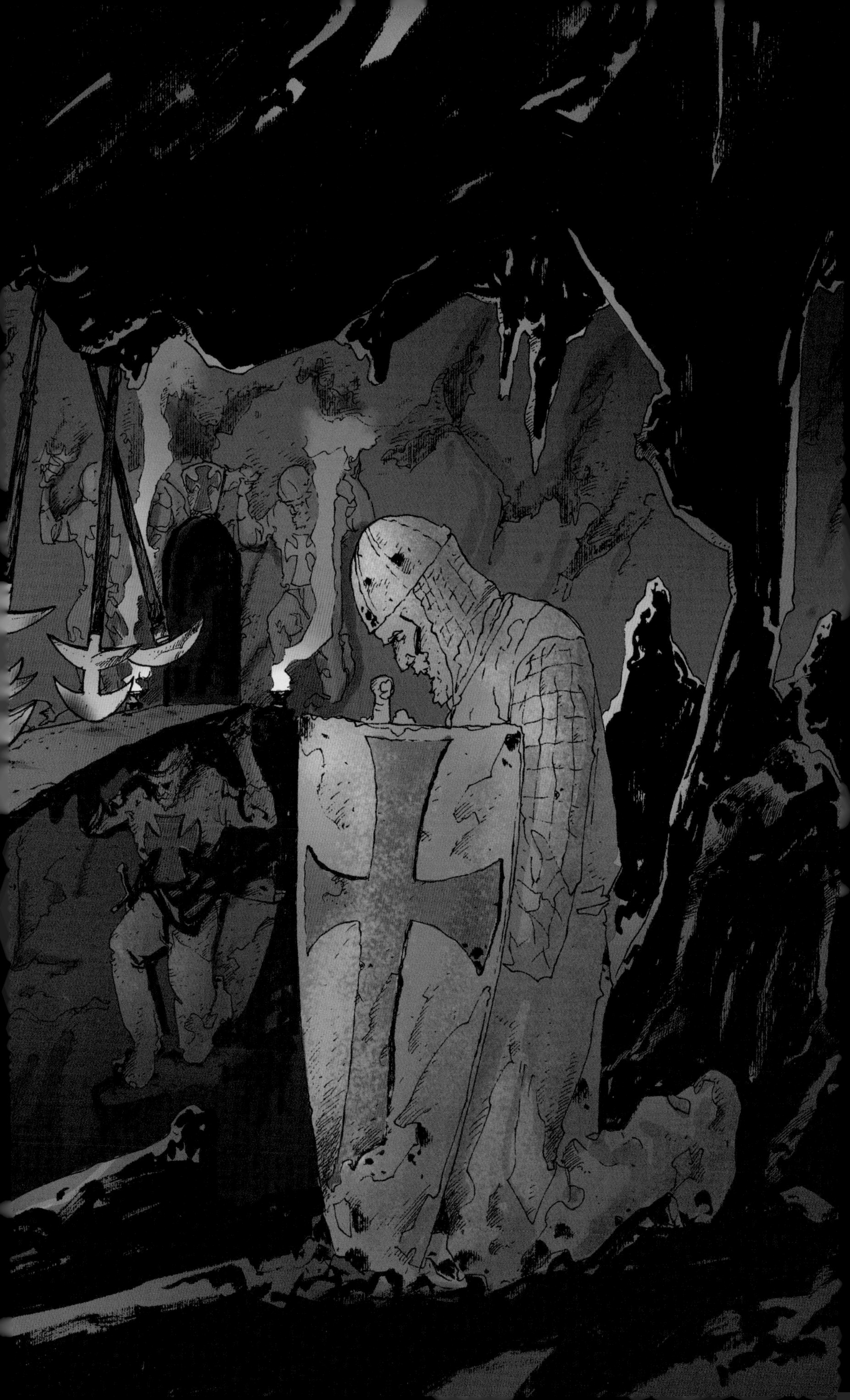

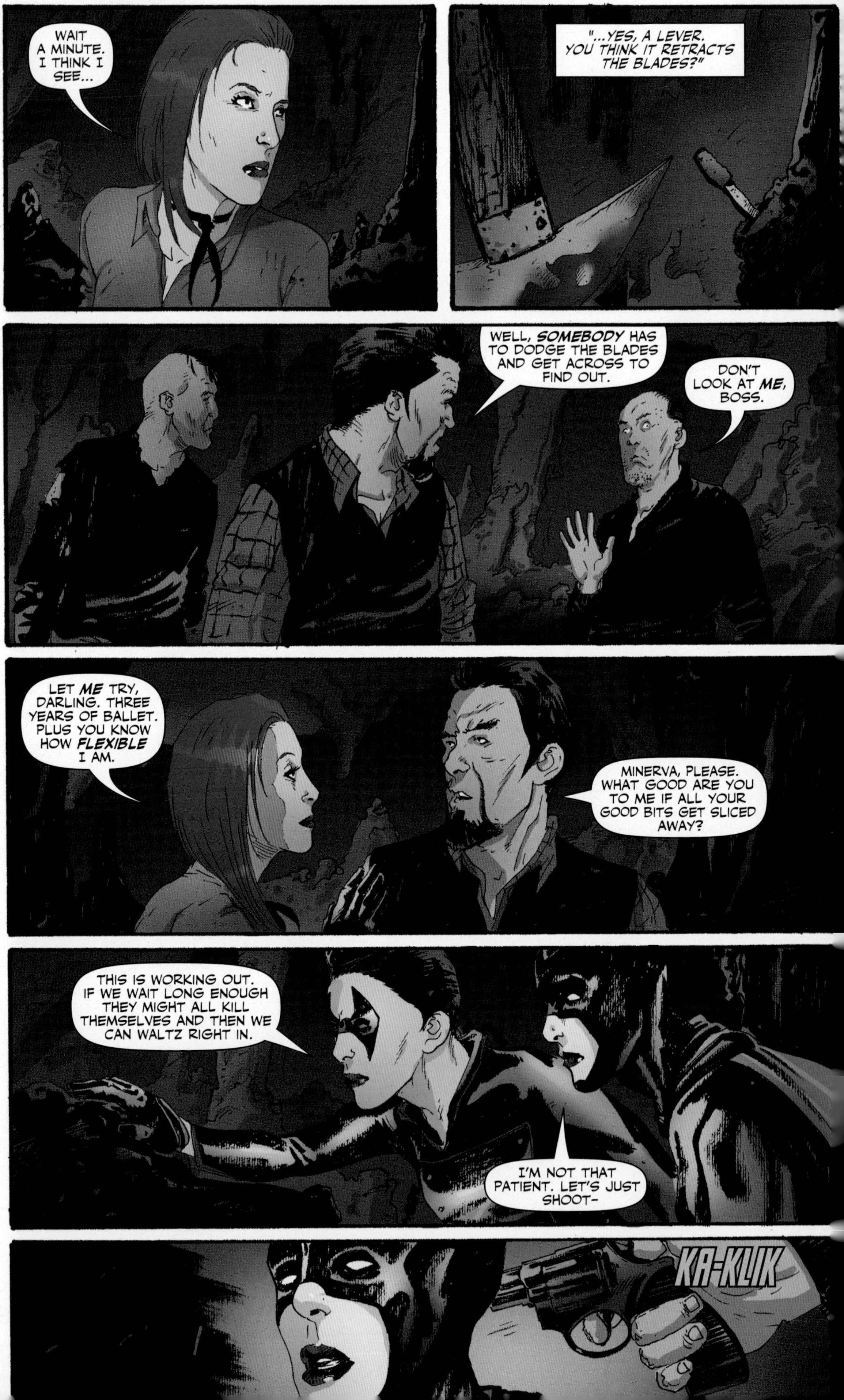
WAIT A MINUTE. I THINK I SEE...
"...YES, A LEVER. YOU THINK IT RETRACTS THE BLADES?"
WELL, SOMEBODY HAS TO DODGE THE BLADES AND GET ACROSS TO FIND OUT.
DON'T LOOK AT ME, BOSS.
LET ME TRY, DARLING. THREE YEARS OF BALLET. PLUS YOU KNOW HOW FLEXIBLE I AM.
MINERVA, PLEASE. WHAT GOOD ARE YOU TO ME IF ALL YOUR GOOD BITS GET SLICED AWAY?
THIS IS WORKING OUT. IF WE WAIT LONG ENOUGH THEY MIGHT ALL KILL THEMSELVES AND THEN WE CAN WALTZ RIGHT IN.
I'M NOT THAT PATIENT. LET'S JUST SHOOT-
KA-KLIK

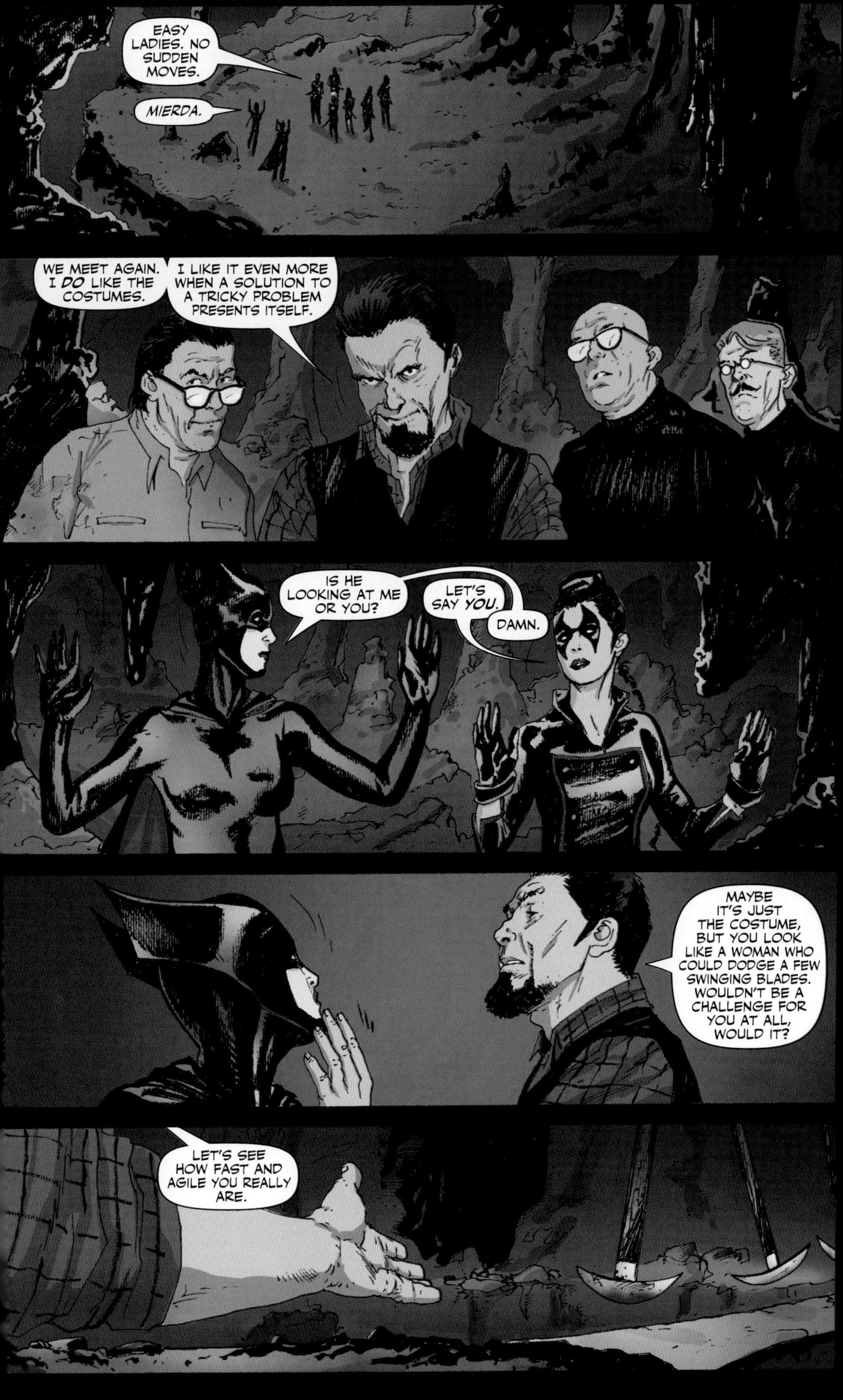
EASY LADIES. NO SUDDEN MOVES.
MIERDA.
WE MEET AGAIN. I DO LIKE THE COSTUMES.
I LIKE IT EVEN MORE WHEN A SOLUTION TO A TRICKY PROBLEM PRESENTS ITSELF.
IS HE LOOKING AT ME OR YOU?
LET'S SAY YOU.
DAMN.
MAYBE IT'S JUST THE COSTUME, BUT YOU LOOK LIKE A WOMAN WHO COULD DODGE A FEW SWINGING BLADES. WOULDN'T BE A CHALLENGE FOR YOU AT ALL, WOULD IT?
LET'S SEE HOW FAST AND AGILE YOU REALLY ARE.

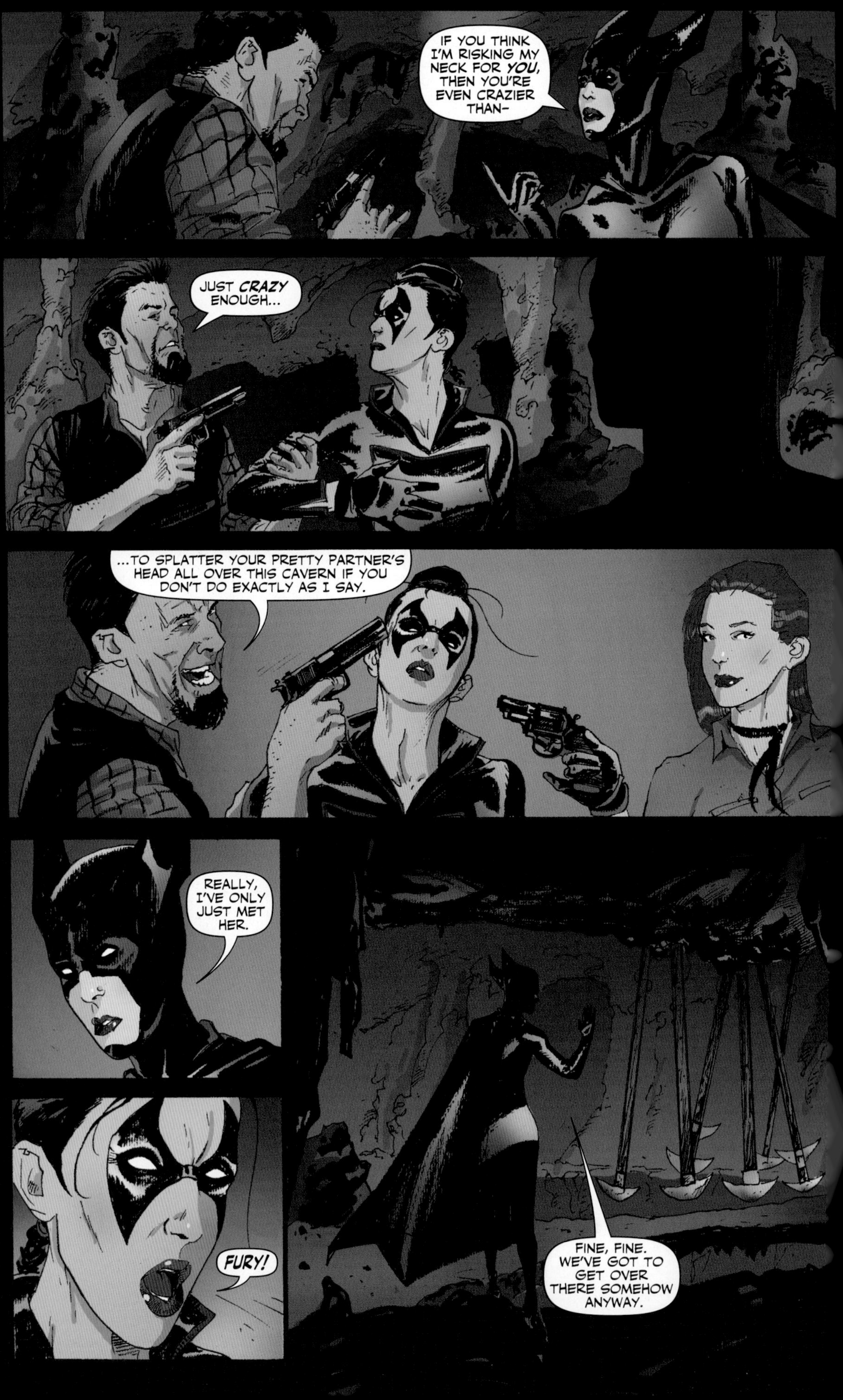
IF YOU THINK I'M RISKING MY NECK FOR *YOU*, THEN YOU'RE EVEN CRAZIER THAN-
JUST *CRAZY* ENOUGH...
...TO SPLATTER YOUR PRETTY PARTNER'S HEAD ALL OVER THIS CAVERN IF YOU DON'T DO EXACTLY AS I SAY.
REALLY, I'VE ONLY JUST MET HER.
FURY!
FINE, FINE. WE'VE GOT TO GET OVER THERE SOMEHOW ANYWAY.

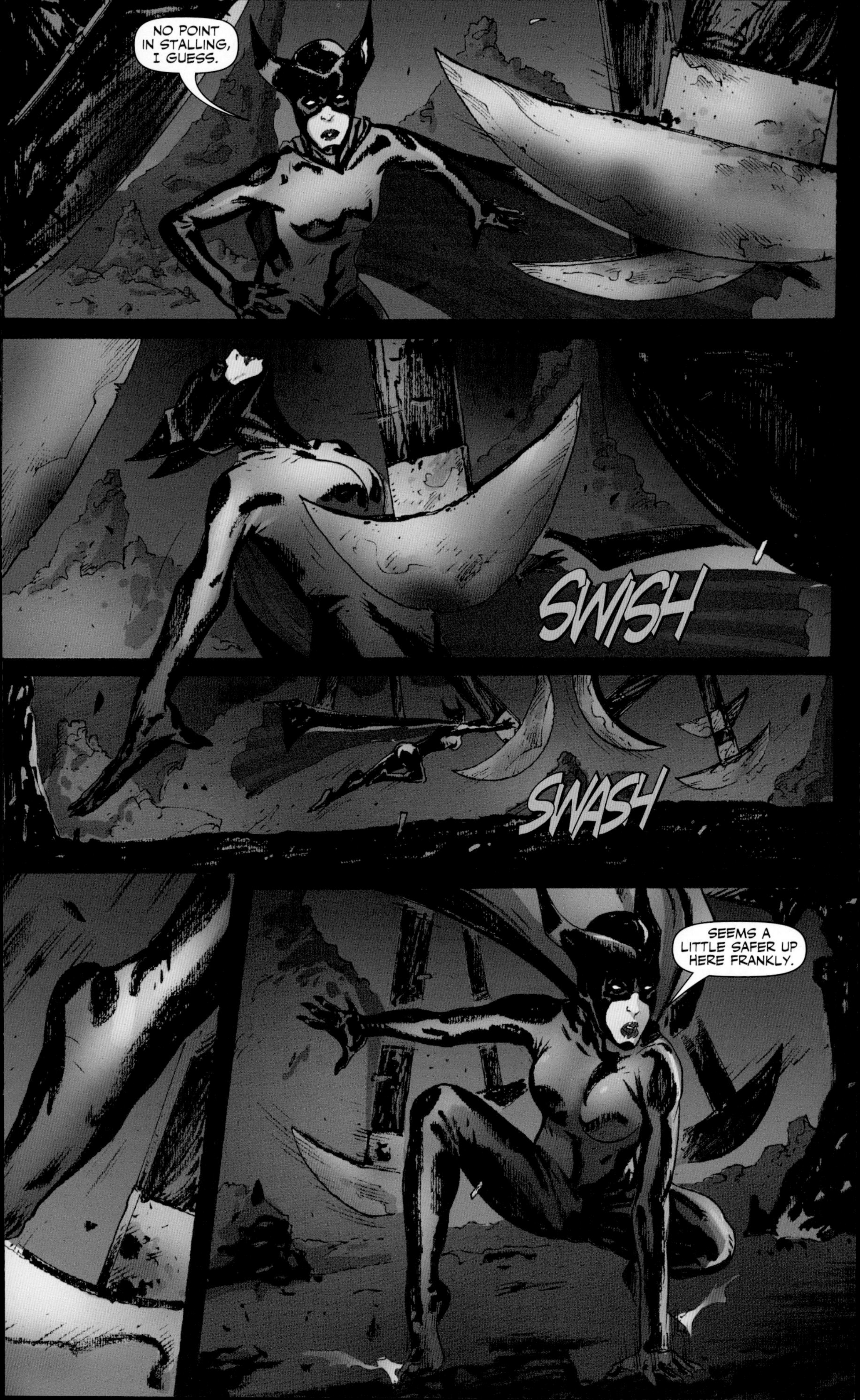
NO POINT IN STALLING, I GUESS.
SWISH
SWASH
SEEMS A LITTLE SAFER UP HERE FRANKLY.

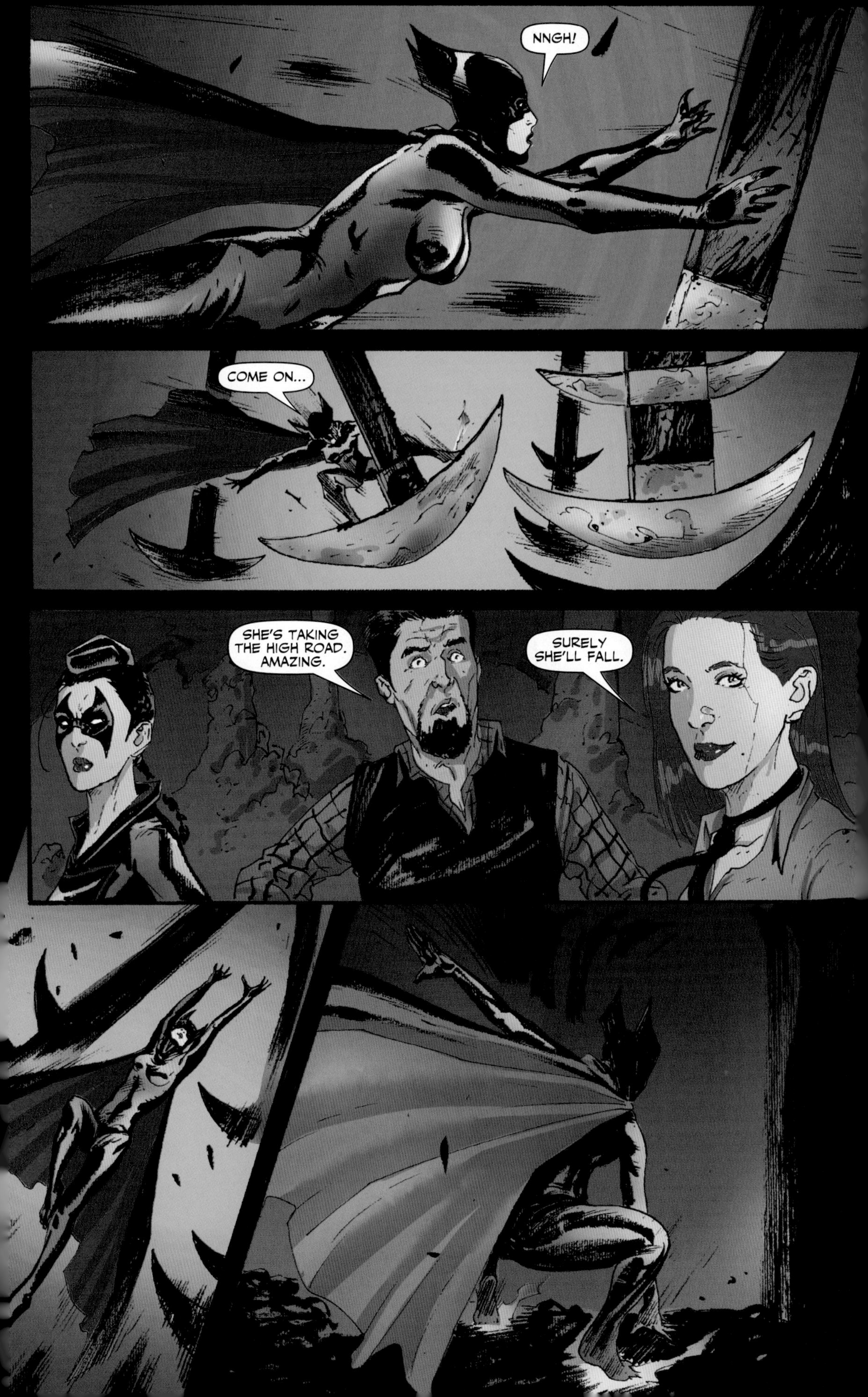
NNGH!
COME ON...
SHE'S TAKING THE HIGH ROAD. AMAZING.
SURELY SHE'LL FALL.

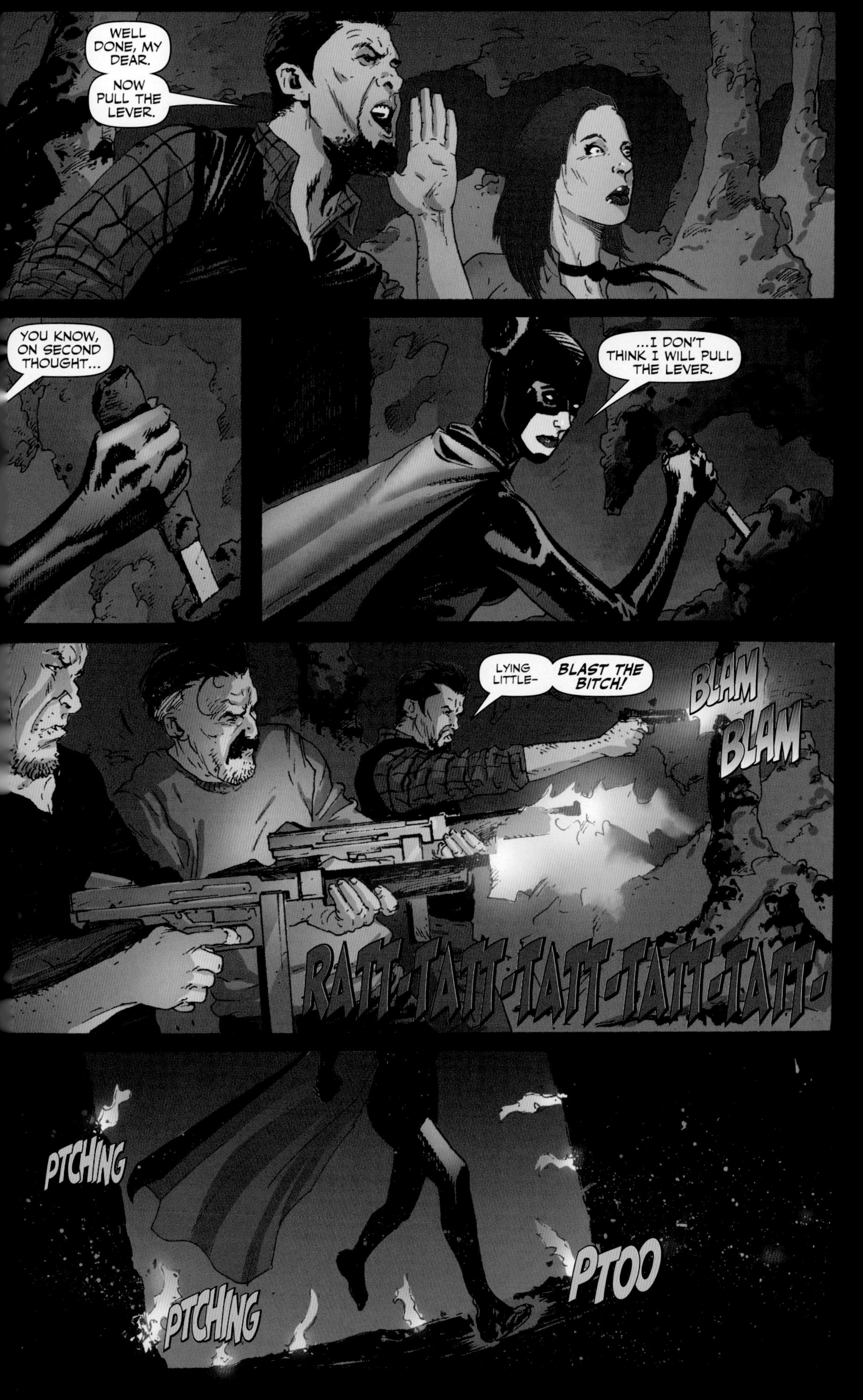
WELL DONE, MY DEAR.
NOW PULL THE LEVER.
YOU KNOW, ON SECOND THOUGHT...
...I DON'T THINK I WILL PULL THE LEVER.
LYING LITTLE-
BLAST THE BITCH!
BLAM
BLAM
RATT-TATT-TATT-TATT-TATT-
PTCHING
PTOO
PTCHING

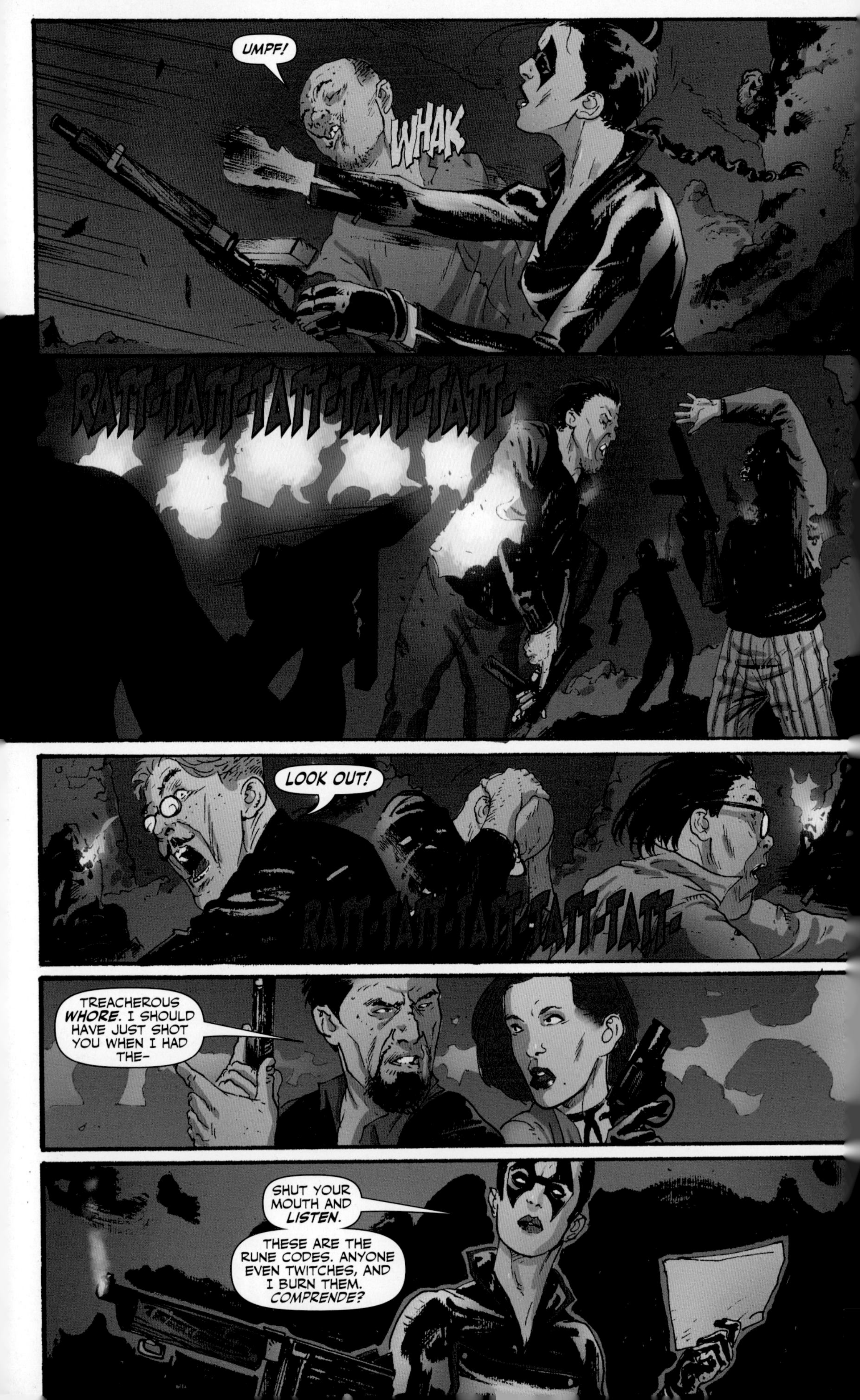
UMPF!
WHAK
RATT-TATT-TATT-TATT-TATT-
LOOK OUT!
RATT-TATT-TATT-TATT-TATT-
TREACHEROUS WHORE. I SHOULD HAVE JUST SHOT YOU WHEN I HAD THE-
SHUT YOUR MOUTH AND LISTEN.
THESE ARE THE RUNE CODES. ANYONE EVEN TWITCHES, AND I BURN THEM. COMPRENDE?

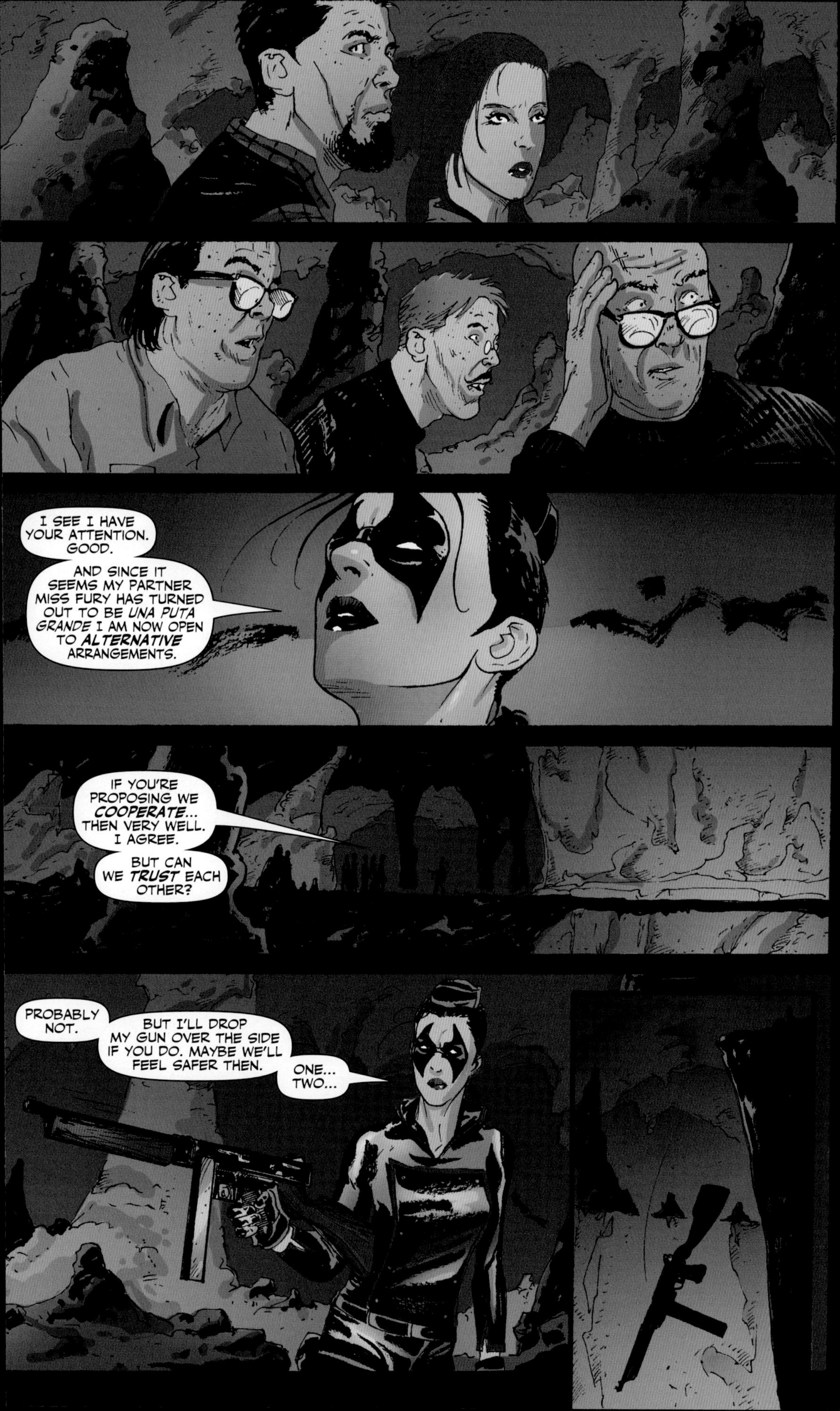

I SEE I HAVE YOUR ATTENTION. GOOD.
AND SINCE IT SEEMS MY PARTNER MISS FURY HAS TURNED OUT TO BE *UNA PUTA GRANDE* I AM NOW OPEN TO ***ALTERNATIVE*** ARRANGEMENTS.
IF YOU'RE PROPOSING WE *COOPERATE*... THEN VERY WELL. I AGREE.
BUT CAN WE ***TRUST*** EACH OTHER?
PROBABLY NOT.
BUT I'LL DROP MY GUN OVER THE SIDE IF YOU DO. MAYBE WE'LL FEEL SAFER THEN.
ONE... TWO...

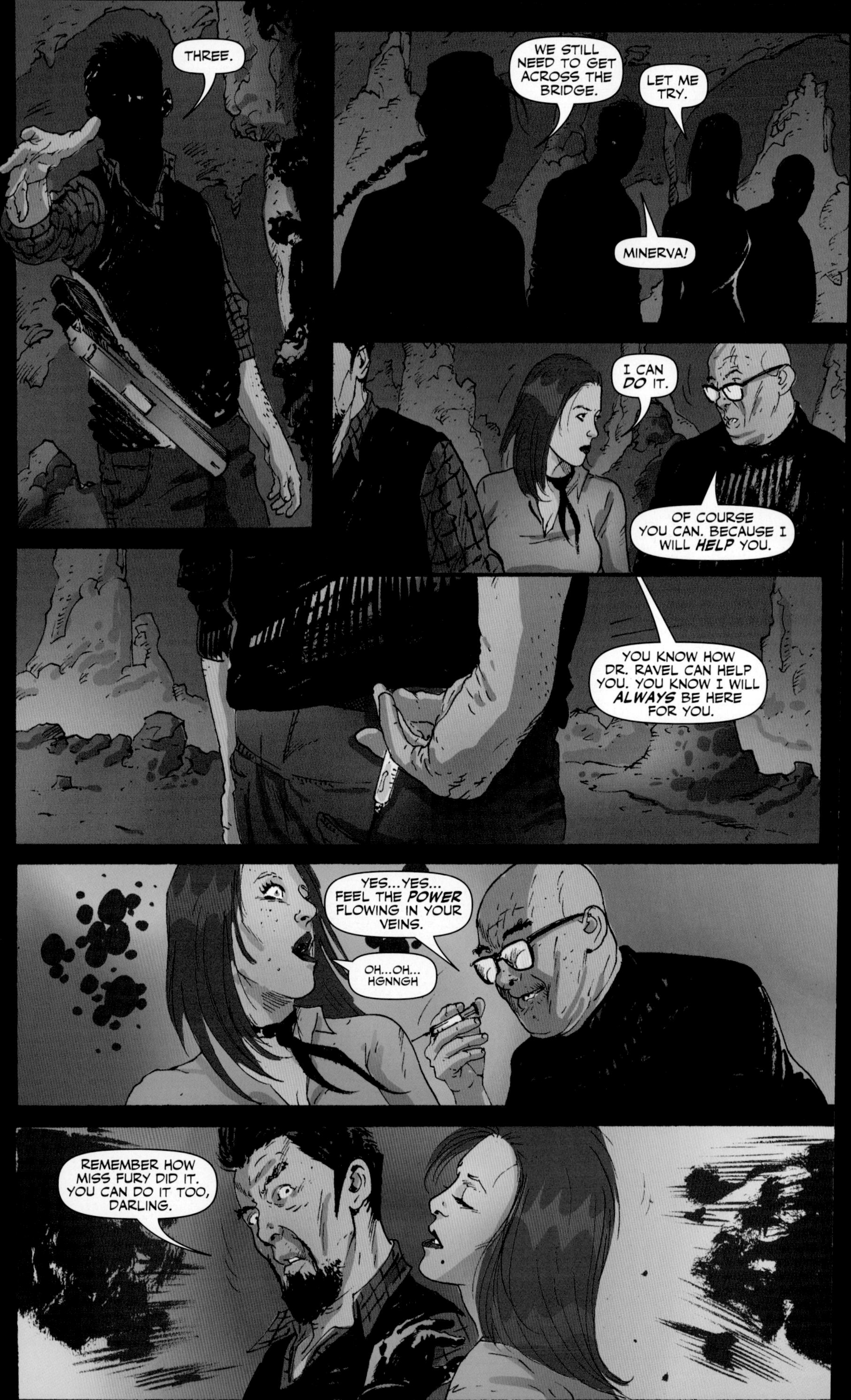
THREE.
WE STILL NEED TO GET ACROSS THE BRIDGE.
LET ME TRY.
MINERVA!
I CAN *DO* IT.
OF COURSE YOU CAN. BECAUSE I WILL ***HELP*** YOU.
YOU KNOW HOW DR. RAVEL CAN HELP YOU. YOU KNOW I WILL ***ALWAYS*** BE HERE FOR YOU.
YES...YES... FEEL THE ***POWER*** FLOWING IN YOUR VEINS.
OH...OH... HGNNGH
REMEMBER HOW MISS FURY DID IT. YOU CAN DO IT TOO, DARLING.

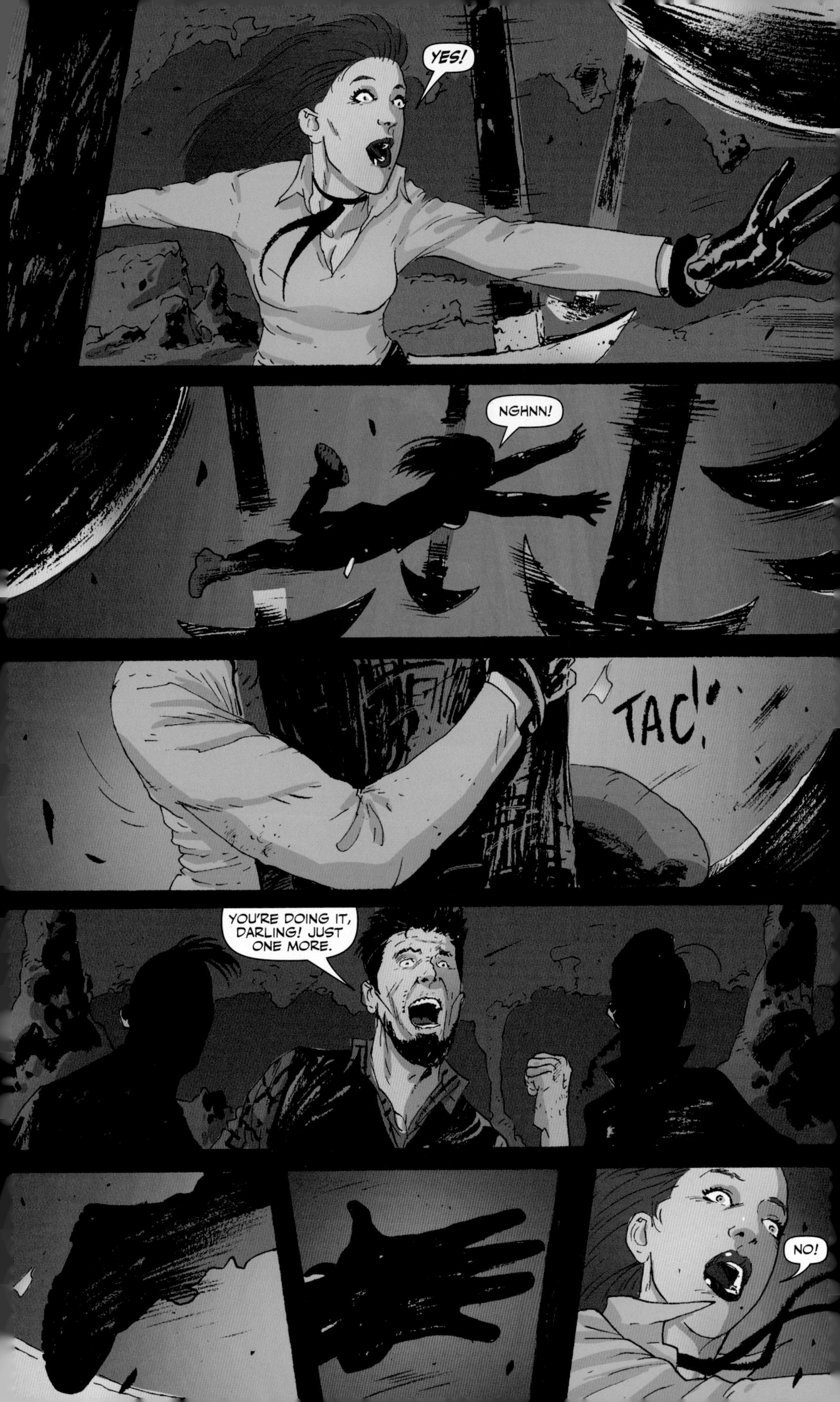
YES!
NGHNN!
TAC!
YOU'RE DOING IT, DARLING! JUST ONE MORE.
NO!

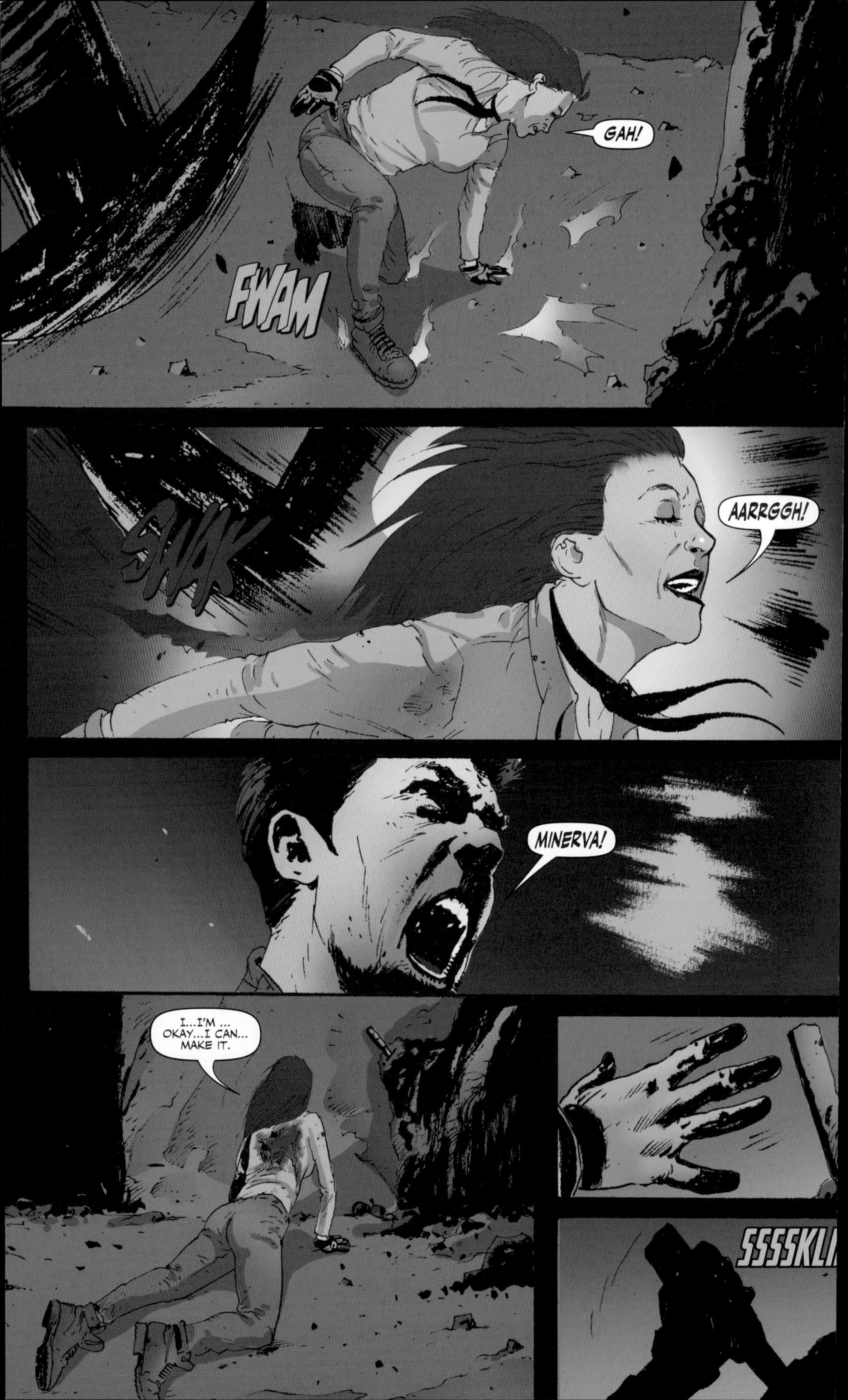
GAH!
FWAM
SWAK
AARRGGH!
MINERVA!
I...I'M ... OKAY...I CAN... MAKE IT.
SSSSKLI

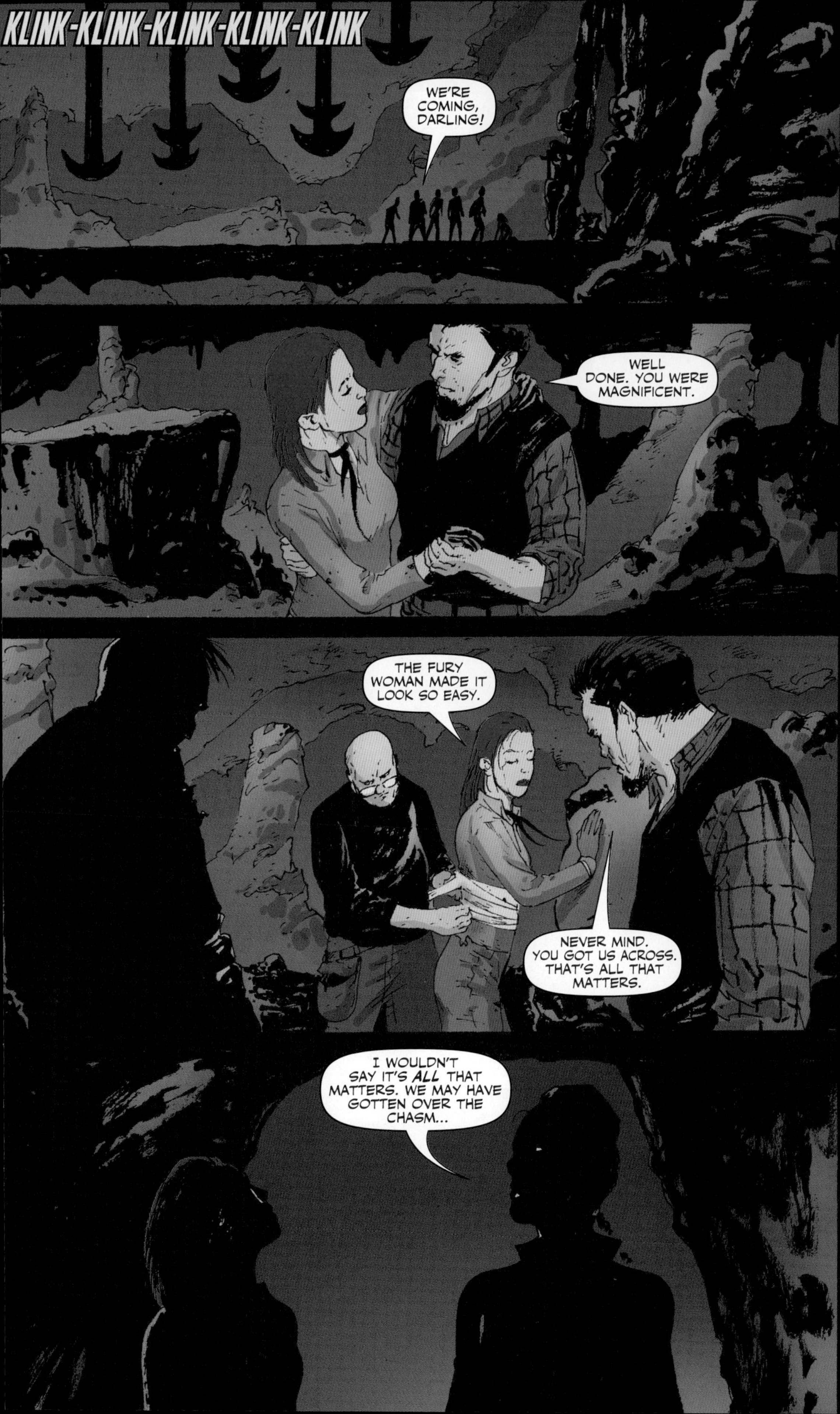
KLINK-KLINK-KLINK-KLINK-KLINK
WE'RE COMING, DARLING!
WELL DONE. YOU WERE MAGNIFICENT.
THE FURY WOMAN MADE IT LOOK SO EASY.
NEVER MIND. YOU GOT US ACROSS. THAT'S ALL THAT MATTERS.
I WOULDN'T SAY IT'S ALL THAT MATTERS. WE MAY HAVE GOTTEN OVER THE CHASM...

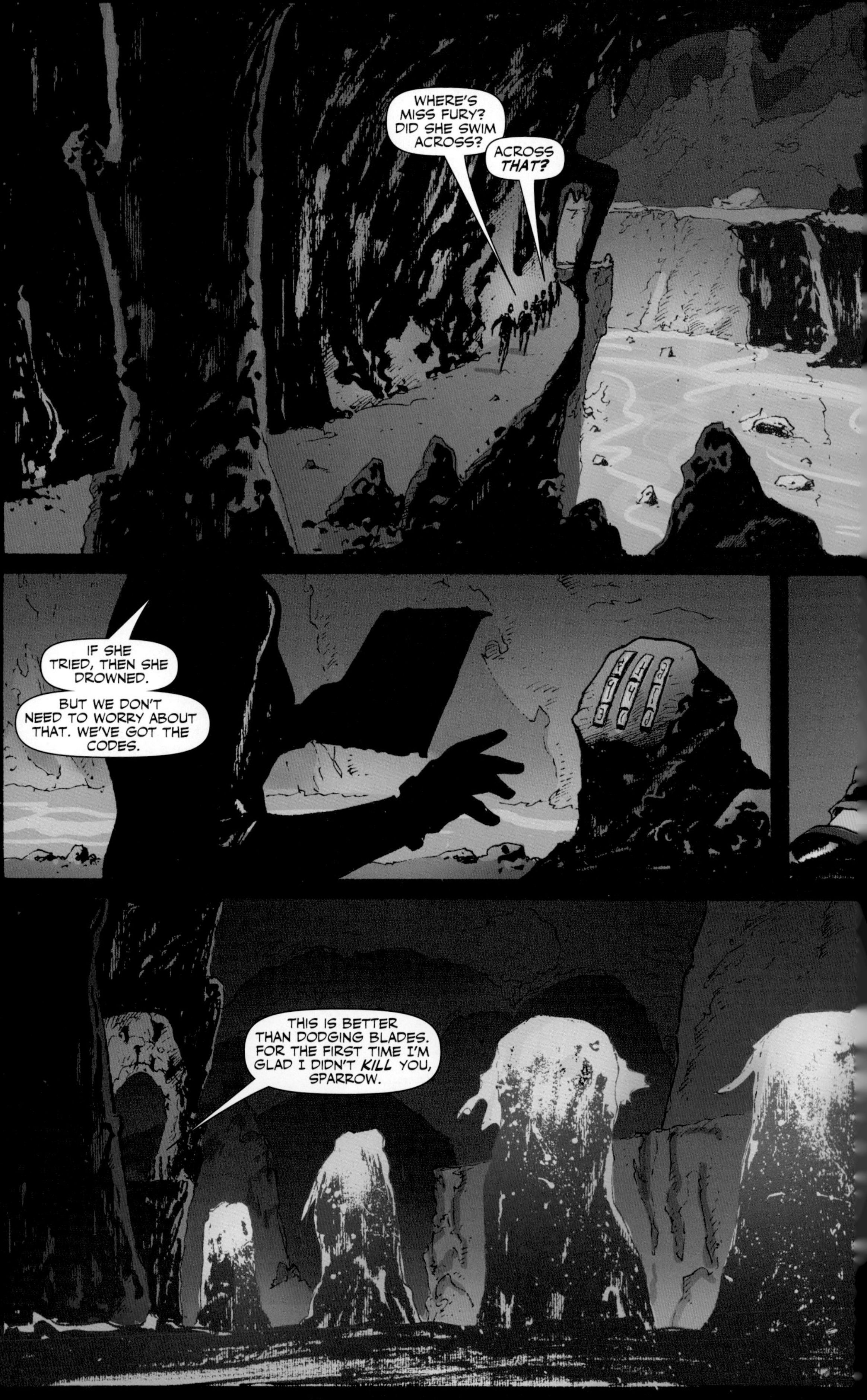
WHERE'S MISS FURY? DID SHE SWIM ACROSS?
ACROSS *THAT?*
IF SHE TRIED, THEN SHE DROWNED.
BUT WE DON'T NEED TO WORRY ABOUT THAT. WE'VE GOT THE CODES.
THIS IS BETTER THAN DODGING BLADES. FOR THE FIRST TIME I'M GLAD I DIDN'T *KILL* YOU, SPARROW.

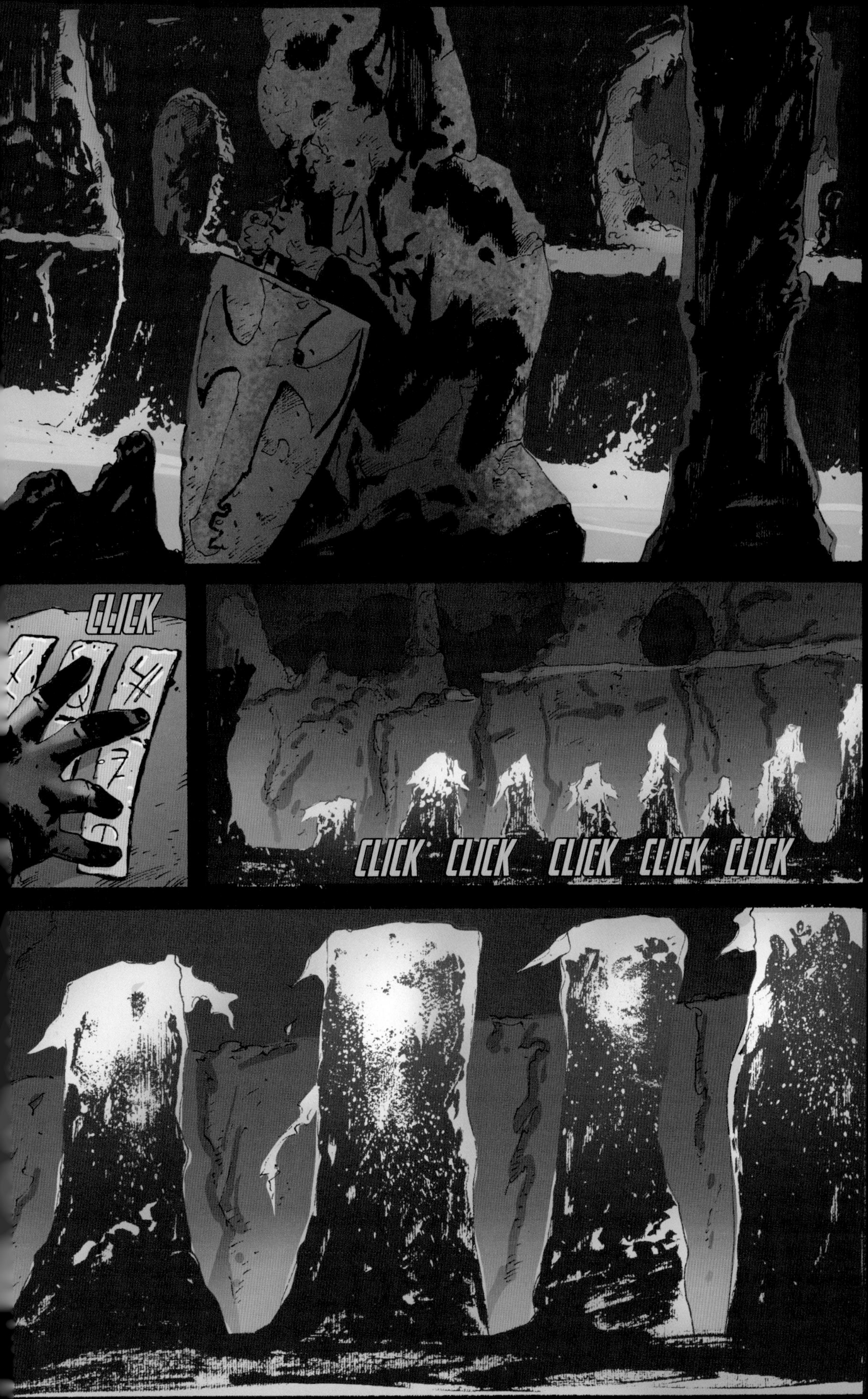
CLICK
CLICK CLICK CLICK CLICK CLICK

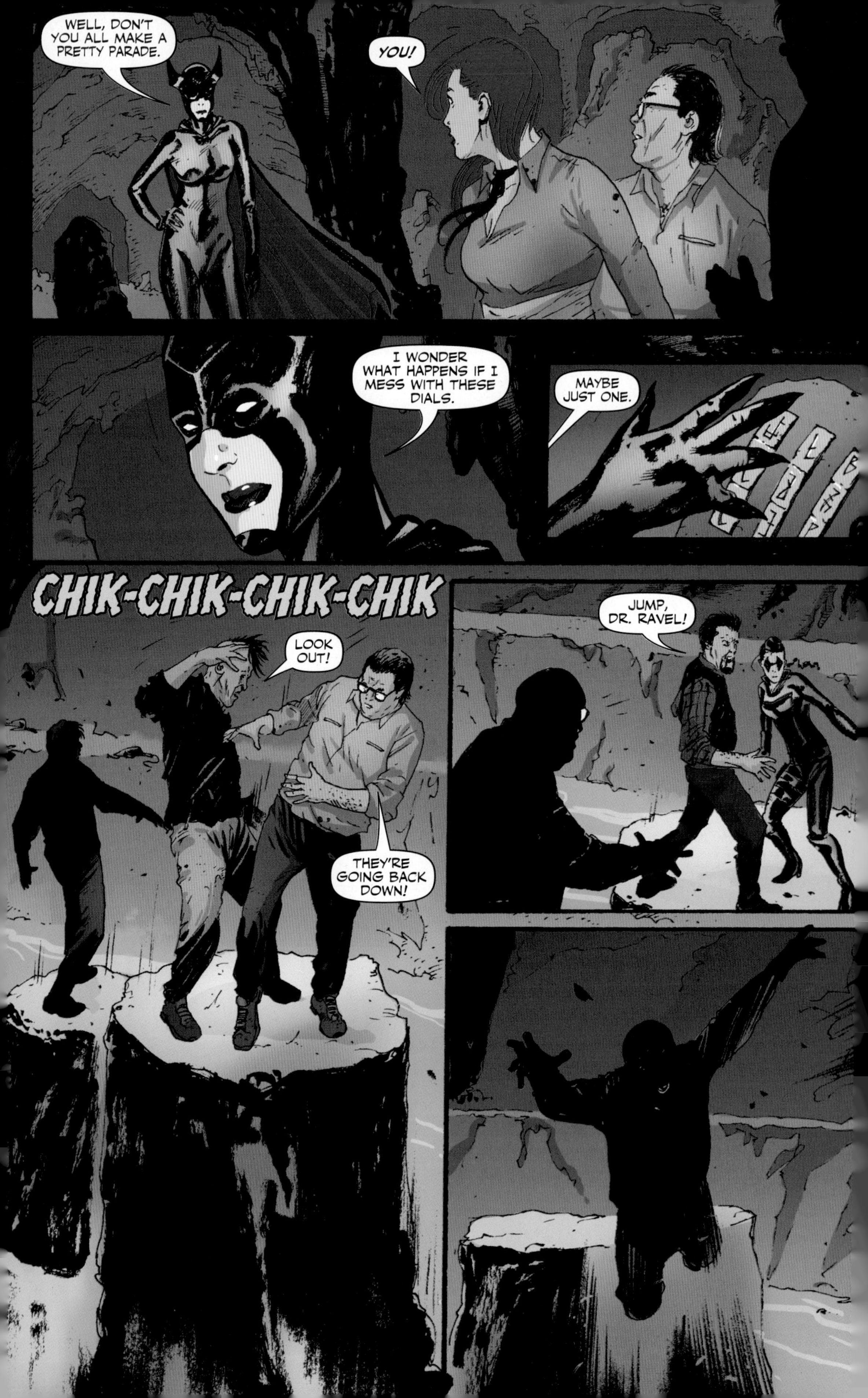
WELL, DON'T YOU ALL MAKE A PRETTY PARADE.
YOU!
I WONDER WHAT HAPPENS IF I MESS WITH THESE DIALS.
MAYBE JUST ONE.
CHIK-CHIK-CHIK-CHIK
LOOK OUT!
THEY'RE GOING BACK DOWN!
JUMP, DR. RAVEL!

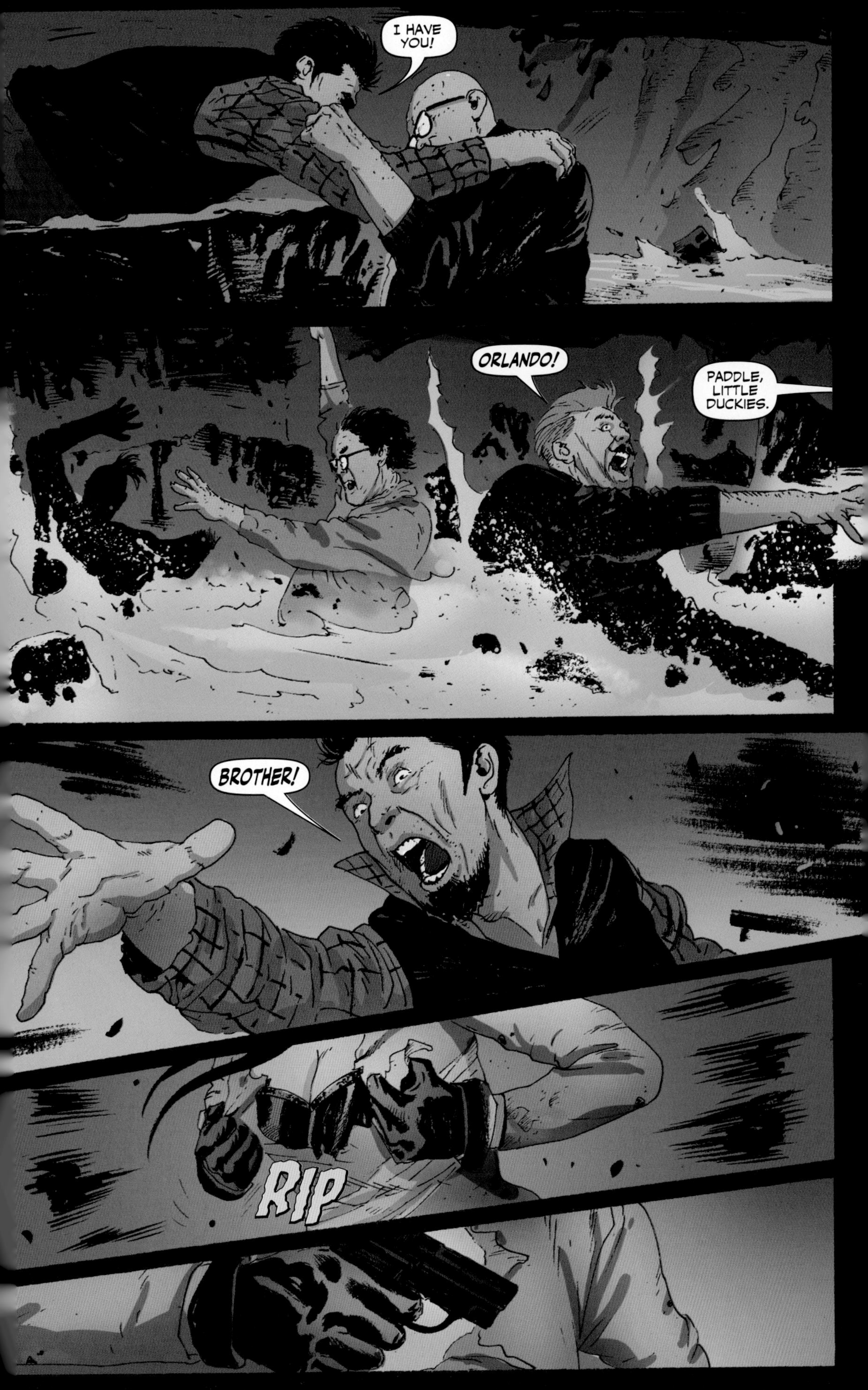
I HAVE YOU!
ORLANDO!
PADDLE, LITTLE DUCKIES.
BROTHER!
RIP

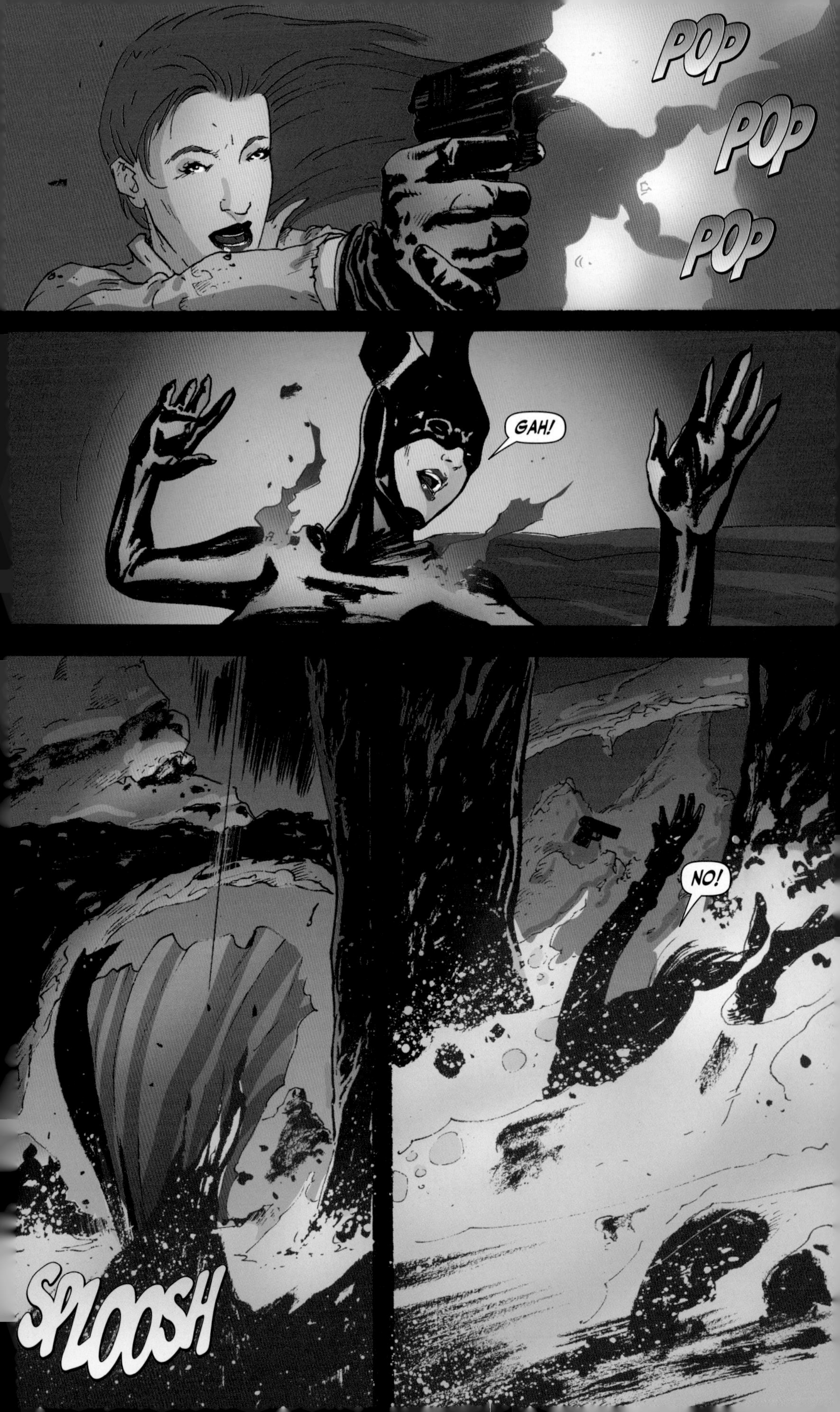
POP
POP
POP
GAH!
NO!
SPLOOSH

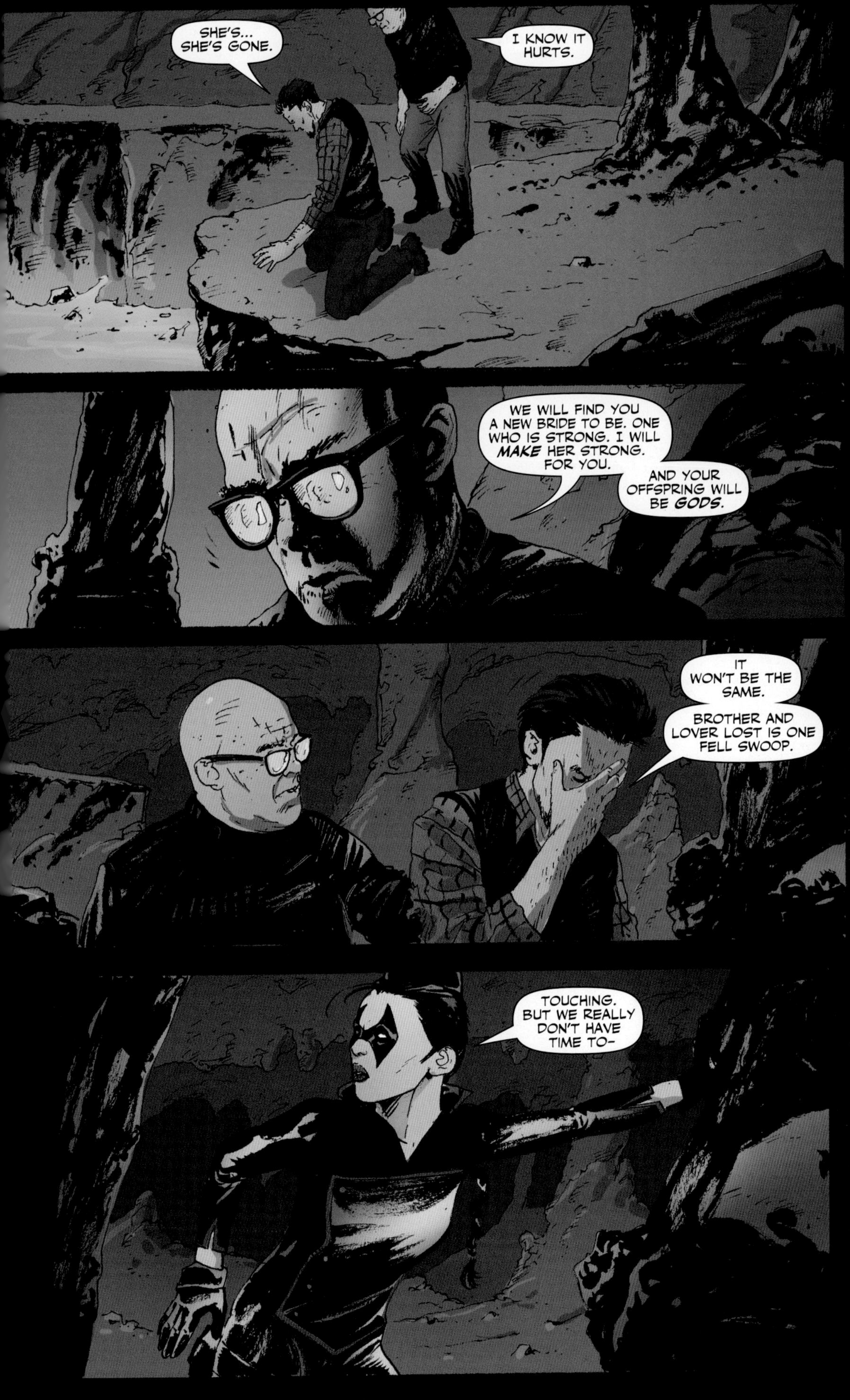

SHE'S... SHE'S GONE.
I KNOW IT HURTS.
WE WILL FIND YOU A NEW BRIDE TO BE. ONE WHO IS STRONG. I WILL MAKE HER STRONG. FOR YOU.
AND YOUR OFFSPRING WILL BE GODS.
IT WON'T BE THE SAME.
BROTHER AND LOVER LOST IS ONE FELL SWOOP.
TOUCHING. BUT WE REALLY DON'T HAVE TIME TO–

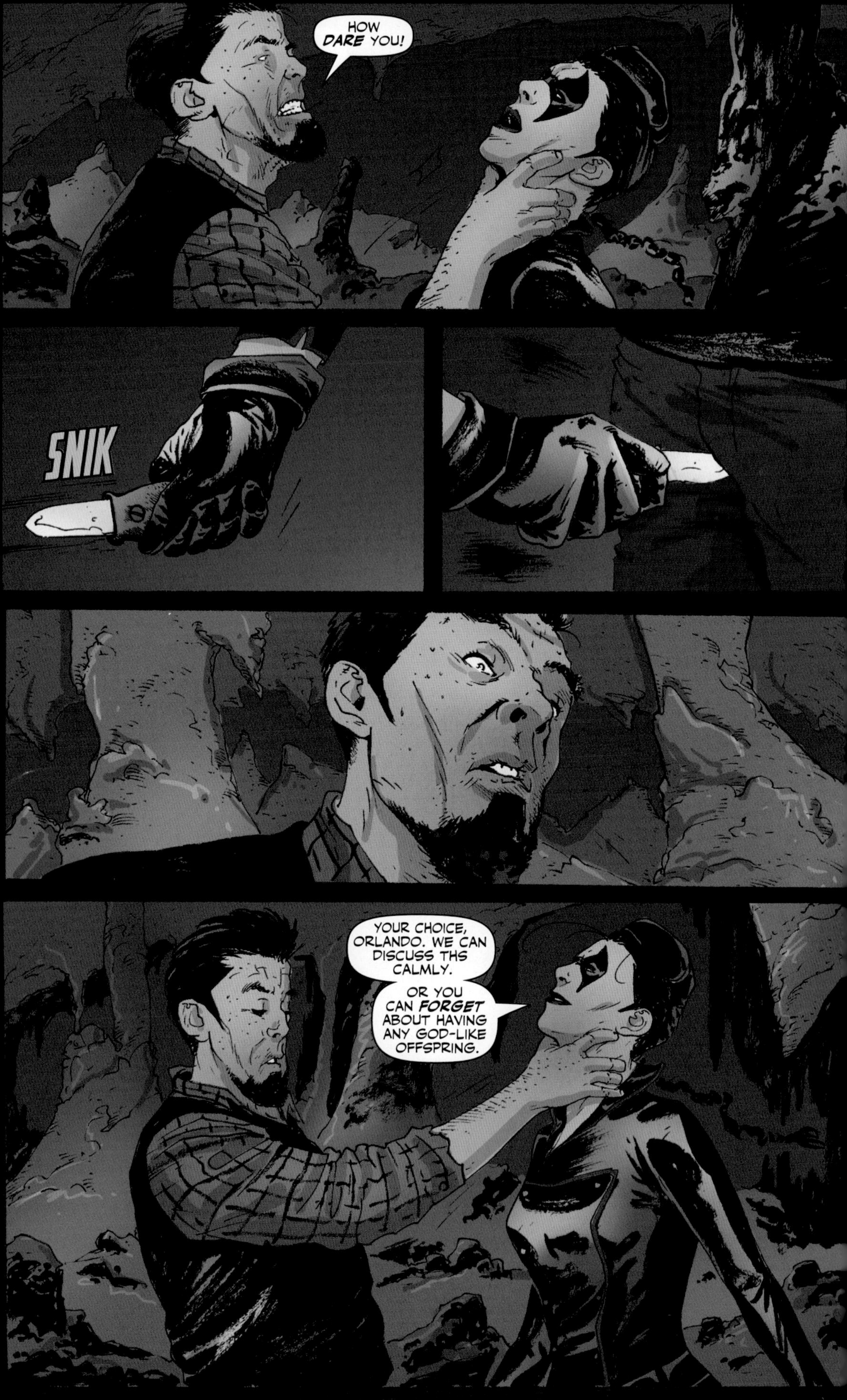
HOW DARE YOU!
SNIK
YOUR CHOICE, ORLANDO. WE CAN DISCUSS THS CALMLY.
OR YOU CAN FORGET ABOUT HAVING ANY GOD-LIKE OFFSPRING.

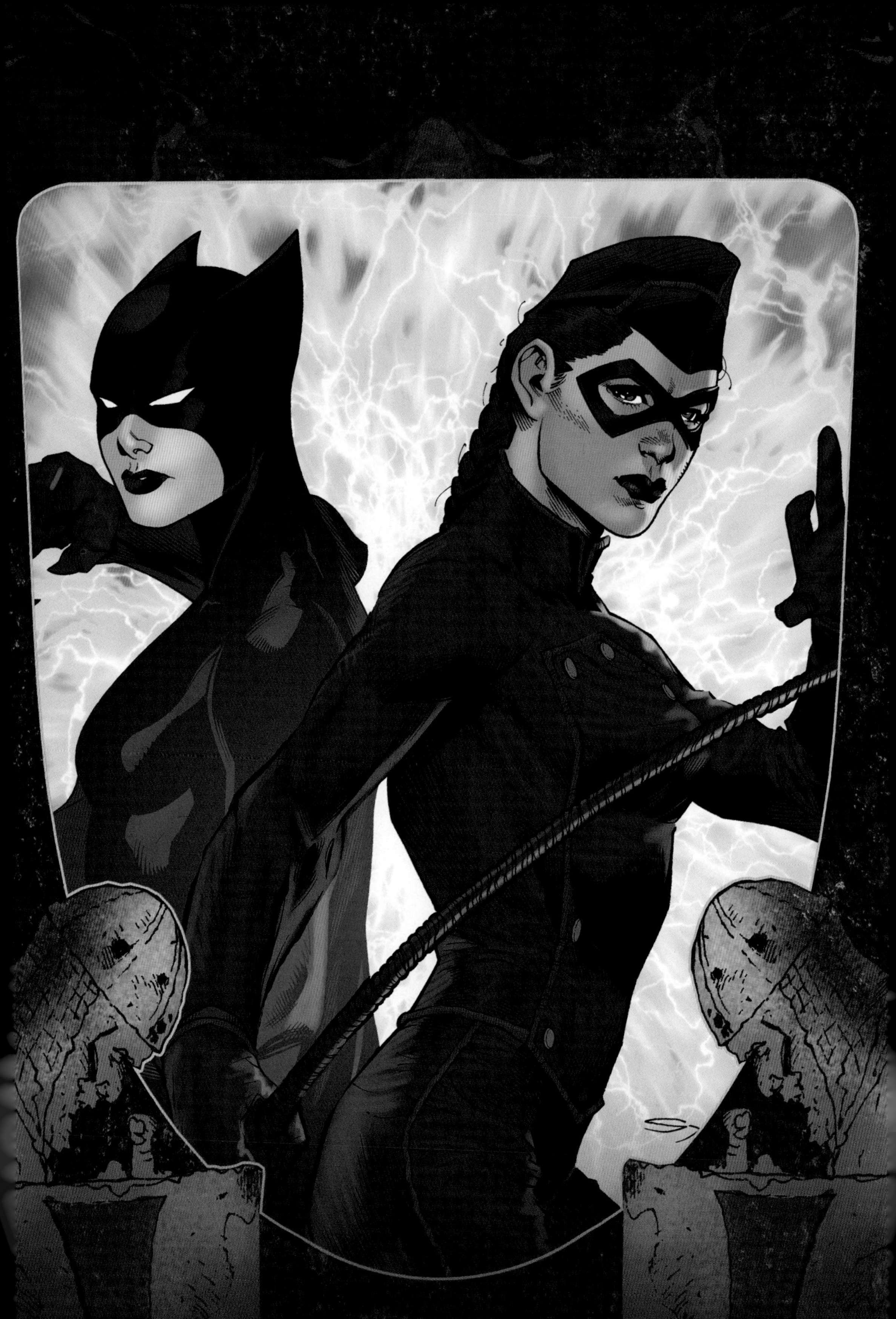

ISSUE 5

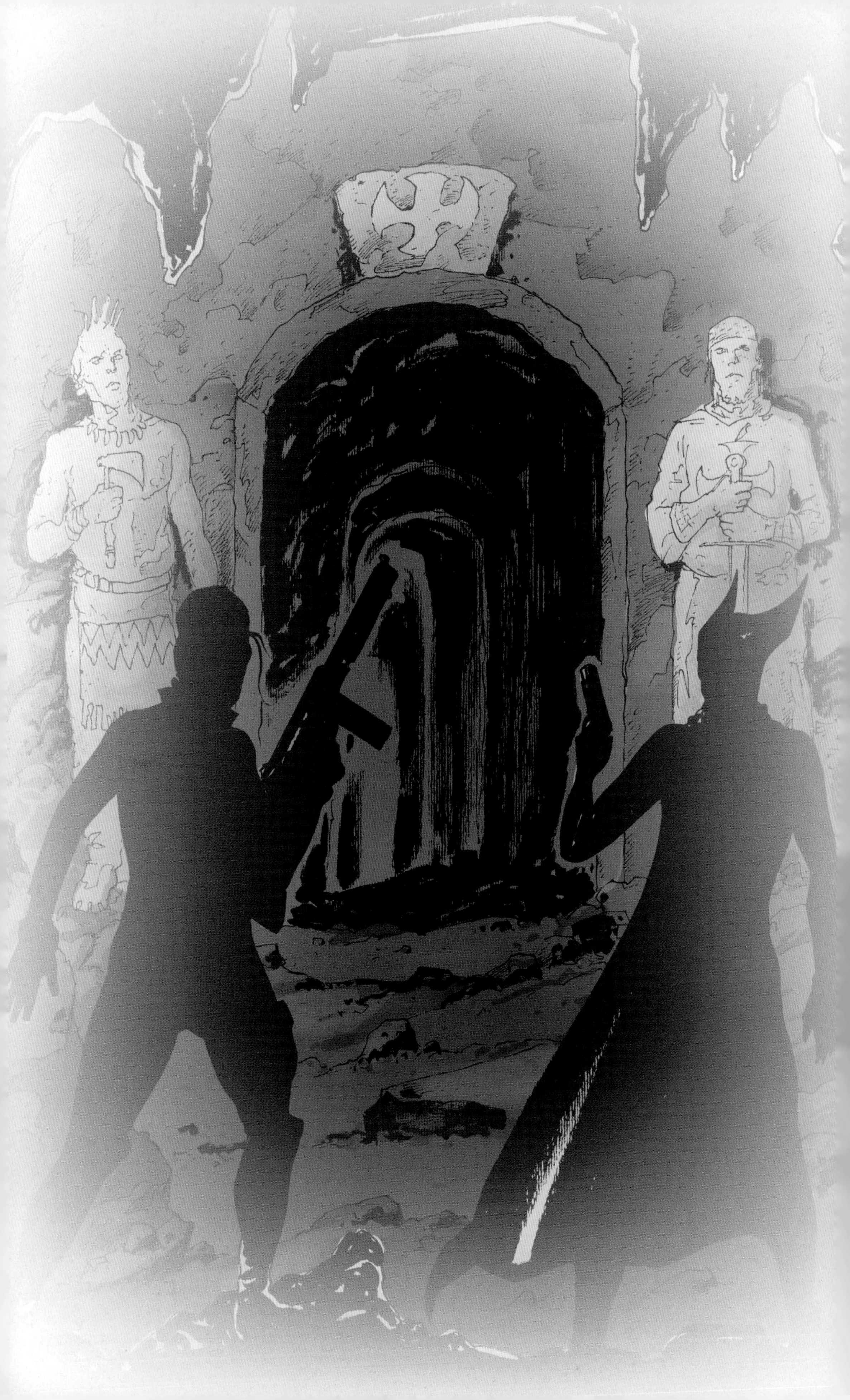

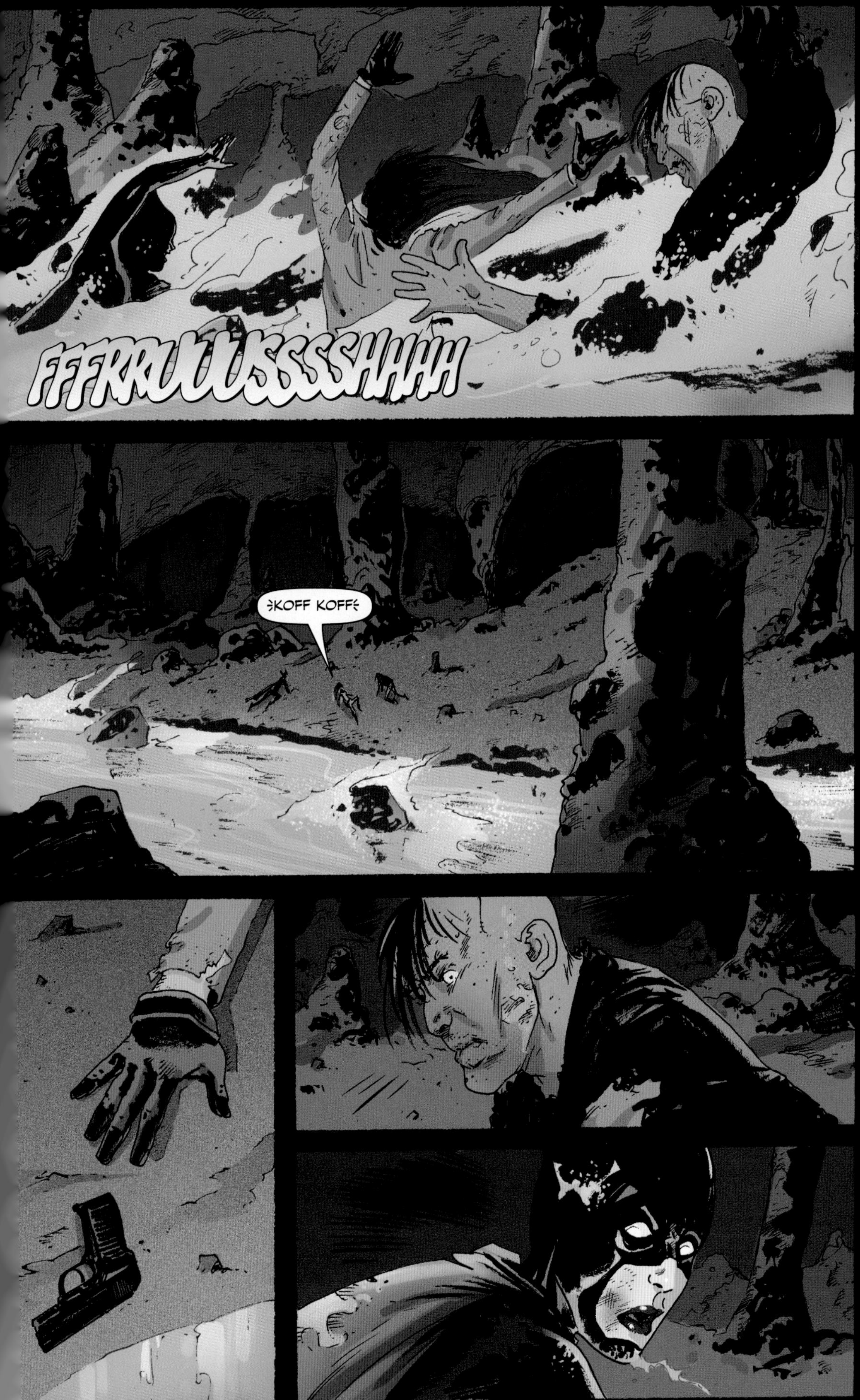
FFFRRUUUSSSSHHHH
KOFF KOFF

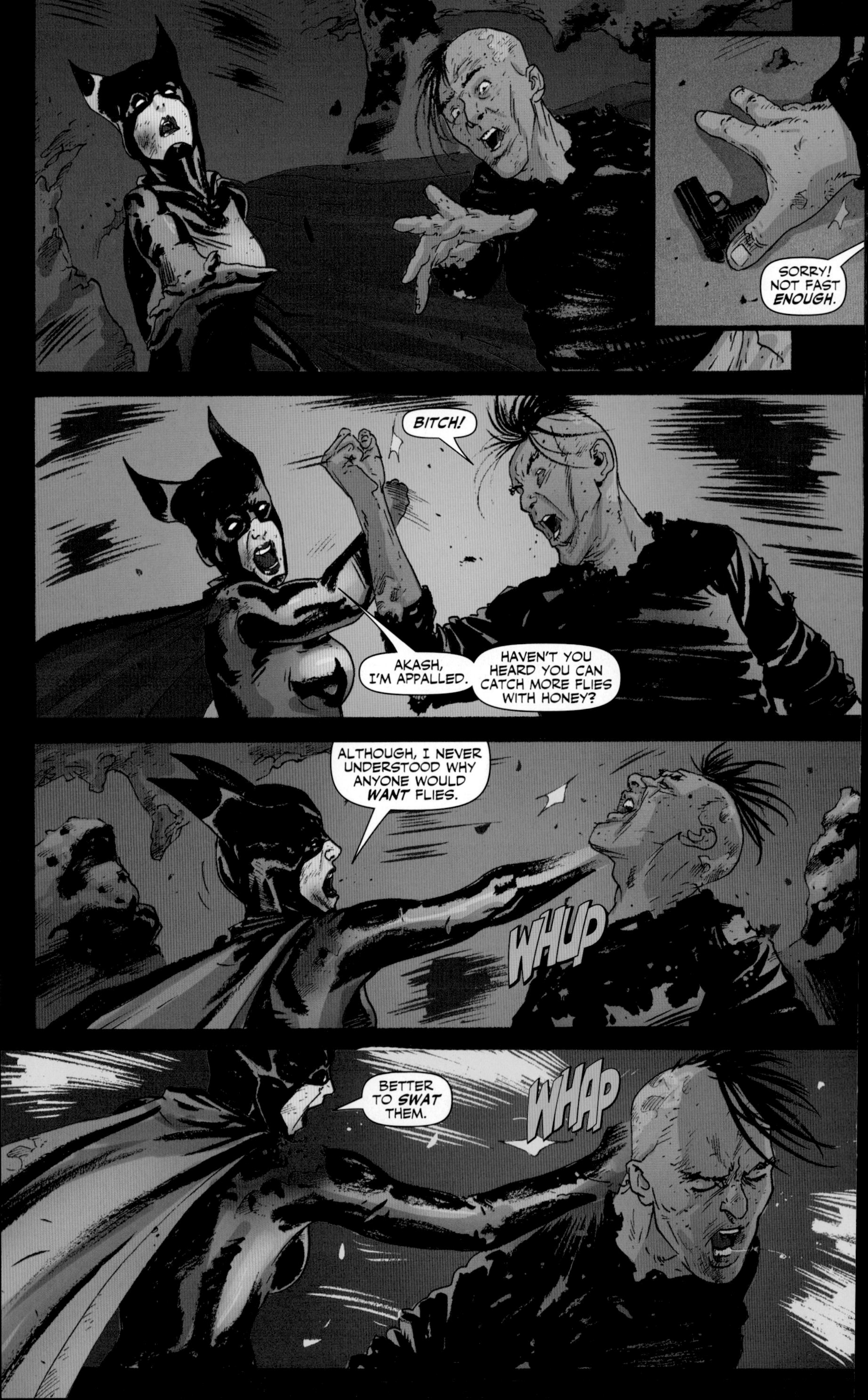
SORRY! NOT FAST ENOUGH.
BITCH!
AKASH, I'M APPALLED.
HAVEN'T YOU HEARD YOU CAN CATCH MORE FLIES WITH HONEY?
ALTHOUGH, I NEVER UNDERSTOOD WHY ANYONE WOULD WANT FLIES.
WHUP
BETTER TO SWAT THEM.
WHAP

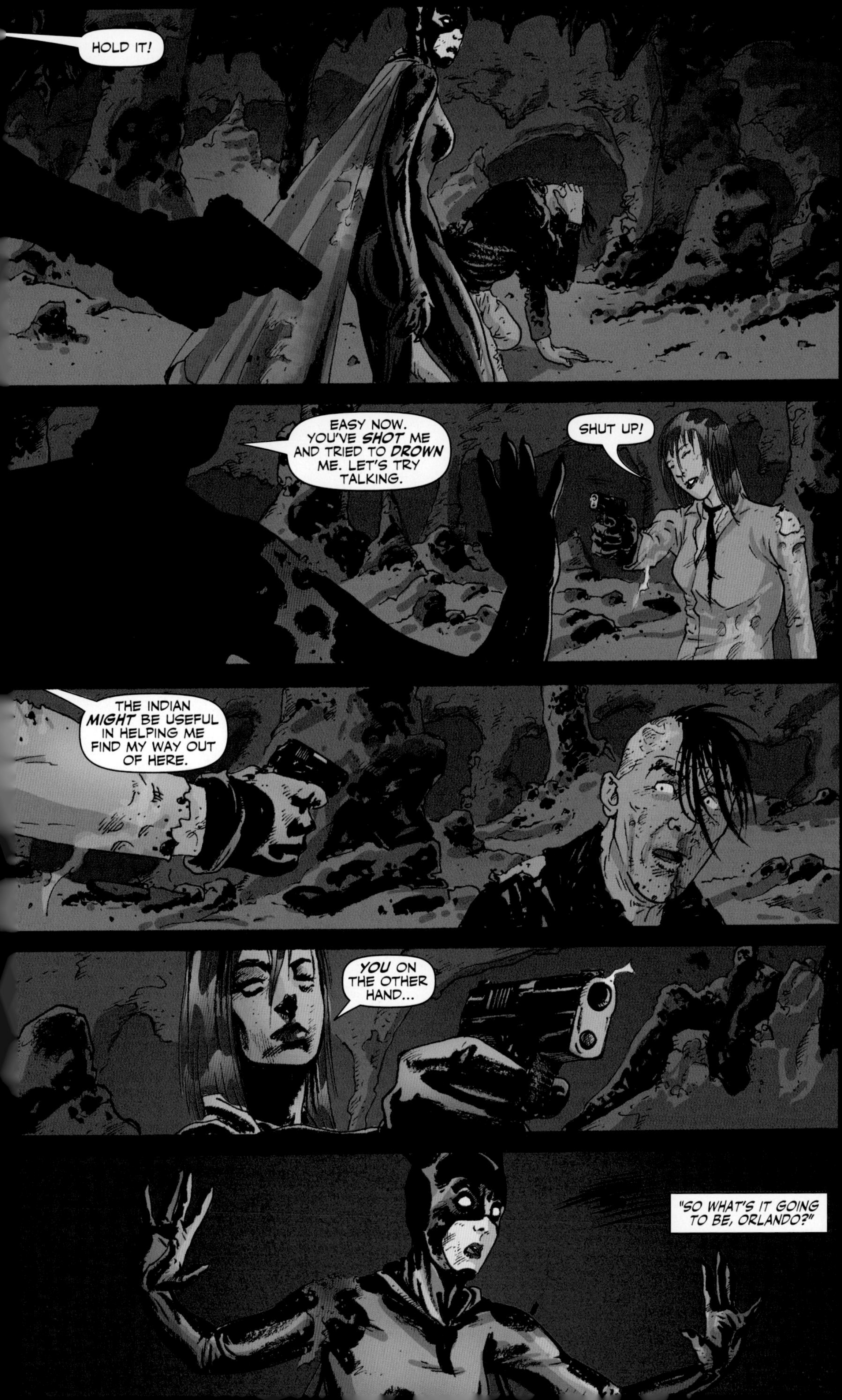

HOLD IT!
EASY NOW. YOU'VE SHOT ME AND TRIED TO DROWN ME. LET'S TRY TALKING.
SHUT UP!
THE INDIAN MIGHT BE USEFUL IN HELPING ME FIND MY WAY OUT OF HERE.
YOU ON THE OTHER HAND...
"SO WHAT'S IT GOING TO BE, ORLANDO?"

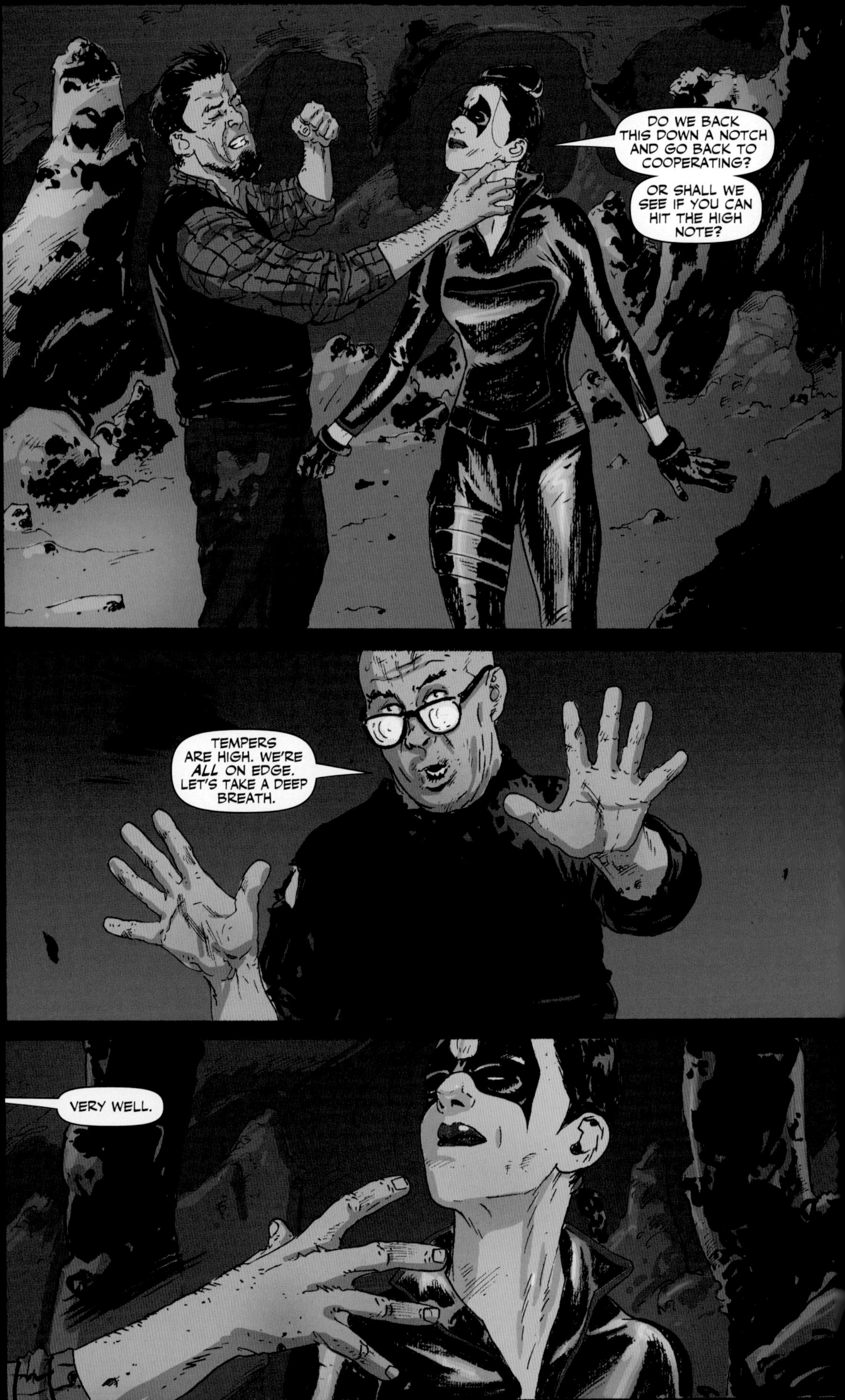
DO WE BACK THIS DOWN A NOTCH AND GO BACK TO COOPERATING?
OR SHALL WE SEE IF YOU CAN HIT THE HIGH NOTE?
TEMPERS ARE HIGH. WE'RE *ALL* ON EDGE. LET'S TAKE A DEEP BREATH.
VERY WELL.

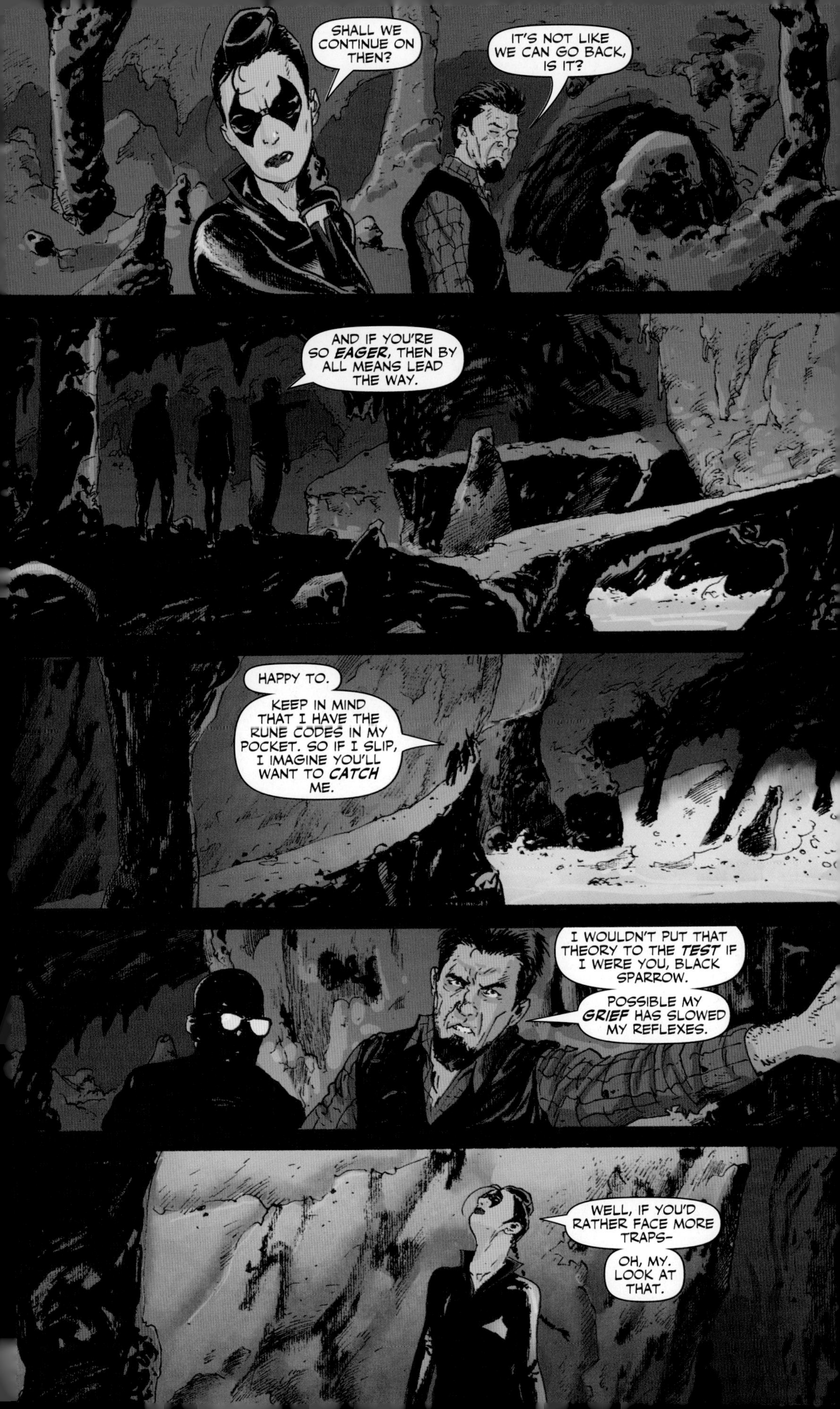
SHALL WE CONTINUE ON THEN?
IT'S NOT LIKE WE CAN GO BACK, IS IT?
AND IF YOU'RE SO *EAGER*, THEN BY ALL MEANS LEAD THE WAY.
HAPPY TO.
KEEP IN MIND THAT I HAVE THE RUNE CODES IN MY POCKET. SO IF I SLIP, I IMAGINE YOU'LL WANT TO *CATCH* ME.
I WOULDN'T PUT THAT THEORY TO THE *TEST* IF I WERE YOU, BLACK SPARROW.
POSSIBLE MY *GRIEF* HAS SLOWED MY REFLEXES.
WELL, IF YOU'D RATHER FACE MORE TRAPS–
OH, MY. LOOK AT THAT.

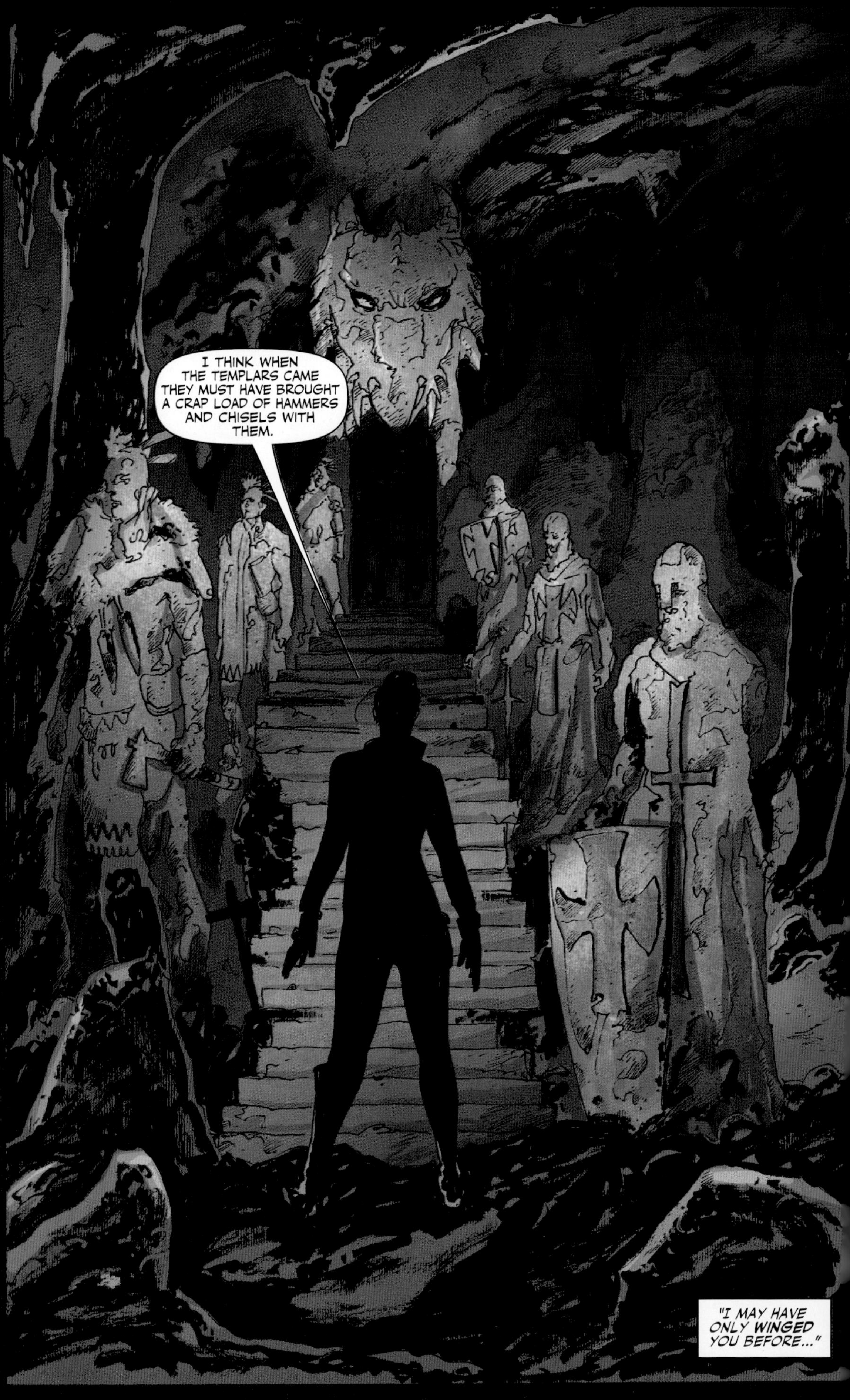
I THINK WHEN THE TEMPLARS CAME THEY MUST HAVE BROUGHT A CRAP LOAD OF HAMMERS AND CHISELS WITH THEM.
"I MAY HAVE ONLY WINGED YOU BEFORE..."

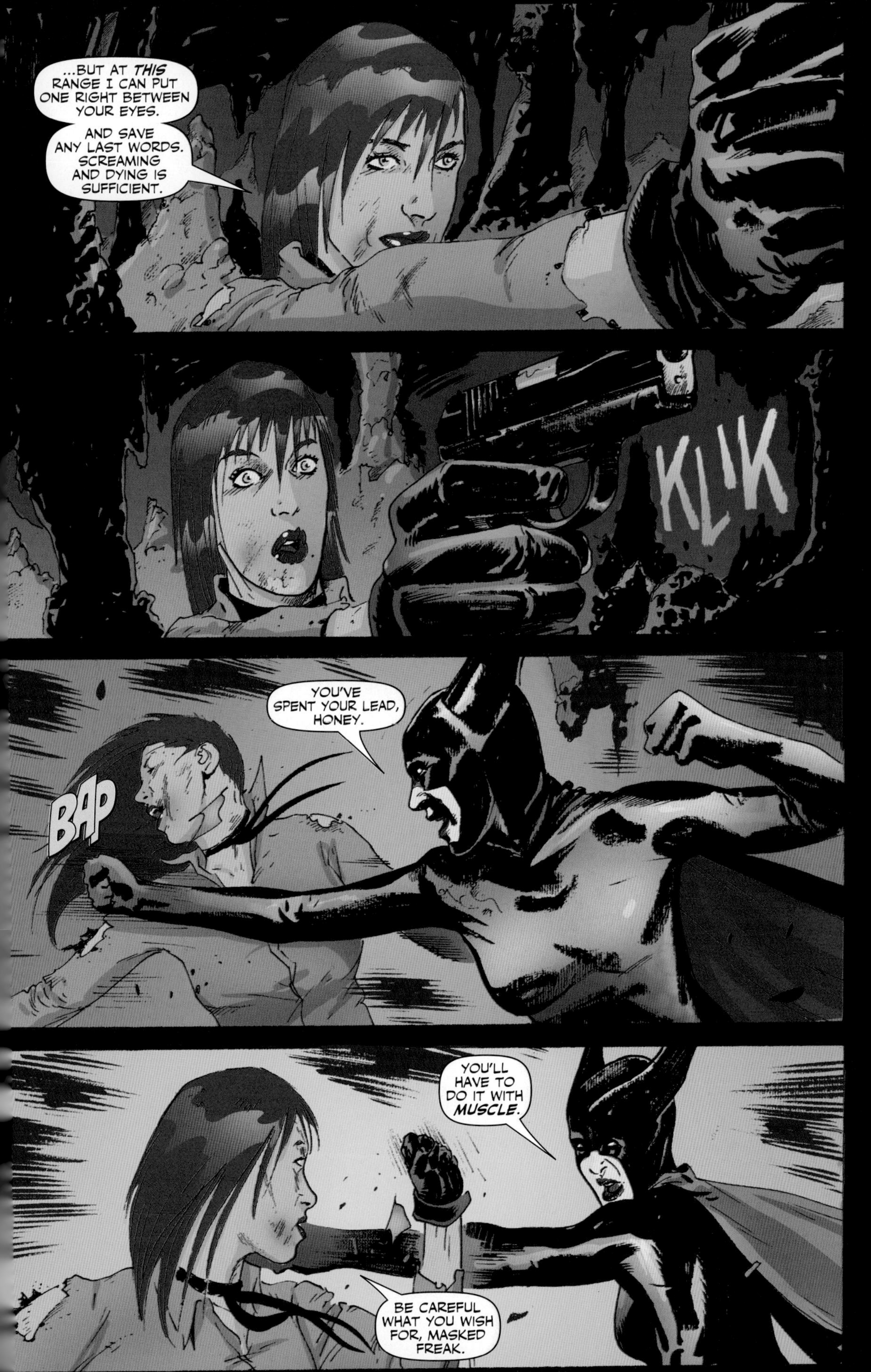
...BUT AT THIS RANGE I CAN PUT ONE RIGHT BETWEEN YOUR EYES.
AND SAVE ANY LAST WORDS. SCREAMING AND DYING IS SUFFICIENT.
KLIK
YOU'VE SPENT YOUR LEAD, HONEY.
BAP
YOU'LL HAVE TO DO IT WITH MUSCLE.
BE CAREFUL WHAT YOU WISH FOR, MASKED FREAK.

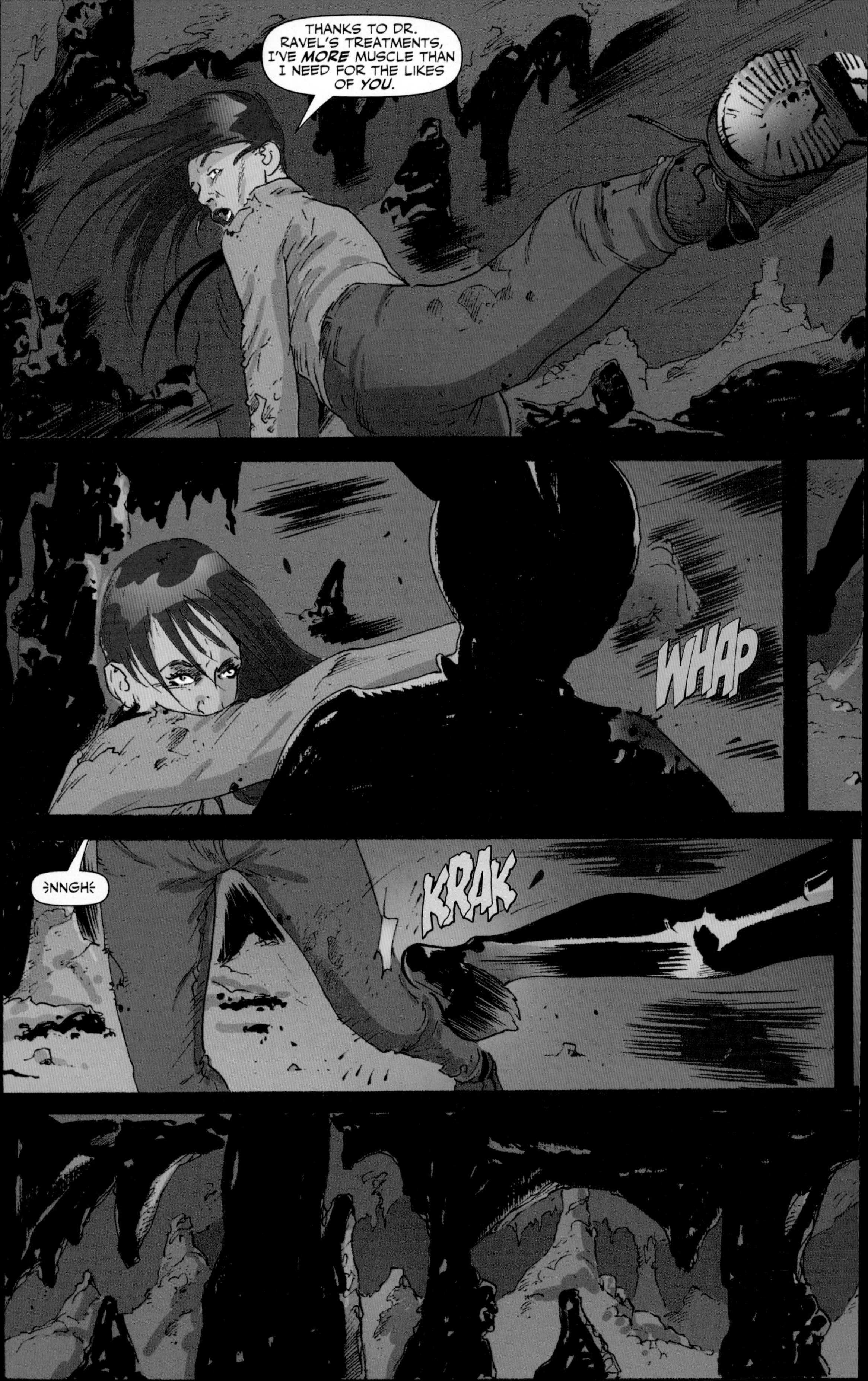
THANKS TO DR. RAVEL'S TREATMENTS, I'VE MORE MUSCLE THAN I NEED FOR THE LIKES OF YOU.
WHAP
NNGH
KRAK

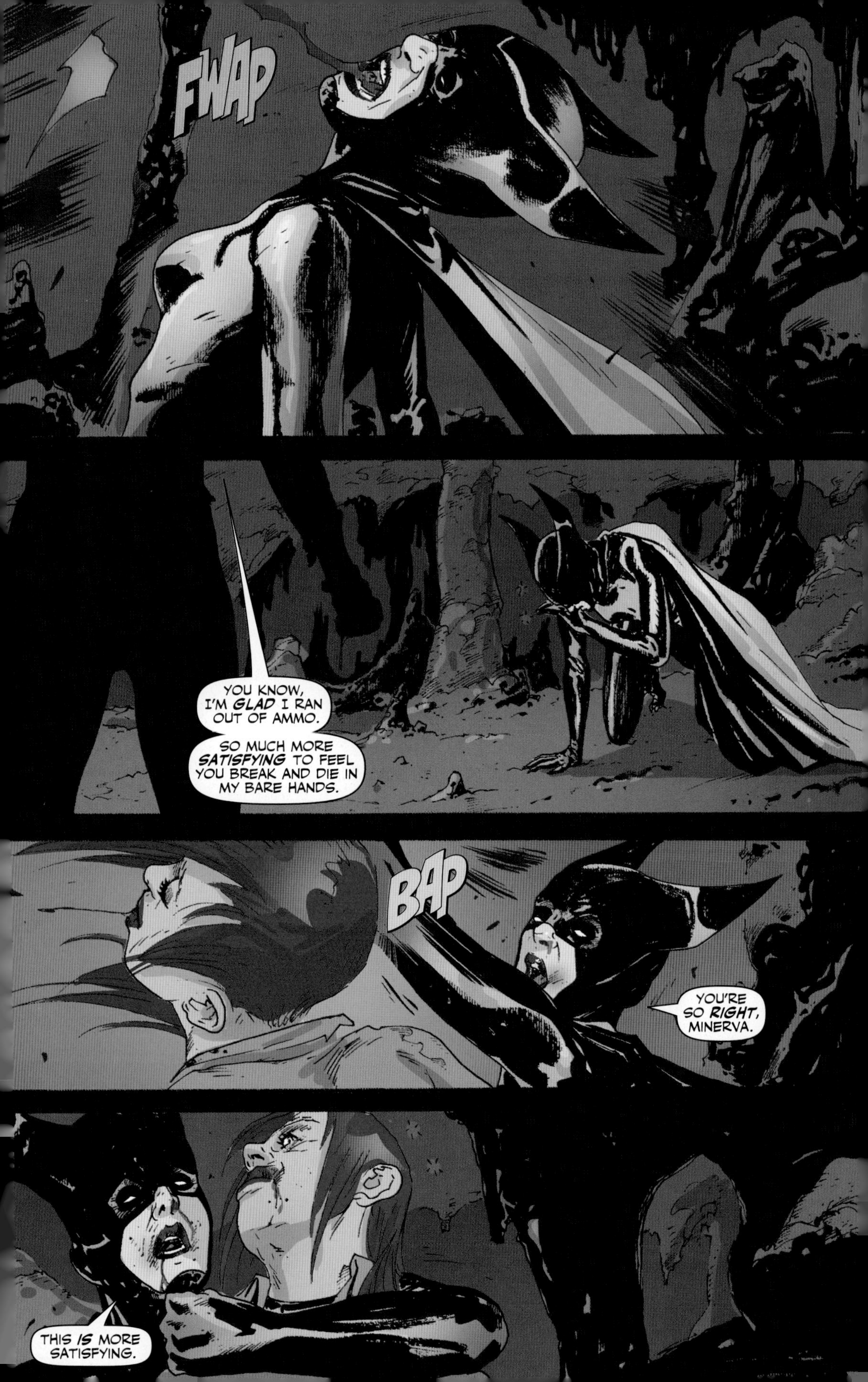
FWAP
YOU KNOW, I'M GLAD I RAN OUT OF AMMO.
SO MUCH MORE SATISFYING TO FEEL YOU BREAK AND DIE IN MY BARE HANDS.
BAP
YOU'RE SO RIGHT, MINERVA.
THIS IS MORE SATISFYING.

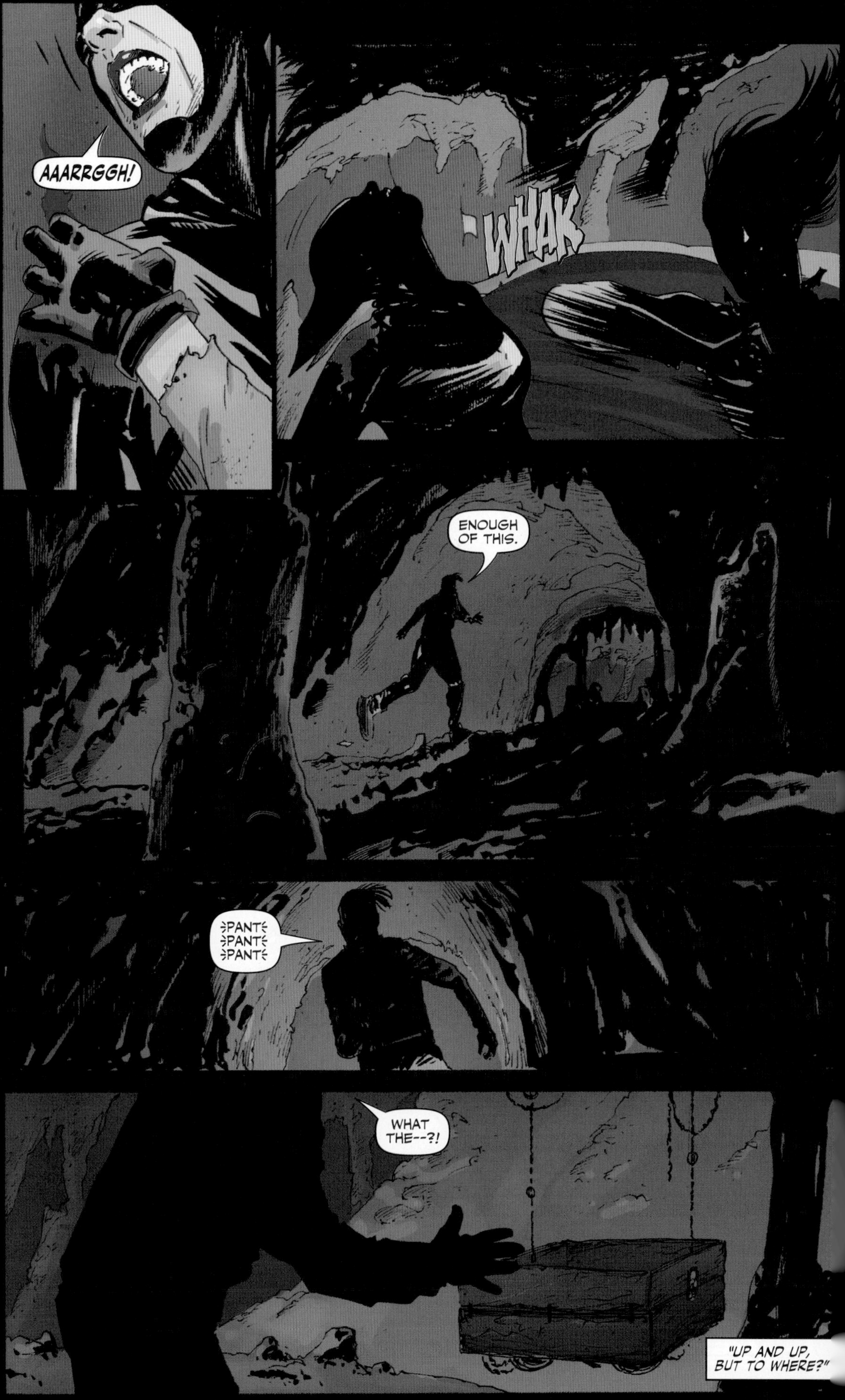
AAARRGGH!
WHAK
ENOUGH OF THIS.
PANT PANT PANT
WHAT THE--?!
"UP AND UP, BUT TO WHERE?"

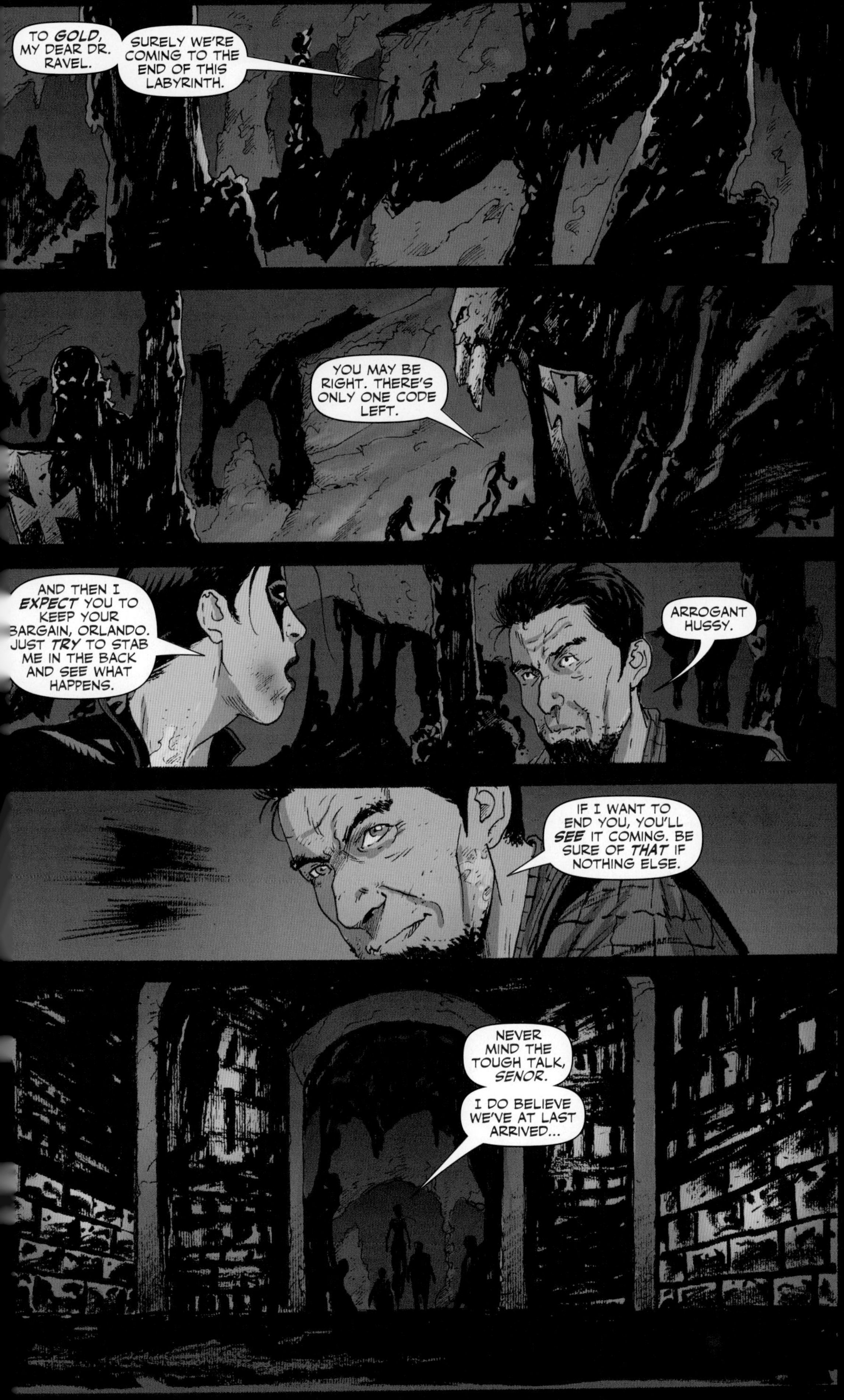
TO GOLD, MY DEAR DR. RAVEL.
SURELY WE'RE COMING TO THE END OF THIS LABYRINTH.
YOU MAY BE RIGHT. THERE'S ONLY ONE CODE LEFT.
AND THEN I EXPECT YOU TO KEEP YOUR BARGAIN, ORLANDO. JUST TRY TO STAB ME IN THE BACK AND SEE WHAT HAPPENS.
ARROGANT HUSSY.
IF I WANT TO END YOU, YOU'LL SEE IT COMING. BE SURE OF THAT IF NOTHING ELSE.
NEVER MIND THE TOUGH TALK, SENOR.
I DO BELIEVE WE'VE AT LAST ARRIVED...

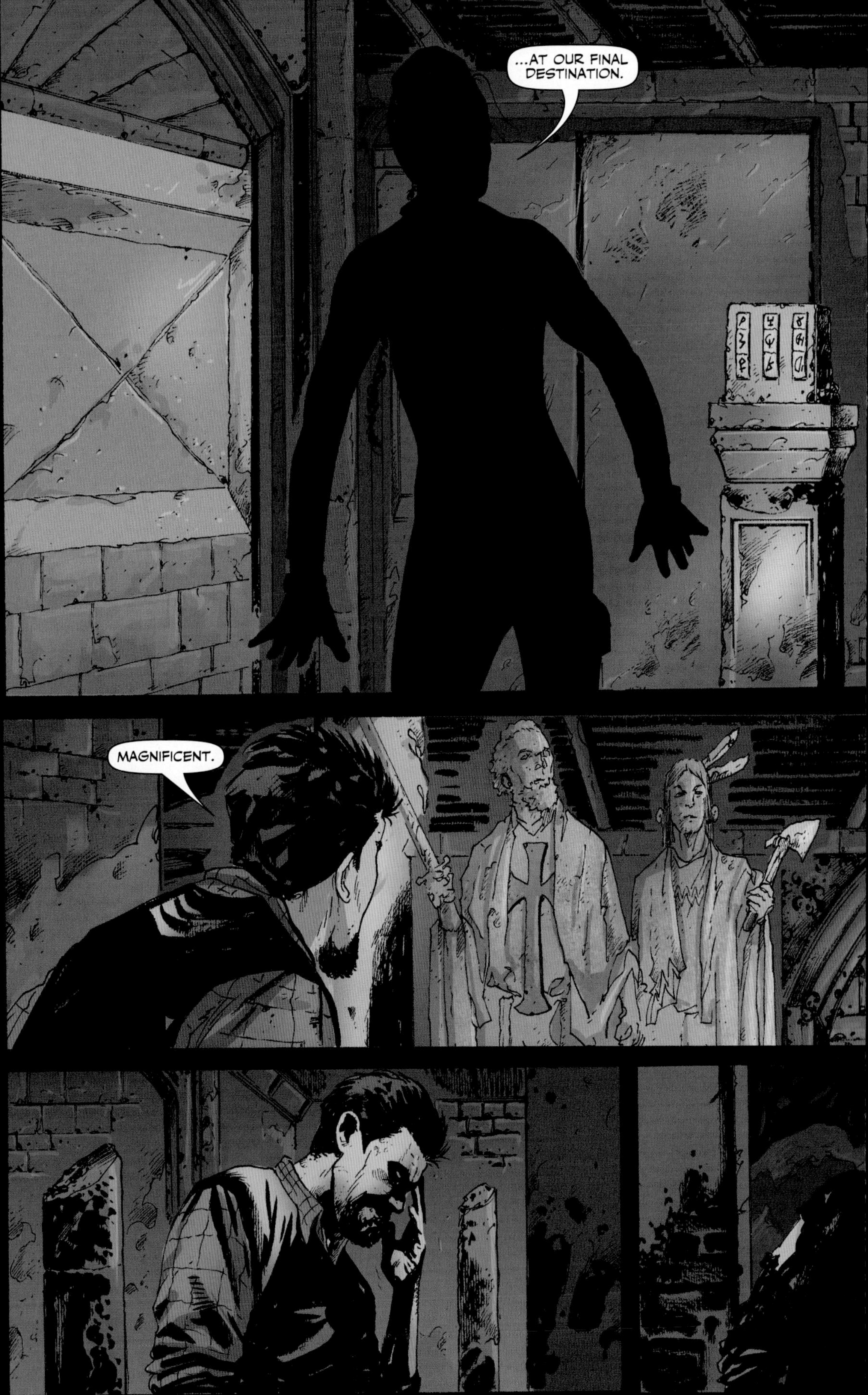
...AT OUR FINAL DESTINATION.
MAGNIFICENT.

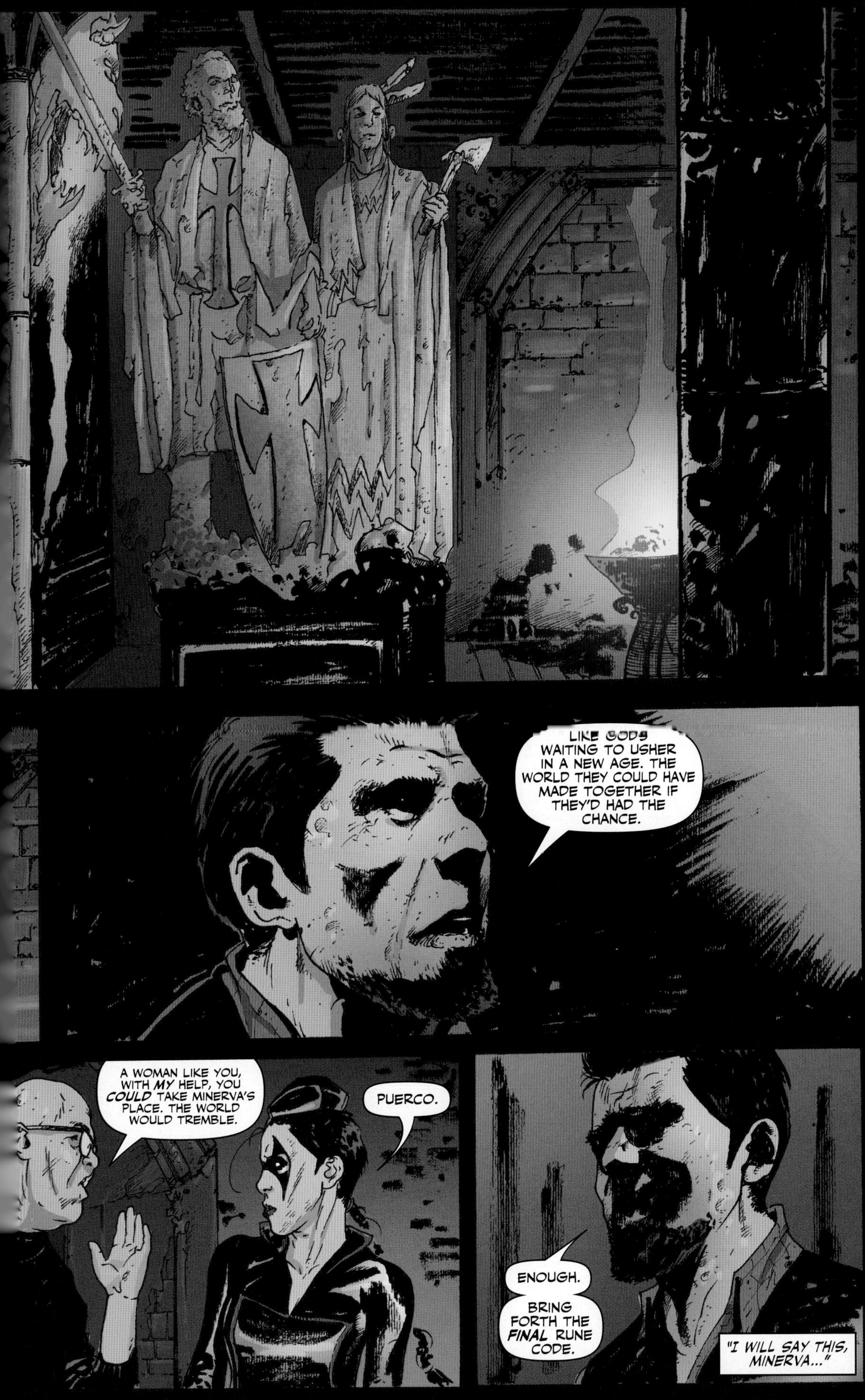

LIKE GODS WAITING TO USHER IN A NEW AGE. THE WORLD THEY COULD HAVE MADE TOGETHER IF THEY'D HAD THE CHANCE.
A WOMAN LIKE YOU, WITH *MY* HELP, YOU *COULD* TAKE MINERVA'S PLACE. THE WORLD WOULD TREMBLE.
PUERCO.
ENOUGH.
BRING FORTH THE *FINAL* RUNE CODE.
"I WILL SAY THIS, MINERVA..."

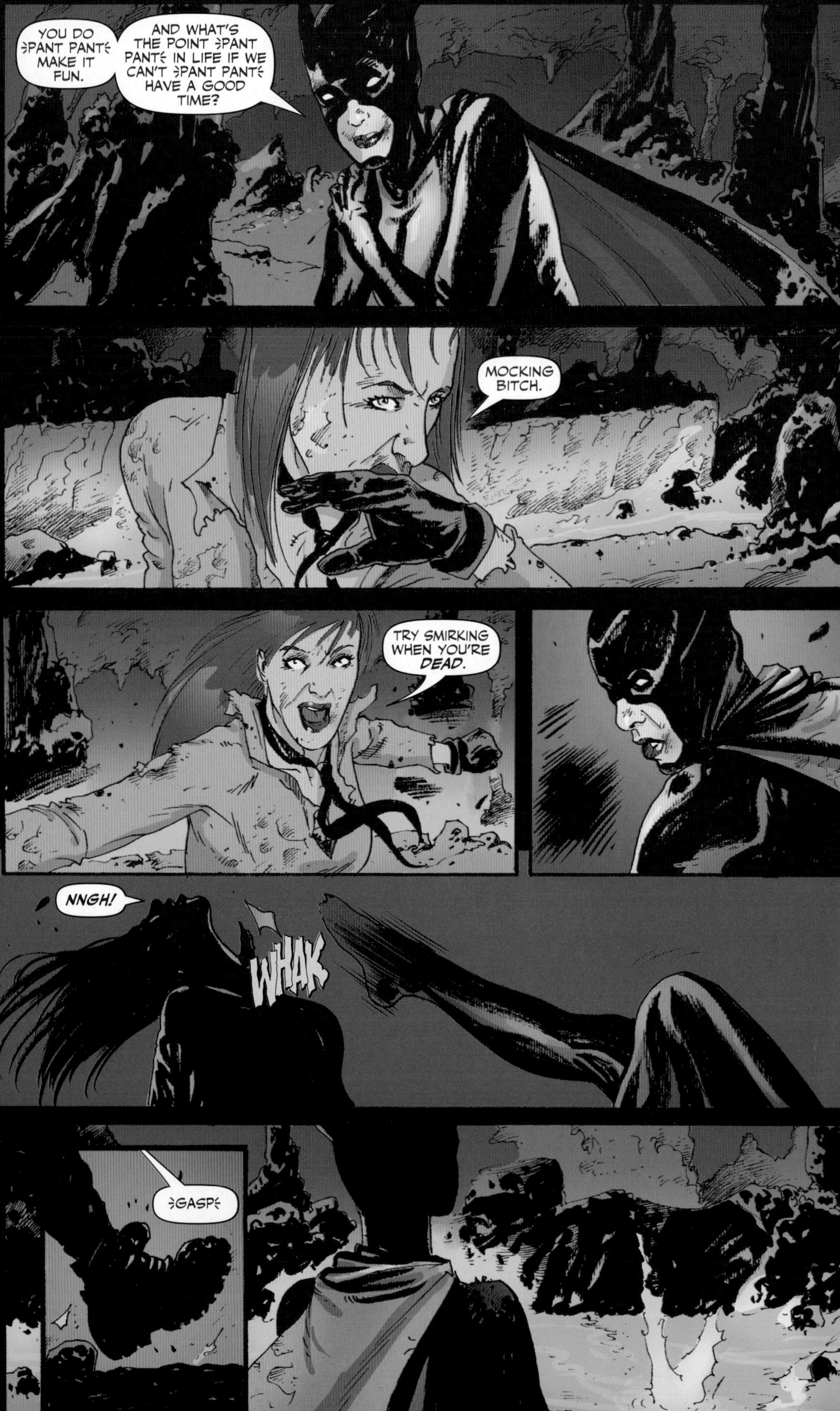
YOU DO ⋮PANT PANT⋮ MAKE IT FUN.
AND WHAT'S THE POINT ⋮PANT PANT⋮ IN LIFE IF WE CAN'T ⋮PANT PANT⋮ HAVE A GOOD TIME?
MOCKING BITCH.
TRY SMIRKING WHEN YOU'RE *DEAD*.
NNGH!
WHAK
⋮GASP⋮

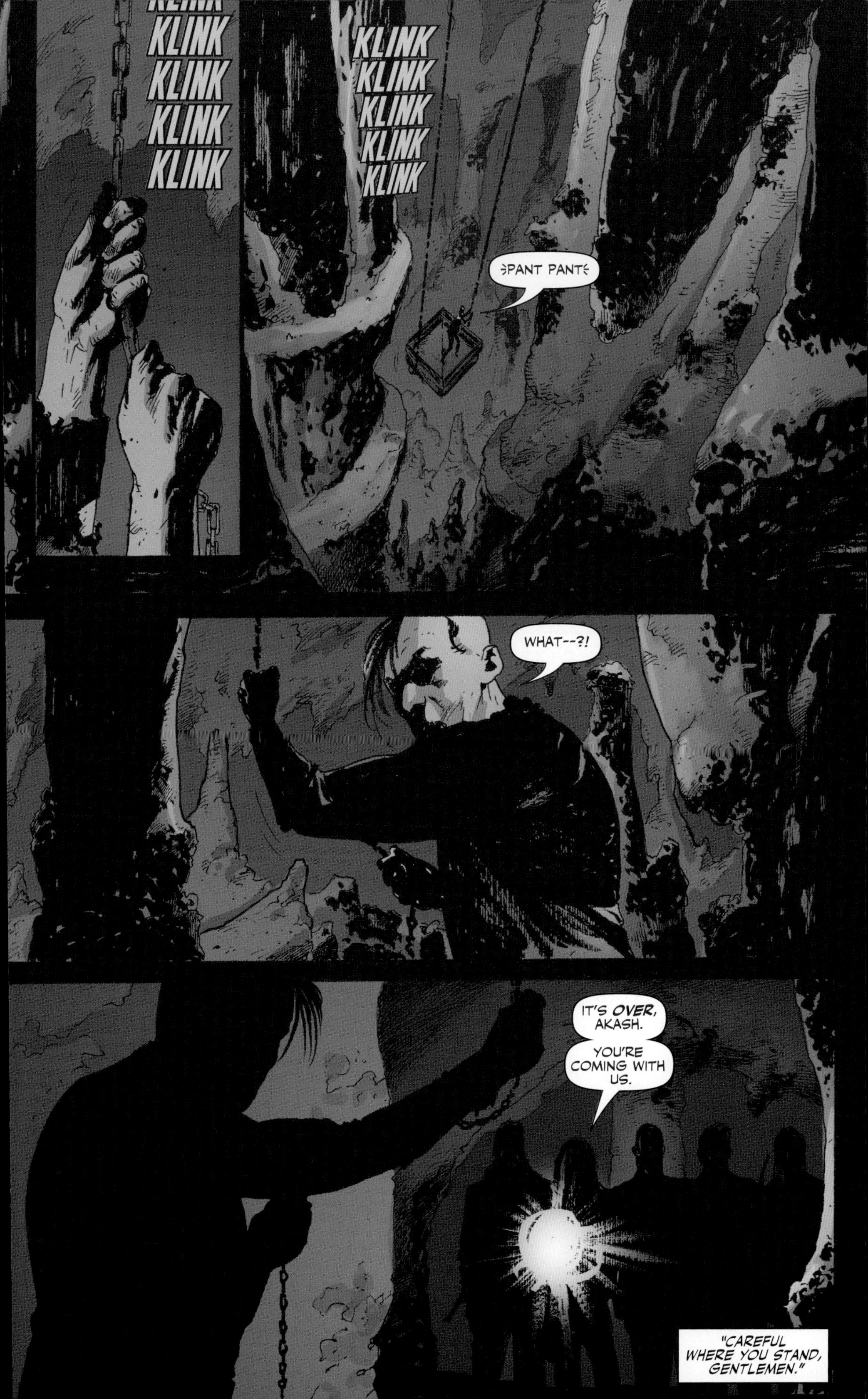
KLINK
KLINK
KLINK
KLINK
KLINK
KLINK
KLINK
KLINK
KLINK
PANT PANT
WHAT--?!
IT'S *OVER*, AKASH.
YOU'RE COMING WITH US.
"CAREFUL WHERE YOU STAND, GENTLEMEN."

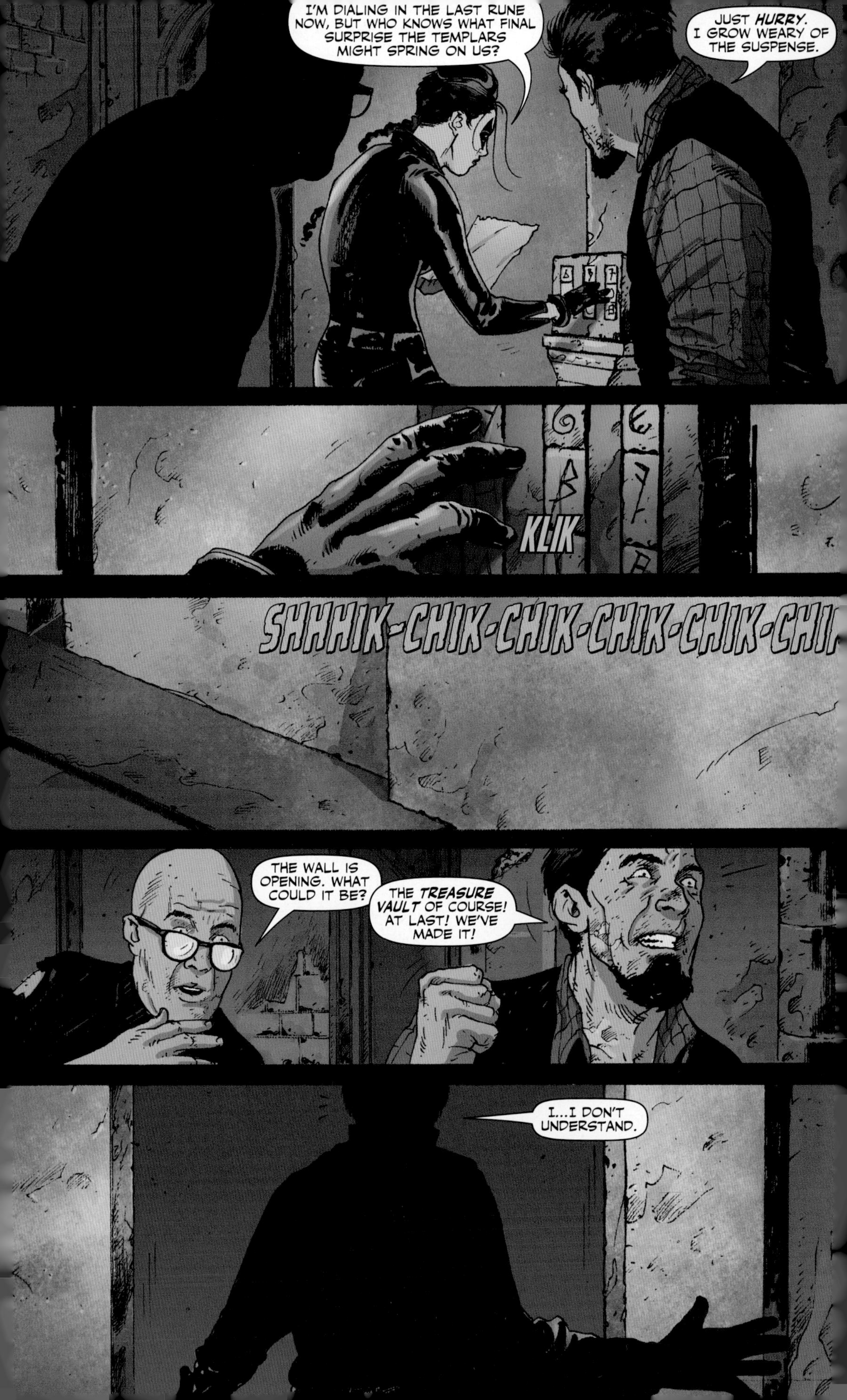
I'M DIALING IN THE LAST RUNE NOW, BUT WHO KNOWS WHAT FINAL SURPRISE THE TEMPLARS MIGHT SPRING ON US?
JUST HURRY. I GROW WEARY OF THE SUSPENSE.
KLIK
SHHHIK-CHIK-CHIK-CHIK-CHIK-CHI
THE WALL IS OPENING. WHAT COULD IT BE?
THE TREASURE VAULT OF COURSE! AT LAST! WE'VE MADE IT!
I...I DON'T UNDERSTAND.

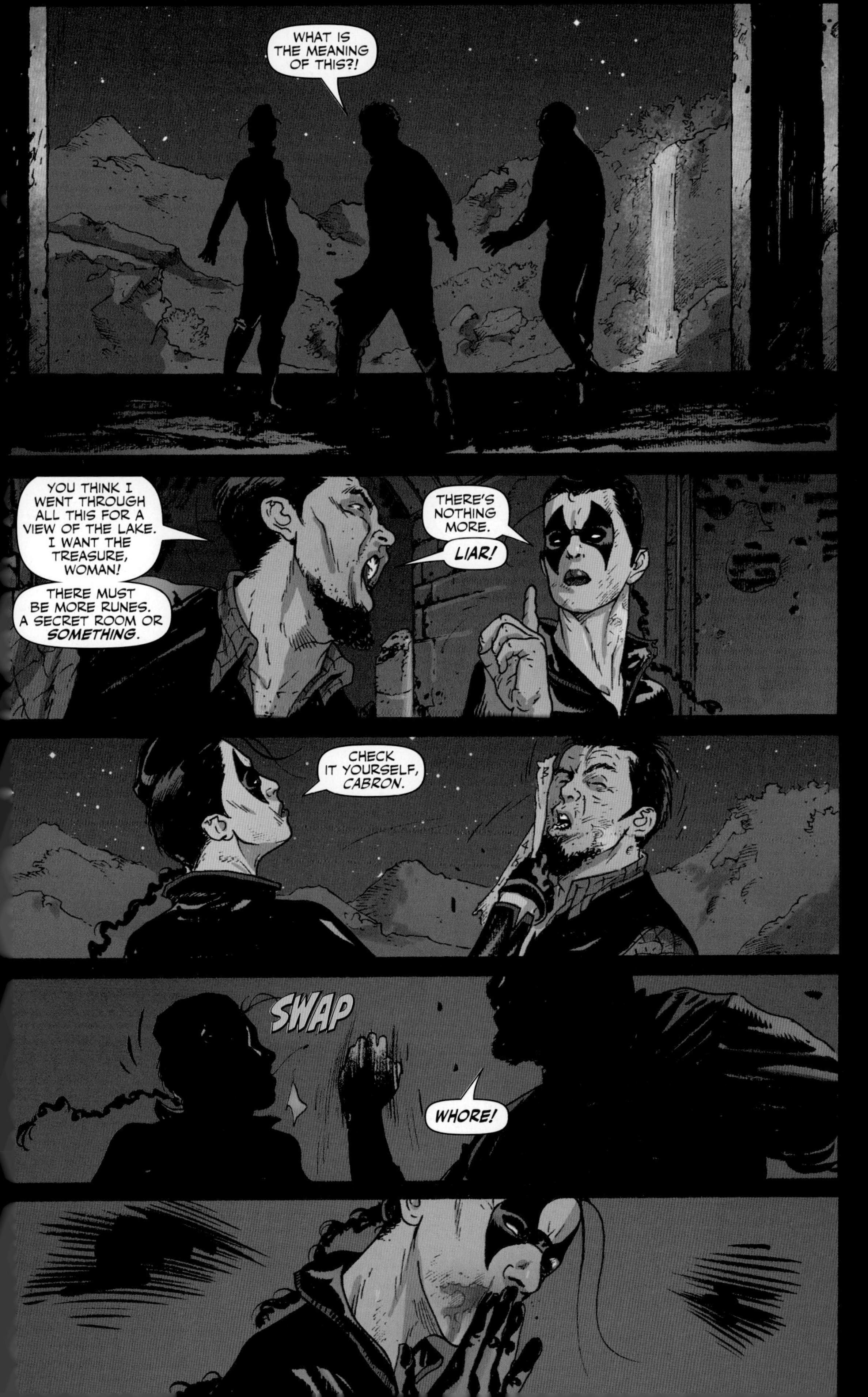
WHAT IS THE MEANING OF THIS?!
YOU THINK I WENT THROUGH ALL THIS FOR A VIEW OF THE LAKE. I WANT THE TREASURE, WOMAN!
THERE MUST BE MORE RUNES. A SECRET ROOM OR SOMETHING.
THERE'S NOTHING MORE.
LIAR!
CHECK IT YOURSELF, CABRON.
SWAP
WHORE!

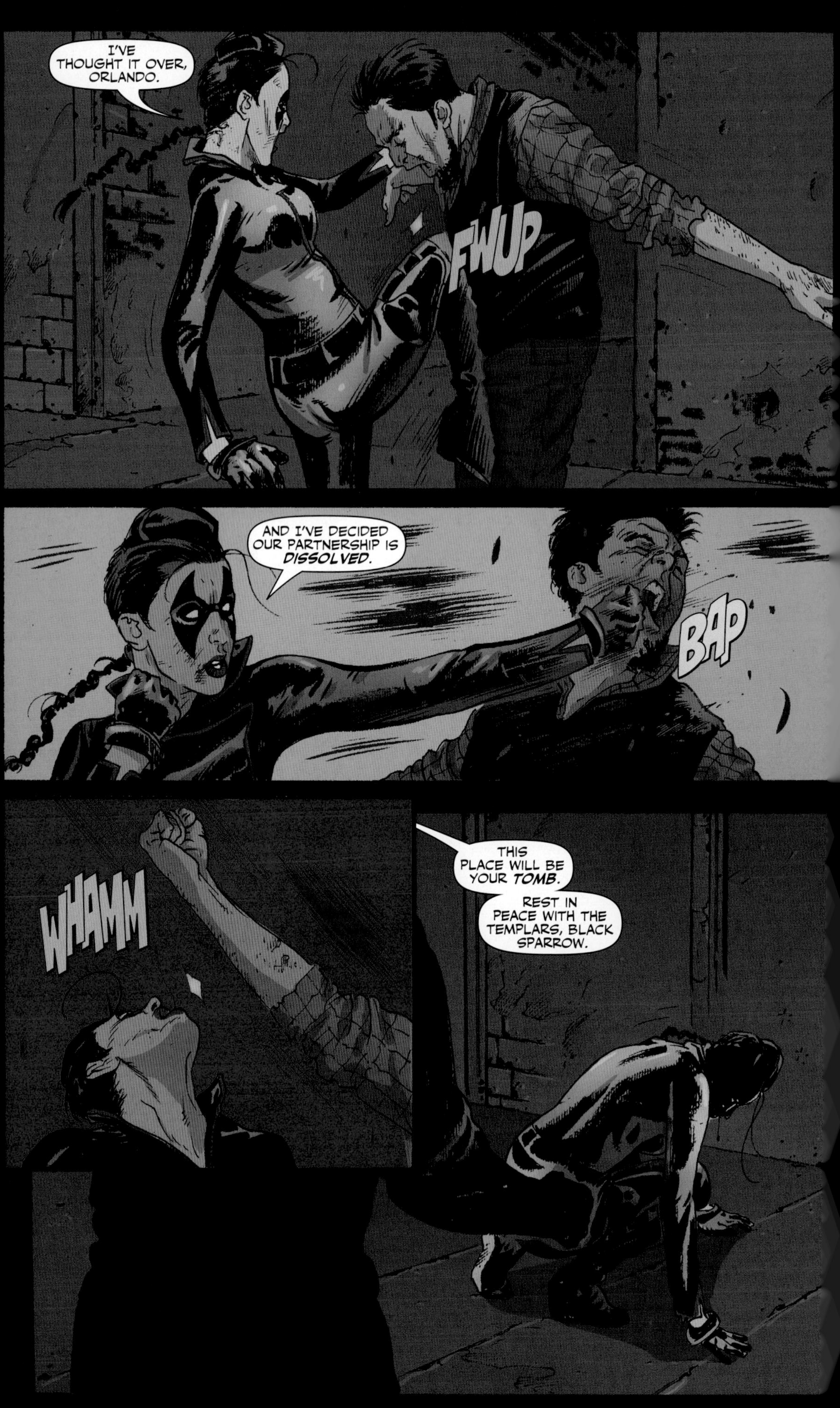

I'VE THOUGHT IT OVER, ORLANDO.
FWUP
AND I'VE DECIDED OUR PARTNERSHIP IS *DISSOLVED*.
BAP
WHAMM
THIS PLACE WILL BE YOUR *TOMB*.
REST IN PEACE WITH THE TEMPLARS, BLACK SPARROW.

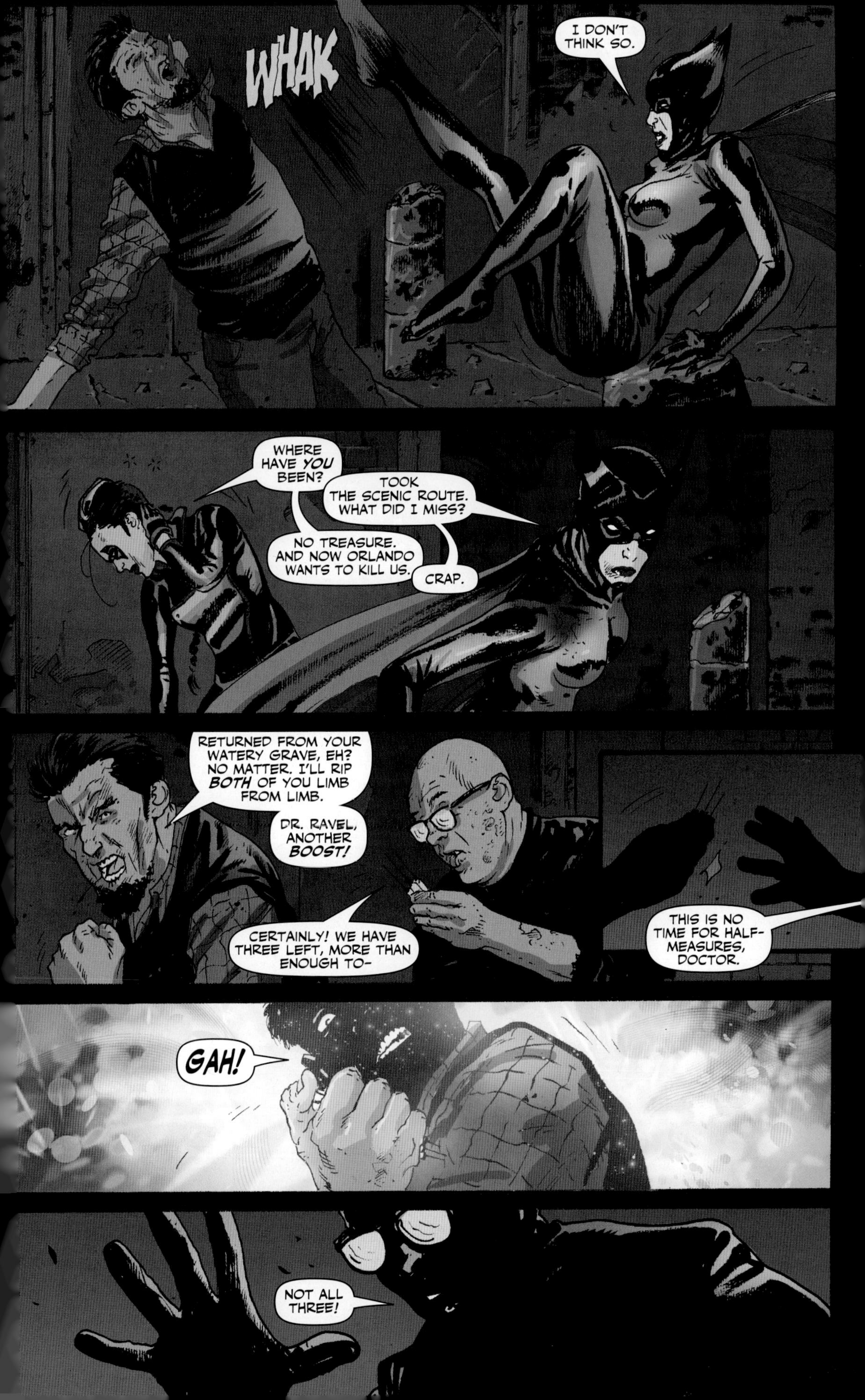
WHAK
I DON'T THINK SO.
WHERE HAVE *YOU* BEEN?
TOOK THE SCENIC ROUTE. WHAT DID I MISS?
NO TREASURE. AND NOW ORLANDO WANTS TO KILL US.
CRAP.
RETURNED FROM YOUR WATERY GRAVE, EH? NO MATTER. I'LL RIP *BOTH* OF YOU LIMB FROM LIMB.
DR. RAVEL, ANOTHER *BOOST!*
CERTAINLY! WE HAVE THREE LEFT, MORE THAN ENOUGH TO-
THIS IS NO TIME FOR HALF-MEASURES, DOCTOR.
GAH!
NOT ALL THREE!

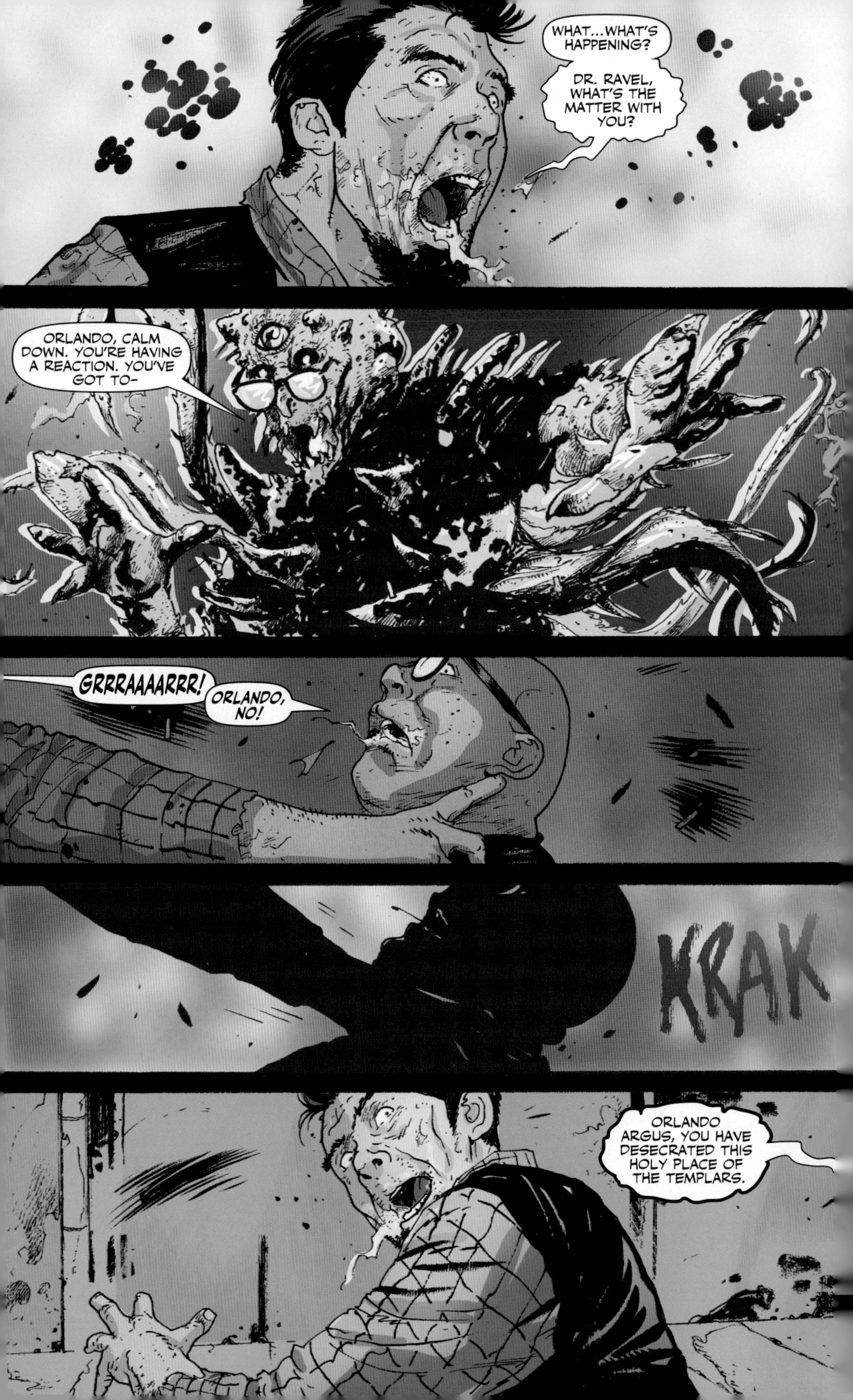
WHAT...WHAT'S HAPPENING?
DR. RAVEL, WHAT'S THE MATTER WITH YOU?
ORLANDO, CALM DOWN. YOU'RE HAVING A REACTION. YOU'VE GOT TO-
GRRRAAAARRR!
ORLANDO, NO!
KRAK
ORLANDO ARGUS, YOU HAVE DESECRATED THIS HOLY PLACE OF THE TEMPLARS.

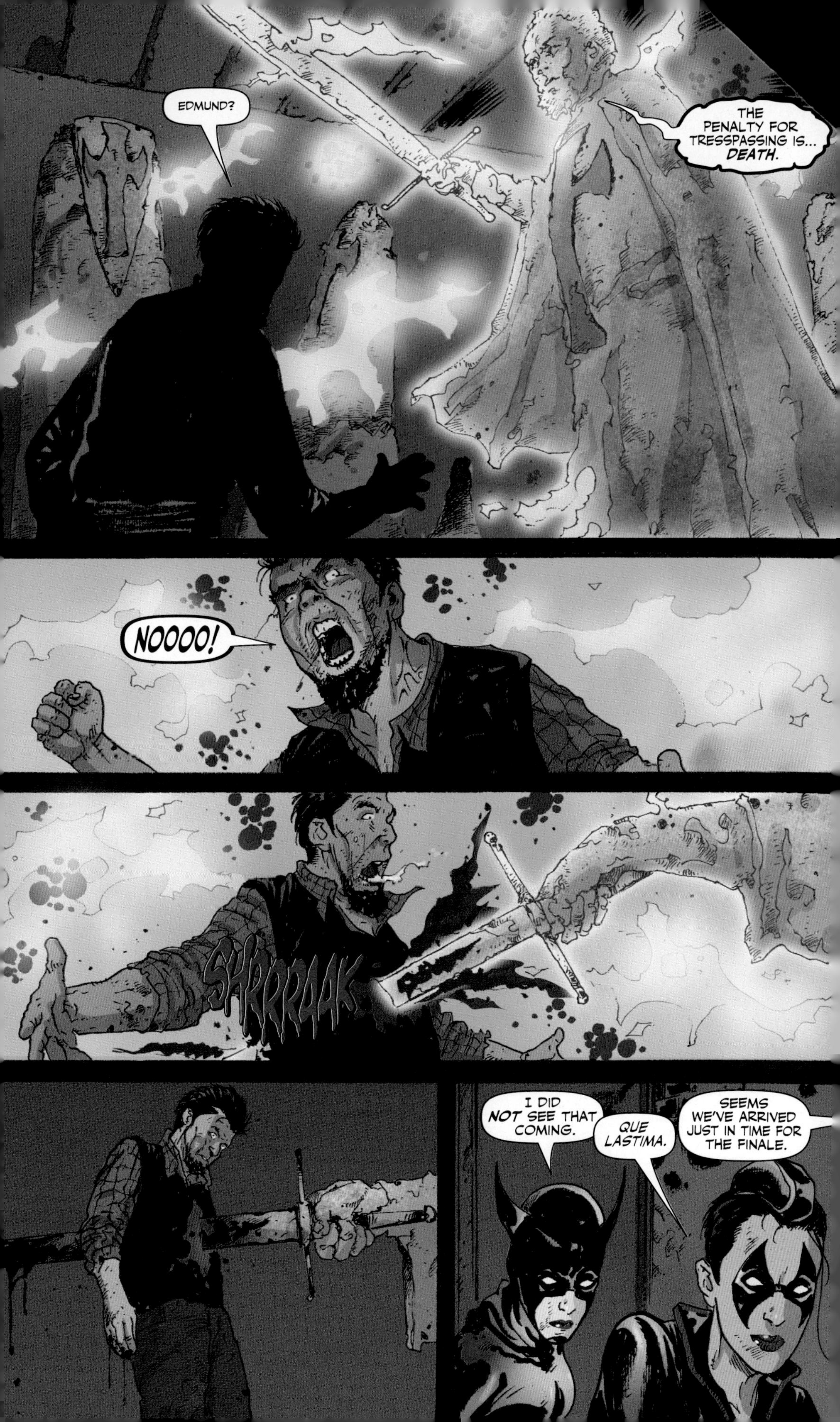
EDMUND?
THE PENALTY FOR TRESSPASSING IS... DEATH.
NOOOO!
SHRRAAK
I DID NOT SEE THAT COMING.
QUE LASTIMA.
SEEMS WE'VE ARRIVED JUST IN TIME FOR THE FINALE.

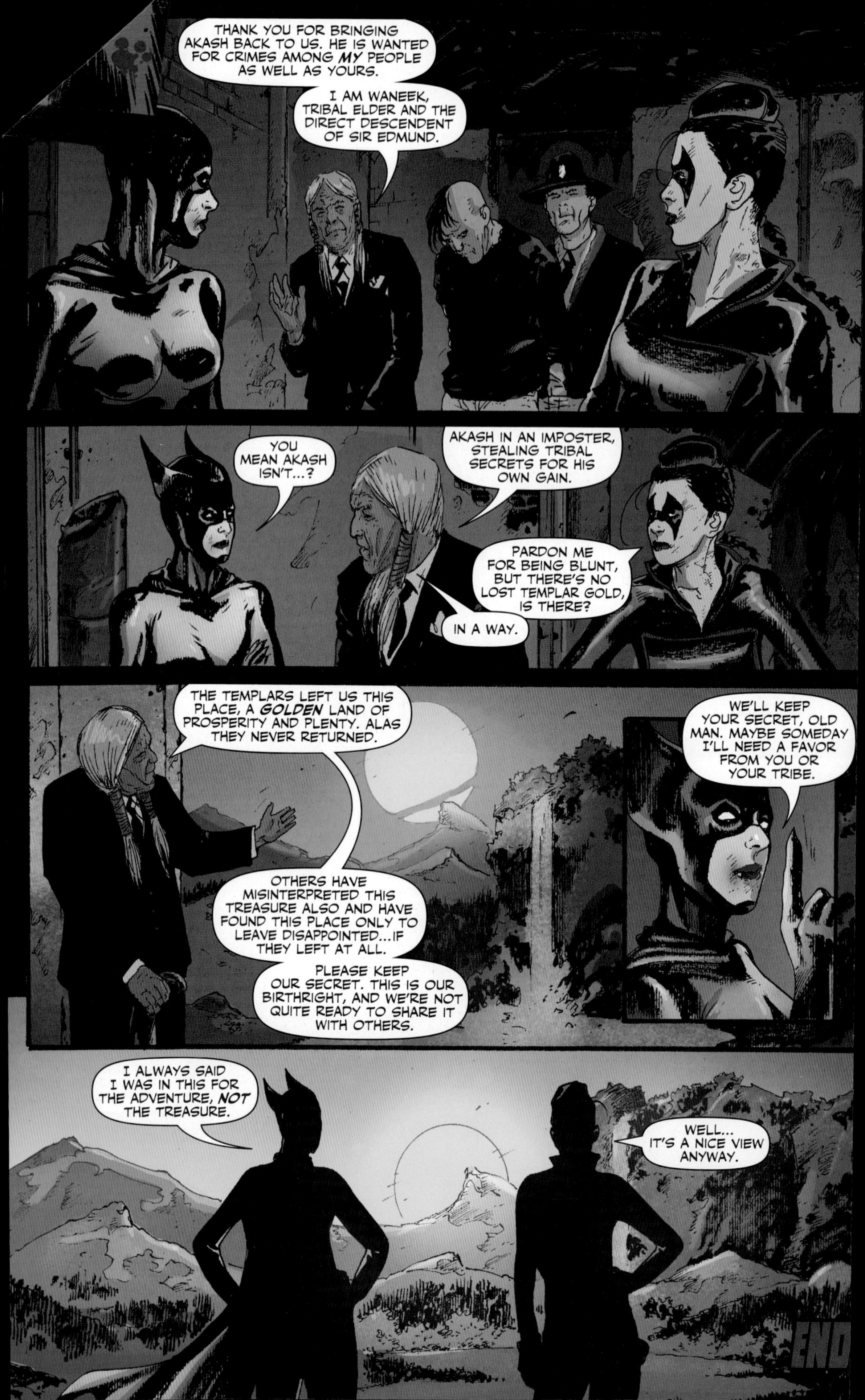
THANK YOU FOR BRINGING AKASH BACK TO US. HE IS WANTED FOR CRIMES AMONG MY PEOPLE AS WELL AS YOURS.
I AM WANEEK, TRIBAL ELDER AND THE DIRECT DESCENDENT OF SIR EDMUND.
YOU MEAN AKASH ISN'T...?
AKASH IN AN IMPOSTER, STEALING TRIBAL SECRETS FOR HIS OWN GAIN.
PARDON ME FOR BEING BLUNT, BUT THERE'S NO LOST TEMPLAR GOLD, IS THERE?
IN A WAY.
THE TEMPLARS LEFT US THIS PLACE, A GOLDEN LAND OF PROSPERITY AND PLENTY. ALAS THEY NEVER RETURNED.
OTHERS HAVE MISINTERPRETED THIS TREASURE ALSO AND HAVE FOUND THIS PLACE ONLY TO LEAVE DISAPPOINTED...IF THEY LEFT AT ALL.
PLEASE KEEP OUR SECRET. THIS IS OUR BIRTHRIGHT, AND WE'RE NOT QUITE READY TO SHARE IT WITH OTHERS.
WE'LL KEEP YOUR SECRET, OLD MAN. MAYBE SOMEDAY I'LL NEED A FAVOR FROM YOU OR YOUR TRIBE.
I ALWAYS SAID I WAS IN THIS FOR THE ADVENTURE, NOT THE TREASURE.
WELL... IT'S A NICE VIEW ANYWAY.
END

BONUS MATERIAL

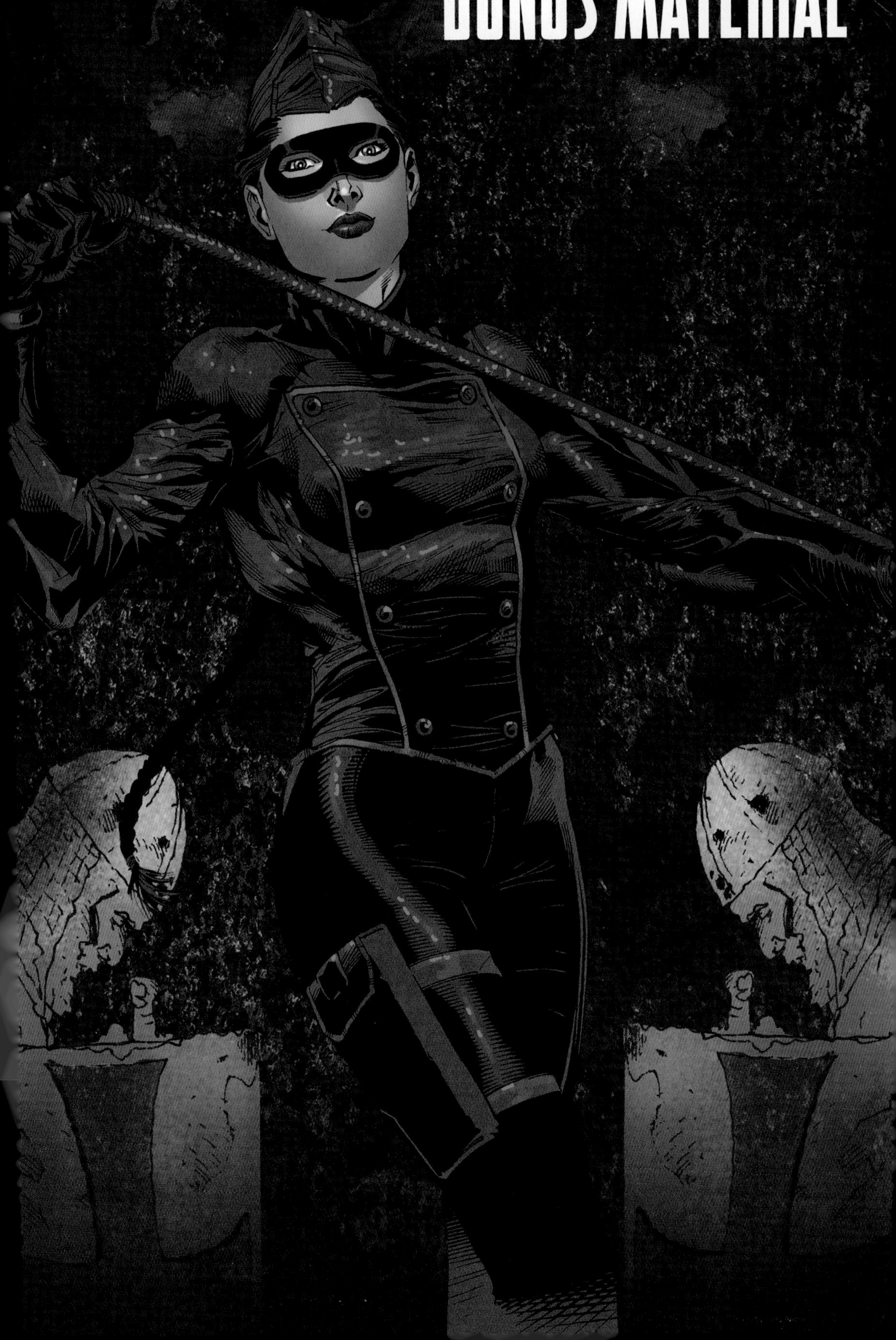

NOIR #1

VICTOR GISCHLER

"The Moon Stone Legacy"

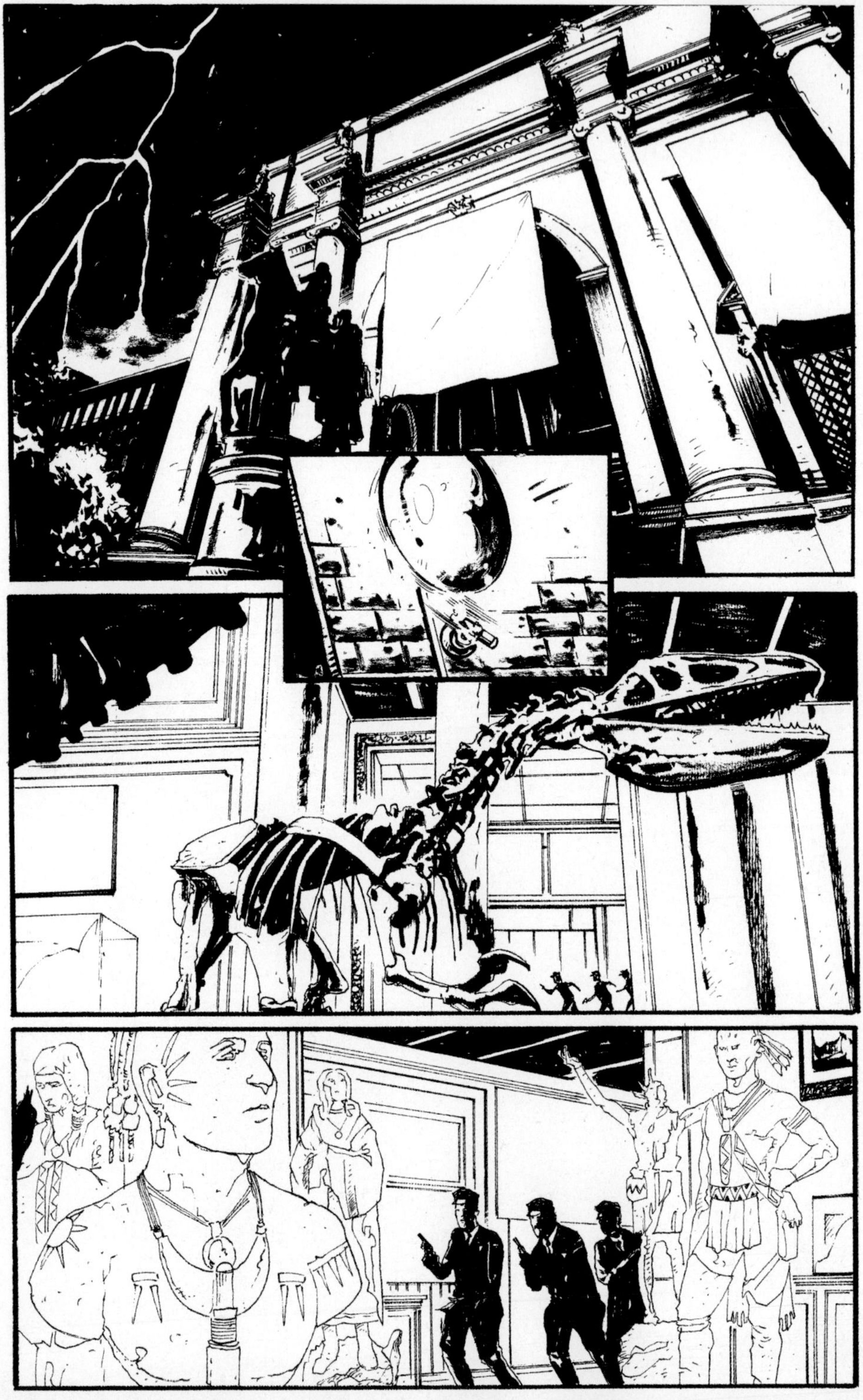

PAGE ONE

Panel 1
Establishing shot of the American Museum of Natural History in New York City. Late at night.

1 SFX: RINGAringaRINGAringaRINGAringaRINGA

Panel 2
Close on an old time alarm bell ringing. Small panel.

2 SFX: RINGAringaRINGAringaRINGAringaRINGA

Panel 3
CUT TO: Big panel. The dark lobby of the museum but light enough to see what is going on. Three uniformed security guards run past the big skeleton of the dinosaur. They are wielding flashlights. The flashlight beams stab into the darkness.

3 Guard: THIS WAY! GET THE LEAD OUT, YOU
                                         BUMS!

Panel 4
CUT TO: A hallway with display mannequins of Mohawk Indians on either side. The guards run up this hall. They have pistols drawn.

4 Guard: COME ON! THE MOHAWK EXHIBIT!

PAGE TWO

Panel 1
The guard, with the other two standing behind him, shines his flashlight on a broken dome of glass on a pedestal. The glass dome is obviously a display for something, but it's been broken into and whatever was under the dome is gone.

1 Guard:	THE MOON STONE!
2 Guard:	OKAY, SPREAD OUT. WHOEVER TOOK IT CAN'T HAVE GOTTEN TOO FAR SO –

Panel 2
A length of bull whip lashes out of the darkness to snap a pistol out of one of the guard's hands. (We do NOT see who is wielding the whip on this page ... but we can guess.)

3 SFX:	*WUP-SNAP*
4 Guard:	**HEY!**

Panel 3
The bull whip lashes out again at a different guard and his pistol goes flying to

5 SFX:	*SNAP*
6 Different Guard:	*>GAH!<*

Panel 4
The whip lashes out again and the flashlight goes flying from the hand of the other guard, the beam of light flashing around wildly as the flashlight spins in the air.

7 SFX:	*WIP-SNAP*

Panel 5
Close on the flashlight hitting the floor, the glass part breaking as the flashlight winks out.

8 SFX:	*KISH*

Panel 6
CUT TO: A kitchen. Day. Close on the kitchen floor as a juice glass hits the tile and shatters. We also see an attractive pair of women's feet. These are Margo's feet, but we don't know that yet. This panel should somehow mirror or match the one above to help us transition to the next scene in Cranston's kitchen.

9 SFX:	*KISH*

PAGE THREE

Panel 1
The kitchen of Cranston's swanky penthouse apartment. Cranston is standing in the doorway of the kitchen, looking in at us. He is wearing an expensive robe over silk pajamas, cinched at the waste. He has one hand behind his back ... try to make this look natural although, yes, he's got a gun back there.

1 Cranston:	I HOPE THAT WASN'T THE SOUND OF ONE OF MY **GOOD** CRYSTAL GLASSES BREAKING ON THE TILE –

2 Cranston: OH.

3 Cranston: WE HAVE COMPANY.

Panel 2
Reverse angle. **BIG** panel to show off the ladies. The Black Sparrow is sitting on the kitchen counter next to the sink. Over the sink is a window, thin curtains blowing in to show the window is open. (We also want to suggest that maybe the window is how Sparrow got inside.) Margo stands in front of Sparrow. She is wearing a sexy period nightgown. Maybe:
http://img1.etsystatic.com/009/0/6216065/il_fullxfull.446570593_2lgh.jpg

Margo's chin is up, an expression on her face like she refuses to be rattled by this situation ... and here is the situation: Sparrow is sitting behind her, her legs wrapped around Margo. One of Sparrow's hands gently grabs Margo by the shoulder/neck, sort of half caress half domination hold. Sparrow's other hand holds her trademark Mauser pistol pointed at Margo's face. Pistol:
http://www.warmuseum.ca/cwm/exhibitions/guerre/photos/2800/19920246-001.jpg

On the counter on the other side of the sink (space permitting) maybe we see a state of the art 1939 kitchen appliance of some sort. A blender or mixer or something.

4 Black Sparrow: GOOD MORNING, MR. CRANSTON.

5 Black Sparrow: SORRY IF I'M CATCHING YOU OFF GUARD,
                                          BUT I DIDN'T THINK YOU'D MIND IF AN
                                          OLD FRIEND POPPED IN FOR BREAKFAST.

Panel 3
Closer head-n-shoulders two-shot of Margo and Sparrow. They are almost cheek to cheek. Sparrow's expression is sultry but also somewhat like she might be a little crazy. Sexy-crazy. Margo's eyes slide to the side to consider Sparrow. She has a snooty look on her face like Sparrow is some kind of trash from another social class that Margo is being forced to socialize with.

6 Margo: YOU **KNOW** EACH OTHER?

7 Margo: HOW DELIGHTFUL.

PAGE FOUR

Panel 1
Behind Cranston now. We can see he's holding one of Shadow's .45 automatics behind his back. Looking past Cranston, we glimpse Sparrow and Margo.

1 Cranston: I ADMIT I AM A **LITTLE** SURPRISED TO SEE
                                          YOU.

2 Cranston: THE LAST TIME I SAW YOU, YOU WERE ...
                                          WELL ... **PLUMMETING**.

Panel 2
On Margo and Sparrow. Slightly wider than the previous two-shot. The gun wavers from Margo's face as the Sparrow offers us a slight shrug. Margo looks like she's just starting to pull away from Sparrow.

3 Black Sparrow: YOU PUSH ME OFF A TOWER. I TOSS YOU FROM AN AIRPLANE.

4 Black Sparrow: HAZARDS OF OUR PROFESSION, YES?

5 Margo: SEEMS I'M NOT STRICTLY **NEEDED** FOR THIS CONVERSATION SO MAYBE I'LL JUST TODDLE OFF AND –

Panel 3
Sparrow pulls her back, presses her nose against the side of Margo's face so she can speak directly into Margo's ear. Sparrow has a slightly wild look in her eyes – but don't go over the top. Margo has a look on her face like she's just smelled a fart.

6 Black Sparrow: BUT IT WOULDN'T BE A PARTY WITHOUT **YOU**, BRIGHT EYES.

Panel 4
Cranston casually enters the kitchen, close enough to include all three of them in the shot.

7 Cranston: I'VE OFTEN EXPRESSED THE SAME SENTIMENT. SHE DOES TEND TO LIGHT UP A ROOM.

8 Cranston: BUT YOU'RE HERE TO SEE **ME**. I SUGGEST WE RETIRE TO NEUTRAL GROUND WHERE WE CAN DISCUSS WHAT'S ON YOUR MIND IN A CIVILIZED FASHION.

9 Margo: I VOTE FOR **THAT**.

Panel 5
Tight on Sparrow's face. A tight smile totally devoid of humor. Eyes narrow.

10 Black Sparrow: VERY WELL.

11 Black Sparrow: NAME THE TIME AND PLACE.

12 Black Sparrow/CAP: "IT WAS WHILE CLINGING TO A GARGOYLE IN THE FOG THAT I BEGAN TO PLAN MY BRUTAL, VIOLENT REVENGE UPON YOU."

PAGE FIVE

Panel 1
CUT TO: A swanky Manhattan watering hole. Late afternoon. Interior. This is where all the big shots and swells get a head start on happy hour.   Rich wood paneling. Plush chairs. Could this be at the Plaza? Someplace like that. Bartender in a swanky white coat with a bow tie. Cranston leans against the bar, looking suave in classy jacket and tie. Black Sparrow – now Esmeralda – stands in front of him like she's just arrived, smiling. She wears a very nice cocktail dress which offers a hint of cleavage. She has a blasé smile/smirk on her face. Cranston is looking at her but signaling the bartender (LOU) with a casually raised hand.

1 Cranston: VIOLENT REVENGE, EH? MIND IF WE HAVE
                                 A **DRINK** FIRST?

2 Cranston: LOU, HOW ABOUT A BOTTLE OF
                                 CHAMPAGNE? TWO GLASSES. BRING IT TO
                                 MY USUAL TABLE.

3 Lou: YES, MR. CRANSTON.

Panel 2
On Cranston and Esmeralda walking side by side through the lounge/club. To either side of them we see rich people drinking and conversing. No tuxedos or ball gowns please. This is late afternoon casual drinking. But it's still a very ritzy place.   Her eyes flick toward him with amusement.

4 Esmeralda: DON'T FRET, YOU BAD MAN. MY ANGER
                                 SUBSIDED AS SOON AS MY FEET WERE ON
                                 SOLID GROUND AGAIN.

5 Esmeralda: AS I SAID BEFORE, THESE THINGS HAPPEN
                                 IN OUR LINE OF WORK.

6 Cranston:
YOU'VE **PLENTY** TO ANSWER FOR, MAJOR, BUT I'LL RESTARIN MYSELF FOR THE MOMENT. I'LL ADMIT I'M INTRIGUED.

Panel 3
Cranston pulls out a chair for her to sit at his table as Lou pours champagne into two glasses.

7 Esmeralda:
CALL ME **ESMERALDA**. I RESIGNED MY COMMISSION WITH THE SOCIALISTS IN FAVOR OF PRIVATE ENTERPRISE.

Panel 4
Two-shot. Cranston and Esmeralda sit across the table from one another, holding up glasses like maybe they are about to toast.

8 Cranston:
OBVIOUSLY YOU THINK I CAN BE OF SOME USE TO YOU. **SOCIAL** CALLS SELDOM COME THROUGH MY KITCHEN WINDOW.

9 Esmeralda:
IT SEEMED THE MOST EXPEDIENT WAY. AND YES, YOU – OR PERHAPS YOUR **ALTER EGO** – CAN HELP.

10 Esmeralda:
MAYBE YOU'VE READ ABOUT THE MUSEUM OF NATURAL HISTORY BREAK-IN. THAT WAS **ME**, I'M AFRAID.

Panel 5
On Cranston, holding up his glass and about to drink, looking bemused, a raised eyebrow.

11 Cranston:
YOU CONFESS? VERY WELL. WOULD YOU LIKE TO COME QUIETLY OR DO YOU PREFER **HANDCUFFS**?

Panel 6
On Esmeralda. A wry smile. About to drink her champagne too.

12 Esmeralda:
REALLY, DARLING, WE CAN DISCUSS ROLEPLAY LATER.

13 Esmeralda:
RIGHT NOW ... A STORY.

PAGE SIX

Panel 1
COLOR ALERT. We're entering flashback mode until further notice, so let's do something with the color palette to indicate this.

.CUT TO: Establishing shot. A big luxury motor yacht docked among some shabbier ships and boats. The yacht could be something like:

http://uk.boats.com/motor-boats/mathis-yacht-building-co-llc-fantail-motor-yacht-12080524/

1 Esmeralda/CAP: "HIS NAME WAS GUSTAV ARGUS AND HE WAS KNOWN TO THE LEGITIMATE WORLD AS AN IMPORTER AND EXPORTER.

2 Esmeralda/CAP: "EVERYONE ELSE KNEW HIM AS A BLACK MARKET DEALER OF STOLEN ANTIQUITIES AND RARE CURIOSITIES.

Panel 2
CUT TO: Interior of yacht. A fancy lounge area. We're looking at Argus who wears a double-breasted white suit. He has a fancy curly moustache and round rimmed glasses and a ruby ring on his pinky finger. Fancy middle-aged guy. Drink in one hand, smoldering cigar in the other. Behind him we see two of his thugs in dark suits standing at ease.

3 Esmeralda/CAP: "HE SUB-CONTRACTED THE MOON STONE JOB OUT TO ME. AN EASY OPPORTUNITY FOR QUICK CASH.

4 Argus: ONCE YOU HAVE THE STONE, WE'LL MEET, AND I'LL PAY YOU. I BELIEVE TEN THOUSAND WAS YOUR PRICE?

Panel 3
Reverse angle. On Black Sparrow, hands on hips, looking sassy and kick ass.

5 Black Sparrow: I SAID **TWENTY**. IN CASH.

6 Black Sparrow: AND WORTH EVERY PENNY.

Panel 4
Small panel on Sparrow holding the Moon Stone up to her eyes and grinning at it. It's the size of a baseball, a curious combo of diamond and pearl and has a subtle glow to it.

7 Esmeralda/CAP: "AS YOU ALREADY KNOW, THE CAPER CAME OFF WITH LITTLE TROUBLE.

Panel 5
CUT TO: Establishing shot of the Plaza Hotel in NYC.

8 Esmeralda/CAP: "I RETIRED TO MY HOTEL SUITE TO BASK IN MY ACCOMPLISHMENT ...

Panel 6
CUT TO: Interior of Sparrow's hotel suite, although we don't see much of it in this panel. Close on a note she's holding in her hand, written in a woman's penmanship. The note reads: *Black Sparrow, Do not give the Moon Stone to Argus. I will pay you triple for it. Wait to be contacted. F.*

9 Esmeralda/CAP: " … AND FOUND A MESSAGE WAITING.

Panel 7
On Sparrow, still holding the note. A sly smirk on her face. She's interested.

10 Esmeralda/CAP: "I'LL ADMIT I LET **GREED** GET THE
                                    BETTER OF ME.

PAGE SEVEN

Panel 1
A wider shot of the hotel suite. Black Sparrow has stripped down to a black lacy
bra and panties which barely contain her. She is lounging on a divan or maybe an
easy chair with a foot rest. Next to her is a champagne bucket with an open bottle
in it. She tilts her head back as she drinks champagne from a glass. Two other
empty champagne bottles are visible on the floor. French doors leading out to a
balcony are open and we glimpse the skyline beyond. Resting on a small pillow
on a table is the moon stone. A slight subtle glow around it. The stone should be
as far from Sparrow as possible yet still pictured. Her holstered pistol hangs on
the back of the chair or corner of the divan or arm of the chair or whatever. As
long as it is visible and within easy reach. Big-ish panel to show off the goods.

1 Esmeralda/CAP: "I SKIPPED MY MEETING WITH ARGUS. I
                                    HAD THE MOON STONE AND COULD FIND
                                    HIM AGAIN IF I WISHED. SIMPLE ENOUGH TO
                                    MAKE UP SOME EXCUSE.

2 Esmeralda/CAP: "I WAS MORE INTERESTED IN THE
                                    MYSTERIOUS NOTE WRITER, SO I DID AS I
                                    WAS INSTRUCTED, AND WAITED TO BE
                                    CONTACTED.

3 Esmeralda/CAP: "AND WAITED …

Panel 2
Three guys bust through the door of the hotel suite. Two are huge thug types
with Tommy Guns. The third is a little weasel looking guy. All in gangster suits.
They bust in, the door swinging open on one hinge.

4 Esmeralda/CAP: "I WAITED TOO LONG. ARGUS'S MEN
                                    FOUND ME.

5 SFX: *KRASH*

6 Esmeralda/CAP: "I'M A **CAREFUL** WOMAN AND HAD
                                    CHECKED INTO THE HOTEL UNDER A
                                    FALSE NAME.

Panel 3
Closer on Esmarelda as she frantically twists to make a grab for her pistol.

7 Esmeralda/CAP: "BUT A LADY CAN NEVER BE **TOO**
                                    CAREFUL, I GUESS.

Panel 4
The two thugs cut loose with the Tommy guns, barrels belching fire at us. The little weasel guy is reaching between them to snatch the Moon Stone off the little pillow.

8 SFX:	*RATT TATT TATT TATT TATT TATT TATT*

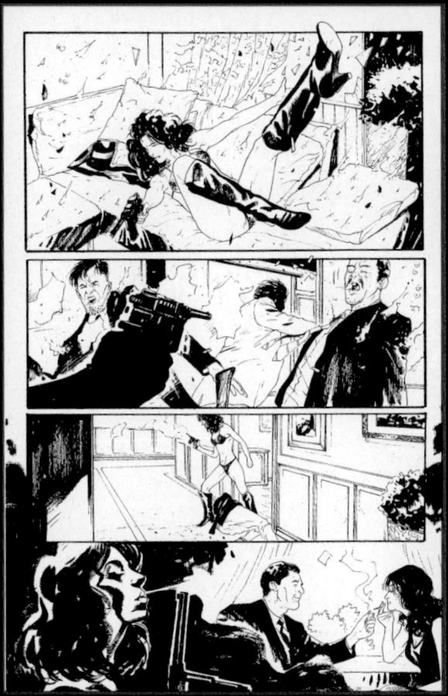

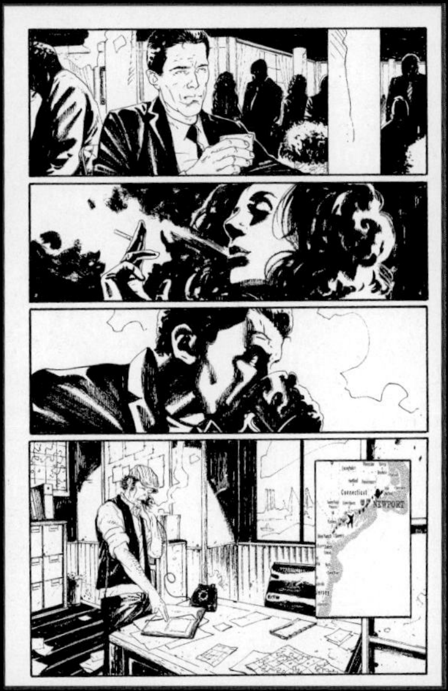

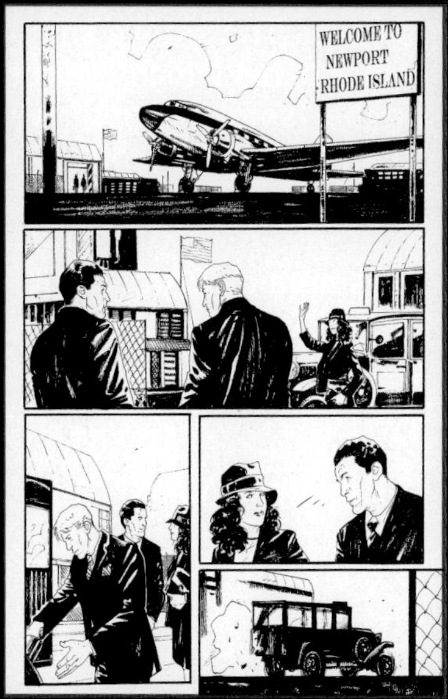
WELCOME TO
NEWPORT
RHODE ISLAND

PAGE EIGHT

Panel 1
Back on Sparrow. She is doing a sort of one-handed gymnast move to spring herself off the divan/chair. Her pistol is in her other hand. The Tommy gun bullets shred the divan/chair, stuffing flying all over the place. A few of the shots pass dangerously close to Sparrow. Feel free to shoot up whatever walls or windows are in the background.

1 SFX:	*RATT TATT TATT TATT TATT TATT*
2 Esmeralda/CAP:	"THEY WERE GOOD ENOUGH TO CATCH ME OFF GUARD.

Panel 2
Video game POV. Looking down Sparrow's pistol arm as she fires off several rounds at the thugs who contort and spray blood and die. Behind them we get a glimpse of the weasel guy escaping back through the door.

3 SFX:	*BLAMM BLAMM BLAMM BLAMM*
4 Esmeralda/CAP:	"**NOT** GOOD ENOUGH TO LIVE THROUGH IT.

Panel 3
CUT TO: The hallway outside the suite, but we're looking back inside at Sparrow standing over the bodies, smoke leaking from the barrel of her gun. She is looking out at us in the hall, but nobody is there.

5 Esmeralda/CAP: "BUT WITH THEIR LIVES, THEY PURCHASED
                          THE SECONDS NEEDED FOR THE THIRD
                          MAN TO SLIP AWAY WITH THE MOON
                          STONE.

Panels 4-5
Closer on Sparrow, lifting the barrel of the gun to her mouth to blow away the
smoke. The smoke she blows away drifts to the right and expands to form the
other panel which returns us to the present and our NORMAL COLOR PALETTE.
In the "smoke panel," we return to the present, a two-shot of Esmeralda and
Cranston at the table. She is leaning toward him with a cigarette in her mouth.
Cranston reaches to light it with a fancy gold lighter.

6 Esmeralda/CAP: "NOBODY STEALS FROM THE BLACK
                          SPARROW, SO I PLOTTED MY RETALIATION.
                          BUT I WAS IN A STRANGE CITY. I NEEDED
                          HELP.

7 Esmeralda/CAP: "I NEEDED THE SHADOW."

8 Cranston: SO ... TO RECAP ...

PAGE NINE

Panel 1
On Cranston, leaning back in his chair, holding his drink. The look on his face is
one of somebody who is amused by an especially precocious child.

1 Cranston: A SHADY CHARACTER HIRES YOU TO STEAL
                          THE MOON STONE. YOU THEN DOUBLE-
                          CROSS HIM. THEN THEY GET THE DROP ON
                          YOU AND STEAL IT BACK.

2 Cranston: AND NOW YOU'RE ASKING FOR HELP.

3 Cranston: FROM SOMEBODY WHO'S ALREADY TRIED
                          TO KILL YOU ONCE.

4 Cranston: DID I LEAVE ANYTHING OUT?

Panel 2
Close on Esmeralda. She's holding her cigarette close to her face, so the smoke
wafts up past her in a noir way. A sexy mysterious half smile on her face. Eyes
blazing with inner mystery and whatnot.

5 Esmeralda: JUST THIS.

6 Esmeralda: ALL I WANT IS WHAT I STOLE FAIR AND
                          SQUARE.

7 Esmeralda: BUT ARGUS HAS A NETWORK OF THIEVES
                          AND SMUGGLERS ALL UP AND DOWN THE

EAST COAST. YOU TURN A BLIND EYE TO **MY** MINOR INDISCRETIONS, AND I SERVE **HIM** AND HIS OPERATION UP ON A SILVER PLATTER.

Panel 3
Back on Cranston. He's turned his head somewhat away from us to sip his drink, but his eyes slide back to look right at us. He's considering.

8 Caption: FOR A LONG TIME NOW I'VE BEEN **TWO** MEN.

9 Caption: WELL, ONE MAN AND ONE **SHADOW** OF A MAN.

10 Caption: TOO OFTEN PEOPLE THINK THEY NEED THE ONE WHEN THEY REALLY NEED THE OTHER.

Panel 4
CUT TO: The office of a petty pencil pusher. Out of his window we can see the shipping yards and docks and boats. With one hand, he's talking on the phone. With the other hand, he has a finger on a spot to the open pages of a log book on his desk. In the background on the wall, maybe shipping and nautical charts, things like that.

11 Caption: THE BUREAUCRATS OF NEW YORK KNOW EVERYTHING REALLY. YOU JUST NEED TO KNOW WHICH ONE TO ASK. AND THE CLOUT TO GET AN ANSWER.

12 Caption: AFTER ESMERALDA GAVE ME THE NAME OF THE YACHT, THE REST WAS EASY.

13 Pencil Pusher: YES, I HAVE THE MANIFEST AND LOG FOR THE *THALIA* RIGHT HERE. SET SAIL FOR NEWPORT THIS MORNING.

14 Pencil Pusher: ONLY TOO HAPPY TO HELP, MR. CRANSTON.

Panel 5
Now we need an old-time B-movie map with dotted lines going from New York to Newport with a map icon of an airplane leading the dots.

14 Crofton: "BOSS, DO YOU **REALLY** NEED ME TO TELL YOU THIS IS A BAD IDEA?"

PAGE TEN

Panel 1
CUT TO: Newport Airfield. Day. Cranston's private plane is parked on the tarmac in the background. Cranston and MILES CROFTON walk toward us each carrying

a small suitcase. Their heads lean slightly toward one another as if talking low so nobody else can hear. Maybe we can work in a WELCOME TO NEWPORT, RHODE ISLAND sign someplace.

1 Cranston: YOU DON'T THINK I CAN TAKE CARE OF MYSELF, MILES?

2 Crofton: I THINK EVERY TIME YOU TURN YOUR BACK ON THAT BITCH YOU RISK GETTING A **BULLET** IN IT.

Panel 2
Now behind them. They are walking towards the fence/gate that leads away from the tarmac. Esmeralda is on the other side of the fence, waving over Cranston and Miles. Behind her is a parked Taxi. She is close enough that she is easily recognizable but far enough not to hear Miles and Cranston's conversation. Put her in an expensive, period-appropriate traveling dress. (Give her a very small purse or clutch and remember to show her with it occasionally.)

3 Cranston: MILES, I'M SURPRISED AT YOU. DON'T TELL ME YOU'RE THE SORT TO HOLD A GRUDGE.

4 Crofton: I LOST AN EYE OVER FRANCE. I STILL WON'T EAT A **KAISER** ROLL.

5 Esmeralda: OVER HERE, GENTLEMEN. I'VE SNAGGED US A TAXI.

Panel 3
At the Taxi. Miles is loading bags in the trunk while Cranston and Esmeralda converse.

6 Cranston: YOU CALLED THE MARINAS?

7 Esmeralda: YES. THE *THALIA* HASN'T PUT IN ANYWHERE.

8 Cranston: HELL. THIS MIGHT BE TOUGHER THAN I THOUGHT. THEY COULD BE ANCHORED **ANYWHERE** UP OR DOWN THE COAST.

Panel 4
Closer two shot. She looks up at Cranston with a knowing smirk.

9 Esmeralda: WHEN DID YOU BECOME SUCH A **PESSIMIST**, DARLING?

10 Cranston: I SUPPOSE **YOU** KNOW WHERE ARGUS AND HIS THUGS ARE?

11Esmeralda: NO. BUT I KNOW WHERE THEY'RE **GOING** TO BE.

Panel 5
A wide shot. Give us a little elevation. The taxi pulls away from the airfield and heads into town.

12 Esmeralda/CAP: "DRIVER, TAKE US TO TOURO PARK."

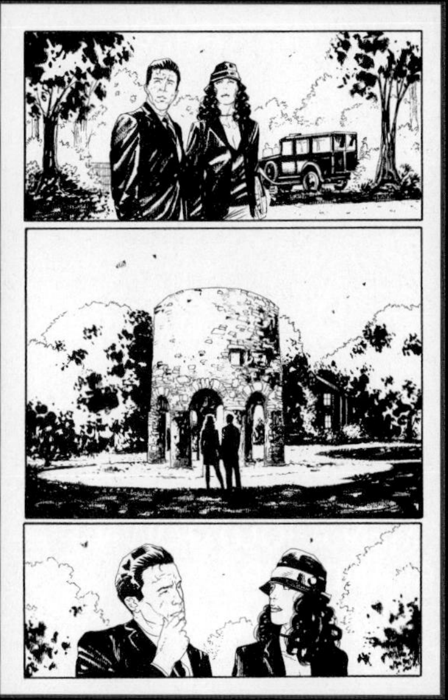

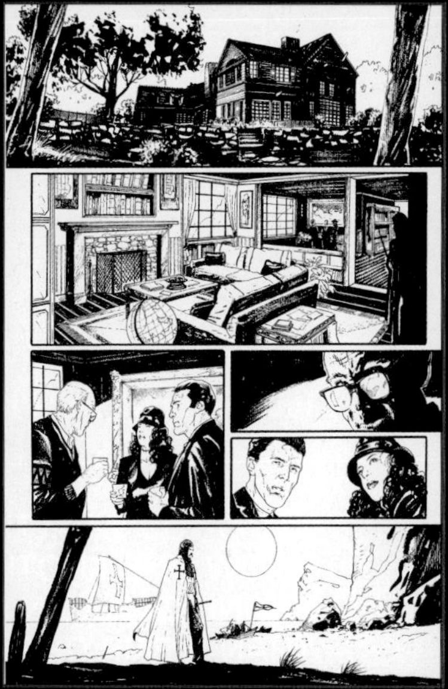

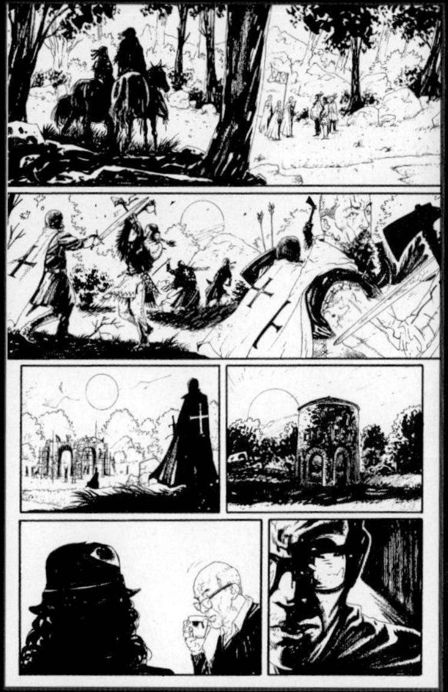

PAGE ELEVEN

Panel 3
Small panel, maybe an insert. Just a two-shot of Esmeralda's and Cranston's heads talking to each other.

6 Esmeralda:
I WAS READING ABOUT IT WHILE PLANNING THE HEIST. THE STONE AND THE TOWER ARE CONNECTED IN LOCAL HISTORY, BUT I CAN'T REMEMBER HOW.

7 Cranston:
HMMM. TIME TO MAKE ANOTHER PHONE CALL.

PAGE TWELVE

Panel 1
CUT TO: Establishing shot. A very nice colonial style house. Night. The home of professor Edgar Jenks.

1 Caption:
ALL OF US WEALTHY MEN ABOUT TOWN KNOW ONE ANOTHER, AND FOR US A PHONE CALL CAN BE MORE POWERFUL THAN A PAIR OF PISTOLS.

2 Jenks/CAP:
"YOU APPEAR TO BE A WELL-CONNECTED MAN, MR. CRANSTON."

Panel 2
CUT TO: The interior of the house – a study or den of some kind. There are a few chairs and shelves with leather bound books and a globe in the corner, maps and old paintings on the wall. Important: Show at least one window (if not in this panel then later). Professor Jenks is a man in his mid-sixties wearing a cardigan sweater over a white shirt and looking like an old professor. He's at a sideboard, pouring three glasses of sherry from a decanter for himself and his guests. Cranston and Esmeralda are there also.

3 Jenks:
I DON'T USUALLY SEE PEOPLE AFTER OFFICE HOURS, BUT MY DEAN TOLD ME ONE OF THE UNIVERSITY'S MORE INFLUENTIAL ALUMNI **SUGGESTED** I MAKE TIME FOR YOU.

4 Cranston:
WE APPRECIATE IT, PROFESSOR JENKS. WE WOULDN'T HAVE DRIVEN UP FROM NEWPORT IF IT WASN'T IMPORTANT.

Panel 3
New angle. They all have their drinks now. Cranston is sipping.

5 Esmeralda:
WE'VE BEEN TOLD YOU'RE THE MAN TO ASK WHEN IT COMES TO THE NEWPORT TOWER.

6 Jenks: IT'S THE REMAINS OF AN OLD WINDMILL. I
                                 HOPE THAT WAS WORTH THE DRIVE.

7 Esmeralda: BUT ISN'T THERE **ANOTHER** THEORY? ONE
                                 INVOLVING THE MOON STONE?

Panel 4
Close on Jenks. His head is turned as he brings his glass up for a drink. But he
pauses, eyes coming back to us, one eyebrow raised in semi-amusement.

8 Jenks: AHHH. SO YOU WANT TO HEAR ABOUT THE
                                 TEMPLARS.

Panel 5
Two-shot of Cranston and Esmeralda. Her eyes slide toward Cranston, comically
frowning.

9 Cranston: DO WE?

10 Esmeralda: **YES**. WE DO.

Panel 6
Jenks' face is all the way to the left of the panel. Spreading out to the right is the
beginning of the flashback story he's telling. This flashback is going back much
farther in time than the earlier flashback, so rather than just changing the color
palette, let's make the whole thing MONOCHROME. In the flashback part of the
panel, we see an old Templar knight on the beach with his sword and wearing
armor, the symbol of the Templars on his tunic:
https://upload.wikimedia.org/wikipedia/commons/1/10/Cross_Templar.svg
Behind him, more knights climb out of a beached longboat. Farther in the background we see the knights' anchored ship.

11 Jenks: THE LEGEND **CLAIMS** THAT AN
                                 EXPEDITION OF TEMPLAR KNIGHTS SET
                                 FOOT ON NORTH AMERICAN SHORES A
                                 HUNDRED YEARS BEFORE COLUMBUS.

PAGE THIRTEEN

Panel 1
Still in monochrome flashback mode. A scene on the edge of a forest with the
Knights peacefully meeting with a group of Indians.

1 Jenks/CAP: "THE STORY GOES THAT THEY MET WITH A
                                 NUMBER OF INDIAN TRIBES. SOME WERE
                                 FRIENDLY.

Panel 2
Continue flashback. CUT TO: A battle scene between the Knights and a different
tribe of Indians. Change their clothing or something to show they are a different
tribe. NOTE: Neither tribe should be Mohawk. That tribe comes later. Swords
and spears and whatnot.

2 Jenks/CAP: "OTHER TRIBES ... NOT SO MUCH.

Panel 3
Continue flashback. CUT TO: the site that would later be Touro Park but is now
just woods around a clearing. In the middle of the clearing, the construction of
the Newport Tower is underway. It is maybe two-thirds finished and easily recognizable. Under the supervision of the knights, Indian laborers are carrying stones
to the construction site. The lead knight stands in the foreground consulting a
map he's unrolled and is holding in front of him.

3 Jenks/CAP: "ARMCHAIR HISTORIANS ARGUE ABOUT
                                      WHAT THE TEMPLARS' MISSION TO
                                      AMERICA MIGHT HAVE BEEN. THEY ALL
                                      SEEM FARFETCHED TO ME.

4 Jenks/CAP: "BUT MOST AGREE THE VISITORS BUILT
                                      THE TOWER AS A MARKER, A MESSAGE
                                      FOR TEMPLARS WHO MIGHT COME AFTER
                                      THEM.

Panel 4
Continue flashback. Pull back for a view of the finished tower, but let's add some
kind of simple, medieval looking roof. Something pointy and maybe simple old
style wooden shingles. The setting sun is shining its light into the square window
of the tower.

5 Jenks/CAP: "BUT THIS WE DO KNOW. THE TOWER'S
                                      SMALLER WINDOWS LINE UP WITH
                                      SIGNIFICANT ASTRONOMICAL BODIES.
                                      CREATING SOME KIND OF MAP POSSIBLY.

6 Jenks/CAP: "FURTHERMORE, WHEN THE SUN SHINES
                                      THROUGH THE WEST WINDOW AT THE
                                      SUMMER SOLSTIC, THE BEAM TARGETS A
                                      NICHE ON THE OPPOSING WALL WITHIN.

7 Jenks/CAP: "SOME THEORIZE A SORT OF REFLECTING
                                      DEVICE IN THE NICHE. WHO KNOWS?"

Panel 5
End Flashback. CUT TO: Professor Jenks' study. He is pouring himself another
sherry. Esmeralda is visible over his shoulder.

8 Esmeralda: OR A MOON STONE PERHAPS?

9 Jenks: MY DEAR GIRL, YOU CAN'T SHINE
                                      SUNLIGHT ON A MOON STONE. HOW
                                      INELOQUENT. NO NO NO ...

Panel 6
Small panel, very tight on Jenk's face. He has a kind of half-creepy grin on his
face like he's suddenly enjoying telling this outrageous story.

10 Jenks: YOU'D NEED MOONLIGHT.

PAGE FOURTEEN

Panel 1
Two-shot of Cranston and Esmeralda. Esmeralda looks very interested and attentive. Cranston's head is down slightly. His eyes are closed tight and his pinching the bridge of his nose between thumb and forefinger in a gesture of impatience.

1 Cranston: AND **WHY** IS THIS IMPORTANT?

Panel 2
Back on Jenks. Pouring yet another glass of sherry for himself. He is getting a little rosy cheeked.

2 Jenks: IT'S **NOT** IMPORTANT. IT'S ALL **BUNK**.

3 Jenks: THE STONE IS SUPPOSED TO AMPLIFY AND REFLECT MOONLIGHT, REVEALING ... **SOMETHING**. A MESSAGE. A TREASURE MAP. ALL PURE FANTASY.

4 Jenks(small):   I SUPPOSE **ONE** MORE GLASS WOULDN'T HURT ...

Panel 3
On Esmeralda.

5 Esmeralda: FORGIVE ME, PROFESSOR, BUT YOU SEEM TO KNOW **A LOT** ABOUT THESE LEGENDS FOR SOMEONE WHO DOESN'T BELIEVE THEM.

Panel 4
Wide shot of the room. Let's put some distance between Jenks and the others. Cranston and Esmeralda watch as Jenks moves across the room to gesture to a framed map hanging on the wall next to a large window. (More about the map later.)

6 Jenks:	IN FACT, I'M WRITING A BOOK DEBUNKING A MYRIAD OF RHODE ISLAND FOLK TALES AND LEGENDS. THE LOCAL HISTORICAL SOCIETY IS SPONSORING ME.

7 Jenks:	THEY GAVE ME THIS MAP AS A TOKEN OF ESTEEM.

Panel 5
On the framed map. We see Jenks' hand touching the corner of the frame as if absently straitening it. The map itself looks old, maybe on parchment. A river, a forest, some hills, but nothing labeled like a town. In the upper part of the map and off to the right is a red Templar cross ... marking the spot!

8 Jenks/Off:	IT DATES BACK TO 1770 AND WAS RECENTLY DISCOVERED AT AN ESTATE SALE. AS YOU CAN SEE, THERE ARE NO TOWNS OR LANDMARKS, SO IT'S REALLY QUITE USELESS.

9 Jenks/Off:	BUT IT HAS THE MARK OF THE **TEMPLAR** ON IT, AND THE SOCIETY THOUGHT I MIGHT BE AMUSED.

Panel 6
Jenks turns back to face us, the map still visible over his shoulder and also some of the big window to the side.

10 Jenks:	A NUMBER OF PEOPLE HAVE OFFERED TO BUY IT, BUT AS I TOLD THE YOUNG GENTLEMAN THIS AFTERNOON, I HAVE **NO** INTENTION OF SELLING. GROWN RATHER FOND OF IT ACTUALLY.

PAGE FIFTEEN

Panel 1
On Cranston and Esmeralda suddenly looking interested and concerned.

1 Cranston:	SOMEBODY **ELSE**?

2 Esmeralda:	WHO WAS IT?

Panel 2
Back on Jenks. He is standing somewhat in front of the window now but NOT blocking the window. We should still be able to see what's out there. At the moment it's just the blur of a street lamp across the road.

3 Jenks:	DIDN'T I MENTION HIM? HOW SILLY OF ME. I THOUGHT MAYBE HE WAS WITH YOU IN SOME WAY SINCE HE WAS **ALSO** ASKING ABOUT THE TEMPLARS.

Panel 3
Same shot, but we see the dark, vague blur of somebody in the window. Jenks is gesturing as he talks, spilling a little sherry from his glass – but not TOO comically.

4 Jenks: A YOUNG INDIAN FELLOW FROM ONE OF THE NEARBY TRIBES, I THINK.

5 Jenks: FUNNY THING, REALLY, SINCE THE MOON STONE LEGEND HAS A **CONNECTION** BETWEEN THE TEMPLARS AND A LOCAL TRIBE OF –

Panel 4
Same shot. The silhouette in the window is much more clearly now the outline of a large dude. We get the smallest hint of the man's face in the flash of muzzle fire from the gunshot. The gunshot punches a hole in the glass and the bullet comes out of Jenks's chest with a spray of blood. Jenks's eyes go wide and his mouth falls open.

6 SFX: *BLAMM*

Panel 5
Floor level. In the foreground, Jenks' dead body falls, the side of his face hitting the floor hard, his eyes rolling up. In the background, Cranston and Esmeralda look on with alarm.

7 SFX: *FLIMP*

8 Esmeralda: **OH, $#!+!!**

PAGE SIXTEEN

Panel 1
BIG panel. A REALLY BIG guy comes flying through the window, scattering glass and basically making a hell of an entrance. He is a Mohawk Indian and his name is Akash. He wears a cheap brown tweed-ish sports jacket and slacks. But no tie. Instead his collar is open, revealing a bit of Indian jewelry, some kind of choker maybe. He also has an earring in one ear, a small dream-catcher. His face looks tough and rugged. He has the tribal Mohawk haircut, but not a crazy punk rocker Mohawk, but rather a more subdued Native American version. He holds a revolver in one hand. Again, big panel.

1 SFX: *KRASH*

Panel 2
Now that he's inside, we see what Akash wants. He's grabbing the map off the wall with one hand, blazing away with the revolver with the other hand. Muzzle flashes all dramatic and whatnot.

2 SFX: *BLAMM BLAMM*

Panel 3
Pan around to see Cranston diving behind a chair. I don't know if there is a cool way to do this, but try not to make him look too clumsy or anything. A bullet flies but misses him ... maybe breaks a lamp or something.

3 SFX: *BLAMM*

PAGE SEVENTEEN

Panel 1
On Esmeralda. She flinches and dodges to the side a step as bullets fly past her and wreck whatever is behind her. As she dodges, she reaches into her purse/clutch. Her face looks hard and pissed.

1 SFX: *BLAMM BLAMM*

2 Esmeralda: **BASTARDO!**

Panel 2
Small panel. Maybe an insert of the above. Your call. Close on Esmeralda's hand coming out of the purse/clutch with this single-shot Derringer: http://www.rock-islandauction.com/photos/51/p_standard/VLP41-L-F2C-H.jpg
She is cocking back the hammer with a thumb as she pulls it out.

3 SFX: ka-klik

Panel 3
Pull out for wider shot of Esmeralda. Her arm is straight out, aiming the Derringer. A little burp of fire coming out the barrel as she squeezes the trigger. She has a slight snarl on her face, eyes narrow.

4 Esmeralda: HOLD STILL FOR MAMA, *HIJO DE PERRA*!

5 SFX: *POP*

Panel 4
Back on Akash. He's halfway back out the window with the framed map under his arm. Esmeralda's shot hits him on top of his shoulder with a spray of blood. His face grimaces in pain.

6 Akash: >GAH!<

Panel 5
CUT TO: Outside. In the foreground, Akash races past us on a motorcycle. Maybe something like: http://www.bikeexif.com/wp-content/uploads/2012/08/crocker-motorcycle.jpg
In the back ground, we see Esmeralda and Cranston at the window, watching him go.

7 SFX: VVVVRRROOOOOOMMM

8 Esmeralda: HE'S GETTING AWAY!

9 Cranston: NEVER MIND. WE KNOW WHERE HE'LL GO.

Panel 6
Small panel. Tight on Cranston's face. He's expression is hard, eyes intense.

10 Caption: EVENTUALLY, THERE COMES A TIME WHEN
                                 THE MAN HAS TO SIT, AND **THE SHADOW**
                                 COMES IN OFF THE BENCH.

PAGE EIGHTEEN

Okay, I want the first five panels on this page to be a quick back and forth montage kinda thing.

Panel 1
CUT TO: The interior of a hotel room, but don't worry about that. The focus is not on the room. Shadow puts on his trademark coat. But we don't see his face. We just focus on his hands buckling his trench coat belt or whatever it's called.

1 Caption: I'LL LEVEL WITH YOU. I'M NERVOUS
                                 EVERY TIME, JUST FOR A SPLIT-SECOND.
                                 NOT MUCH.

Panel 2
CUT TO: Another room ... again the room doesn't matter. Just letting you know it's a different location. Black Sparrow pulls on one of her boots. Again, just focus on the leg and hands and boots.

Panel 3
CUT TO: A belt to shoulders view of Shadow. One of his pistols is in the holster. He's holding the other pistol and slapping in a fresh magazine with tho palm of his hand.

2 SFX: *CHIK*

3 Caption: THE NOTION THAT THE MAN ISN'T GOOD
ENOUGH RUBS ME THE WRONG WAY.

Panel 4
CUTTO: On Black Sparrow's hands as she fastens her gun belt. Her coiled whip
hangs from the belt also.

Panel 5
CUT TO: Shadow puts on his hat. But his head is down. We don't see the face.

4 Caption: BUT WHEN CRANSTON TAKES YIELDS,
AND I'M FULLY **HIM**, THE MAN IN THE HAT,
I CAN FEEL IT'S RIGHT. I WONDER HOW I
COULD EVER BE SATISFIED JUST BEING A
GLIB, GIN-SWILLING MAN ABOUT TOWN.

Panel 6
CUT TO: A rooftop. Night. Black Sparrow is partially turned away from us, but
turns back to smile warmly at us, like she's been waiting for us to come along.

5 Caption: AND **THAT** THOUGHT MAKES ME NERVOUS
TOO.

6 Black Sparrow: **THERE** YOU ARE, DARLING.

7 Black Sparrow: SUCH A BAD MAN TO KEEP A LADY WAITING.

PAGE NINETEEN

Panel 1
CUT TO: A rooftop in Newport. Night. This is a VERY BIG panel. The payoff
we've been waiting for. Two cool costumes ready for action. The moon is big
and full and low and close in the background. Shadow stands tall and proud and
kick-ass looking. Black Sparrow looks sleek and graceful and sexy in her costume.
She is moving close to Shadow, her hand coming up like she is about to caress
his face.

1 Black Sparrow: **THIS** IS HOW IT SHOULD BE. THE TWO OF
US **TOGETHER**. THE LORD AND LADY OF
THE NIGHT.

2 Black Sparrow: DON'T TELL ME THAT BIT OF FLUFF I
FOUND IN YOUR KITCHEN COULD EVER
MAKE YOU HAPPY LIKE I COULD.

Panel 2
Closer two-shot of Shadow and Sparrow. Shadow grabs the wrist of the hand
Sparrow was about to caress him with. (Wow. What a lousy sentence.) He twists
slightly as he moves her hand away from his face. She grimaces, showing teeth,
eyes flashing anger.

3 Shadow:	MY HAPPINESS IS NONE OF **YOUR** CONCERN. YOU AND I WILL SETTLE ACCOUNTS SOON ENOUGH.
4 Caption:	IT WAS ALWAYS **CRANSTON** WHO WAS THE FLIRT, THE PLAYBOY, QUICK WITH A WINK AND A QUIP.
5 Caption:	**THE SHADOW** IS MORE DIRECT. LESS FORGIVING. CLARITY OF PURPOSE IS HIS STRENGTH.

Panel 3
On Black Sparrow. She's pulling back, rubbing her wrist, mouth tight, eyes narrow.

| 6 Caption: | AND YET A SMALL, DARK , UGLY PART OF ME WORRIES SHE'S RIGHT. |
| 7 Akash/CAP: | "GUSTAV ARGUS, SHOW YOURSELF!" |

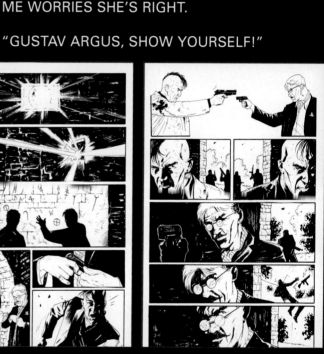

PAGE TWENTY

Panel 1
CUT TO: The Newport Tower. We're outside the tower, but we can see the dark figures of two men inside. Off to the side, we see Akash's parked motorcycle. One of the dark figures is Akash shaped. The other is Gustav Argus shaped.

| 1 Argus: | RIGHT HERE, AKASH. AND **ALONE** AS INSTRUCTED. |
| 2 Akash: | YOU BROUGHT THE STONE? |

Panel 2
CUT TO: Within the tower. It's night, but a combination of street lamps and moon-

light makes it easy enough to see what's going on. On Argus. He's holding up a small canvas bag.

3 Argus: YOU GET THE MOON STONE, **IF** YOU HAVE THE MONEY. THIS LITTLE ITEM WAS **NOT** AS EASY TO COME BY AS PREDICTED.

4 Argus: YOU LOOK LIKE **HELL**, AKASH. WHAT HAPPENED?

Panel 3
On Akash. He looks sweaty and a bit green, lost a lot of blood. He has one hand grasping his shot shoulder, but the bloodstain on his shirt and jacket is clearly visible. He's in bad shape. His other hand is out, palm up. He wants the Moon Stone.

5 Akash: NEVER MIND ... **ME**. I'M F-FINE.

6 Akash: JUST HAND OVER ... THE DAMN ... STONE. I NEED TO M-MAKE SURE IT'S ... THE REAL THING.

Panel 4
Two-shot. Argus hands the stone to Akash.

7 Argus: TWO OF MY MEN **DIED** GETTING THIS THING. I'D LIKE TO KNOW WHY IT'S SO IMPORTANT.

8 Akash: I'LL **SHOW** YOU.

Panel 5
There is a large stone block under a niche high up on the wall. Sorta like an altar but nothing too garish. There is no actual thing in the real tower, so keep it low key. Anyway ... Akash has climbed up on this block so he can reach over his head to slide the Moon Stone into the niche.

9 Akash: CENTURIES AGO, THE TEMPLARS MADE A PROMISE TO MY PEOPLE.

10 Akash: THE MOON STONE IS THE KEY TO **UNLOCKING** THAT PROMISE.

PAGE TWENTY-ONE

Panel 1
CUT TO: Outside. A wide shot. Far enough back to see the moon shining down into the little window of the tower.

1 Akash/CAP: "WHEN THE MOON BEAMS HIT THE STONE ..."

Panel 2
CUT TO: Back inside the Tower. The moon beams come through the square win-

dow and zap across the interior of the tower to hit the Moon Stone in the niche. Smaller beams reflect out from the stone to fill the room.

2 Akash/Off: ... IT REFLECTS, REDIRECTS, AND BATHES THE INTERIOR OF THE TOWER IN MOONLIGHT.

Panel 3
Behind Argus and Akash. They are both looking up to what is happing high up on the side of the tower wall. Glowing runes are becoming visible in the wash of moonlight. Use some of these random symbols: http://2.bp.blogspot.com/-Jg7SjUKdM_U/TlwSfk2NUdl/AAAAAAAAGag/7dNK3h883QE/s1600/phoenician-runes.jpg
Try to give the impression that the runes are just beginning to form and there are more that we don't see continuing to form beyond this panel.

3 Akash: UP THERE!

4 Akash: THE BUILDERS WORKED **SHARDS** OF MOON STONE INTO THE MUNDANE STONEWORK TO CATCH THE LIGHT AND REVEAL THE MESSAGE.

Panel 4
Bring us around the front of the two men. We're looking at Akash. He's scribbling frantically in the notebook, his eyes still looking up. He is smiling weakly. He's still in a bad way but happy to be so close to solving the mystery. Over his shoulder, we see Argus also still looking up at the runes, his mouth hanging open in surprise.

5 Akash: YES, YES ... AT LAST, THE **FINAL** PIECE OF THE PUZZLE.

6 Argus: MY GOD. IT'S SOME SORT OF **TREASURE** MAP, ISN'T IT?

7 Akash: SOMETHING LIKE THAT, YES.

Panel 5
Close on Argus's hand coming out of his jacket with a small, silver automatic pistol. Maybe something like:
http://1.bp.blogspot.com/_6PbD56mSkS8/TlgWTWmt9WI/AAAAAAAABTQ/HJEInMFstPQ/s1600/europellets2.jpg

8 Argus/Off: THAT'S ALL I NEEDED TO KNOW.

Panel 6
Akash is turning, seeing what Argus is doing. He drops the notepad and pencil and fumbles frantically to pull his own revolver.

9 Akash: WHAT THE – ?!

Panel 1
Akash and Argus face each other, arms straight out, guns in each other's faces.
Akash is still looking shaky but he manages to keep his revolver up.

1 Akash: OKAY, IF **YOU** PULL THE TRIGGER, THEN SO
                                  DO I?

2 Akash: I THINK WE'RE AT A **STALEMATE**, FRIEND.

3 Argus: I SUPPOSE THAT WOULD BE TRUE. EXCEPT
                                  FOR ONE THING.

Panel 2
Looking down Argus's gun arm at Akash, but we ease the camera a bit to the left
to see two thugs suddenly appear in on e of the tower's archways. Akash's eyes
slide to the left. One thug holds a pistol. The other has a pump shotgun and is
pumping in a shell.

4 Argus: I HAVE MORE TRIGGERS TO PULL THAN
                                  YOU DO.

5 SFX: *SHLUK-SHLAK*

Panel 3
Same shot, but now we ease the camera a bit to the right. Two more thugs full
the archway on that side, one with a pistol and one with a Tommy Gun. Akash's
eyes slide that way now. His facial expression indicates he is realizing he might
be fucked.

5 Argus: WHEN THE BLACK SPARROW DOUBLE-
                                  CROSSED ME, I **SUSPECTED** THERE MIGHT
                                  BE MORE TO THE STORY.

Panel 4
On Argus, pointing the gun at us. Over his shoulder we see another thug just out-
side of one of the other archways. (So yeah, we get that surrounded feeling now.)
The thug holds another Tommy Gun.

6 Argus: NOW, **I'LL** TAKE THE STONE AND
                                  WHATEVER ELSE I NEED TO FIND THIS
                                  TREASURE.

7 Argus: IF I WERE **YOU**, AKASH, I'D DROP THE GUN
                                  AND FIGURE OUT A WAY TO BE USEFUL.

Panel 5
Same shot, but now Argus is half-shrugging and smirking at us as he still points
the gun at us. In the background, we see the thug drop his Tommy Gun as a
length bullwhip shoots down from above and wraps around his neck. The thugs

hands come up to uselessly paw at the whip around his neck.

8 Argus: MAYBE IF YOU **TRANSLATE** THESE SCRIBBLES FOR ME, I COULD SEE MY WAY CLEAR TO PATCH YOU UP. MAYBE EVEN CUT YOU IN FOR A TOKEN PERCENTAGE OF WHATEVER WE FIND.

9 Thug(small): *>ACK<*

Panel 6
Same shot as above, but Argus's eyes go wide as he starts to turn his head. We only see the thugs legs now as he's yanked up out of sight.

10 Thug/Off: *>AAIIIIEEEEE<*

11 Argus: WHAT THE F—?!

PAGE TWENTY-THREE

Panel 1
BIG, garish panel! The Shadow drops down from above, his cape spread out and looking awesome, fire in his eyes. He lands in between Argus and Akash, bringing down a pistol butt on the back of each of their skulls, knocking them for a loop.

1 SFX: *WHAP*

2 Argus: *>NNGGHH<*

3 Akash: *>UHMMPH<*

Note: Next couple of pages are going to be action heavy. We have an interesting space here with this tower: http://news.beloblog.com/ProJo_Blogs/architecture-hereandthere/egantower.jpg

Being "inside" the tower and "outside" the tower is often a matter of just a few steps. So some panels could be outside the tower looking in, or inside looking out. I'll suggest the basics as we go along, but feel free to stage things as you think will make them look the most super-fly awesome. However you stage things, just make sure Black Sparrow and Shadow are both INSIDE the tower by the top of page 25.

Panel 2
The other thug with a Tommy Gun sprays the interior of the tower with bullets, and Shadow dives underneath the shots, a few maybe piercing his fluttering cape. Let's wash the interior of the tower in muzzle flash.

4 SFX: *RATT-TATT-TATT-TATT-TATT-TATT-TATT*

Panel 3
Shadow comes up on one knee and blazes away at the thug with both of his automatics. Fire spouting from the barrels. The thug contorts and sprays blood.

5 SFX: *BLAMM BLAMM BLAMM BLAMM*

Panel 4
The thug with the shotgun lifts it and aims.

6 Thug: TRY A FACE FULL OF **BUCKSHOT**, YOU SON
                                OF A –

PAGE TWENTY-FOUR

Panel 1
The bullwhip wraps around the barrel of the shotgun, yanking it up as it goes off. The thug looks surprised.

1 SFX: *THIP-THIP*

2 SFX: *POOM*

Panel 2
On Black Sparrow. With one hand she is yanking back strongly on the whip. Her other hand is out to catch the shotgun flying toward her.

3 Black Sparrow: THAT LOOKS **FUN**. MIND IF I TRY?

Panel 3
Small panel, close on Sparrow's hands pumping another shell into the shotgun.

4 SFX: SHLUK-SHLAK

Panel 4
Black Sparrow blasts the guy to hell with the shotgun. Blood!

5 SFX: *POOM*

Panel 5
Another small panel of her pumping in a new shell, the old one ejecting. These "pump in a shell" panels can be very small or inserts or whatever. Just trying to suggest a quick cinematic rhythm of her firing, pumping, firing, etc.

6 SFX: *SHLUK-SHLAK*

Panel 6
She whips the shotgun around to blast another thug coming at her from a different direction.

7 SFX: **POOM**

PAGE TWENTY-FIVE

Panel 1
Another very small "pumping a shell" panel.

1 SFX: *SHLUK-SHLAK*

Panel 2
Wide shot. The final thug flying through the air, trailing an arc of blood.

2 SFX: **POOM**

Panel 3
On Black Sparrow. She's looking down at the shotgun in her hands with a grin. Smoke leaks from the barrel. (Reminder, we should be inside the Tower by now.)

3 Black Sparrow: OH MY. I DO BELIEVE I NEED TO ADD ONE
                             OF **THESE** TO MY CHRISTMAS LIST.

Panel 4
Behind her now. She turns to look at us over her shoulder, the grin dropping from her face. A gloved hand holding an automatic comes in from the side of the panel to point at her head. The Shadow's hand and one of his pistols. He thumbs back the pistol's hammer. All we see of the Shadow is the hand and the gun.

4 SFX: *ka-klik*

Panel 5
Reverse angle. Looking at Shadow, pointing his pistol at us and looking badass.

5 Shadow: NICE SHOOTING.

6 Shadow: NOW DROP IT.

PAGE TWENTY-SIX

Panel 1
They face each other, Black Sparrow casually tossing aside the shotgun. He's still pointing a pistol at her.

1 Black Sparrow: WHAT IS THIS? I THOUGHT WE HAD AN AGREEMENT.

2 Shadow: YOU **PROPOSED** AN AGREEMENT. I LET YOU THINK WHAT YOU WANTED.

3 Shadow: AFTER ALL YOU'VE DONE, YOU DON'T REALLY THINK I'LL LET YOU JUST WALK AWAY AND –

Panel 2
A smoke grenade comes flying though the Tower's little square window, trialing gray smoke. Something like: http://gunshowgoods.com/zencart/images/M18%20Smoke%20Grenade.JPG

4 SFX: *FSSSSSSSS*

Panel 3
The grenade lands between Sparrow and Shadow. Smoke rising around them. Shadow looks down at the grenade, distracted for a second.

5 SFX: *FSSSSSSS*

Panel 4
Zoom in a bit. Sparrow knocks the gun out of Shadow's hand with a backhand swipe. Smoke is thicker.

6 SFX: *SWAP*

7 Caption: IT'S ONLY A **SECOND'S** DISTRACTION.

Panel 5
Now the smoke is so thick that we only see silhouettes, although we can clearly see Sparrow doing a martial arts leg sweep on Shadow, upending him.

8 Caption: AN **ETERNITY** FOR SOMEONE WITH HER SKILLS.

9 SFX: *SWUP*

Panel 6
Small panel. Amid the smoke, Sparrow's hand reaches down to pluck Akash's notebook from the ground.

PAGE TWENTY-SEVEN

Panel 1
On Shadow as he emerges from the Tower, both guns up and ready, smoke billowing out around him. He's turning his head side-to-side, obviously searching for Sparrow.

1 Caption: THE BOX SCORE WILL READ A **WIN** FOR THE SHADOW.

Panel 2
CUT TO: On an unconscious Akash. The smoke is clearing.

2 Caption: MURDERER APPREHENDED.

Panel 3
CUT TO: On an unconscious Argus. Smoke almost completely gone now

3 Caption: SMUGGLER FOILED.

Panel 4
CUT TO: The glowing moon stone in the niche. No smoke at all now.
4 Caption: STOLEN PROPERTY RECOVERED.

Panel 5
CUT TO: The roof of a nearby building. Maybe 5 or 6 stories up. We are standing behind Black Sparrow, looking down with her at the tower where there is now an ambulance parked and 3-4 police cars, lights blinking, etc.

5 Caption: SO WHY DO I HEAR FATE LAUGHING AT ME AGAIN?

6 Miss Fury/Off: I SENT YOU A LETTER ASKING YOU TO WAIT. BUT I **GUESS** I DON'T BLAME YOU FOR BEING IMPATIENT.

Note: This page is basically a Splash. But the first and third panels can be very small inserts.

Panel 1
Very close on Sparrow, turning to look at us, surprised.

1 Sparrow: WHAT --?

2 Sparrow: WHO ARE **YOU**?

Panel 2
BIG BIG panel ... basically a splash. We want to show both Miss Fury and Black Sparrow in all their sexy bad-ass splendor. So arrange them on the rooftop, facing each other in whatever way is super cool.

3 Miss Fury: HOPE YOU DON'T MIND THAT I TOSSED
THAT LITTLE SMOKE BOMB IN THERE, BUT
IT LOOKED LIKE YOU WERE IN A TIGHT
SPOT.

4 Miss Fury: OH, THEY CALL ME **MISS FURY** BY THE
WAY.

Panel 3
Small insert panel down in the bottom right corner. On a wildly grinning Miss Fury.

5 Miss Fury: AND I HAVE A BUSINESS PROPOSITION
                                      THAT **MIGHT** INTEREST YOU.

To be continued ...

NOIR
ARTIST SKETCHES
by ANDREA MUTTI

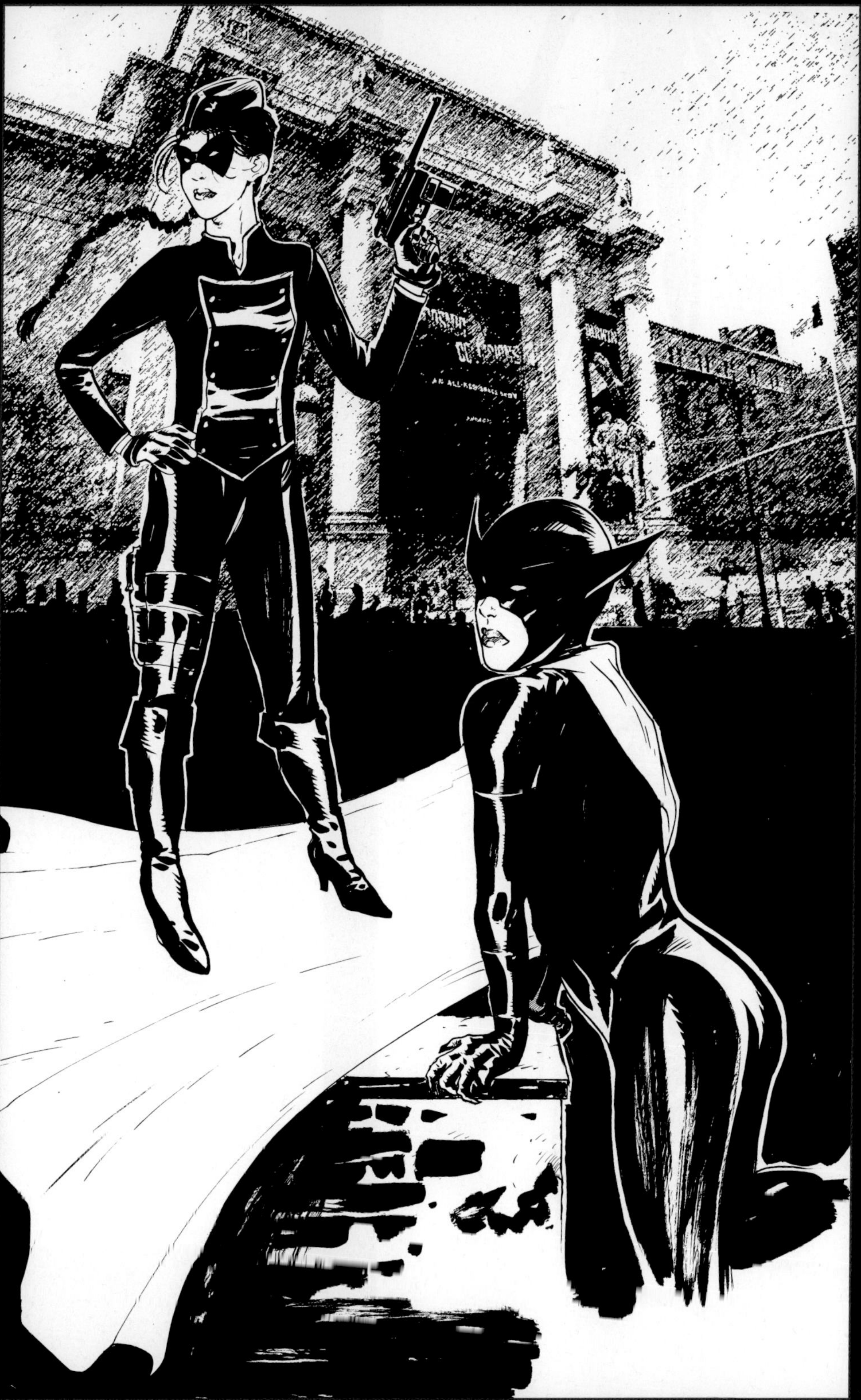

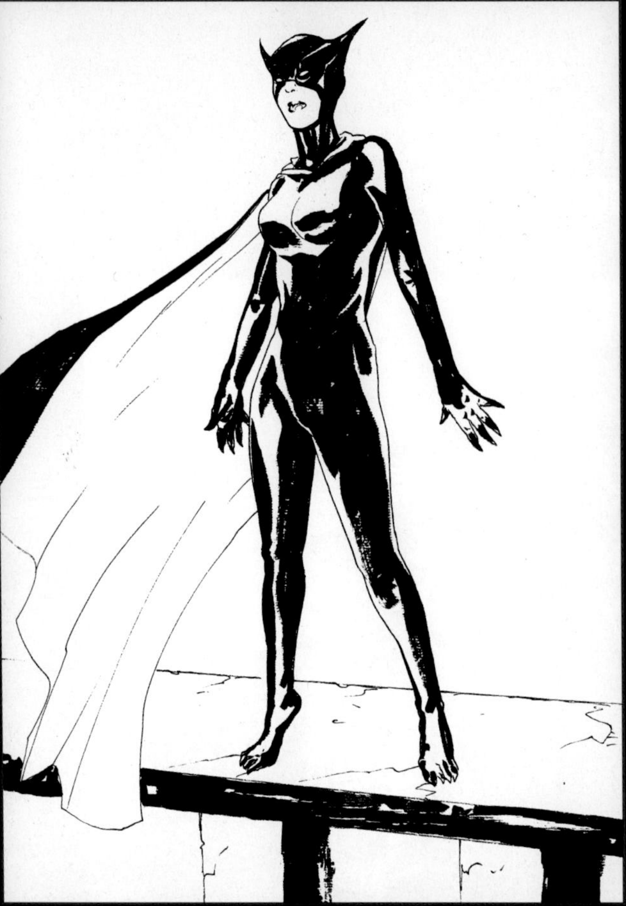

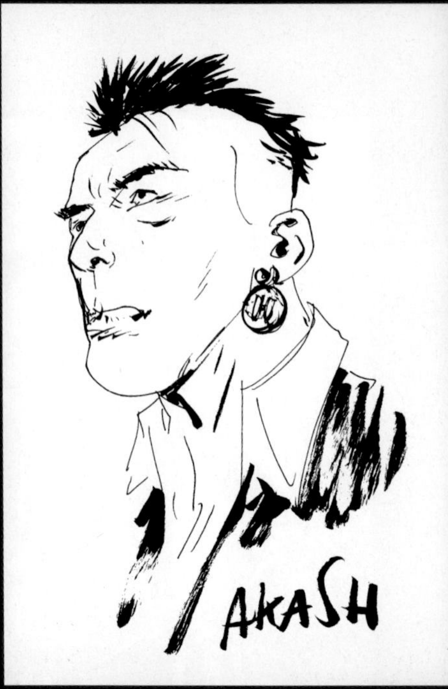
AKASH

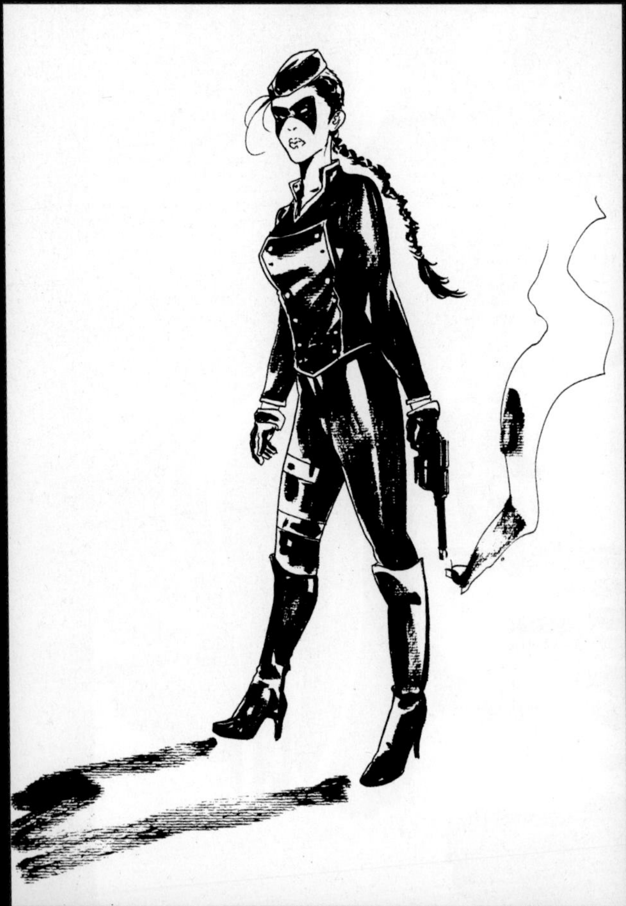

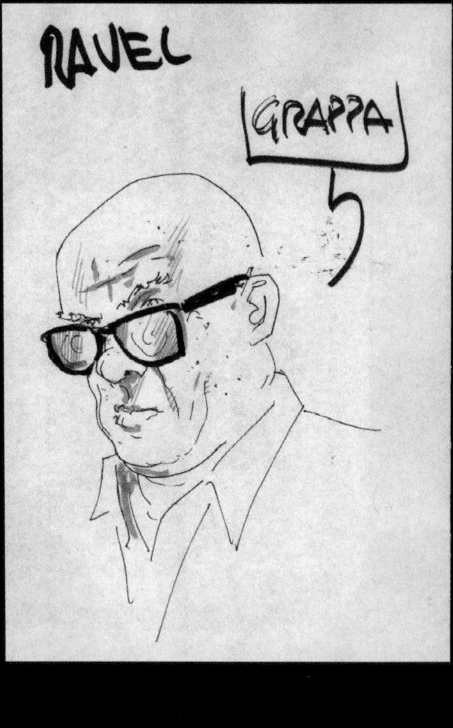
RAVEL
GRAPPA

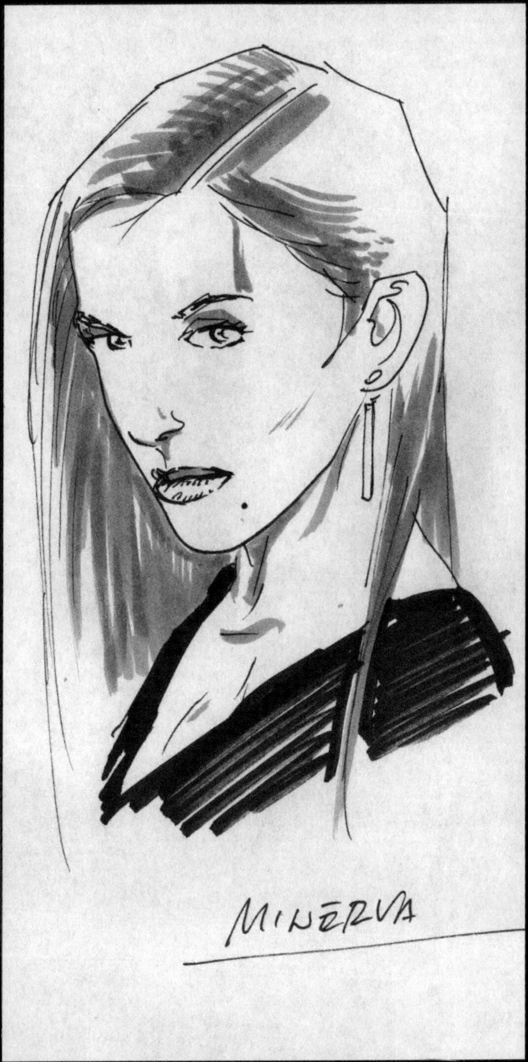
MINERVA

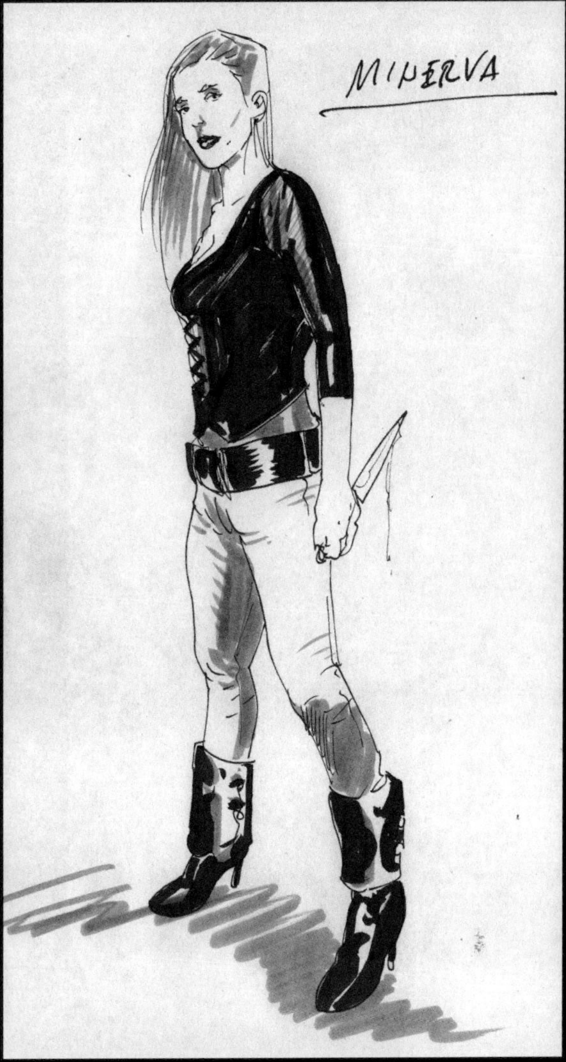
MINERVA

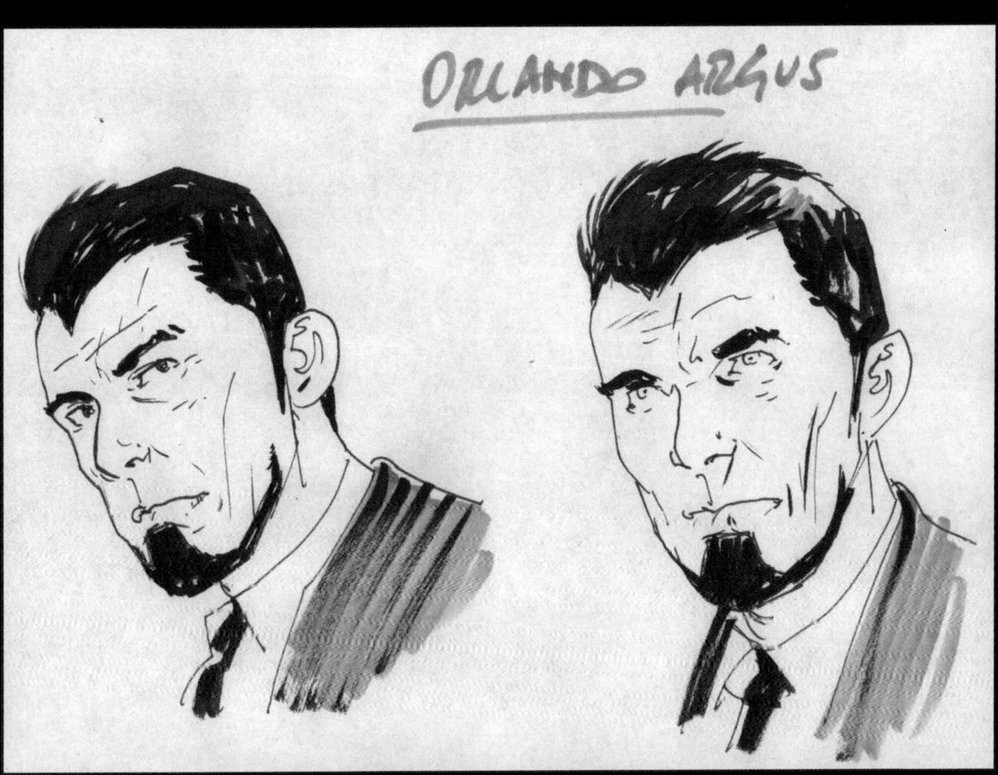
ORLANDO ARGUS

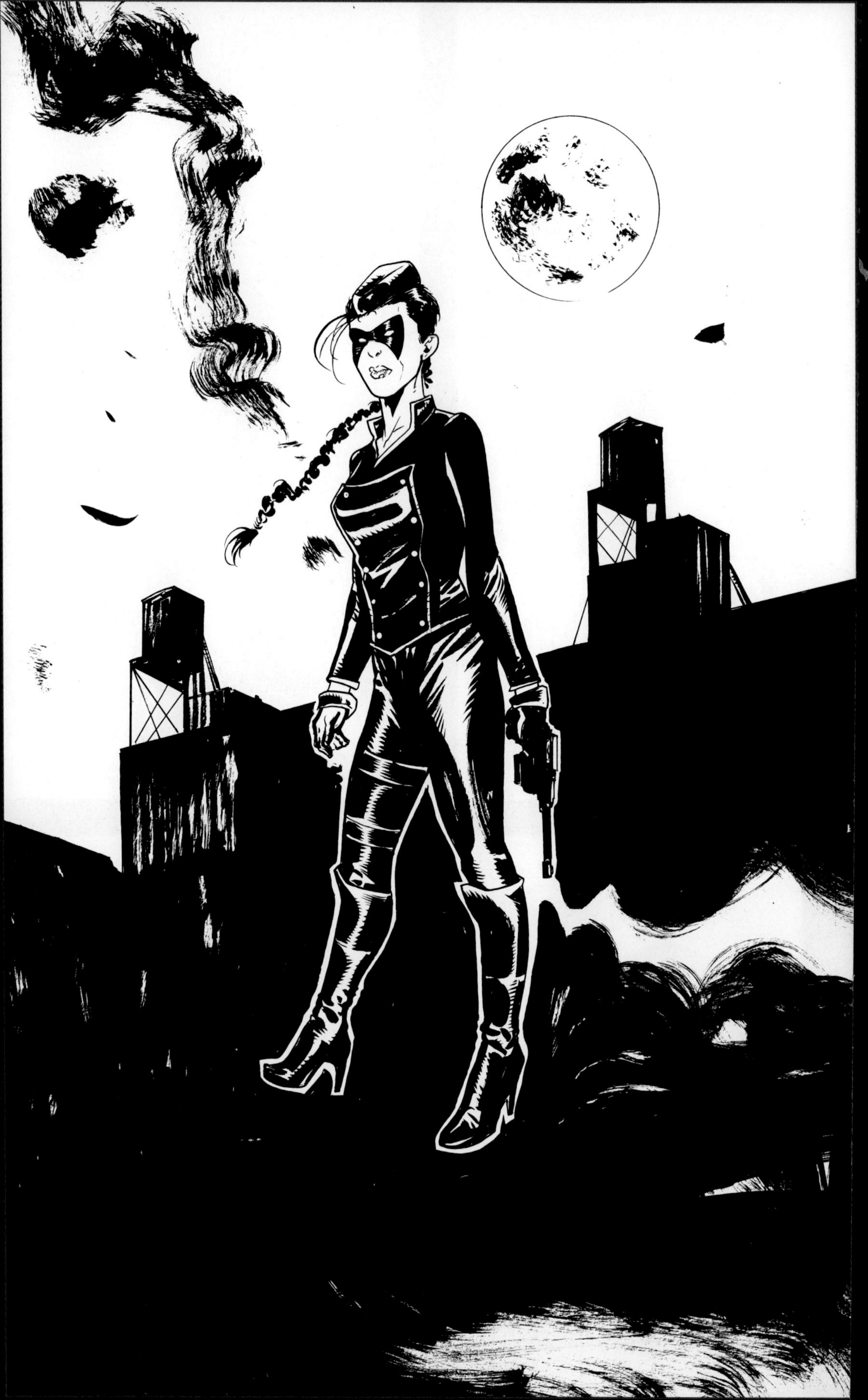

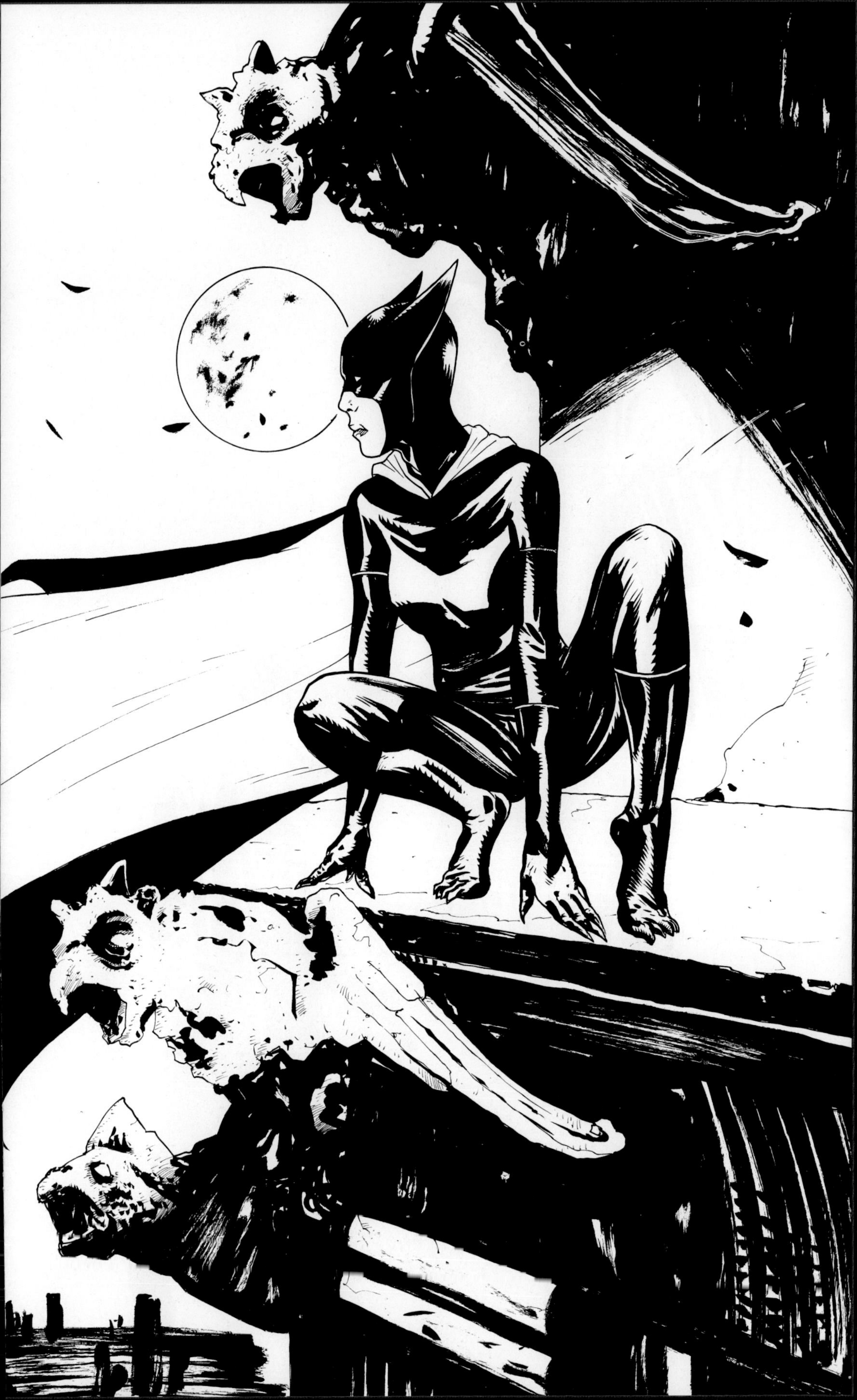

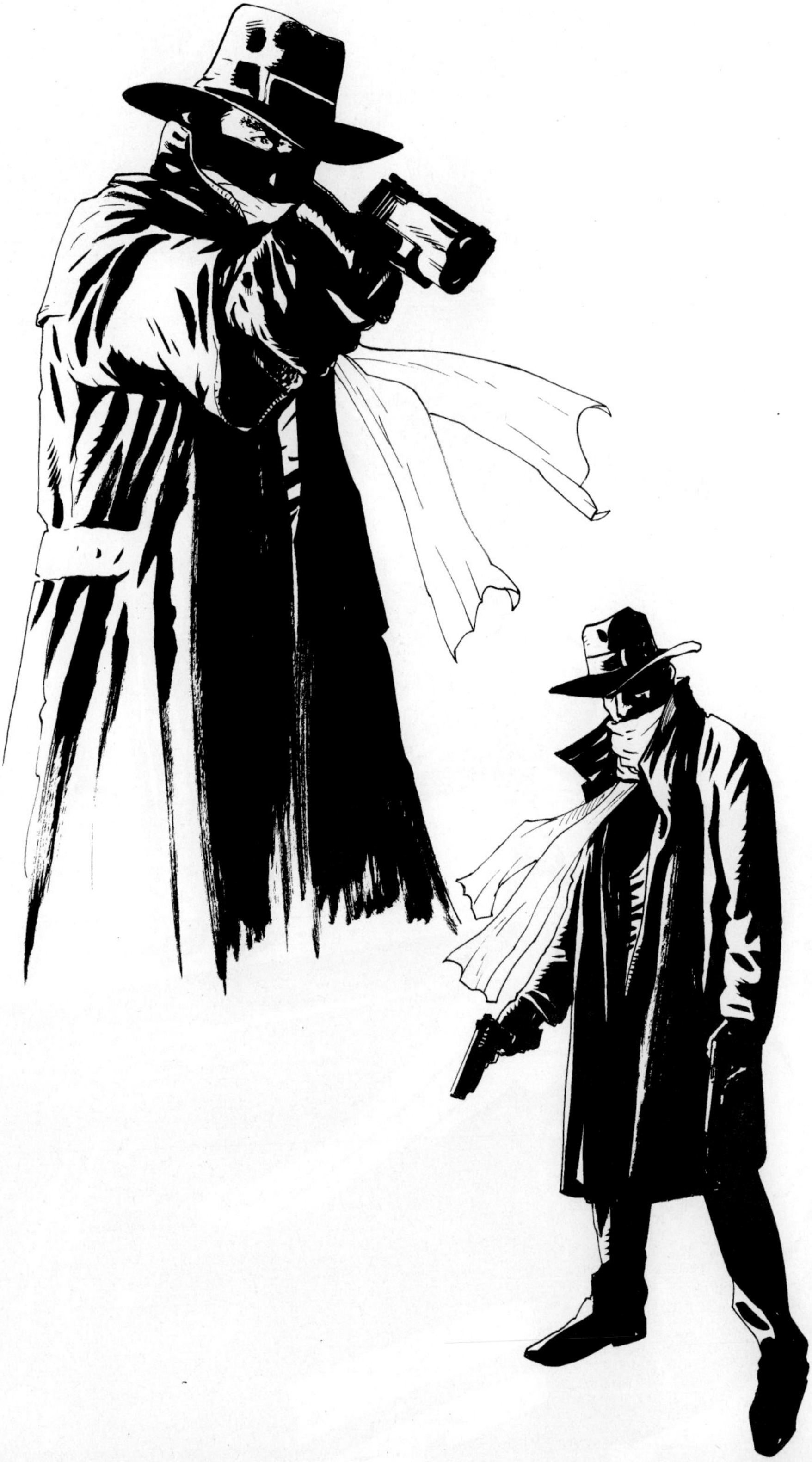

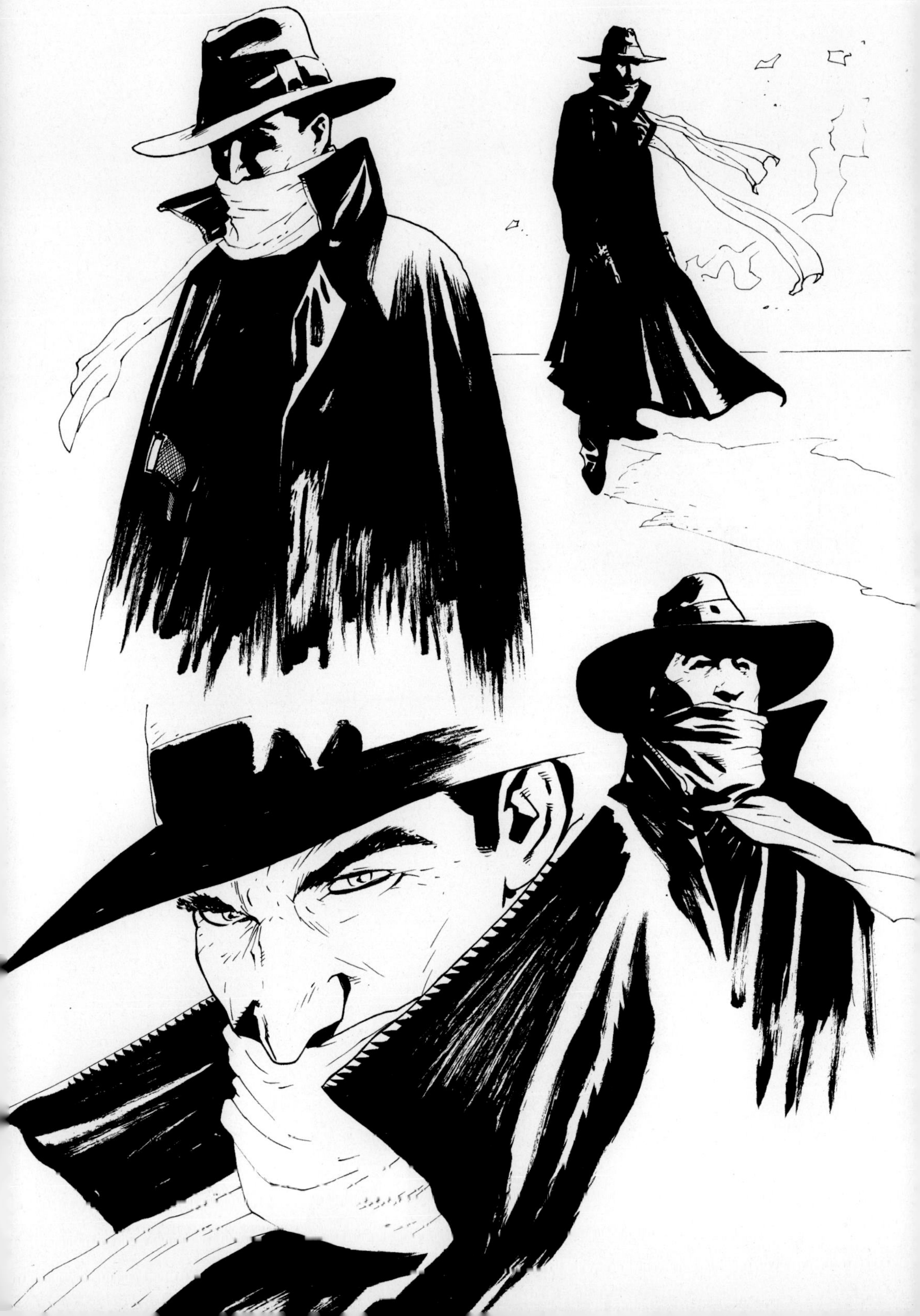

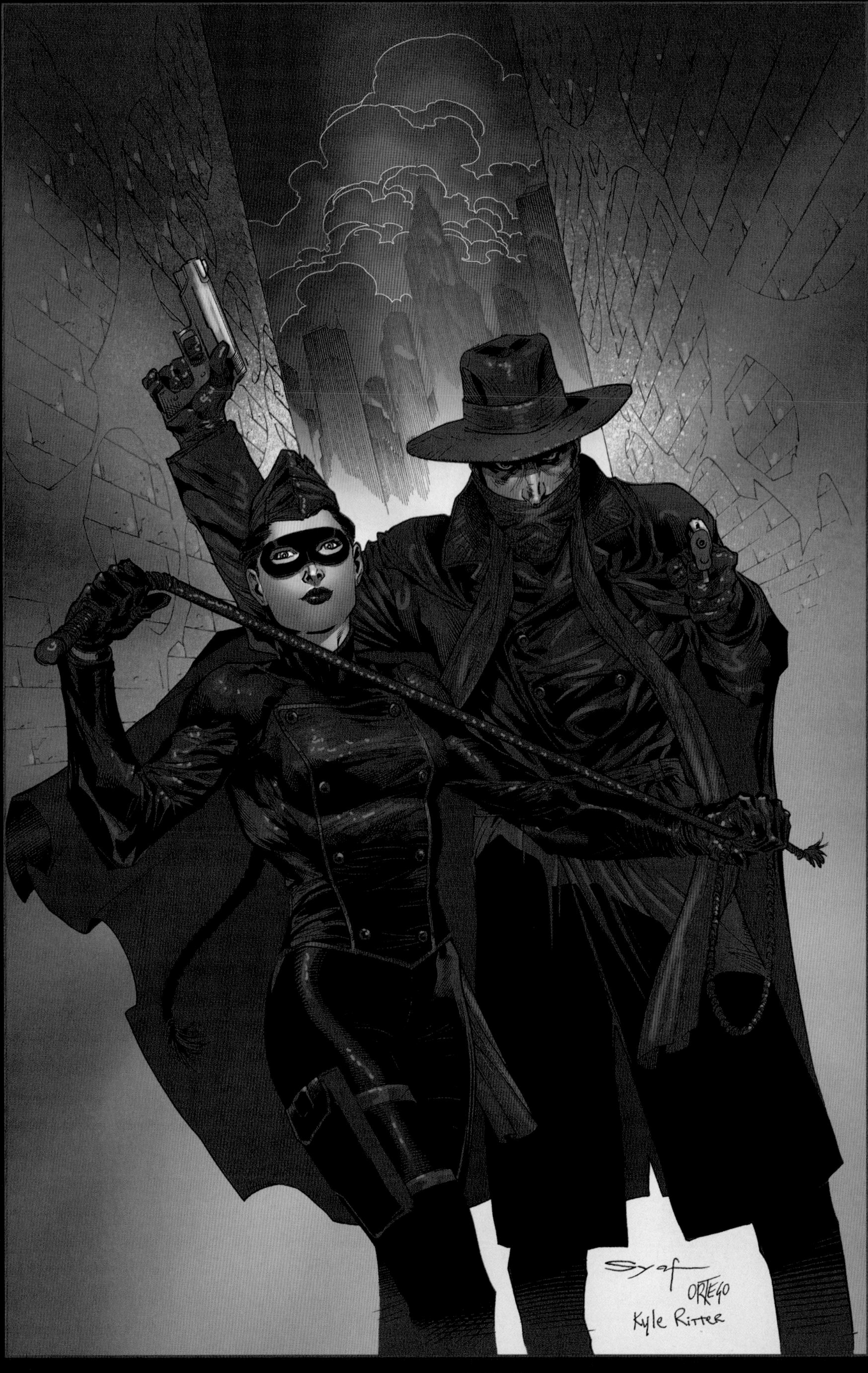
Syaf
ORTEGO
Kyle Ritter

issue #1 cover by ADRIAN SYAF

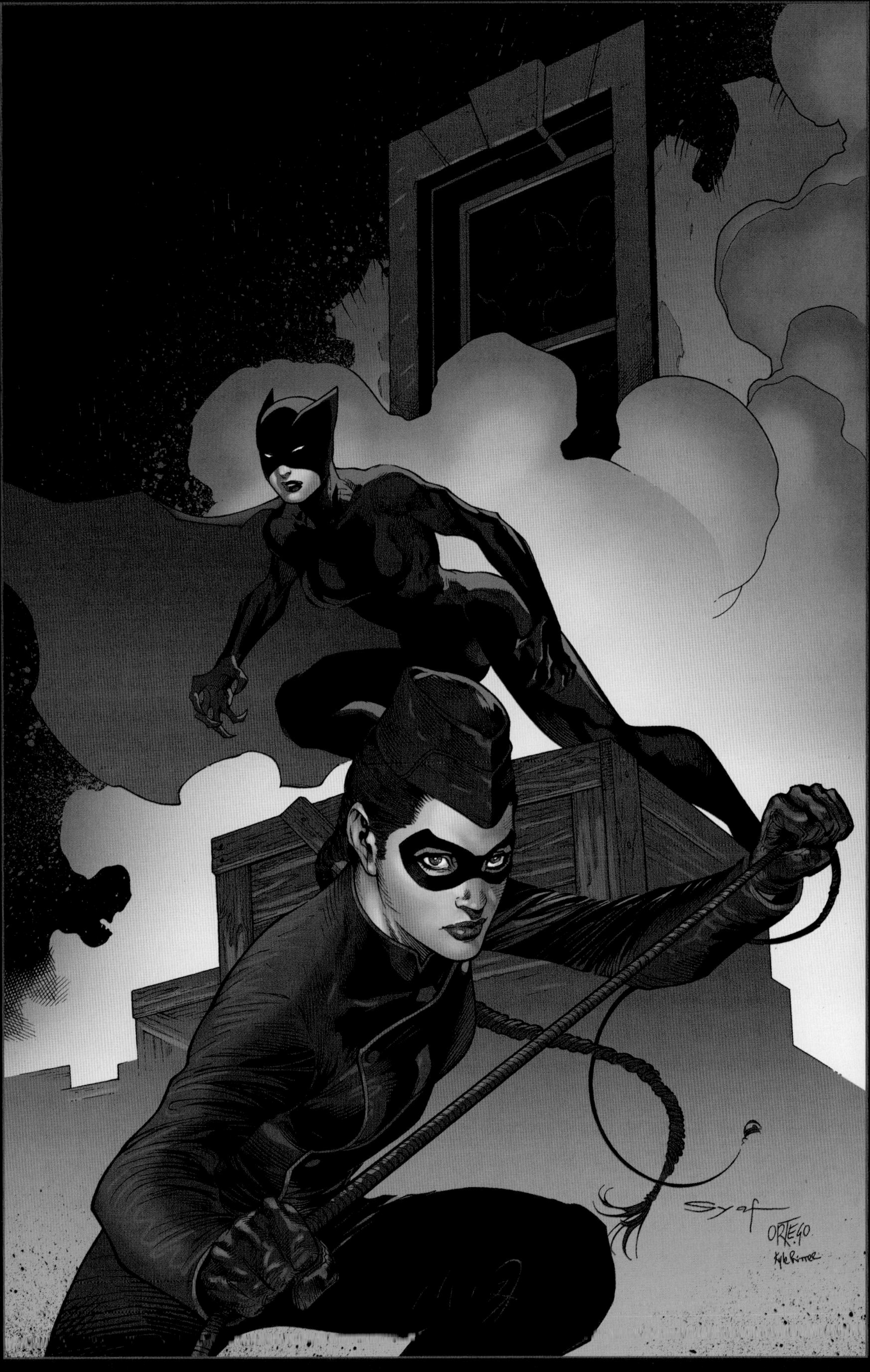
Syaf
ORTEGO
Kyle Ritter

issue #2 cover by ARDIAN SYAF

colors by KYLE RITTER inks by GUILLERMO ORTEGO

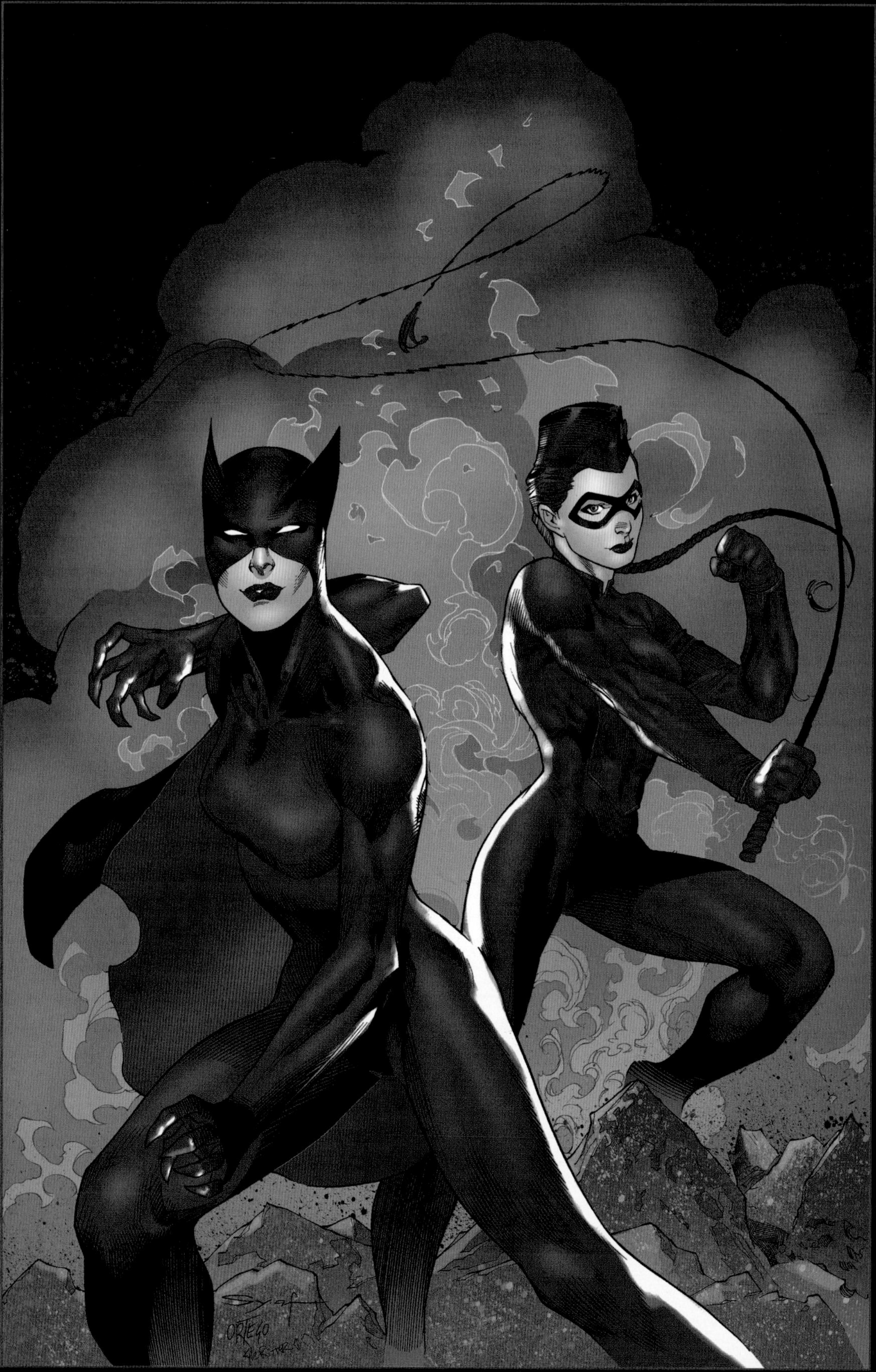
ORTEGO

issue #3 cover by ADRIAN SYAF

colors by KYLE RITTER inks by GUILLERMO ORTEGO

issue #4 cover by ARDIAN SYAF

colors by KYLE RITTER   inks by GUILLERMO ORTEGO

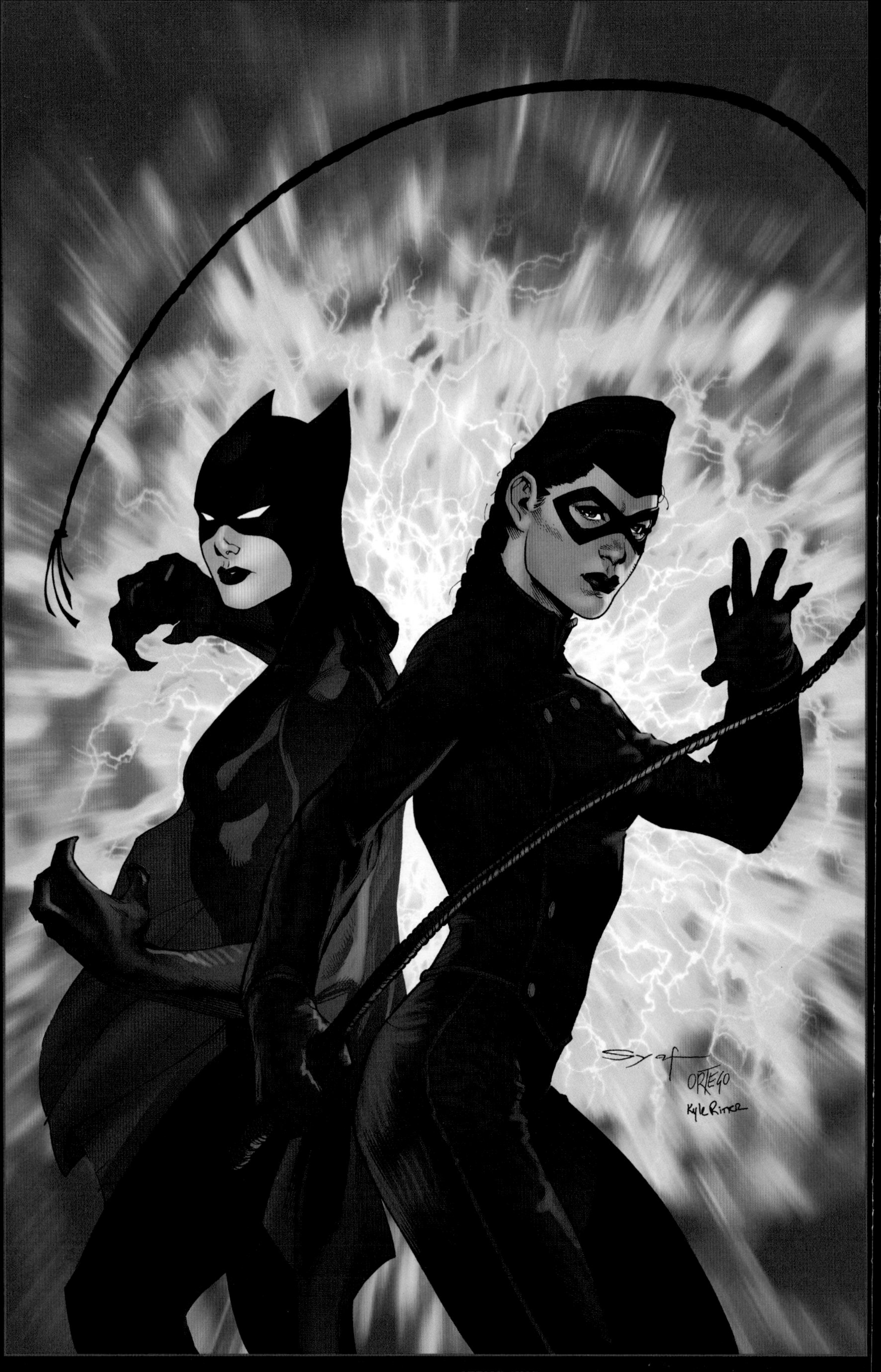
Syaf
ORTEGO
Kyle Ritter

issue #5 cover by ARDIAN SYAF

colors by KYLE RITTER inks by GUILLERMO ORTEGO